James Runciman

Skippers and Shellbacks

James Runciman

Skippers and Shellbacks

ISBN/EAN: 9783743308640

Manufactured in Europe, USA, Canada, Australia, Japa

Cover: Foto ©Thomas Meinert / pixelio.de

Manufactured and distributed by brebook publishing software
(www.brebook.com)

James Runciman

Skippers and Shellbacks

Skippers & Shellbacks

By James Runciman.

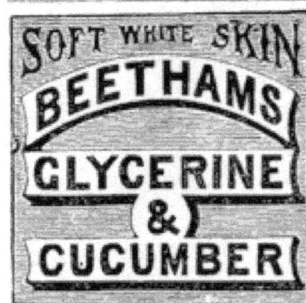

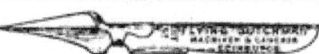

SAMARITAN FREE HOSPITAL
FOR WOMEN AND CHILDREN.

LOWER SEYMOUR

STREET,

PORTMAN SQ.,

W.

SUPPORTED ENTIRELY BY VOLUNTARY CONTRIBUTIONS · ESTABLISHED 1847

Branch:

1, DORSET ST.,

MANCHESTER SQ.,

W.

Patron.—H.R.H. The Duke of Connaught, K.G.
President.—The Right Hon. the Lord Leigh.
Treasurer.—Richard B. Wade, Esq.

OBJECTS OF THE HOSPITAL.

This Hospital is a Home for the Reception of Poor Women afflicted with diseases peculiar to their sex.

Poor Women suffering from such diseases, and Children from all diseases, treated in the Out-Department.

Children received as In-Patients to the Branch. Ages, between 2 and 12. Medical, Surgical, and Accident Cases admitted.

All Patients are received into this Hospital without any payment whatever.

No Governor's Letter required by either In- or Out-Patients, the admission being entirely free.

No payment demanded for Medicine from Out-Patients.

Since its foundation no less than 265,725 Women and Children have been treated in the Out-Department, and 8,472 Women as In-Patients, of whom 1,036 were operated upon for Ovarian Tumour, with 863 recoveries, and only 173 deaths.

Bankers—Sir Samuel Scott, Bart., & Co., 1, Cavendish Square.

Contributions *are earnestly solicited*, and may be paid to Messrs. Barclay & Co., 54, Lombard Street; Messrs. Coutts & Co., 59, Strand; Messrs. Glyn & Co., 67, Lombard Street; Messrs. Ransom & Co., 1, Pall Mall East; Messrs. Hatchard, Piccadilly; or to

GEORGE SCUDAMORE, *Secretary*.

FORM OF BEQUEST.

I give and bequeath unto the Samaritan Free Hospital for Women and Children, *Lower Seymour Street, Portman Square, London, the sum of to be raised and paid, free of Legacy Duty, by and out of my ready money and personal effects, which by Law I may or can charge with the payment of the same (and not out of any part of my Lands, Tenements, or, Hereditaments), to be applied in and towards carrying on the Charitable designs of the said Institution.*

TO

DR. W. F. FOSTER,

OF NEW CROSS.

Dear Foster,

These stories would never have been written but for your skill. I inscribe the book to you, and I am

Yours sincerely,

J RUNCIMAN.

CONTENTS.

PART I.

OVER SEAS.

PART II.

ALONGSHORE.

CONTENTS.

PART III.

SALTINGS.

SKIPPERS AND SHELLBACKS.

PART I.

Ober Seas.

I.

LITTLE TEXAS.

MOST of the steerage passengers on board the ocean-liner *Roumania* were huddled below, and sounds of lamentation echoed faintly through the grim, bare cabin ; for the ship was slashing her way through a powerful head sea, and a bitter storm of rain was discharging its slanting volleys on the sodden deck. Ahead there was nothing to be seen but a wrathful trouble of grey mist and swooping spray, while astern, the wake coiled away like a pale riband over furious rollers.

A few men were crouching in the fiddley amid the clouds of rank steam that belched up from the stokehole, but out in the dripping gangways not a soul was in sight save one tall girl who stood with her back to the blast and swayed gracefully as the ship dived and rose.

She was gazing over the wild tumult of the sea, and she looked dreamy. Her face was not wet at all, for she had folded a bright shawl over her head like a hood, and her pale cheeks gleamed from out a ring of gaudy colour. Her eyes were large and brown, her parted lips had an expression of deep sadness, and the pose of her head, as she kept up her steady forward gaze, was almost devotional. Her

delicate pallor and air of still abstraction made her seem
like one of the prayerful women that you may see figured
in old Florentine pictures. The girl was coarsely dressed
in a ragged brown frock, and she had looped up her skirts
till her strong legs were shown with liberal simplicity.
A merry sailorman came clattering along the alley in his
heavy sea boots ; his oilskins and sou'wester poured multi-
tudinous streams from all their crinkles as he walked, and
his face shone with the wet.   He was singing :

> "Says she, ' My love, I'm dead and gone !
>   Lowlands, lowlands,
> And on my head they've put a stone ;
>   Good-bye, my love, in the lowlands.' "

He sang this sorrowful ditty as if it were quite a comic
affair, and he was evidently a high-spirited fellow.   He
came up behind the girl, and shouted, " What cheer, Texas?
Had your breakfast yet, old lady ?"
    She turned her saintly face and observed, " Texas be
damned !   You git callin' o' me out o' my name, and I'll lay
you out 'fore you know what hoss kicked you."
    " Here, sling it quieter, now, you little cat !   I ain't going
to call you only what I know you by.   Why don't you give
a genelman your bloomin' card, and git your parents and
guardians to interdoose you if you wants to be so blanked
perlite ?"
    " You git !   I want to look at the water."
    " Tell me if you've had breakfast ?"
    " No ; I can't git away with that horse-feed.   They give
us gruel this mornin'."
    " There now, be a good old girl, and I'll fetch you a pan-
nikin of tea out of the galley.   Serve you better right if I
whanged you with a rope's-end, you little rip."
    The sailor interrupted the straightforward conversation
by lurching round to the galley.   He peeped in at the door
and winked affably at the cook.   Then with diplomatic
suavity he said, " Billy, my boy, tip us a dose of tea out
here.   Nobody's lookin'   We're just relieved, and the
bo'sun's messin' about aft."
    Billy, the cook, was a morose person whose general dis-
course was totally unfit for publication, and can only be
given here in a severely expurgated form.

" Who do you want the tea for ?   Ain't you got no coffee ready forrard ?"

" Come on, sonny ; it's for a gal."

" You get caught speaking to any of them steerage judies, you'll be up on the bridge and logged."

" I'll chance that."

So the seaman got a big pint jug of tea, which he secreted in a most perilous way under his huge oilskin.   He then crept to the baker's shop and managed to beg two or three of the exquisite little cakes meant for the after-cabin. Delicately bearing his precious burden, he approached the girl and presented his gifts after glancing cautiously round.

" Look sharp, now, missy ; I've got to slide quick. Hand the mug to Billy yourself."

" Here, you stuck fool ! you're all wet and cold.   Why don't you have a drink yourself ?"

" No ; I brought it for you.   Wade in."

" I'll sling it overboard if you don't drink first."

So the sailor took a sip, and pretended to be vastly refreshed ; then he went forward and dived into the forecastle.

The girl leaned against the deck-house, and enjoyed her breakfast placidly.   She broke her cakes daintily, and showed none of that indecent voracity which one notices among the coarse women who are often found in the steerage.   After that she resumed her long melancholy gaze over the sea until the driving rain had drenched her through.   Without any support from handrail or rope, she strode to the companion with a kind of incipient swagger, but you could see that on solid ground her walk would be free and majestic.

The women who were not wet hailed her draggled appearance with a shrill babble of wonderment ; but she made no sign, and sat down, without speaking, after she had changed her dripping clothes.   There was light enough to knit by, and Texas made herself very busy on a long, thick piece of woolwork that looked like a comforter.   When the jolly steward came past he inquired, " Making a wrap for your sweetheart, missy ?" and she answered, " You best mind your own business, daddy."

It will be seen that Texas was a young lady who somewhat lacked feminine graces. She had been born and brought up on a remote ranche ; her father was a stockrider, and Texas had learned all the lessons that the rude gang in the shanties could teach her. The bold rider had saved a little money, so he determined to start for England. At Galveston he died, and left his daughter friendless. She pushed on to New York, and tried to settle for a while there, but, after a month or two of work in a rough boarding-house, she resolved to seek out her father's relations in England, and she took a steerage passage.

The sailors soon strike acquaintance with the girls, and they were not long in addressing this strange, wild creature. With their ordinary irony they christened her "Little Texas," because she was so big and strapping, and they were fond of inviting her to haul on a rope when the bo'sun was not within hearing. Her real name was Polly Beck, and she was a perfectly untaught, untamed being. It was quite natural to her to swear, but a red gleam came into her large, melancholy eyes if lower forms of brutality were spoken before her, and the clumsiest of the ruffians who slily addressed her dared not go too far.

All the dreary day she knitted at her comforter, and when the second dog-watch began at six o'clock she sighed with pleasure, for her work was done. She went on deck and sauntered about, trying to look as though she were thinking of nothing in particular, but her eyes were very keenly occupied all the while. The dusk soon fell, and the breeze dropped, so that all was quiet.

Texas strolled steadily round and round within the limits till she was arrested by a low whistle from the galley. Her sailor friend once more said, " What cheer ?"

But Texas walked on to the boundary rope aft. Having rendered this tribute to maidenly reserve she came back, and suddenly inquired, " Well, what do *you* want there ?"

The sailor answered, " Only just a word with you, my honey. Is that swine on the bridge looking over ?"

" No. Shouldn't care a cuss if he was. How do you keep your neck warm nights, loony ?"

" Don't try."

" Why, ain't yer got proper clothes ?"

" What ud the grog-shops do if I wasted my money on clothes, my girl ?"

" I ain't your gal. You best keep a straight tongue in your head. Here, shove that round yer silly neck, and don't go shiverin' round like Solomon's old breeches."

This idyllic conversation was checked by the steward, who came up to drive the women down below. The sailor said, "Good-night, and thank you. I'll dance at your wedding, Texas ;" but the damsel walked off without deigning a reply.

Bill Farwhite, the sailor, spat out his quid, whistled, and said, "There's a little cat for you ! Who'd thought it ? Blowed if I don't hang up my hat there 'fore long." Then he lit a pipe, and sat smoking in the reeking galley until the watch was called at eight o'clock.

I don't believe that ordinary sailors ever think at all in the proper sense of the word ; they are so entirely men of action that the habit of contemplation is unknown to them. They can sit still for hours at a time ; but, although they may stare into a fire or look solemnly over the side with an air of deep wisdom, you will find that their thoughts have no sequence. I have sat smoking for two hours with a man whom I liked, and I counted the number of topics which he started. His conversation was only a series of brief grunts followed by long silence ; but he changed his subject six times, and in no case did he finish a sentence. I give this explanation so that you may follow the course of Bill Far-white's meditations.

First he remarked to his shipmate, who sat on a bucket beside him, " What's the grub to-morrow ?"

" Measly pork again."

Then a vision of brown eyes arose, and, in a second, there came before the man a pale face that seemed to waver and shimmer in the dusky light from the furnace. " My blanked seaboots take in water."

" More blank fool you."

Then once more Bill's mind wandered, and he heard the sweet voice of his brusque friend Texas.

At last he felt that he must say something about the thing next his heart. After spitting with complicated skill, he grunted, "Seen that big girl with the red stockings, steerage ?"

"M'm, blanked fine blank petticoats she is, too.   Should like to cart her round a bit at Liverpool."

"Would you ? You blank well won't.   Guess that's goin' to be my judy, or I'll sweat for it !"

This was all, and this is the way sailors talk.   I never yet heard a real conversation among them that would bear full reproduction in print.   All metaphors, ornaments, literary graces, and emphasis, are replaced by oaths and improprieties.   The man's feeling is measured by the number of naughty words which he uses, and the curious thing is that the blasphemer's mind may be essentially healthy and manly.   His swearing is innocent, and merely answers to the alliterations and turns of speech with which poets and other writers embellish their work.

This is a digression.   Bill Farwhite went on the watch till twelve, and again from four till eight.   As he was coming off he once more met Texas, and smuggled her a little breakfast.   She smiled on him, and the sudden gleam of her white, strong teeth was very pleasant to see.   Her whole face seemed illumined with pure kindness, and Bill felt a strange pang run through his whole being.   She called him a damned fool with much gentleness, and graciously accepted his gift.

Morning after morning and evening after evening the pair had brief meetings.   Bill would have been entered in the log-book had he been caught speaking too long with a passenger, but he knew his times pretty well, and escaped with ease.

Texas was one of those women who seldom smile, but her rare and beautiful look of pleasure always came when Bill drew near.   Of course, she did not smile when any of the firemen or passengers were looking ; that would have provoked rude observations.   But when they met in the alley her face seemed like sunshine.

Bill once said, "I never seen nobody like you, Texas."

"Got nary sister, then ?"

"No. My old dad gave me the dirty kick-out fifteen years since, and I swore I'd go back no more, and I ain't."

"Where do you stop when you're off the ship, then ?"

"Anyways.   Sometimes in a grog-shop and get drunk all the time ; sometimes in a crimp's, where you gets your bill

—here's for what you've had, here's for what you're goin' to
have, here's for what you'll never have ; you owe me three
pound—and then they shunts you. That's how I live."

"Guess you live like a hog, my sonny."

"Someways that way. So long, old fellow."

Bill had ceased to say "old girl"; he called Texas "old
fellow" as a term of endearment, and she recompensed his
tenderness by rarely swearing at him.

A lovely afternoon came, and the *Roumania* was nearing
home. The keen wind blew over a gladsome stretch of
great rollers, and as the sea struck the starboard side of the
vessel little rollers flew back and tossed up clouds of spray.
While the fine spray hung in the air the sun struck on it,
and every cloud broke into myriad rainbows. The
monster ship seemed to surge along through some fairy
realm where the very air was shot with purple and crimson.
For mile after mile the path of the steamer was painted
with delight. Texas gazed at the sea with thoughts past
utterance, but she often took a sly look aloft, for the men
were tarring the rigging, and Bill was hoisted in a sling till
he looked like a dot far up in the glad blue air. As he
worked at a forestay Texas admired the lithe strength which
he showed when he swung himself coolly around at will ; he
was plucky at any rate, she thought, to twirl and clamber
on that dizzy eminence.

On a sudden something went wrong with the engines ;
there was a crack, a long wheeze, and then the throb of the
propeller ceased. Gradually the vessel lost her way, and
the rumour spread that a slight accident had happened. The
engineers went hard to work, and the vessel crawled ahead
under trysails. Of course, she could scarcely make a knot
per hour, but still she was kept moving. So far as the send
of the sea was concerned, the *Roumania* was a mere hulk ;
she threw herself about with enormous rolls that seemed
likely to shear the masts and funnels right out of her.
The men up aloft were hard put to it to keep their grip,
for the final jerk as the vessel reached her limit and steadied
herself for the return was something terrific. Nevertheless,
the hands went on tarring away, and Texas looked kindly
again and again at her grimy admirer.

The *Roumania* fell down the side of a swift roller, and

lurched to port. There was a crash ; the little boy at the
belaying-pin gave a stagger and fell. Then Texas heard a
long whirr-r-r-r, and the rope which held Bill flew whirling
and wriggling aloft ; a black arc seemed to cut across the
blue of the sky ; then came a sound like Soss ! and Texas
knew that Bill was overboard.

There was a roar. The tremulous scream of the boatswain's whistle rose high, and a few hands trampled aft,
cursing at the passengers as they came. Texas sprang over
the barrier and ran right to the taffrail. She saw a black
shape wallowing close by the ship's quarter, and she
clenched her teeth as she looked round to see how the men
were getting on with the boat. There was a sad amount of
bungling, for these liners are abominably undermanned in
many cases. Texas saw one fellow fumbling at the falls, and
then, quick as lightning, she swung herself on to the rail
and clambered to a rope where a line of life-buoys hung by
their thin ropeyarns. She whisked her scissors from the
bag at her waist, snipped off two buoys, sprang like a cat
to the deck, and flew to the taffrail.

Taking good aim, she slung one buoy, which landed near
Bill's head ; then, putting her hands to her mouth, she
yelled, "Keep up, sonny ! These damned old women won't
be down for a Dutch month yet. I'll come and take my
chance along o' you. Look out !"

Before anyone could stop her she mounted the rail and
took a flying spring into the sea with the buoy under her
armpits. The green hissing depths boiled above her ; she
felt herself rushing up, and at last, with a roar in her ears
like muffled thunder, she mounted into the light. One
dazed look round and she saw that the vessel was not far
off. Then she looked for Bill, but she had not to look long,
for he came panting up alongside of her. Neither could
speak for a little, but at last Bill gasped, "Here she is."

Poor Texas was cruelly hampered with her clothes, but
the life-buoy helped her, and she paddled quietly until the
shock was over and her wind came. Then she stuttered,
"How long are you good for ?"

Bill answered, "All right. I've worked my boots off. I
can do for a bit. Shall I help you ?"

"No ; they'll not be more than an hour, the cows ?"

She was very disdainful of the sailors, but, as a matter of fact, the boat came hissing up to them within two minutes and a half after Bill went overboard. The sea was not troublesome, and Texas was soon hauled aboard. She was strong enough to mount the ladder when they got back to the ship's side ; and her first words as she lit on the deck were, " One of you give that chap a good drink o' whisky. He's been longer in nor me."

Bill was really not a whit the worse for his ducking, and he was chiefly concerned about the girl.

Texas went below, disdaining to notice the greetings of the excited crowd. After supper she came up in her best clothes and strolled round the deck as usual.

The cabin passengers came forward to stare, and one polite and kindly gentleman said in a patronising manner : " 'Pon my soul, you're a monstrous plucky girl ; but I can't tell why on earth you risked your life for nothing."

Texas looked the polite man calmly in the face and said, " All right, boss. If you can't tell, don't trouble yourself. You kin bet I know my own business."

The polite gentleman afterwards made various comments on the matter. " Doosid good-looking ; but I fancy there's a tile off." This summarised his conclusions.

It mattered little to Texas what he thought ; she had jumped overboard under a sudden impulse, and she did not care to form any opinion as to whether she was wise or foolish in so doing.

She met Bill in the dusk of the same evening. The warm sun had gone, and a chill rain drove all the passengers below save the one restless prowler who loved the mystery of the brooding night and the fierce lash of the driven rain.

Bill whistled low, and Texas approached him. " What did you go for to come over the side for, Texas ?"

" What's that to do with you ? How was I to know you could swim ?"

" But suppose both of us had went ?"

" No fear of me. The boys used to chuck me into the water when I was five years old. I could swim like a Kanaka when I was just a chick. Tom the Bummer made me a bathing suit before I was ten year gone, and I'd a done

the Fork at flood-times if my dad would let me. If I'd had
time to cut my clothes off to-day I'd swum to you without
them rings. That is so, you kin lay."

A passion of gratitude was in the man's soul. His voice
shook, and he said : " Oh, my sweetheart ; I wish I'd a
chance ; I'd die for you right away !" With a quick movement he drew her to him, and kissed her lips before she
could move away.

Texas sprang back ; then she prowled with her feet like
a wild cat, and lashed out with a heavy blow that caught
Bill in the throat and made him stagger. " You dare ! you
dare ! How dare you do that ! I've a good mind to give
you one with the left as well. Who do you reckon I am ?
Not a man in the station durst a-done that, or I'd murdered
him. You git !"

Her eyes glittered as she stood waving poor Bill off ; she
was a magnificent virago. The instinct of maidenly re-
pulsion which a civilized girl would have shown in delicate
fashion flared out violently in this handsome barbarian.

Bill was aghast. The blow confused him, for Texas had
by no means a light hand, and the volcanic savagery of the
action transcended all his previous experiences of feminine
vagaries. Bet and Sue in the Highway had often taken off
a shoe to chastise him, but they were only rowdies ; the
majestic fury in front of him was altogether different.

He breathed hard, and said : "Look here, Texas, I didn't
mean to rile you. What for do you want to hit a chap
that cares for you ? Why, blow me ! I'd be over the rail
after *you*, if she was going fifteen knots. What's a kiss here
or there when a man can't sleep for thinking about you ?"

Texas put out her hand. She had a good mind to step
up and kiss him, but she held herself in. "Now shake
hands. My kisses ain't cheap. Suppose I was your gal, and
I held myself cheap to you, how do you know I wouldn't
be cheap to the other boys when you wasn't round ? I'm
sorry now. There ! make that do for you."

Bill hastened ruefully aft. The scene hadn't lasted more
than a few seconds, but it had changed the man's whole
mind. He wasn't frightened of Texas ; he felt no sense of
wrong ; he only knew that he was in presence of a gigantic
puzzle. The watch was a very easy one, for the rain kept

the wind down, and there was no need for the incessant fiddling on with the sails, which is about the only night-work done on board steamers. Bill leaned against the engine-house, and gave himself up to many inconsequent reveries. Before he turned in he muttered, "I'm glad she give me that clout."

  *   *   *   *   *

When the "Channel fever" was over, and the green Mersey glittered as the boat ripped her way up to the dock, Bill and Texas had become confidential in a queer way, Texas had mended a woefully ragged guernsey for her favourite, and she finished footing two pairs of stockings for him just before the tender came alongside.

When the luggage was being rattled down the shoot, Bill handled his sweetheart's trunk as though he loved it, and he stood glowering with pathetic intensity as the boat churned away from him, until the second officer aroused him by a perfect typhoon of ornamented language. When the men were paid off, all the unmarried hands were very anxious to take Bill with them on the rampage, but he steadfastly refused, and went straight off to seek lodgings. At night I fear he was not precisely sober, but as he usually slept in his clothes on the first night ashore, the fact that he merely fell upstairs this time and went to bed decently afterwards must be accepted as evidence of increasing virtue.

Texas had said before going, "I reckon I shan't look up my people till I'm broke. They may think I've come to live on them, and I ain't; I'll get one thing or another to do in Liverpool and take my chance for a while. Dare say I'll drop across you, and then I'll tell you my address."

So Farwhite wandered about during several days, looking rather wearily at the flitting faces that passed him. A good deal of the fun was gone out of him for the time, and he shocked some of his intimates by his comparative austerity.

Nothing came of his search, and at length he began to look for a ship. Hundreds of unemployed men were tramping hungrily about, and some who had run regularly for years in the ocean steamers were thrown out by the general re-duction made in the complement of hands. Bill's shoes wore thin, and his money ran down till he owed two weeks' lodging and had sixpence to pay with.

He spent one desperate day in toilsome lounging, and at night he was choking with thirst, hungry, and very footsore. He was far from home, and he did not know how he should manage to get under a roof for the night. The glitter of a great bar drew his eye, and the sense of his violent thirst came home to him. He passed the swing door, and stood in the clamorous area where gas and glass, glare and glitter, make the eyes ache till alcoholic dimness blunts the nerves.

He was peering round in a dazed manner when a sweet voice said : " Well, sonny, I told you I'd drop across you."

Little Texas was behind the bar. She was dressed in decent black that showed her splendid bust in modest beauty ; her large solid hands looked ruddy against her snowy cuffs, and her strange, melancholy face seemed to remove all the vulgarity from the clashing, reeking ring in which she stood.

" Speak to you in a minute," she went on, and then Bill saw her serve out a dozen glasses in succession with a dexterity that appalled him. How had she learned ?

When Texas was at leisure, she leaned over and affably inquired : " So, boy. How are you making out up to now ?"

" Bad ! Give me a drink, or I can't talk. I'm choked !"

" All right, only mind, I shan't let you get full. I won't have it in this bar. Soon as I see a boy like to come off his perch, out he goes."

" Not much fear o' me getting full, old fellow. Give me the biggest drink you can for twopence, and that leaves me fourpence."

Texas whistled, and looked grave. " Can't you get a ship ?"

" Not a chance just now."

" Well, I'll stand this liquor, and you sit down till I can talk to you."

When a lull came Texas resumed the conversation, and went very speedily to the point. " See here, sonny. I tumbled into this job as soon as the boss saw me with my shawl off. I'm all right, and I ain't broke into dad's money yet. Now, you take fifty dollars, and get yourself a first-rate coat and pants, and sling those boots into the dock. Then you come right round here to-morrow afternoon when we're quiet, and I want some straight jaw with you."

Bill flushed. "Easy, Texas. I'm a rough sort o' boy, but I ain't got to letting a girl give me coins yet."

"Oh, ain't you? Well, you don't want number two clout like the last one I gave you, do you? You don't take the money, and I guess I'll lay you out, for as fine as I am."

Bill couldn't keep from laughing, and he went away with a joyous heart.

Next day he appeared at the bar nicely dressed, and a very good-looking, well set-up fellow he was. Texas nodded brightly, and her ineffable smile made her face beautiful as she glanced Bill over from head to foot.

"How much for that lot, sonny?" she inquired.

"Twenty dollars the suit—that's four pound. Eleven the boots, and the other things seven."

"Where's your checks?"

Bill stared.

"Your receipts, I mean, from the store."

"Never had a receipt in my life."

"I always said you were a fool. Who ever bought things without a writing for the money? I'm only looking after you, you know. It don't matter to me what you done with the money. Never mind, sit down. Now, sharp, I'm going to tell you what you've got to do. I've had lots of officers about, and I know all about it. You've got to go to school."

"You're silly, Texas. How can I?"

"Don't shove your jaw in where you ain't wanted. I say you've got to go to school. There's lots of men makes all their money by teaching sailors the thingumbobs that them sharps wants before they lets you be officer. You go. See me every week on Saturday night, and live on three dollars a week. I'll give you the dimes here, and you pay your man when the job's over."

Bill shuffled, and his bronzed face grew almost purple.

"You're making me out a scurvy lump, Texas. I wouldn't let up like that on a chap that's out of luck. What do you think any man would say at me for taking a girl's money? You don't know how our chaps are for that sort of thing. They'd turn me out of the forecastle, and send me to lie on the hatches."

"I tell you again, you were always a fool. Do you go

for stopping in the forecastle? Don't you think of your children?"

"You're tying me up into knots."

"Well, suppose you don't care about *your* children, how about mine? Guess you're going to marry me, and you can bet I don't marry a common sailor. It's money that does it—dollars, my sonny. You'll have to keep me a mighty long while, and keep me well too, so you needn't rile up if I want to keep you a bit for a start. You and I are chummies. If you don't like the bargain, leave it alone, and leave me alone."

The woman was the master. There was something so pure and fine in her directness that Bill gave in.

*   *   *   *   *

On a fine summer morning Bill Farwhite might have been seen (as the old novelists say) trying *not* to run past the Sailors' Home. His face was red, his eyes were moist, and his hands quivered. He reached the bar, and Texas coolly said, "All right; I see you've done the trick."

"Give us a drink to wet my ticket. You've made me be teetotal for three months, and I must have a turn now."

"No you won't. Come round into the parlour before you make yourself smell of beer."

In the parlour Texas stood, with a quiet smile on her lips. Bill faced her, and she spoke. Her voice seemed sweeter than ever, and her eyes were moist. "You would like that kiss now, would you not? No, stand still. I hit you a bang in the jaw last time you tried, and I'm going to make it up."

Then she made the first advance, and put her arms round Bill's neck. "There—there. Guess you don't think I'm cheap now."

Bill was a sly rascal. He waited till Texas had stepped back, and then he said, "That's not the right way. It isn't proper for young ladies to kiss officers and gentlemen like I am. I'll show you how the aristocracy manages it," and then the fellow took quite a surprising number of kisses without receiving a single clout.

The education of Texas was proceeding satisfactorily.

*   *   *   *   *

Six years after this a splendid clipper was lying at anchor.

She was bound for New Zealand, and she carried a large number of emigrants. Her cargo was made up of steel rails, and a hundred hulking navvies were going out with her to aid in laying a new railway. The evening was calm with a light haze hanging over the water, and the high lights of far-off steamers blinked over the white sheet-like stars that had lost their way. The people were nearly all down below, and the captain sat easily in his state-room. A tall and noble-looking woman came in. She bent gently over the jolly skipper and kissed him. He winked comically, and said, " I must put a stop to this kissing. Any gentleman of proper modesty ought to hit a person a bang in the jaw when they take liberties like that." He emphasised the " bang in the jaw " slily, and his wife laughed with a low, happy ripple of sound.

" We're getting on," said the lady. " I've ticked it up, and I find we have a good eight hundred in the bank now."

" Ah ! I should have been a measly pauper if it hadn't been for you, my dear old lady."

Just then a loud clamour of many voices resounded. Captain Farwhite could hear one man yell, " Where are you coming to ? Hard-a-port ! Hard over !"

He rushed on deck, and presently his wife heard his stentorian voice cry, "Stand to the boats."

Then he came and softly cried, " Bring up my revolver, my dearest."

Texas rushed to the companion.

Crash !

Then a long grind, and a huge formless bulk drew back into the gloom. Texas ran forward. One boat was down, and a mad rush of clumsy navvies threatened to swamp her.

Texas lifted the revolver, and her voice rang clear. " The women first. I'll plug the first man that crosses that rope. You will have it then, will you ?"

One navvy fell, shot through the head.

" Now, men, help the passengers in. Come aft to me, Bill !"

Farwhite whispered, " We've only time to get two boats out. The scoundrel has left us to drown. Into the boat, my darling !"

Then Texas answered, " Oh, Bill Farwhite, what do you

take me for ? Get those poor women in, and then come
and we'll die together after you have done."

A furious coward shouted, " I *will* be in !" and sprang on
the rail.

" You'll be dead meat, then," said Texas. She fired, and
the fellow dropped into the boat badly wounded.

The ship gave an awful lurch, and the two overloaded
boats drew clear. Bill Farwhite rushed to his wife.
" That's the last roll, my woman. When she draws level
she goes down."

Texas put her arm round her husband, and stood there
proud, pale, defiant.

She waved to the rescued people, and then silently waited
through the few dread seconds that went before the end of
all. So that was the last of Little Texas.

II.

AN UGLY RISK.

THE steamer *Penelope* was very busily employed during the
spring in collecting wine and oil on the coast of the
Adriatic.

The peasantry bring down their loads on rough, jolting
waggons, and the clumsy barrels, from the various little
villages that stand by the green waters of the narrow sea,
are planted in rows on the jetties. The *Penelope* scoured
all the ports from Venice to Brindisi, but she was unable to
obtain a full cargo. The French agent at Messina was able
to stow a few casks of oil aboard, but when the boat threaded
her way through the dangerous cluster of islets to the north
of Sicily she was not more than half loaded, and she behaved
herself in a very lively manner when she met the northerly
sea on her run to Gibraltar.

In going through the Gut she met a strong westerly
breeze, and she punched at the short seas without making
much headway. As she swung round to the north she
rolled to such an extent that the men could neither stand,
sleep, nor sit. Washing was out of the question, for the
basins and buckets were emptied as the steamer took her
great slants down the sides of the Western Ocean rollers.

Harry Glanton, the chief mate of the *Penelope*, did not like the look of things at all. He was not much given to making a fuss about danger, but he had never in his life been on board a ship which seemed so much disposed to take charge of herself. When the wind took her on the port side it required the most violent exertions on the part of the two men who were put at the wheel to prevent her from falling away and driving nose-end on to the low, hard cliffs.

After passing the Burlings the vessel met a northerly wind, with a very powerful head sea. The distressing roll was moderated, but she threw herself from wave to wave with jerks which threatened to pitch the masts out of her with every fresh swing.

Twenty-four hours after passing the Burlings, Glanton was on the bridge, and he had very gloomy thoughts indeed. He was a rough fellow, not by any means given to sentiment, and, like the rest of his class, he was somewhat fond of drink, and apt to use improper language on occasion. His education had been a little neglected, but he could read the slim paper-covered novels which are so much in favour among sailors, and he had certain undefined poetic notions. He liked to read about heroic actions ; and, although the language in which he criticised the deeds of his heroes was not fit for the drawing-room, his rough comments showed that he knew a man when he met him in the flesh, or only looked at his pale shadow reflected on the pages of a book.

I hate and utterly detest and despise the sailor of the sentimental songs, the creature who is always talking about his dear, and saying, "Yeo, heave yeo," and "Hilly-hilly, hilly-ho," and all the rest of the made-up twaddle that pleases the ears of the music-hall. But the real sailor, with his rank coarseness, his fierce friendship, his superb strength and animalism, his dogged and narrow brutality, is a man all over. I like to live with such, either at sea or ashore ; I like to sit and hear them grumbling in the fo'c's'le when the guttering lamp shines dimly through the haze, and when the clash of falling seas sounds like muffled drums overhead ; I like to meet them in their drinking places ashore, and hear their jolly roaring nonsense, and all the

2

boyish and stupid extravagance engendered by the hard free life in the salt air.

Harry Glanton was a true specimen of his class—quick with an oath, quicker still with a blow, ready to drink, fight, work, or engage in debauch. He had the vices of a man, the courage of a man, and he was faithful even to death in discharging his duty.

On that wild evening, after the smooth swell of the Burlings had been left behind, Glanton was gazing uneasily to the westward, where a streak of chill grey light shone like a gleam from a dying fire. A lurid, coppery flush had overspread the westerly sky as the sun sank, and there was a troubled look about the horizon on the vessel's port bow as though multitudes of undefined and shadowy objects were whirling above the dim smoking tumult of the waves.

Glanton never liked to shift responsibility, but the look of the weather at last prompted him to say, " I must have the old man up ; there is something there I have never seen before, and it is going to be ugly."

He blew his whistle, summoned one of the men, and told him to ask the captain to come on deck at once.

The old man came, blowing and wheezing, and not too well pleased at being disturbed in the middle of the first sleep he had had since the vessel blundered past the African shore ; but when Glanton pointed out to him the mysterious, threatening aspect of the west, he looked grave, and said, " You did quite right to fetch me up. I have never seen a sky like that since the gale of '66. I was knocking about here for ten days then, and it got so bad that we were swept, and I called the men aft for prayers. Now, I tell you what, Mr. Glanton. I am going to shove her head round to the west ; you will find there is something very bad coming from there presently."

The vessel's head was put round, and she received the whole weight of the northerly breeze on her starboard side.

At near midnight there came a sudden lull, and the long march of the waves went smoothly by without a single gust coming to pluck the crests from the black tops and fill the air with arrowy spray.

After waiting on for a quarter of an hour in this deadly

and startling lull, Glanton shouted, "Here she comes, sir!" and with a sudden roar a great squall struck the big steamer with a sound like a volley of musketry. The rigging shrieked, the swift, violent wind reverberated with bellowing noises as it blew across the mouth of the funnel, and the *Penelope* stopped, shuddered, and almost entirely lost her headway for a few seconds.

Within the hour a tremendous westerly sea was marching in mountainous heaps; it seemed as if every fresh wave that came was bound to smother the *Penelope*, and the peevish, short, northerly sea combined with the westerly drift to throw up irregular hills of water. "If she gets on the top of one of them and tumbles off," said the captain, "it will be a bad job with us. If one of those casks gets loose and hits her it will be very apt to knock a plate out of her, and then it'll be, 'Good-morning, ladies all,' for the lot of us."

The *Penelope* simply refused to steer. When she headed a little to port or starboard so that the wind obtained a purchase on the expanse of her side, it was almost impossible to fetch her round with head to wind, and again and again Glanton feared that they would be obliged to let her drift.

At seven in the morning a big sea caught the steamer just as she was recovering from a tremendous lurch to port. The sea came crashing along, caught her nearly amidships, and ripped away aft, carrying the starboard boat in fragments, and demolishing the funnel as though it had been a carrot.

Then came the catastrophe the captain had feared. The green sea from the west was met obliquely by a strong northerly roller, and a vast eddy formed by the swirl of the two waves was met in turn by a jumping backwash that seemed to fall right in the very teeth of the wind. A monstrous hill of water rose, and on the very crest of it the top-heavy steamer balanced for an instant, and then literally fell off on her broadside with a crack that set everything shaking.

A loud rumbling was heard in the hold. "I thought so, sir," said Glanton; "one of them casks has got adrift. As long as they only hit her with the soft side there will be no harm done, but if one of them falls end-on, I guess we have got to go."

At nine o'clock, while the *Penelope* was lying with a nasty list, a little brig went labouring by under the foretopsail. Just as she had got well away under the *Penelope's* stern the brig broached to; a couple of waves caught her in quick succession, and she came up no more.

At noon the look-out man sang out, "Vessel away half a mile on the port bow, sir!" And the captain said, "Ah! he has got his rags out. Very sorry for him, but we can't help him. If we can save our bacon that is about all we can do. We will try and steam a bit nearer to him and see what is up."

When the *Penelope*, after half an hour's hard steaming, got near to the distressed vessel, Glanton saw that it was a steam yacht. The yacht signalled, "Crank shaft broken and plate started. We are settling by the stern."

The old merchant skipper shook his head as he read off the signals, and in response to Glanton's eager look he said, "It is no good; they will have to drown, poor souls, and I don't suppose we shall be very long after them."

The mate answered, "But don't you think we could get up and make a lee, and then try and send a raft or something down to them?"

"Raft be damned!" said the captain. "How many of them do you suppose could hang on the raft as we haul her back?"

"Well," Glanton answered, "we must either not look at them or else do something. I can't see them drown. See there now! She's hardly got a foot of freeboard right aft; it is only the fore compartment, I fancy, that is keeping her up at all."

"I have got a plan, sir," he added, after a pause. "Suppose you put the lifeboat over the side and pay out a coir rope? I can drift down on her in less than a minute, and then if you give us steam to the winch you can haul me up when I have got some of them on board."

The old skipper looked very gloomy. He said, "Well, if it was my case, I would not like to see a vessel go away and leave me. If you like to try it on you can go."

Glanton put off his shoes and stockings and stripped to

the shirt, and left the knee-strings of his drawers slack, so that he might make some sort of a fight for it if the boat happened to capsize.

The *Penelope* was swung round till she approached perilously near to the yacht. Then Glanton said, "Neck or nothing; over with the boat!" and in an instant the lifeboat slipped from the davits. She had hardly touched the water when Glanton sprang on board, and before the huge lurch of the vessel could strike him in the return roll, he had given a shove with a big oar that sent the boat far away amid the boiling milky crests.

The wind was blowing a perfect hurricane, and the lifeboat flew like a cork.

Glanton used the oar to steer with, and sometimes he had to tear with all his might to prevent his little craft from flying away out of the road of the yacht. He had to stand up to his work, and he was afraid that the iron rowlock might snap under the strain of his violent exertions. When he had run down within about fifteen yards of the sinking boat he was trembling in every limb, and felt as though his last ounce of strength had left him.

The yacht was heavily down by the stern, and could rise to the sea no more. A lady was lashed to the stump of the mainmast, and a huddled group of men hung on as they best could.

Glanton sang out, "I dare not come near you, else we'll get stove in. I shall go under your stern, and you must jump as I pass."

He then signalled the men on the steamer to pay out a little more rope. The sea took him within a yard and a half of the yacht, and he yelled, "Jump for it now, men!"

The young lady made a spring, leapt lightly on the thoft, and fell into the boat with a sprained ankle.

By that time the lifeboat had gone about five yards to leeward of the yacht. Glanton signalled to the men of the steamer to haul him forward again, and as the boat plunged he said, "Four of you jump as I go past, and I will come back for the rest."

Five men jumped; one was hit in mid-air by a comrade, but fell into the boat, breaking two ribs across the seat; another man fell into the streaming gulf, and went away to the east. Nothing could be done for him, and he soon threw up his hands.

It was wild work getting back to the steamer, for the men hauled without any caution whatever, and although the lady and the four seamen baled as hard as ever they could, the little boat was nearly full of water when she was brought up under the bow of the *Penelope.*

The skipper had rigged up a boom, with a block and tackle, and the rescued people were bowsed up as though they had been casks.

After the boat was baled out Glanton prepared for his second trip, and he got a little Norwegian sailor to accompany him, so that somebody might be handy for baling purposes in case the boat shipped too much water.

There was a terrible bother when the yacht was reached, for the gentleman who owned her was rather faint-hearted, and hesitated again and again to jump.

With blunt directness Glanton roared, " If you don't want to drown, why don't you jump ? You can either jump and not drown, or stay and drown. Jump at once, or else we'll haul ahead and leave you."

The faint-hearted owner screwed up his courage at last, and soon lay in a limp and shivering coil at Glanton's feet.

While the mate was jockeying round the stern of the yacht, the captain hailed him very loudly through the speaking-trumpet, telling him that he must hurry up, or the *Penelope* would be lost for a certainty.

The task of keeping the huge and unsteady hulk broadside on was one of the highest danger, and no one who has not stood amid the awful clamour of a real gale of wind, while the blocks clash, and strong ropes give way, and the masts groan with tearing noises, can form an idea of the task that the captain had set himself to perform with that big clumsy mass of iron.

Glanton had a stiff job in getting back, and when the last of the crew had been put on board, he fell down on his face in the chart-house, and lay like a log until his chief forced a little brandy between his teeth.

The yacht soon pointed her bowsprit skyward, and before the *Penelope* had been forced round once more into the teeth of the gale the little craft had disappeared.

The big steamer had a long and bad time of it before she reached Bordeaux, but she got there with the loss of a boat, one man, and a large quantity of wine.

The owner of the yacht behaved handsomely, so neither the skipper nor the crew had any reason for regretting their unselfishness and simple daring.

No one can be much in the company of seamen without hearing many such stories which never get into the newspapers, for Jack treats every incident in his life at sea as part of the day's work, no matter how thrilling and romantic it may be; and, after performing some feat which would set all the newspaper people talking if it were only known, he very probably never alludes to it in the course of his life, except in bluff and indifferent phrases.

Glanton is now a captain. He married a very good-looking barmaid, and that lady is not in the least aware that her husband is a hero, although she knows that he is a "master man." She is very proud of his great fierce beard and his corded limbs. She takes care of his money, and if any anecdote of her man's bravery ever gets into the journals in the future she will not know about it, for her reading is confined to penny novels.

III.

THE LOST SKIPPER.

The *Mariana* was swung outside the bar, in order that her compass might be adjusted.

While she was travelling slowly round in circles Thomas Hardy, the skipper, stood on the bridge with his wife, and received the directions of the man who was making out his new compass cards.

After an hour's delay the pilot boat came alongside, and Tom said: "Now, Jenny, my dear, we shall have to get you over the side. Good-bye; I will send you a letter from Port Said."

Jenny Hardy put her arms round her husband's neck, and said: "You will find us just the same when you come back; and mind, Tom, not a drop! I think I shall break my heart if you take it again."

Hardy replied, with a tremor in his voice : " I cannot promise anything, my dear, but I will struggle my very hardest. If I can get over the first week of the hot weather without touching the drink, I will come back without breaking the pledge. It is the confounded heat that always tempts me."

There was a good deal of reason for Mrs. Hardy's caution.

Tom was one of the finest seamen on the coast ; he had been brought up in the old school, and when he was only eleven years of age he knocked up and down in a clumsy old collier brig. Before he was twelve he was shipwrecked on the *Galloper*, and landed home on a bitter winter day in his shirt-sleeves. While he was second mate he was once blown north to the verge of the Arctic Circle, where two of the crew lost their feet through frostbite. There was no kind of adventure usual to merchant seamen that he had not gone through, and there was nothing connected with his trade that he did not know better that most other men. He was an active fellow, of the blonde Scandinavian type— red-bearded, yellow-haired, deep of chest, and muscular to an extraordinary degree : he could go up a backstay hand over hand with hardly a wriggle of the legs ; he could jump over a rope-yarn held four feet ten inches above the deck, and when he performed this feat he came down with a light, buoyant thud which testified to the springiness of his limbs. No danger ever scared him ; and when he was in a sailing-vessel he let neither wind nor weather delay him when once the hatches were on. He was the terror of timid mates, on account of his way of carrying sail. He made a little fortune for the owners of one fine barque, but it was at the expense of almost tearing her to pieces. He once carried away two suits of sails in the course of a single voyage ; and he kept the barque going at eleven knots from the Rock of Lisbon to the Downs. He might have been a wealthy man before he was forty years old, for his luck was wonderful, and his skill was only equalled by his good fortune. But he had one failing.

It happened that when he was an apprentice he fell off the main-yard and hurt his head. There was a big ugly indentation just over his right temple, and there was no doubt that his brain was affected to some degree. He had no particular craving for alcohol, but if he once so much as tasted spirits, he became silly, and was no more responsible for his own actions until it was out of him. That was his little failing. Times out of number he had been pardoned, for the fellow had the knack of inspiring affection and confidence, even among those who had seen him during his maddest fits of drunkenness, yet no one knew when or where he would break out again.

He was once running a smart little brig on a roundabout voyage to Malta, Venice, Naples, and Cardiff; he was rattling up the Adriatic at about eight knots, when one of the men happened to displease him. Hardy had taken a glass or two of spirits, and his mad temper got the better of him; he picked the man up and threw him overboard. Then, with incredible heartlessness (which he repented in his sober moments), he cracked on and left the poor drowning wretch. It happened that a pilot-boat was running under the stern of the brig, and the man was picked up. The felucca carried the waif into Venice, and a prosecution was ordered. Mr. Tom had to pay a fine of £25, which considerably lessened the profits of his voyage. At Cardiff he threw a man down the hold, and very narrowly escaped a prosecution for manslaughter.

By the time he got round to London his crew were up in arms against him, and one dark night he heard one man say to another : " Can you see the swine ?"

"I don't know whether you can see, but I am going to let you feel me," said Tom, and he thereupon inflicted such a terrible beating upon the poor squealing Dutchman that he made a case for the hospital.

Hardy was very heavily fined for this, and not a penny was left to him when he came to reckon up accounts.

Such was the skipper of the *Mariana*—a wild, undisciplined man, a compound of tenderness and ferocity, stupidity and shrewdness, cruelty and kindness, gallantry and superstition—in short, a kind of man who might have been a pirate or a Scripture reader, according to the circumstances in which he was thrown, for his ferocity was strongly tempered by intense religious feeling. He would have been the most brutal pirate in the whole of the Spanish Main, and he would have been a kindly and helpful visitor had his fate compelled him to labour among the poor.

The *Mariana* had a very good run to Port Said, and then Tom wrote home to his wife thus :

"DEAR JENNY,—I write these few lines, hoping they will find you in good health, as they leave me at present. We have had a good run, and she is a nice smart boat. We can get twelve knots out of her when the wind is dead astern and we can put the square sails on her, and she goes nine very easy. I was very near having a drink as we were passing Gibraltar, but you will be glad to hear that I have managed so far without taking any stuff, and I believe I shall get through the voyage all straight. Tell Nance that I can't wear the comforter, because the weather here is so hot that you could sleep on deck at night if it were not for the moon making you blind. I go on deck in pyjamas, but not, of course, here, but after we left Malta and our decks was all frizzling like anything with the heat. Dear love, I hope we shall have a good haul this voyage, because I want to see you dressed as well as the rest of them, and if we stop at Marseilles on the way home I will get you a lump of silk, so you can cut all the lot of them out. We have got to take a lot of Arab firemen, and I doubt if the beggars vex me I shall be breaking some of their backs. The queer thing about Arabs is that if you hit them they tumble down directly, and you have to be pretty rough on them to do any good. With best love, I am your faithful husband,

"THOMAS HARDY."

Not long afterwards a telegram from the owners reached Jenny. The message simply said : "*Mariana* arrived at Bombay. She is to run for two years between Shanghai and Hong Kong. Charter arranged this day."

Jenny was very glad, although she hardly liked to think of poor Tom frizzling out on that scorching coast ; but two years at £20 a month meant a lot of money, and the woman's heart was rejoiced.

Things went on very smoothly, and Mrs. Hardy drew her half-pay quite regularly. Once the owner said : "I am glad Captain Hardy is doing so well ; we are quite satisfied with him, and we have a strong notion of renewing the charter."

Tom was very lucky in certain private speculations of his own, and in four months he earned eighty pounds over and above his wages. Every letter that reached England carried the same cheering tale of temperance and success, and the wife was as happy as the day was long, for she thought to herself, " If he can only go on for five years like this he will be able to retire, and not have to go to sea any more in the stormy weather."

On one glorious summer morning she went up the river in a passenger-boat to the great town where the owner's office stood. Everything seemed hopeful, and even the grimy banks were almost joyous under the pouring discharge of sunshine.

One of the clerks in the outer office looked ominously at Mrs. Hardy as she took her seat, and presently a messenger said : " Mr. Brown would like to see you privately in the inner office."

The colour faded from the woman's face, and a black foreboding seemed at once to blot out the brightness of the sunshine.

Mr. Brown motioned his visitor to a chair. With a sudden effort he came right to the heart of the business. " Mrs. Hardy, I am sorry to say there is no half-pay for you this month ; I thought everything was going on well. The fact is, we have been obliged to unship your husband, for conduct which you will probably understand."

Jenny fell back on the chair, and the good-natured owner stuttered, " Nay, nay ! take a glass of water. You see, we have to be strict in these matters, and we could not keep a man who might lose our vessel any day. I'll strain a point and give you five pounds ; but of course you must see we have our own interest to consider. Good-morning, madam ; I am very sorry it has happened."

Jenny felt as though a bar of iron had been bent across her head, and she walked home in a dazed condition. All night long she sat in a dream in the little parlour, surrounded by the quaint ornaments that Tom had collected from all parts of the world. She saw nothing, thought nothing ; and even the babble of her little girl fell upon her ears as if she had been deaf.

The owner was quite right—Tom Hardy had broken out

with a vengeance. During a sudden fit of temper he had
been induced to take a glass of champagne with a genial
stevedore, who wanted to "pull him round." One bottle
led to another, and before midnight Tom Hardy was mad
drunk. Next day he carried on the most extraordinary
capers : he hired a carriage with four ponies, and occupied
himself with driving full gallop until his beasts were
foundered, and he had to hand over a pretty fair sum by
way of compensation for broken knees. He went on board
the vessel and invited a jolly party of seven skippers, who
kept up a carouse until eight o'clock next morning. By
that time Hardy was frantic. He kept his legs, it is true,
but his brain was absolutely distraught, and his actions were
those of a lunatic. He began with his old practice of knocking men about ; and one poor wretch whom he shot overboard with a terrific left-hander would never have risen
again if the drags had not been promptly employed by the
English water-police.

After three days, during which time he never ate any
solid food, he was on the verge of an attack of delirium
tremens, and the vessel had to go to sea, with Hardy drunk
on the bridge. In running out through a very difficult
water-way he slapped the pilot's face, bade that functionary
hold his jaw, and proceeded to put the engines full speed
ahead.

A smart Yankee brigantine was towing out in front of the
Mariana; the sailing vessel yawed slightly, and Hardy, who
was attempting to accomplish a close shave, struck her on
the quarter with the bulge of the steamer's starboard bow,
and surged forward, bumping heavily, and making frightful
havoc amongst the standing rigging.

After tearing his way clear he gave a wild halloo of
defiance, and plunged ahead at twelve knots.

Of course the *Mariana* was detained at her port, and, as
Hardy was scarcely sober even then, his explanation of the
affair to the agent was so very lame that a telegram was
sent to England. The reply came promptly : "Discharge
him instantly."

The *Mariana* was lying at her moorings when the prim
agent stepped aboard about eight o'clock in the morning.
Tom had a fearful headache ; his eyes were bleared ; his

hand was shaking, and he was casting anxious glances over his left shoulder as if he expected some one was coming behind him.

The agent said, "I must ask you to go ashore, Mr. Hardy. I have orders to put another captain aboard at once." And on that very afternoon the drunken skipper took his baggage ashore.

*　　　*　　　*　　　*　　　*

Two years went by, and Jenny Hardy's savings were completely exhausted. She had written to her husband saying :

"DEAR TOM,—I don't care what you do ; you are always the same to us. I will live as well as I can until you get back, and nobody shall ever know that anything is wrong with you. We shall have to go short, I expect, of things to eat ; but I shall always be nicely dressed when I go out. It's a bad job, but there is no use moaning about it ; and I will try and keep your fault from being made public as well as ever I can. Do come home, dear, as soon as you can, and you will find us just the same if you have not a penny, or a coat to your back. We send you kisses, and I am your own faithful wife for good luck or bad."

Little by little the store of savings had dribbled away, and at last poor Jenny came to the end of her hoard. One morning Nance said, "I am so hungry, mother. As I came along the street I saw a lump of bread close beside the gutter, and if no one had been looking, I should have picked it up. I seem as if I could eat my bootlaces."

The woman put her arms round the girl, and said, "My bonnie bairn, I have not a bite to give you, and I dare not go and sell my shawl, or all the folks in the town would know it. We will starve just one day more, and perhaps God will be good to us if we say our prayers to-night."

With hunger biting at her very vitals, the brave little body went out day after day, and kept a cheery face in the presence of all the townsfolk. Some few of our people knew the real state of affairs, for gossip travels fast in so small a community, but no one could get a word out of Mrs. Hardy.

She was fainting with hunger after two days' starvation, when her big, burly brother came home from sea.

She met him smiling, and he sat down in the kitchen.

His first inquiry was rather startling : " No fire, Jenny ! what's up ?"

" I didn't think it was cold enough for a fire, Ralph dear."

" By George ! you must have a harder skin than I have got, then. Let us have a cup of tea, old girl."

Then Jenny fell on the strong man's breast and buried her face against him. She said, " Oh, Ralph dear, we are starving ; we have not a penny, nor a bit of bread, nor a morsel of coal."

" The blazes you haven't !" said the sailor, jumping up.

" Oh, my dear, it is all through drink, the drink, the weary drink. He has lost his ship, and he has never written for more than two years, and I didn't like to tell you, or else I would have written out to you to America. Just keep it quiet, Ralph honey, for I pray to God every day, and I go to the church every Sunday and pick out pieces in the Prayer-book like what I wish to say ; and I know my lad will come back to me, for all his being so cruel as to leave us so long without a word."

When she finished the sailor man was sobbing heavily.

He said, " Damn ! God forgive me. I have got my two years' voyage-money here. Now, look here, you must let me lodge with you, and take care of my coin ; and mind it's your own. I have a good mind to skelp you, you little duffer—starving your bairn for fond pride, and leaving all the lot of us in the dark. Why, my chums would have thought me a pretty scoot if they had known I let my sister go a-hungering."

Within an hour a load of coals drew up at the door, and little Nance and her mother had the first mouthful of meat they had tasted for many a long day.

*   *   *   *   *

When Tom Hardy woke to a sense of the situation after his discharge, he felt as though suicide was his only resource. He fixed his bleared eyes on the slimy water as he tramped up and down the quay, and again and again he had an impulse to throw himself forward, and end everything in those black depths. His reputation was gone ; he was friendless in a foreign land ; and his wild debauch had left him with very little money. He stayed in a low tavern amidst a riotous set of English sailors, but the shock had sobered him, and he clenched his teeth.

" Never another drop, not if I have to lie and grovel. And I will not go back to my wife and children until I have regained my character." So he growled in his extremity.

It happened that the Chinese Government was occupied just then in routing out a nest of pirates, who frequented the winding waters of the marsh lands, and preyed ferociously on the trading boats.

Tom was wandering aimlessly among the shipping, when he met a smart, aristocratic-looking man, dressed in a naval uniform.

The aristocrat politely raised a finger and touched his hat ; he then said, "Pardon me, sir; you are of the merchant service, are you not ?"

Tom answered, " Yes, sir ; late captain of the *Mariana.*"

" Ah ! are you the fellow who got us into the mess with the Yankee Government ?"

" Well, sir, I am afraid I am, and I have suffered for it. I have lost my ship, lost everything, and now I don't care what I do."

The officer said, " Well, I fancy you are just my man. I am trying to pick up a crew for a gunboat, and I should think you and I might strike up some kind of a bargain. You can fight, I suppose ?"

" Well, sir, I don't know about fighting, but I never saw anything in my life that I was frightened of ; I can say that much, if you won't fancy I am bragging."

" All right, then; now, look here, these affairs are managed very informally. I want to get together a lot of desperadoes, and it strikes me you are the kind of fellow I could trust. Will you ship ?"

Tom's heart bounded as he said, " Like a shot, sir ! I will stand to you as long as the life is in me."

And so for many months Tom Hardy was engaged among the wild crew of reckless and forlorn blackguards who formed the ship's company of the gunboat *Mandarin.* Even amongst that dare-devil lot he was conspicuous from his absolute insensibility to danger, and his prodigious strength.

His chief one day said to him, "By Gad ! Hardy, I wish you and I had lived in the old times. I guess that we and our boys would have taken the starch out of the Frenchmen."

Tom laughed with a burly roar at the notion, and said : " We certainly are giving Johnny Chinaman fits. I hear that some of the beggars pray to us. They call me the ' big devil ' and you the ' little devil.' "

From this fragment of conversation it will be seen in what kind of enterprise our sailor was engaged.

Shortly afterwards the *Mandarin* was sent out to punish a set of scoundrels who had lately massacred the entire population of a village.

At nightfall the gunboat lay at anchor in a very awkward part of a deep sluggish channel. The flats to right and left were covered with tall, rank reeds, which grew to a great height, and completely obscured the view from the vessel.

Towards midnight the captain went forward. On his return Hardy said, "I heard a frog just now. Damned funny kind of frog. He croaked three or four times, and he was answered by another round the bend of the river. If you will excuse me, sir, I should say we had better strengthen the watch."

"Oh, I don't think it is necessary," answered the captain ; "the marshes are swarming with frogs."

About an hour afterwards a Yankee sailor sang out, " Stand by, all of you ; we are going to get sky-blue fits in half a minute."

The captain rushed to the bows and looked anxiously into the murky darkness ; there was a flash, a sound of confused yelling, and before Tom Hardy had time to collect himself a perfect horde of men jumped over the bows of the gunboat and swarmed aft.

Tom didn't depend upon a sword ; he picked up an enormous handspike, and dashed into the crowd just in time to find the captain in extremity. With crashing blow, right and left, he cleared a lane amongst the marauders ; then with a hoarse roar like that of a wild beast he yelled, " Come on, *Mandarins*, murder the lot !"

His tremendous figure, and the fearful power of the blows

he delivered, fairly scared the pirates. The gunboat's crew rallied, and in five minutes not a pirate was left on board, excepting five who had been struck down by Tom Hardy's club.

The captain was wounded, but not seriously, and he said, " You shall have the command of a boat for yourself, my boy, after this job is over."

And sure enough Tom Hardy was promoted to high rank in the Chinese service.

*   *   *   *   *

Ralph and Jenny were chatting over their supper and speaking many kind words of poor Tom, when a knock came to the door.

Jenny shrieked, "Oh, it's him, it's him! I knew that God would not let us lose him. Run, Nance, to the door; I can't trust myself on my feet."

Then entered a jolly, broad-shouldered fellow, whose face was burnt almost to blackness by the tropical sun.

The boom of his deep voice sounded tremulously in the kitchen as he said, " Well, old girl, you thought I was behaving badly; but I will make up for it now, and never go away from you any more."

Jenny tottered to her giant, and the tears ran down his rough face as he strained her hard in his mighty arms.

Tom had been very lucky in the service, and he did not need to go to sea any more. He bought a few houses, and eked out his little income by acting as ship's husband for a small private company.

He is now a temperance lecturer, and it is worth going a long way to see strong men fall sobbing under the thrill of his great voice and his rude eloquence.

IV.

TOM BOWERY'S LITTLE GIRL.

Tom was very drunk. He had just offered to argue any man in the room on any subject that the universe supplied; he professed himself willing to discuss history, the Old Testament, Mr. Bradlaugh, politics, or theology, and he

3

implored the company to appoint a jury of rational men to
pronounce a verdict on the intellectual combat.

The landlord, a quiet Shetlandman, knew that Tom was
nearing the last stage, and he said, "Ah, then, Maister Bowery,
will it no pe time for you to pe makin' to your ain hoose ?"

Tom considered the matter during two solemn minutes,
and then volunteered to walk a chalk line with Mr. Wild-
goose, the landlord.

His challenge was not accepted, so he rose cheerily and
shouted, "No offence, any of you ! Argyment's argyment,
and no bad blood after. I'm off home."

Six inebriated mariners at once offered their services as
guides, and Tom accepted the convoy of the whole lot.
Two of the guides stopped to discourse on a knotty question
of nautical etiquette ; the other four continued the conversation which had been going on for the last hour, and, as
they all spoke at once, and all took different views of the
mixed set of questions under consideration, the passage of
the company along the street caused some commotion. The
four controversialists finally became so excited that they
formed themselves into a compact group, and roared at each
other like a set of rival bookmakers. Tom Bowery gazed
with sadness on the noisy logicians, and, after saying, " Not
the intelleck of a single buck rabbit to divide amongst the
four of you. You haven't, I tell you—word of honour—
the intelleck of one well-educated tom-cat. No !"—he
lurched off in drunken majesty.

Tom's progress homeward was marked by few incidents.
It is true that he thought the church clock in the market-
place was laughing at him, and he expressed his intention of
demanding satisfaction for the insult ; but a good-natured
policeman explained that the flippant clock would be sure
to apologize in the morning, so Tom went off satisfied.

Bowery was a sailor of the intellectual class. He was a
fine fellow to look at ; indeed, he was fitted both bodily and
mentally to take a very high place in the world, but he had
managed to slide out of the right groove somehow or other.
He stood over six feet high, and the stern, thoughtful head
that topped his athletic body drew attention wherever the
man went. His eyes were light grey, and they flashed like
steel when he was excited or intent on talk ; his brow was

very heavy, and a beetling prominence came sharply out over the cavernous sockets whence his wonderful eyes gleamed. A yellow moustache hid his flexible lips, and his rather weak chin was covered by a thick red beard, so that the real feebleness of his face was disguised. Looking at him casually, you would have thought that such a massive, imposing head must belong to a man of action; yet, in truth, a fatal infirmity of will rendered poor Tom's intellect almost abortive. Under perfect guidance he would have become a social force, but he was left to the mercy of violent passions, inordinate desires, and greedy sensuality, so that he drifted wildly hither and thither. Had he been a university professor, his extraordinary intellect and his personal fascination would have made him eminent; but he was a sailor, and his furious appetite for all the indulgences of life was uncurbed amid manifold temptations.

Tom was a poet, and I often wondered that he did not strike suddenly into fame, like Robert Burns. In a hundred ways he resembled the Scotch ploughman (though he had no humour), and his rough, half-grammatical verses had something of that piercing intensity that takes you by the throat when you first plumb the heart of Burns's mystery.

I want to put my man before you alive, that you may understand him, so I will copy some of his poetry for you, and you will then be able to understand his after-life better. I may say that he always laughed at himself for writing "poetry and muck," as he called it, but when the impulse was on him it mastered his mind till his song was done. Here is a poem which he wrote on the back of a discharge-sheet one morning when he had brought up in that nasty anchorage at San Francisco. He was incredibly dauntless, yet the fear of death sometimes seized his soul like a vice, and his verses are a confession.

AT ANCHOR.

The wind is pouring from the sea,
　And life and joy are in its breath,
But all its gladness saddens me,
　For I am thinking of my death.

When the white dawn rose up to-day
　And shone upon my drowsy eyes;
I couldn't keep the thought away—
　It poisoned all my Paradise.

3—2

It isn't sleeping that I dread;
  I fear the waiting moments when
The sword shall poise above my head—
  Ah! Jesus, give me courage then.

If we are drowned at dark to-night,
  I do not think my soul will quail
When the last wave, with aimless might,
  Charges our boat before the gale.

'Twill be like fighting when the spray
  Whirls its sharp arrows on the blast,
And the long waves in huge array
  Tramp with their sullen thunder past.

But waiting, waiting for the hour
  That takes me from the homes of men,
It makes my very pulses cower—
  Ah! Jesus, give me courage then.

Tom laughed at this, but I have no doubt that it was
done with a shuddering soul. All his reading (and he was
a voracious reader) only emphasized the melancholy on
which his nature was founded, and he often rushed off to
meet his curse just because the alcohol prevented him from
thinking of the terror and darkness of extinction. He had
his tender moods, and he often used his knack of verse-
writing to send sweet, prattling letters to his little girl.
This wild man had not shrunk from shedding blood in his
time—he was a savage when the passion was on him—and
he once dashed his bowie clean through a Spaniard's
jugular at Callao; yet there was a fund of unutterable
tenderness in him.

Here is a letter that he sent to his tiny pet when she was
five years old. He said, "I had such a long talk with the
sea and the birds and the wind the other night, and it was
all about you, and you must get your mother to read it to
you, for it is as true as ever can be. This is what the sea
and your father said:

    "'Oh! where are you flying, flying,
        You birds, with your bright white wings,
    And why are you sighing, sighing,
        You waves, with your curly rings?'

    "'We're flying away to the river
        That flows so far from here.
    We waves go sighing for ever;
        We'll laugh if you bring your dear.'

" 'My darling is sleeping, sleeping,
 Her dear little eyes are still ;
But why are you weeping, weeping ?
 I'll fetch her here, if you will.

" ' You birds must carry a letter,
 And say that it came from me,
And tell her I can't forget her,
 I want her here by the sea.'

" 'The wind it is blowing, blowing,
 So we will not go to-night ;
The tide it is flowing, flowing,
 But we'll go when the sun is bright.'

" The birds will fly till they hover
 Just over your darling's door ;
They'll wait until school is over,
 And the night has come once more.

" Then they'll drop the note through the curtain,
 And there they'll let it lie ;
They'll peep just once to be certain,
 And then they'll whisper ' Good-bye.'

" And the waves will go crying, crying,
 ' Oh ! when will Jenny be here?'
Till the birds come flying, flying,
 And they'll say, ' We've seen your dear.'

" Her queer little face was ruddy,
 Her queer little eyes were bright,
And her queer little shoes were muddy,
 But she'll clean them and come to-night.

 " Then the waves will be glad,
  They will dance just like mad ;
 And the fishes will flop,
  And now I shall stop."

This kindly fooling was often repeated in different forms as Tom reached port after port, and little Jenny Bowery did not care at all for a letter unless it was written in rhymes.

This was the man who was reeling home, muttering senseless brutalities to himself and facing the beauty of the sacred night with a bleared glare of his sodden eyes.

Little Jenny stayed up with her mother, and the two watched the clock with quick, quiet glances.

" I doubt your father's not coming home, my bairn. Get thee away to thy bed."

" Nay, mother. Daddy said he would come in, and he

said I was to sit up, and he's had none of the nasty drink this week yet. So I'll just stop."

The little girl was a perfect beauty. She had a clear, faintly tinted face, with golden-brown eyes that always seemed to be looking at something ever so far away. All her father's poetry had descended to her, and she always looked dreamy, but she was by no means delicate, like the poetic children of fiction. In her bath she looked like an exquisite statue, and her father used to say that there wasn't a young 'un with better legs anywhere north of the Head.

Little Jenny knew that her father drank, and she had weary thoughts about it, but she was keen beyond her years, and she always pretended that she did not notice. During several hard bouts the family had been impoverished, and Jenny had to go with darned stockings and shabby frock, but she used to cheer her mother up at the worst times, and she would say, "Never mind. You see, we'll make him better. I put it into my prayers every night, and you must come and hear me say them, 'cos if I don't say it right maybe God won't understand." She once wrote a letter, and addressed it to God, but her mother said it couldn't go. Jenny thought this was very hard, because, as she said, "If God had the paper on the table in front of Him, it would be far better than when there's such a lot of people talking all at once." She had written:

"DERE GOD,—don't let my fahver take enny nasty wisky and no bere, and no rum, and bring all his munny home, for my mother says we got no munny, and pleese do it for yure little girl, for jesus christs sake amen.

"JINNY BOWRY."

Jenny idolised Tom, for he had never spoken a cross word to her, and the child somehow knew that the big, strong man had a passion of love for her. Mrs. Bowery despaired, but Jenny was full of childish confidence. She once said, "What's the good of heaven if they can't keep daddy right?" and after every spell of drinking she lavished her care on the prodigal, and invented pet names for him in loving profusion.

The little girl was feeling drowsy, when a heavy, flapping step sounded in the street, and a thick voice roared :

> " Oh ! Sally Brown is a Creole lady ;
> Way, O, my rolling river,
> Sally Brown is like a May-day ;
> I'll spend my money on Sally Brown."

Then the latch was lifted, and a heavy fall echoed in the passage. Muttered ejaculations followed, and at last the kitchen door was opened. Tom swung to and fro, and blinked at the light ; his wife gazed at him with dull terror and rising disgust. Here was her man that used to be so clean, and alert, and bonny. She remembered how she liked to kiss the cool freshness of his cheeks ; she remembered when his breath was pure and his eye like a falcon's. And now a brutal mask was over his face ; the lustrous, poetic eyes were like the soulless orbs of a ruffianly bully ; the mouth that used to be compact and bright as a cherry was loose and slobbery. All the soul was gone from that fine front, and you would never have thought that this man was a splendid seaman, a master of men, a deep thinker. Poor Mrs. Bowery !

Tom said gravely, " Why deuce not go-bed my d—d—darlin' !"

Mrs. Bowery answered, "Sit thee down, honey, and get thy supper."

"Don't care cuss summer. Wha's summer to me ? Summer. Get thy summer ! Gimme winter."

Then with swift ill-nature Tom inquired, " Wheresh pet ? My angel. Wheresh she gone to ?"

He sank into a chair as he made this inquiry.

Little Jenny had stood behind her mother all the while. Her heart was throbbing so hard that she felt throttled, and her sweet soul was all in a turmoil. A sudden desperate resolve came into her childish mind. She raised her hands above her head ; her golden eyes shone with unearthly light as the excitement mounted in her ; her lips had gone pale, and they trembled as she parted them. With strange deliberation she advanced towards the startled man, who glared at her, and the unconscious, convulsive movement which made her lift her arms gave the tiny figure a weird look. She threw herself on her father, and cried, "Oh, daddy, daddy, my dear old boy! Oh, darling, don't drink, don't drink any more! My heart, darling. Here—see—your own little girl's heart. Look you, it's broken, broken, broken. Take me in your arms, and go and throw us both in the river, and I'll cuddle you all the time, and there'll be no nasty public houses in the river, and you'll take your little girl right away. But don't drink any more, my own, my boy, my dear, dear daddy! Oh, I could just die for you!"

Tom Bowery struck his forehead with both fists clenched, and the woman said, "Oh, Tom honey. No one put that into her head. It's a warning from heaven, my man. Come back to us, and don't touch it any more."

Bowery got up with Jenny in his arms; he strained her hard. He shook his head as if he were trying to clear his eyes; then he set Jenny down on her mother's knee, and burst out crying. The shock, the awful gesture of the child, the tearing passion of her voice, had struck through his nerves, and he was half sober. When his fit of sobbing was over he paused, and then said with low, strong tones, "I'll promise nothing to-night, when the drink's in me, but to-morrow I start fresh. I've got a lesson to last me till I'm dead and buried."

Mrs. Bowery faltered, "Come thy ways, then, to bed;" but the little girl stepped up, and, assuming an air of extreme authority, said, "No you, mother. He's my boy, and I'm going to make him good. You go in the back bedroom all alone by yourself, and I'll sleep with him, 'cos he wants to be petted."

Tom went meekly upstairs with his peremptory little guide, and the dumbfounded mother followed as if she were a minor person in the establishment.

As soon as Tom had laid down, Mrs. Bowery lifted Jenny in beside him, and the little thing murmured, "Come to me, my poor boy, and I'll say my prayers for you." Then she nestled her head on her father's strong breast, and he heard her murmuring her petitions.

Tom was uneasy in the night, but whenever he moved his strange little nurse waked quickly and patted him—crooning all the time as if she were soothing a child. There was something magnetic in the touch of the small, soft hand, and a blessed thrill went through the drunkard's heart as he gradually came to measure the might of the love that this sweet creature bore him.

In the morning Jenny was quite brisk. She bounced out of bed, and said, in her pretty guttural way, "Now, lie still, like a good boy, and I'll go and get you a cup of tea ; I hear mother downstairs."

She soon brought up a tray, and as she put it down she asked very proudly, "Now, am I not a clever one ? There, now, I'll watch you all the time till that's done, and then I'll run for another. Wait a bit. Don't wet your moustache yet. Now give me a kiss ! There ! Now whisper in my ear, ' I'll never, never, never take any whisky no more, and I'll please my little girl, 'cos she loves me.' Whisper nice."

And Jenny played round her father and coaxed him till he forgot his headache and his mental depression.

She danced down with Tom, and putting on the most delicious airs of coquetry, she shouted, "Here he is ; and he's made me a promise, and he's never going to be a bad boy any more, and I'm going to be his sweetheart altogether !"

Tom went out, and in the market-place he met one of the six orators who had escorted him homeward on the night before.

"What cheer, tintacks ! How's the coppers this morning ? Oh, lor' ! I went to bed in my boots, and I've got a thirst on me now I wouldn't take ten shillings for. Come on and let's have our lives saved. I am just in for a whole sixpenn'orth of Scotch."

Tom's nerves were agitated ; the vision of cool tankards, of glittering glasses, came before him, and his burning mouth moistened at the thought. Every muscle of him was charged with alcohol, and every molecule of the stuff was craving for a companion.

He dug his nails into his hands, and gasped, "I can't, Jimmy, I can't. Don't ask me. Be a friend now, or 'pon my soul I'll never speak to you more."

"What's up ?"

"I've sworn to my little girl I won't touch it ever again,

and I'll die on the flags with the jim-jams before I'll wet my lips with it again."

The rough sailor looked grave, and replied : " All right, sonny, I commend you. You keep to that and you're right for life."

It is a popular notion spread by weak drunkards that sober men are " chaffed " till they give way. This is pure rubbish, born of selfishness and cowardice. I have lived with the roughest and hardest-drinking sets in England and Scotland, and I can safely say that any drinker would be scouted if he tried to press a teetotaler into tasting. As a matter of fact, a man who drinks always respects a man who doesn't drink. I am not speaking of moderate and decent persons who know when to stop ; I am speaking of the tremendous soakers among whom my lot has often been cast. In their worst moments they know that they are on the wrong road, and they never try to coax another man to join them. With my own eyes I have seen a half-drunk man empty into the fire a glass which had been called in for one who was trying to "take the turn." The new teetotaler had never been tempted ; his glass was merely brought as a thing of course, but his tipsy guardian said : " No, no. We don't want him to be the same as us again."

Tom Bowery was fearfully depressed that evening, and he was unspeakably comforted by the presence of the soft little dove who nestled by him, and cooed her lovely little words of comfort.

He stood out till his vessel was ready for sea, and by that time his face was clear, the whites of his eyes were without a speck, and his superb mental and bodily power had come back to him.

It is nonsense to talk about the hopelessness of curing a drinker. When the first week of abstinence is over, a well-nourished man feels no craving of a violent nature, and it is only whimpering poltroons who go home and say that they were "tempted." They begin afresh of deliberate purpose, and they rouse a craving that would perish if it were not stimulated by a man's own crass selfishness and weakness.

Little Jenny hung on her father's neck when the pilot-boat came alongside, and she had a light of pure joy on her face when she jumped ashore at the landing, for Captain Tom Bowery had whispered : "I'll blow my brains out before I vex you again, little sweetheart."

When Tom was gone, the necessity for acting as "mother" existed no more, and little Jenny resumed her old childish life with perfect contentment. On the second morning Mrs. Bowery opened a big parcel at breakfast time, and showed the most ravishing doll that ever was seen. "There, my lass," she said (and the tears ran down her face), "we're none too well off just now ; but I would a bought thee that if it had been our last sovereign, my canny wee daughter."

Jenny paraded the house and the front street with a pride which passes description. She used to murmur her confidences to the doll, and her talk ran all on one subject. She would say : "And didn't we make him better ? And when he comes home, you and me'll go down to the dock, and I'll make him kiss my dolly, and I'll show you what a good boy he is ; and you'll be pleased with him, won't you, dear ? and we'll make him nurse you when he's smoking his pipe." So she went on, and her good heart was full of happiness.

  *   *   *   *   *

Tom Bowery was in command of a fine steamboat, for, of course, he was too high-class a man to go in an ordinary merchant sailing-vessel. He was bound for New York, after calling at Cardiff, and he met with pretty heavy weather. On one cruel day, when everything was awash, and the scuppers were flushed continually by a rushing, creamy torrent, the steward said : "Would you like your whisky after dinner, sir ?"

"No, steward. I've knocked it off."

The man stared, because he knew only too well what Tom's former habits had been like, and he had often been kept up all night when a party of noisy captains came to play cards on board. He stammered and asked : "Would you like to have these locked away then, sir?"

"Locked away ! No. Do you think I might give in ? No fear. If a fellow can get through a day like this without a nip I should think he might manage in any weather. No. But I'll tell you what I'll do. Open a bottle of brandy, and stick it over my washstand. I know what you're thinking, but if you find that stuff touched at the end of a year I'll give you a five-pound note. I'm going to fight it, and I'll take a lot of licking."

Bowery's mind grew finer and more powerful ; he read with increasing enjoyment, and he felt irresistibly inclined to literary work. He had a touch of genius in him, and now that the lulling influence of his curse was gone, and he had escaped from the house of Circe, his mental activity was overpowering. All nature took a different colour in his eyes, and he learned by degrees the inestimable value of small and simple pleasures. The transformation was like magic. He was as good a sailor as ever, but there was something in him besides. A master intellect struggled to find expression, and on wild nights, when the hoarse winds called and the illimitable mystery of clamorous darkness folded him round, Tom Bowery had thoughts in him that raised him high, and made him look with loathing on the beastly slough that had fallen away from him. His passionate love for little Jenny grew daily, but the hysterical element of mere animal fondness died out, and instead of thinking of her as a brute might think of its cub, he felt that pure and reasonable affection which is the loveliest light poured on the troubled darkness of life.

At New York he went unscathed amid the hurrying debauchery that marks the seafarer's life in that goodly city. When the usual offers of drink were made, Tom quietly declined, and the good-natured Yankees merely said : "All right, Cap. So long as you feel good, you take your own way."

He wrote a sweet letter to little Jenny, and I transcribe one fragment :

" You must not be too proud to meet me when I come home, for all your doll and the rest of it. I am quite right up to now, and I kiss your portrait every time I come off the bridge. Since we came here I have not spent half a dollar on myself, and if we go on like this we shall soon have a fine house, and your mother shall be dressed as well as the mayor's wife, and my little girl shall have such a rig-out as never was known. When I come back I shall do nothing but go out with you at nights, and I shall give you and your

mother the most awful nailings at crib that you ever dreamed
of. And now good-bye. I left my heart with you, dear
little sweetheart, and I must get back to find it. Here is a
pretty verse which you must take all to yourself. It isn't
my own writing, but I got it out of a book :

> " 'Then come to my grave like a good little lass,
>   Where'er it may happen to be,
> And if any daisies should peep through the grass,
>   Be sure they are kisses from me.'

Don't you like that ? But I am going to stay out of my
grave for a good bit yet."

Jenny kept this letter folded carefully in a piece of newspaper, and she put it inside her pinafore lest it should get
too much crushed. At night she put it under her pillow,
and in all ways she treated it as though she were in possession
of her first love-letter.

Tom Bowery bought a vast heap of foolscap paper before
he left New York, and as soon as his leisure began he engaged
in mysterious scribblings which occupied him many hours
every day. A captain on board a steamer has abundant spare
time, and Tom employed his in earnest study. For during
one of his long meditations the thought struck him, "I see
that all these men who write books never do well unless they
are talking about what they know thoroughly. As soon as
they start with imagination and that nonsense they go all
wrong together. Why should I not write what I know ?
There isn't a change in the sky or the sea that would not be
worth describing if we could only set that Mr. Ruskin on
and make him squat on deck till his sketch was done. Our
life would be just as interesting to other people as theirs is
to us. I'm going to try."

Tom found that his style was dismally awkward, and he
set himself to cure his deficiency. He said, "I'll copy out
some of these good men's work, and I fancy I'll get the
knack directly. I can do poetry. Why shouldn't I do the
other all right ?"

And work he did with fierce assiduity. He would copy a
page of Ruskin, or Thackeray, or Charlotte Brontë; then
he closed the book, and tried to reproduce all he had copied ;
then he opened the book again, and corrected minutely all

the errors into which he had dropped; then he tried again
until he succeeded in approaching his original. This
drudgery lasted him all the way home, and he felt himself
acquiring facility every day—nay, every hour.

When the boat surged into the dock, Tom saw his idol
dancing with delight on shore, and he thought she looked
like some beautiful fairy as she carried on her antics among
the grimy chains and lowering scaffolds. After he had
kissed her, Jenny said, "All right, my boy?" and the big
sailor replied, "You needn't ask; I'm right for life, my
lady."

While the vessel lay in port, Tom passed his spare time
during the day in his new pursuit; but in the evening he
invariably put on his most imposing broadcloth, and prepared to escort his wife and daughter into the town. Mrs.
Bowery wore her satin cape, and a rolling cataract of watch-
chain flowed over her bosom, and resolved itself into a
glittering whirlpool at her waist. Her gloves were uncomfortable to the most fashionable degree, for she had four-
button Suèdes which hurt her hard-working wrists; but
she bore tight boots and long gloves with Christian resigna-
tion in order that her husband's dignity might be kept up.
Jenny trotted alongside, and, while the parents bowed
laboriously to all passing acquaintances, the little girl stole
friendly glances at the children of other captains. Then
came the game of crib, in which Tom outraged all morality
by his scandalous dexterity in cheating, and then the happy
parting for the night. It was a joyous time, and Bowery
felt sudden thrills of keen gladness afterwards when he was
at sea, and remembered the simple quietness of the little
kitchen and the flushed, ecstatic face of his pet.

Jenny was never nervous now, for the change in her
father was complete. The anxious look in her eyes was
seen no more, and she blossomed into a healthy, merry child.
One prosperous voyage after another went by, and Mrs.
Bowery's banking account reached a good figure; but Tom
was not satisfied. The schoolmistress told him that Jenny
was clever to an astonishing degree, and he wanted the girl
to have full opportunities. He heard that there was a
college where young ladies received an education equal to
that of honours' men in the Universities; but £200 a year

was more than he could spare. Doggedly he set himself at
his literary work, and he got through a great deal when the
weather was fine and the boat had a long stretch before her.
You always notice that it is the naturally indolent men who
achieve the most work when they are once spurred into
action. They seem to accumulate energy during their spells
of idleness, and they toil at white heat when the impulse
takes them.

* * * * *

A prim old publisher sat in his comfortable room, medi-
tating about the ruinous losses of a trade which left him a
bare pittance of £5,000 a year to live on.

His son, who acted as reader, hailed him from a side
table. "I have something good here. You're always
telling me to find a new thing. Here it is with a vengeance."

"You have a knack of discovering genius. I wish some
of your geniuses turned up trumps."

"Come now, father, that may do very well outside; but
tell me, have I ever made a blunder yet? I refused
Tamplin's 'History of Mexico,' but you see the book was
five years out before it began to move. No, I don't
blunder."

"What have you got?"

"It's a novel by a sailor. I've run through a volume or
thereabouts, and I never came across such a style in my
life."

"Never mind style. What is the effect? Does it look
as if it had money in it?"

"Why, the fellow's characters seem to burn themselves
on your eyes, and he does some prose that catches me like a
strong wind."

The old man looked thoughtful, and asked, "Does he name
any figure?"

"No. He wants a share."

"Well, take it coolly, and speak to me again when you've
turned the matter over in your mind."

* * * * *

Jenny Bowery was reading a book from the free library.
She looked up with a laugh and said, "Oh, mother, we

must keep this until the boat comes in. I'm sure it's all about our town, and you might think the sailors and the ships were right in front of you. Some of the owners'll go out of their minds."

The novel was called " The Captain's Daughter," and it was rousing much attention in London. The critics were only too delighted to welcome a fresh hand, and they gave the book hearty praise. People talked about it in company, and so much curiosity was excited that the book soon ran through seven editions.

When Tom Bowery came home and settled down for an evening's chat, Jenny said, "Oh, my boy, we've got the most delightful book for you. I believe we're all in it, and the people ask the librarian for it at the rate of forty every day. It's called ' The Captain's Daughter.' "

Tom smiled grimly, and promised to read the book next day ; but before he began his reading the post came, and with it a letter forwarded through his publisher. This letter was addressed to Tom by a shrewd man who was proprietor of a great newspaper. It ran :

"I have read your novel with keen interest, and it has occurred to me that, with a little experience, you might succeed in journalism. We want a man to write articles on nautical subjects, and, should you be disposed to engage yourself exclusively to us, I will guarantee to you a handsome retainer. The sooner the matter is settled the better, and I shall be pleased if you can make an appointment by telegraph."

Tom was in London within twelve hours after receiving this letter, and he returned two days afterwards looking very happy.

In the evening he said, with touching gravity, " My dears, I must tell you my fortune is made, and I go to sea no more. We'll always live together, and there'll be no partings again."

His wife and daughter were like to pull him to pieces with inquiries, before he managed to make them understand how matters stood with him. Then Jenny was too glad to speak ; she remained silent when the full extent of the new life revealed itself to her, and her father thought she looked like a saint.

Tom made a great deal of money, but he never left his own town. Enthusiastic Americans and Londoners made pilgrimages to see him, and all the people in the place were very proud of their man of genius ; but Tom only cared for his success insomuch as it made him able to lavish every luxury and every indulgence on his little girl.

V

THE CHIEF MATE'S TROUBLE.

IN the autumn of 1870 I passed the Board of Trade examination for master after I had stayed ashore four months to attend a nautical school. When I took my ticket home my mother nearly cried, for her heart was full, and she patted me on the back a dozen times over while she was getting tea ready.

All of our people had been sailors ever since the family of Soulsby was known in the town, and I think the head-stones in the churchyard show that there have been five generations of master mariners bearing our name. One very green and rotten old stone is in memory of Simeon Soulsby, who was drowned when the sloop *Elizabeth and Mary* ran ashore south of the Pixie's Gap in 1743, and the newest and whitest of the set was put up for my father, after he went down with his vessel in the January gale of 1867. It didn't seem natural for any one of us to stop on shore, and so my mother knew as much about seafaring business as her lads did, barring, of course, that she couldn't take an observation or pull and haul.

We had a girdle-cake for tea, and the old lady floured my jacket in ever so many places as she kept on turning away from the fire to look at me and clap my shoulders. I never saw anybody so muddled and so proud in my life.

It would not have done for me to hurry out that afternoon, but I fidgeted a bit till tea was over, because I wanted to tell Mary Mather how I had got on. Mary was one of the best-looking girls in the town, and we had walked together from the time when I was an apprentice. It was not usual

4

for people in our position to marry until the man had passed
for master, but old Captain Mather had told me that I
should not wait for the girl a month after I had taken
command of a ship, and I felt safe and joyful now.

My mother at last said, "Now, honey, aw've fashed thee
long enough with my daft talk. Ga away, and get theesel'
made smart-like. Aw's warrant thou wants sair to see her.
Thou minded me of thy father that time when he passed,
and he came right to me, and aw'd putten my ribbons on
for him to see. Eh, me! And thee things is laid ready,
and aw bowt thee a bonny new handkercher."

I put on my new flat cap and my pilot suit, and then I
went away to Mather's. There is no harm in saying that
when I got to the East Lane, where no one could see me, I
ran as hard as I could for three hundred yards.

There was no need to knock. As soon as the gate creaked
I heard a shuffle in the upstairs room, then two or three
thumps on the stairs, and then Mary stood on the doorstep
looking white about the lips. Old Mather declared that she
cleared the stairs in two jumps, and I am certain she had
not come down very carefully. She took me by both arms
and pulled me inside. I clean forgot the door, and she
said, "Oh, you fond lad, they'll see us"; but I cared very
little who saw, and I should have kissed her several times
more if the skipper hadn't roared out, "Ahoy, there, mistorr;
belay, and fetch yoursel' up here sharp!"

Then we went upstairs arm-in-arm till we got to the
parlour door, and I waited till Mary had made her hair
straight. Before we knocked she put her face up to me
and said, "I could just dance," and the old man lifted the
"sneck" quickly and caught us. His own cleverness pleased
him so that he made the glasses rattle, as he lumbered back
to his chair shaking with laughter.

All this time not a word was said about the certificate,
but they knew it was all right, and Captain Mather went
on like a schoolboy—if you can imagine a schoolboy of
seventeen stone weight.

We had some grog from a squat Dutch bottle, and after
the skipper had taken a drink that would have choked anybody else, he said, "Look here, mistorr; what are you going
to pay the schoolmaster?"

This was one of his jokes. I had been obliged to prepare for examination about all the lights round the coast, so in the evenings I used to repeat them to Mary and stand her cross-examination. She would say, "Three red flashes at an interval of thirty seconds, followed by white flash," and then I tried to give her the right name of the light. Sometimes I went wrong on purpose, in order that I might go up and look at the book over her shoulder, and this caused many interruptions, because I never sat down without kissing her. But she didn't mind, and it made a lot of fun. The skipper thought he had found out a really first-rate joke when he christened his daughter "the schoolmaster," and we laughed harder every time he came out with it.

In answer, then, to Mr. Mather's question, I simply said, "She's a tip-top schoolmaster, captain, and if you'll let me offer her my own self I'll say it's a good bargain for me."

He looked serious for a moment, but he replied, "All right, sonny. My word's my bond. Get away the two of you out for a walk,' and the whole business was settled without any more words.

If I were one of the sort to write poetry I should make some up about that evening. The wind was blowing steadily from the west, and the sea lay quiet. Now and again there came a long breath through the coarse grass where we strolled, and it sounded as if somebody was sighing; but neither of us sighed very much except for happiness. The breeze caught at Mary's soft hair and blew it round her face so that she had to turn and go right in the wind's eye, as I said, every now and then, to shake back the cloud over her broad shoulders. She looked splendid as her bright cheeks shone through the tresses, and I don't think she was very much vexed when she had the chance of tossing her head back and showing me what a fine mass of hair she had. She was simple enough, but she knew she looked well when her beautiful locks were disordered a little. The hours went on, and the ships gradually sank into the shadows. One by one the grey towers of canvas seemed to fade round the Point, and the girl said, "Oh, my lad, I'll have to watch you away round there very soon!" The night started out

4—2

of the sea, and we turned homeward just as the lighthouse
began to shoot out its straight red flare.

In the morning I began to look for chances at once. I
had as good discharges as any man need want, and I fancied
that I should get a ship directly; but although the owners
were very friendly, they looked rather shy at my smooth
face. For a fortnight I lived among vague promises and
kindly refusals, and my money dwindled. Night after night
I had to meet Mary without any good news, and my face
was not cheerful, in spite of my efforts to look as if I were
at ease.

When the third week came I happened to stroll into the
Turk's Head Inn, where the sailors used often to meet of a
morning, and I saw a tall, well-dressed man talking to one
of my friends who commanded a steamer.

As I settled down at a table my chum saw me in the
looking-glass, and turned sharply round. He said, " Here,
Jemmy, you know the young 'uns better than we do. Can
you pick us a real likely one to go chief mate up the Black
Sea ?"

I asked, " What's the ship ?"

" Barque. Eleven hundred. Here's the boss. Captain
Haler, Captain Soulsby. Now you know each other."

Haler was a bronzed fellow, with a fine hard face, and a
very clear blue eye. I saw him run me over in a flash, and
he smiled nicely when he had taken my measure.

I deliberated for a few seconds, and then said, "I'm your
man."

My friend was surprised, and asked, "Shan't you hang
on a bit longer ? It's a pity to keep your ticket idle."

I told him I would rather let the ticket lie idle than be
idle myself, and the upshot was that in ten minutes everything was settled. Haler informed me that an agent had got
him a crew, so I needn't trouble myself about seeking for
men. He said, " We have rather a scratch lot, but we'll put
them into shape before we come to Finisterre." The very
mention of the roaring crags of Finisterre made my heart
jump, and I was keen for blue water once more.

We chatted on for a little, and I observed that Captain
Haler drank fast—took his whisky as though he were not
used to it; indeed, his face was too healthy for a drinker,

and his hand was steady when he lifted his glass. Just as we turned to go away he said, "Let's have one more. I'm not right somehow this morning. Here, fill these, and give us decent doses this time."

My friend looked quietly at the captain, as though he were thinking out a puzzle; then he said in a curious tone, "I say, young man, you mean business. Do you know that's your seventh this morning?"

I thought Haler was going to return an angry answer, but he only smiled in a strained sort of way, and said, "Oh, yes; I'm in the humour." Then he drank the fresh glass of spirit raw.

I didn't know the meaning of this scene at the time, but I am certain now that the man was screwing himself up, and his excited state prevented the drink from affecting him on the spot.

My mother moaned a good deal about my going away as mate again, but I humoured her, and she soon forgot her trouble and her dignity in the bustle of packing my sea-chest.

Mary took the thing very well. She laughed to hearten me, and I remember her saying, "It's only another voyage, and you're the same to me if you were to go before the mast again. Don't run off with some of them fine ladies out Russia way, and you'll find me ready by the quay-side when you come back, if so be you don't take up your moorings at night-time."

The last night came, the tug was ordered for ten in the morning, and I slipped ashore in my working clothes to have one word before we started.

Mary walked half-way to the ship with me, carrying a parcel which she wouldn't give up till we bade each other good-bye. Then she said:

"Now here's a guernsey I've knitted for you all by myself. It's cold away down there, and I don't like to think of you being cold. You'll find the other things from me in your sea-chest, and God bless you, and you be sure night and morning I'll say something in my prayers for you. And now go away or I'll cry. There'll be time enough for crying when you're gone."

Our women in the little ports are not very good at

grammar, and things of that sort, but they are practical people, and my sweetheart was one of the best of them. She waved as she turned the corner, and I never got the lump out of my throat till I had to swear at some of the hands. It seemed awful to swear with the touch of her lips on me, but duty is duty.

The barque looked a real dandy as she foamed along in the wake of the tug next day, and the men in the sail-makers' lofts and the building yards cheered us when we swept past.

There was plenty for me to do without thinking of senti-ment ; yet, sweating and breathless as I was, I had time to feel sad when the shanty-man struck up, " Away down Rio." The chorus goes :

> Then away, love, away,
> Away down Rio.
> O, fare you well, my pretty young girl,
> We're bound for the Rio Grande.

We were giving her the weight of the topsails, and all the fellows were roaring hard at the shanty, when I saw what I wanted to see. My bonny was out on the end of the jetty. She looked like a lovely figure-head, for she was all as still as stone, excepting when the flossy brown hair lifted with the wind.

There was good water by the jetty, so I whispered to the pilot, " Sheer us in a bit at the jetty, Lancelot, if you can manage without shaking the tug." Lancey glanced forward, then he winked, and the barque yawed as far as the hawser would allow, so I saw my sweetheart close, and her face was pale. She tried a smile, but found she dare not part her lips. She tightened them, and stared straight forward without even fluttering a handkerchief.

Outside of the bar the steamer came back on us to take off the pilot and the owner, and the barque drew very slowly ahead under the topsails. The cabin boy came forward to tell me that the owner wished to see me. I took off my cap, and went below.

Mr. Hawbrook, our owner, was sitting beside the captain. He said, " Now, Mr. Soulsby, you must drink good luck for us all. I wish you a pleasant voyage and success to your efforts." He handed me the decanter as though I was wanted to perform some kind of religious ceremony, and I bowed and took a second mate's nip of brandy.

Mr. Hawbrook was a very respectable man, and whenever he sent a ship to sea on a Sunday morning he went to chapel and asked a blessing on the undertaking—at least, that is what people used to say. Sometimes, when the men had to lie out on a yard while the vessel was smothering herself in wreaths of white water, the sailors would say, "It's a pity old Jemmy Hawbrook ain't here to spend his Sunday;" but the folks ashore never sneered in that way, for they had a great belief in Mr. Hawbrook, and considered him an institution that the town should be proud of.

When the owner got over the side, he and the captain exchanged glances, and I don't think I ever saw anything that made me wonder so much. Sometimes in a crowd you feel compelled to look in a particular direction, and meet the eye of a distant person who seems to be "ready" for you. It was a quiet glance of that telegraphic sort which passed between Haler and his employer. While we were picking our way down the east coast we had spells of thick weather, and the captain showed himself to be as careful a seaman as ever I sailed with. The decanters were put away, and no drink was brought out at any time excepting a bottle of ale on Sunday after dinner ; but the chief had something on his mind, and although he attended to his work he seemed to be always brooding.

One night a great clumsy screw collier came blundering along through the haze, and we had to burn flares and yell a good deal before we could get the thick-witted skipper to give way. Captain Haler showed the right amount of temper as the vessel shaved past us, and when he had shouted, "Where are you coming to ? Why didn't you bring your grandmother to take care of you ?" and other remarks of a sarcastic nature, he proceeded to swear with a strength and finish which I never heard equalled even in the coasting trade. But as soon as his natural instincts, as a sailor, were satisfied, he sighed, and said to himself, "Lord forgive me for swearing. I wish the beggar had gone through us and ended it."

The second mate thought that Haler referred to the compensation which the owners of the collier would have been obliged to pay had any damage been done, but my notion was different. There was a kind of despair in the words and in the captain's tone of voice which affected me.

After we left the Downs the weather still remained hazy, so that the work all the way down Channel was harassing in the extreme.

One morning at four I relieved the second mate, and the captain went on deck with me. When he had put on his oilskin he shivered and turned to the spirit locker. " We can both do with a nip," he said ; and then he took about half a tumbler of raw brandy at one drink. For three days more he drank, off and on, all day, and his caution and skill as a navigator seemed to leave him.

We were creeping along one afternoon, and her head lay N.N.W., when suddenly the haze lifted, and we saw a long low point away on the starboard bow. Haler was standing beside me at the moment, and he said sharply, " Mercy ! we've fetched the Start." I replied, " No, sir. I beg pardon, but that's the Bill of Portland." He reddened, and muttered something, and then we put her away on the other tack.

This incident rather alarmed me, for I saw perfectly well that the skipper had no idea where we were. In all my experience I never knew such a mistake made by any sailorman, and I set it down to the liquor. However, when we made the run for Ushant, Haler braced himself up again, and by the time we sighted the queer, low rocks he was as active and sensible as ever. We ran a little to the east to seek for a wind, and very soon we were bowling nicely along over the Western Ocean roll.

The captain kept himself sober, yet he never really looked like a man who was altogether right. Nothing could have been better than his handling of the ship, but his work was done almost mechanically. Only once I saw him come fairly out of his depression, and then he showed what a rare fellow he must have been in his best day.

It was my watch below, and I was lying on my bunk outside the bedclothes. We were going along with a good breeze a little abaft the beam, and the captain was carrying all she would stand to comfortably. There came a curious sound ; then the vessel seemed to stop dead, and I jumped up at once. Directly I got my head clear of the companion the wind struck me with a blow like that of a solid body ; and I saw that we were nearly on our beam ends. A white stream of streaky water was pouring along like a cataract, and I am pretty well certain that any crew to starboard of us must have seen our keel. Haler sprang like a cat, and let the square mainsail fly ; there was a clatter like musketry ; and the sail split, but the relief did not ease her quite enough. The captain rushed aft, laid hold of the wheel, and the barque came to an even keel in a very short while. There was no time to save our canvas, so something had to go ; we plunged bows under for an instant ; then the foresail was let fly, and then, with a tearing strain and a long rip, the maintopsail, maintopgallantsail, and foretopsail went, and flew like scraps of paper in the screaming blast. I had to make myself very busy getting in the mainsail, and I thought some of us would have had our brains knocked out, but we managed to make all snug without any further harm, and when I came aft I found the skipper standing quiet and cool, with his feet hard set and his hands gripping the spokes so that his knuckles were white.

He had stepped into the chart-house for a minute, leaving the second mate in charge, and the squall had swooped on us like a ghost, before the officer had time to notice any queer appearance to windward. Haler never lost his head for a moment, and when I went up to him he merely said in a low composed voice, " I haven't seen one come like that before. Get out the second suit of sails, and we'll bend them to-morrow."

Next day he did as much of the sailmaker's and rigger's work as any two of us put together; then directly the crush of work was over he relapsed into his sombre and melancholy mood, and went about once more like a sleep-walker.

I often went forward during the dog-watches and smoked a pipe with the boatswain, for I hold that though you must bustle the men around, yet a little familiarity at proper times does no harm.

One evening my friend said in a hesitating way, " The skipper don't seem very jolly, does he ?"

I replied, " Oh, it's his way.   We all have our own ways
of carrying on, you know."

The boatswain bent forward and whispered, " Look here,
Mr. Soulsby, I'm going to run some risk.   I know what
discipline is, but I've seen a thing .or two in my day, and I
tell you I don't like this.   I once sailed with a captain of
the name of Weatherburn, who put us as near as he could in
a bonny mess.   Went off his head, he did, and we had to
tie him down in his state-room.   Now, I've heard our captain
jawing away to hisself, the same as Weatherburn used to do.
When you're out of the way he sometimes keeps mutter,
mutterin', and jabber, jabberin' enough to fley anybody.
Last night I crept under the boat to get a look at our green
light, and when I was standin' behind the boat peepin'
over, he comes past, and he says, says he, ' Oh that I had
wings like a dove !' and then he says, ' Let this cup pass from
me,' and that don't seem the ticket to me.   Then another
time, when I was goin' past the charthouse I sees him
kneelin', and he groaned somethin' awful.   It isn't the jumps
he's got ; I can tell by his eye when he's had a single tot of
grog.   It is worse, sir ; and now you may be riled, but I
can't help speakin'."

" I think there's some family trouble, Joe.   He wasn't
square before we sailed, and I'm sometimes half in the mind to
steal his razors.   But don't you say a word about this again.
I can't appear to be in confidence with you ; but if anything
very particular turns up, stick a dab of white paint on the
breast of your guernsey frock, and I'll manage to get a word
with you where no one can see us."

We were very unlucky with the winds after our mishap
in the squall, and we even missed the northerly breeze that
usually helps a vessel down from Finisterre to the Burlings.
There was plenty of hard work, and while we were beating,
with yards buckling like whalebone, and towers of water
falling aboard of us forward, I envied the ugly colliers that
toiled sullenly on, without needing to care about head-winds
and head-sea.

The captain attended well to his duty, but his spirits sank
lower every day, and his way of starting when he got over
a fit of brooding was enough to frighten you.

I was standing one very dark night just where the wind

from the courses of the mainsail roared down upon me, and made my hair wave. The darkness was full of wild noises and strange dim shapes. The cordage shrieked and crackled, and the timbers moaned with sharp peevish cries, like the voices of people in pain. Our wake boiled away in a white stream that faded out of view amid the black hurly-burly, and we moved on through a strange region which seemed never to have been shone on by sun or stars. I was thinking kindly about my girl when the captain went past, but that night I thought no more of home, for my superior's face made my heart go cold. He was twisting his hands and muttering, and in the loud confusion of the night he groaned with a throttled sound that pierced my ear through all the wild clamour of winds and water.

At twelve o'clock I turned in, but my nerves would not let me sleep, and I felt chilly with vague fears, for I never had seen a man go on in that way.

The cabin was half lit by the yellow flame of the lamp, and the shadows swung heavily as the ship gave her long swoops down the sides of the seas. I closed my eyes and tried to compose myself, but even the squeak and scuffle of the rats (which at ordinary times no one minds) nearly crazed me, and I fairly sweated. The door of my berth was fastened back, so I could easily see when anyone descended the companion.

At three o'clock Captain Haler came down. His lips were hard pressed, and his hands were clutched like claws on his breast, as though he were in pain. He glanced quickly through my door, and then came in and stood over me for two minutes, while I held my breath and got ready to grip him.

I heard him say, " He's sure to find out," and then he went to the table and bent over a chart.

At four o'clock I made an excuse to enter the main cabin, and before speaking I took one look at the chart which Haler was studying. It was a minute survey of the Straits of Yenikale. How he came by it I cannot tell, but he got it from no nautical stationer in England. There are charts enough, but this one seemed to have been drawn for use in the torpedo service, so carefully was it done, and so closely were the soundings marked.

When I coughed and said, "I'm going to relieve the second mate, sir," Haler looked up, as he always did when his waking dreams broke, and his eyes for an instant had a gleam of fear and horror.

He stammered out, "Ah! I'm just trying to learn the trap," and rolled the chart up rapidly.

I thought to myself, "That's very funny. He can't take the vessel through himself. The pilot will come on board, and the skipper's responsibility ends right away"; and this reflection occurred to me again and again until the morning broke, and the pretty schooners could be seen careering hither and thither.

In the afternoon Joe and I began to rip an old sail to bits, for we wanted canvas to mend the hose. The other hands were busy forward, so I had a long, quiet chat with my friend. I told him all about the chart, and about the captain's wild manner, and he said, "There's some game on. I can't smell it out, but I shall manage it before we're up to Yenikale."

I inquired, "Do you fancy there's anything wrong about the cargo? If there is it doesn't matter. They can hardly make a total loss of us unless we get stove in, and bad weather comes away from the Azoff."

Joe shook his head. "There's rum work been goin' on up there for a long time. I shouldn't wonder if old Jemmy Hawbrook had some of his devil's moves on;" and with this suggestive speech our talk closed.

From that day until we brought up off Kertsch bar we spoke no more about our suspicions. The agent came off, and I did not fancy the look of him at all. He was a flashy Greek, with a carneying voice, and an unpleasant trick of stroking one's arm as he spoke. I hate those soft ways, and I could have struck him when he laid his hand delicately on my elbow.

"You won't have to lighten much, captain," he said. "We've got the channel nicely deepened now, and you can tow through easily. I'll stay on board till we're up."

We were waiting for the lighters to come off, and the dusk had fallen. The agent and the captain were down below, when I stole quietly aft with bare feet.

Somehow I *knew* I should hear something, and sure

enough in passing the open skylight I heard Haler say, "I tell you I shan't stay on deck while it's done. I'll manage the shore business, and I'll put the report to the Consulate right, but nothing else. It's killing me."

"Fiddle, captain, fiddle! You're tenderhearted. Do as you like, however. Moro will do the trick easily enough. Let's go and talk in the chart-house. I'm afraid one of your officers may come in on us and catch one word too much."

I saw it all. The Greek pilot was to put us on the ground, Captain Haler was to make a report, and then a ruffianly set of salvors would claim a tremendous sum to be paid by the insurance clubs. I thought of my people at home. I knew that I couldn't be blamed, yet a taint always clings to any officer who has sailed in a vessel that got ashore, and the luck seems to remain in a queer way. How could I face my girl again if I was mixed up in a bungle?

I ran as hard as I could forward, beckoned Joe, and made him spread the boat's lug sail over me as I lay on the roof of the chart-house.

I had hardly got my breath quieted down, when the captain and the Levantine came silently forward, and, sitting down in the gloomy little hut, began a low, earnest conversation.

Haler's voice said, "And how much does Leonides claim?"

"You must pay him £8,000, and the officials will pass your report all right. You draw a bill on London; the bank will discount it at about four; then you pay Leonides, and he and our sweet friend Hawbrook will arrange about dishing the clubs. I pay you £500, and the rest is out of your hands."

The fluent interpreter went on with several other particulars, and I saw that the owner, the righteous Hawbrook, was in league with a set of the fellows who stole £200,000 worth of British property in three months. Vessels are shoved ashore by the pilots, the captain is beset by a gang of salvors, he is afraid of losing his vessel, and he pays an enormous sum to get her lightened and towed off; then the money is extracted from the insurance societies, and the thieves divide. My saintly owner was in league with the pirates, and his captain had agreed to put the barque into the hands of a salvor who paid Mr. Hawbrook liberally for giving him a monopoly of plunder. Only the clubs suffered from this arrangement, and the business was so cleverly transacted that Mr. Hawbrook's reputation for extreme piety never suffered.

I was stiff and cold when the rascally dialogue ended, but I slipped forward and got into Joe's berth. I told him all about the affair, and we agreed to take the second officer into confidence. My own plan was formed, and when I detailed it the good sailor said, "It's you that's the one to plan things out, Mr. Soulsby; you're a real nailer."

Well, the pilot came on board, and we moved over the long, desolate stretches of pale-coloured water. Mr. Pilot was unarmed, and I looked him over very carefully to see what the chance would be if it came to rough-and-tumble work. I had taken my own precautions, and I never went a yard away from the fellow after the tug had once drawn us ahead.

Suddenly far away on our starboard bow I saw a clump of barges and a second tug.

Our captain turned pale and said, "I'll take a look below, Pilot. I suppose you know your way about?"

The worthy Greek grinned.

I noticed that we were edging to starboard, and I said sharply, "Now, Joe!"

The boatswain ran down below, found the captain in his state-room, locked him in, and mounted guard with a handspike.

The second mate cut away the pilot's boat very quietly, and I jumped right at my man, collared him, and put my revolver to his head.

Then I said, "Don't you shove her another yard that way! If she touches, I fire, and take my chance. I know what you are up to."

The men on the tug waved as we went past, for the place of our stranding had been arranged with precision; but I had my man like a rat in a trap, and I kept him covered till he was pretty well fainting. The men were with us, and Captain Haler was lying, as Joe observed, "groanin', and rammin' his head in the sofa-cushions."

I never slackened till we were clean through the worst of

the channel, and I took no sleep till I had my mind quite easy.

Luckily there was an English gentleman at Yenikale, who had come out on behalf of the clubs, and I at once went to meet him. He said, "Well, young man, you must leave your vessel here. I'm going to take you overland with me, and I shall have the boatswain and the second mate as well. They can get the ship home after she has discharged, and you must break your articles. You've made your fortune, I can tell you. Now I am going aboard with you."

Joe's face was very white when he lent us a hand up the ladder.

"He's done the trick," said the boatswain.

" Who ?"

"The skipper. See here," and he showed us a scrap of paper, on which was written, "I kept my honour till now. I was distressed for money, and I agreed to join a rascally conspiracy. I am about to die."

So poor Haler had taken his own life. He was a man all over, and I came near regretting him.

*   *   *   *   *

We went home *via* Odessa and Berlin, and for weeks we were kept "bottled up" at an hotel, and cross-examined by solemn committees.

At the finish the chairman said, "I am desired to present you, Captain Soulsby, with £500, and I think I may personally say that I shall offer you the command of the first of my own vessels that needs a captain. Your evidence is not sufficient to punish the principal in the fraud, but it is sufficient to deprive him of his membership. You'll be glad to hear that we have forced Mr. Hawbrook to send a man of our choosing to bring the barque home, and we've got the whole nest of pirates pretty well in hand."

That night my mother walked with me to Mather's, and when the door was opened the old woman said, "Eh, hinny! Aw've browt thee round thy good man an' his money, and aw'll just kiss thy canny face and get away."

My girl made a low sound almost like a moan as she nestled to me and said, "Oh, my bonny lad, I'll never let you away no more, and you monnot think me bold for saying we are to be married, for I thought the voyage was never going to get over."

Then Captain Mather uttered his huge roar, and made the glasses shake, and I think you'll understand we had a fine evening.

In a month I got command of a full-rigged ship in the Atlantic trade, and Mary took a sail with me in the summer.

I gave £200 to my mother, and now I don't care twopence if all the Greeks in Kertsch lie in wait for me when I go, for I smashed the gang and relieved British commerce.

VI.

THE HISTORY OF A THOUSAND POUNDS.

CAPTAIN HARKUS lived a very monotonous life for a long time after he took command of a vessel.

These brave fellows, who are the very backbone of our country's commercial greatness, do not come by many of the good things which are picked up by traders ashore. They are as far as possible from bearing any resemblance to the merry seamen of fiction. They are quiet, dull, prosaic men, whose lives are made up of meetings and partings, of long spells of loneliness, and hard, commonplace labour, and of flitting sojourns in foreign lands. They have a very slight perception of the romance of the sea—indeed, one might as well expect a railway-guard to be romantic. In most essential respects the merchant captain's work is very like that of the guard, and, although his trips are somewhat longer, the difference is only one of degree. The guard learns very little of the towns at which his brief halts are made. The merchant captain's experience of strange cities is mostly confined to a walk from the docks to the broker's office and back again. The guard, occasionally, has the unpleasant excitement of a collision; in this respect he fares like the skipper. The guard knows but little about the comforts of home; and the merchant captain's spells of domestic bliss are also very brief indeed.

Since one-half of the world knows not how the other half

lives, the way in which Captain Harkus passed his days may as well be described.

When the return voyage was over, the vessel slowed down, and the mouth of the harbour made, the long, sullen roar of the whistle went reverberating away along the deep banks of the river. Then came a slight bustle at the Pilot Station, and a little coble put off to wait for the big steamer. Meanwhile a boy rushed off into the town to inform the captain's wife that the boat had arrived, and then with slow majesty the big ship moved up to her berth, and the Foy boatmen made her secure. If the whistle sounded at night, Mrs. Harkus waked the children and said, " Your father has come in," and next day the whole family took holiday in order to greet the skipper properly.

Then the household had a few pleasant evenings. Harkus sat in his arm-chair by the side of the kitchen fire, and carried on a quiet gossip with his wife, as she moved hither and thither busying herself with household matters. He never cared to go visiting, and his chief pleasure in life was to take a short evening walk in the crowded main street of the town. But coming and going so irregularly as he does, the sailor passes without much heed in seaports. A man goes round the Horn ; perhaps he suffers shipwreck, or passes through many moving accidents ; he comes back after a year's absence, and his old acquaintance nod to him casually, just as if they had seen him the night before. With particular friends he may stop to have a little gossip, but the talk rarely turns on what has happened during the voyage. A few gruff phrases are interchanged, and then the friends part, perhaps not to meet again for yet another year. Sometimes, when the man has been away so long that his very name has become a memory, a friend will ask, " What has become of old So-and-so ?" If the answer should happen to be, " Oh, don't you know ?—they were given up two years ago," the inquirer will shake his head and say, " Ah, poor fellow ! we must all come to it some time or other ;" and then the conversation changes to considerations respecting freights, or the price of coals, or the prospects of a new building society. Properly speaking, the captains keep no society, and they are usually completely wrapped up in their homes. While they are away they only corre-

5

spond with their own people, and by degrees all their
interests in the world become centred in the one spot.
Before the young fellows get married they go about a good
deal, and some of them frequent billiard-rooms, and even
distinguish themselves at Christmas parties ; but as soon as
the skipper has a home of his own, he generally devotes
himself to his wife and family. He is the best of sweethearts, the best of husbands, and, although his children
during a great part of his life are but as mere shadows to
him, he is an affectionate father ; and when you meet him
in foreign places he is rather apt to be tiresome with his
long-winded descriptions of the various characteristics of his
young people.

There was no prouder man in England than Captain
Harkus on the rare occasions when his wife, equipped in all
her splendour, walked at his side, and shared with him the
greetings of the High Street. Mrs. Harkus wore a silk of
rather an alarming colour ; a cascade of watch-chain fell
over her bosom, and in winter-time she was especially
gorgeous in a sealskin jacket, which almost reached the
dimensions of a man's ulster. She was very proud of her
husband, but her relations with him were purely business-
like : she managed his money affairs for him, economised
strenuously while he was away at sea, and her talk when he
came home was mostly about investments and savings.

These simple souls are, to my mind, the very salt of the
earth. With their gravity, their thrift, their complete
absence of sentiment, and their perfect honesty, they make
up a most valuable element in society. Pretty talk is beyond their powers, and their knowledge of books is extremely
limited ; but I like them infinitely better than wordy people
who can chatter about art and the drama, and if I had to
give advice to a girl of the middle class I should say,
"Choose a ship-captain for a husband if ever you have the
chance ;" and to a man of the same class I should say,
"Marry a sailor's daughter."

But to return to Captain Harkus's mode of existence.
After the short blessed days ashore had come to an end,
there was the parting. Sometimes his little girl would cry
at nights after he was gone, especially if it was blowing
hard ; but his wife had no time to spare for tears. She

shook hands with him at the dock-edge, and sometimes the two kissed; but Harkus was of opinion that kissing was rather a soapy performance, and he mostly contented himself with his rough growl, "Good-bye, old girl. God bless you! Take care of yourself;" and then he went to the bridge, used nautical language until the decks were well cleared, and settled himself down contentedly for the run.

In foreign ports his time was passed in the most commonplace way. Like his peers, he bustled about on quay or jetty, routing out merchants and brokers, and holding most carefully aloof from foreigners.

By the way, let me now digress once more for a little while.

I never can see those sturdy, commonplace sailors of ours in foreign towns without feeling proud of my country. I have gone abroad during a fit of high Toryism, which attacked me with much severity. I had come to the conclusion that a sneaking and sentimental Liberal policy had brought irretrievable ruin upon the State, and that the only thing left for England to do was to wrap the latest thing in shoddy round her recreant limbs, and die with as much decency as might be. I mourned the degeneracy of the race, and I was especially bitter against the miscreants of the Manchester school. But when I saw our own people among the foreigners, I felt that I had been a little hasty in prophesying disasters.

The English sailor regards the "furriner" as a being whose existence is permissible under certain well-defined conditions, but he conducts himself as though he had just annexed each place that he visits in the name of his Queen and country. Somehow or other our men take on a lordly air when they are in the presence of aliens. Their calm belief in their own unmeasured superiority is so fixed, and so entirely independent of reason, that I often find myself becoming infected with it, in spite of my wider training and knowledge.

Once I spent a long day in a little town where a great festa was in progress. Thousands of peasants had assembled from mountain and plain, and every strange street seemed to be filled by a long procession. The men slouched about with their curious weak-kneed walk, the women waddled with that uncouth rocking of the hips which one notices among Italians of the lower class. They all looked care-worn, and haggard, and starved, and their manifestations of gaiety gave a rude shock to all my notions of the joyous life of the sunny South. But they were orderly in the extreme, and, although the wine shops were open until late at night, I did not see a single drunken man or woman.

On going aboard, I said casually to the skipper, "Those people certainly beat our English crowds ; I never saw such a well-behaved lot in my life. I see that some soldiers are told off to keep order, but I have not noticed the least dis-turbance all day. If we could cart over a Boxing Day crowd from the Crystal Palace, the place would be wrecked before midnight."

I shall never forget the outburst of righteous anger which followed my rash speech. I thought the skipper would have spun me away to the uttermost parts of the earth in the whirlwind of his wrath. He yelled in my face ; he used language totally unfit for publication ; he hinted that I was a dishonour to my country, and he finally broke down in the midst of an effort at profanity which was gigantic in conception, and which only failed of completion as a work of art by reason of the scantiness of the artist's breath.

Such fellows as my captain are the men who really repre-sent our country abroad. They are not very agreeable ; in fact, I fear that they are sometimes certainly brutal and overbearing, but such as they are they represent our country in places far away from the mere pleasure cities. They are not liked, but they are feared and respected.

Harkus was never quite sure what foreigners were made for, and to the end of his life he felt annoyed by the per-sistence with which they refused to understand the English tongue. But he got on with them as well as he could, and his contact with them made him prize his own home all the more.

When, after twenty years, his owners asked him to give way to a younger captain, he was rather glad, for he had saved a thousand pounds, and, as he said, "he could live ashore, and there would be no more need to see those Spaniards and Italians and Russians any more."

He took very kindly to shore-life, and soon became

known as a man who was pretty comfortably off. Managing-
owners who were projecting new steamers sought him out,
and the secretaries of building societies were most courteous
to him.

In the aristocratic quarter of our town lived Mr. Buller,
a very great shipowning magnate. Mr. Buller had a great
house, many servants, fine horses, and vast influence ; but,
so far as words went, he was humble in the extreme, and,
like the rest of his type, he was most pious.

Smart business men find it well to identify themselves
with some chapel or other, and the number of new ventures
which have been arranged in the course of the secular talk
which follows a prayer-meeting passes belief. I have no
desire to sneer at religion ; I only state the fact that shrewd
speculators work very successfully among the members of
provincial congregations. Nearly all the miserable swindles
lately perpetrated in the shipowning world were arranged
by persons who were regarded as lights of sanctity. This
only proves that religious men are usually trustworthy, for
the rogues would never pretend to be devout were it not
that the general worldly conduct of devout men inspires
confidence.

Mr. Buller often preached, and he was fond of expressing
his regret that the chances of life had prevented him from
entering the ministry. He was the managing-owner of a
very large shipping company, and his practical skill was
regarded with the utmost faith by small investors, who
were content to buy a sixty-fourth share and trust Buller
with the administration of their property.

In the summer Mr. Buller used to spend two or three
months in some watering-place, and he found that places
like Harrogate, Scarborough, and Matlock were his best
hunting-grounds. The well-to-do spinsters, the retired
officers, the retired tradesmen, and other members of the
leisurely classes were his quarry, and he hunted them down
with such sagacity that he never sent a steamer off the
stocks for a long period without every share being taken
up.

So long as the time of prosperity lasted Mr. Buller did
very well, and he lived up to every farthing of £8,000 a
year ; but as freights fell off he found that all his financial

genius was needed to show decent balance-sheets to his
faithful flock, and, at the same time, to secure a sufficiently
large amount for himself. The depression went from bad
to worse, yet Mr. Buller was more ostentatious than ever,
and people began to think that he would hold on triumph-
antly till the storm blew over. Meantime the financier was
plunging deeper and deeper into the mire. He induced
every one of his captains to become shareholders, and his
mode of dealing with those simple creatures was remarkable for boldness and originality. Some of his men had
not so much as a scrap of paper to show for their investments, and some of them paid for shares which had no
existence. It was found afterwards that the ingenious Mr.
Buller had sold as many as seventy shares in vessels which
were supposed to be "sixty-fourthers." Thus sixty-four
persons held share-certificates, and half a dozen simpletons
paid their money for bogus property.

At last it came about that not a single ship in the Buller
company was paying any dividend whatever. The manager
had swamped the banks with shares until he could not
obtain another penny, and he had mortgaged every ship on
which he could get an advance. The shareholders were
kept quiet by occasional payments, but, without knowing it,
they were really eating up their own capital.

Ready money was urgently needed, and Mr. Buller was
driven to his wits' end. He happened to know Captain
Harkus, and, on one unlucky day, he resolved to see whether
anything could be done with our innocent friend. He
drove up in a fine brougham to the captain's little house,
and the commotion raised in the street was quite remarkable. Mrs. Harkus trembled as she showed the mighty
visitor into the best room, and even the burly skipper was
somewhat awed. Buller greeted Harkus cordially, and soon
came to the point in the most flattering manner.

"I learned to-day, Harkus, that you are unemployed."

"I am out of a ship, sir, and I thought of stopping
ashore."

"Ah! you fellows make your pile out of us poor owners.
I only wish I could retire from business at your age. But
we're tied to the wheel, Harkus—tied to the wheel. Don't
you think, though, that's it's unwise for a hearty man like

you to miss the chance of picking up a bit more? Frankly speaking, I want to secure your services. I want a steady, safe hand to run between Messina and Rouen with the *Mary Buller*. Do you care to take her? Twenty pounds a month, and the gratuity usual with our firm."

"I should not mind, sir; thanking you very much."

"Very well, then—that's settled, captain. There's just one condition. We require all our men to have an interest in their vessels. It ensures diligence, you know. You couldn't place a few hundreds better. Your ship leaves about 24 per cent., and you can't get much more for your money anywhere."

"Well, sir, I don't mind putting a little in. I have a thousand."

Buller's heart beat. The payment on an inconvenient mortgage had to be met within four days, and the capitalist was desperate.

"A thousand! Well, you see, that gives you a very fair income over and above your wages. I think I may confidently recommend you to go in and win."

So Captain Harkus drew his thousand, and became the possessor of four sixty-fourth shares in the *Mary Buller*. The managing-owner tided over a whole three months by dexterously dribbling out the precious ready money, and Harkus worked his vessel back and forth with much contentment.

But Mr. Buller had plunged too hard, and the fates mastered him. Six months after Harkus entered on his new duties he received the following letter:

"SIR,—We observe that since the *Mary Buller* was placed in your charge each successive voyage has shown a diminishing profit. You will see from enclosed that the last two trips have even resulted in very heavy loss. We make no reflections, but we are reluctantly compelled to dispense with your services. On your arrival at Rouen Captain Marshall will relieve you of your duties.—We are, yours faithfully, BULLER AND CO.—Per H. B."

When the true meaning of this note dawned upon the captain's slow mind he staggered under the blow; his strong frame reeled, and the blood started as he convulsively bit his lower lip.

"The scoundrel! The slimy rogue! I'll denounce him in front of the market cross," he muttered.

Long and dreary musings had the poor skipper as he stood on the bridge in the sombre nights when the wind's sorrowful calling and the vast music of the waves filled the air with weird harmonies. Age was coming on ; his savings were planted in a losing steamer, and he was dismissed from his employment. The thought of his wife choked him, and he had visions of poverty that made his heart ache for his children.

When he reached home, he hardly dared speak at first, but his kind partner coaxed him out of his gloom, and persistently put things in the most cheerful light.

He went out on the first morning after his dreary homecoming and visited a broker of his acquaintance. "I want to get rid of some steamboat shares," he said. "Can you help me ?"

"I might. What's the ship ?"

"The *Mary Buller.*"

The broker whistled, and then a kindly and sorrowful look came over his keen face.

"By George, Harkus ! How much have you in her ?"

"A thousand. Every penny I had."

"Mercy on us ! Did you never suspect that things were going wrong in that quarter ? I suppose you really bought a berth on board of her ?"

"I did ; to my sorrow."

"Well, to be plain with you, Buller can't last another week. I tell you, sir, I know for a fact he's even sold his watch. When the smash comes, there'll be such a kick-up as never was. Here, old man, take a nip of brandy. You must keep up, you know, and I won't see you short of a ship, if interest can do anything. Sit down, and face it like a man."

On the very next day Mr. Buller filed his petition. The creditors employed a lawyer, who set on foot an investigation, and the results of Mr. Buller's examination before the receiver were startling. Every ship belonging to the company was frightfully in debt ; the cooking of accounts had been daring beyond anything known in commercial history ; and the pious Buller had, in one way or other, made away with the shareholders' property almost to the last penny. In one year, when the vessels had practically earned nothing, the manager had spent £4,000, and the balance-sheets for that year were among the finest works of art ever signed by an auditor.

Harkus could not sell his shares at £5 each, and he would have starved had not his story been told in the Receiver's Court. A good-natured owner, who was touched by the tale, offered him a mate's berth, and the plucky fellow took it. He had grown stout, and he was hardly so active as a mate ought to be, but he stuck to his work, and the £8 a month which he earned just sufficed to keep his home together.

The *Mary Buller* is laid up, like a good many other ships, and it is doubtful whether she will ever be relieved from her load of debt.

Harkus one night said to his wife, " Eh, my woman, they say that the righteous is never forsaken. I've gone straight, except for swearin' hard at the men in busy times, and I cannot believe that I'm to slave on till it's time to go to the workhouse."

Let us hope he is right.

Mr. Buller is not quite so pious as he used to be. Indeed, after the allusions to penal servitude and other unpleasant things which were associated with his name, he could hardly expound the Scriptures with any very good grace. He was not brought to trial, and he is now once more let loose on the community which he adorned. It is said that he managed to settle a few thousands on his wife, so he will not starve. Captain Harkus probably will.

VII.

THE SIEVE.

MR. JONAS LANDON was received with great respect as he strolled down through the clustering houses that fringed the steep banks of our river.

Mr. Landon was a pillar of the Wesleyan Church, and when he took his walks abroad he carried his head as if it were the Holy Sacrament. The Ten Commandments were impressed on his countenance, and his gesture of greeting as he passed his commercial friends conveyed the impression of a benediction. Mr. Landon conducted his business on the strictest religious principles. He never allowed a vessel to go to sea on a Sunday, and for that reason he often discharged a captain who did not finish his loading by midnight on Saturday. The steamers belonging to his line very often went to sea in bad weather within an hour of midnight on the seventh day of the week; but no scoffer in the town could quote an authentic instance in which the pious magnate had violated the Sabbath.

As he passed through the Market Place on the particular morning we are speaking of, the rough captains bowed respectfully to him, and he bore himself towards the whole population very much as the late Patriarch Job is believed to have behaved in his village.

The steamer *Circe* had just come into dry dock, and Mr. Landon was very anxious to see how the repairs were getting forward. The boat had run down as far as Yarmouth, but there, I am sorry to say, it had been found impossible to keep her floating unless four hands were continually at the pumps. She reeled and lunged in an absurd fashion when she ran into harbour; and when the dock gates were open for her admission there was just eleven feet of water in the well. As soon as she was put on the ground, and the falling tide had drawn the water out of the dock, great pouring cataracts flowed out of staring cracks. A trickling stream ran at the fore-peak, and from a long, nasty gash just above the propeller shaft, a broad stream squirted to a distance of six inches from the line of rivets.

The old captain was using language of an improper nature when Mr. Landon stepped over the dock side.

The owner condensed the whole Commination Service into one look of sublime wrath. "Oh, Captain Lennox, how can frail mortals, poor worms, expect a blessing on any enterprise conducted by persons convicted of using such terms as these?" was what his look implied. But his actual speech was businesslike. "May I ask your reason, Captain Lennox, for not proceeding to the Port of London?"

"Port of London, sir! We should have had to run her on the ground. Where is there a dock that we could have put her in? I knew there was a spare berth here, and I came as fast as I could. Very glad I am we are alive to see the place again."

"But, Captain Lennox, I fear the cause of God is not in your heart, and I fear your seamanship is not all it should be."

The captain became very red in the face. He belonged to the old school, whose main principle in life was conveyed in the chaste and simple motto, "The blow first and the word afterwards." He bit his lip, and when he at last opened his mouth to speak, a white crescent was marked on the broad expanse of his shaven chin. If a mere foreigner had addressed such language to him, Lennox would have thrown him overboard, and he felt that the saddest thing in the present circumstances lay in the fact that he could not rope's-end the owner of the boat.

With an ironic accent he observed, "Seamanship, sir! Did you ever try to navigate a ladder? I will bet you grogs round for the crew that you could not sail a ladder across the river now, and this beast is very little better."

I will not say that Mr. Landon grew purple; I do not believe that any known combination of colours could express his hue. If his own pet clergyman had suddenly chanted "Tommy, make room for your uncle," even that phenomenon, terrible as it would have been, could hardly have shaken Mr. Landon's innermost being so cruelly as did the sudden directness of the old skipper. The accumulated essence of many sermons thrilled in his voice as he said, "Captain Lennox, we must part."

The old man went below to collect his various belongings. He locked himself in his state-room, and when the owner tapped gently at the door, he said gruffly that he must leave his accounts all square before he could think of going ashore.

In half an hour Mr. Landon was joined by a prosperous-looking Jewish gentleman.

"Nasty job, Mr. Landon," said the Hebraic individual. "I thought you were going to do the trick this time."

The pious owner pointed to the state-room door and whispered, "Hush!"

But quite enough had been said to make old Lennox prick up his ears, and the skipper growled to himself, "I thought as much; I will go down this very night and have a look at the bed of that stern-post."

The Jew was the proprietor of the dock in which the *Circe* had been laid. During her last trip her stern-post was sprung, and it was bedded anew under the directions of the very gentleman whose loud exclamation had set Lennox thinking.

The coating of cement looked solid as a rock on each side; it seemed as if Titans might have danced upon it without denting the iron surface, and Mr. Landon would have confidently invited all his congregation to inspect the fixing of this—the very keystone of a vessel's strength. But Lennox had been smitten with incurable suspicions, and as soon as he saw his owner ashore he summoned the carpenter and said, "Now, George, I've got everything to risk, and you stand to lose a good deal. I want you to help me in this little affair, at any rate. You saw the inspector pass the ship before we went, didn't you?"

"Yes," said George, "but they had him pretty full of champagne before they let him go round; and I'll tell you what, captain, now you have opened the subject, it's my belief this craft was never intended to come back any more. I don't say old preachee-preachee had anything to do with it, but if you hang yourself over the side I will show you something that will make you gape."

The water was still dribbling from the seams as George and the skipper proceeded with their scrutiny. George had his hammer with him. Assuming an air of profound sagacity, he dealt the plate a sharp crack with the hammer. Then he whispered, "Do you see it now?"

Lennox gasped, and George went on. "When we were going round the Head, I was leaning over the lee rail, and just as she doubled across a sea I saw a rivet start out of her, same as a button might fall off your shirt. This is one of the bad ones ; now, tell me plainly what is that hole filled up with ?"

"Heaven be merciful to us !" said the skipper, very gravely ; "it is stuffed with plaster."

The Hebraic builder was a good man for certain owners to know. On several occasions, after the shares in a vessel had been underwritten for an extra sixty per cent., she was passed out of Mr. Nathan's dock, and never heard of again. One ship which had received a thorough overhaul was going merrily towards the Downs, when a youthful engineer began pottering about on one of the boilers. Tapping with the hammer, he caved the shell in, and the young experimentalist found to his horror that the iron was about the thickness of a sheet of brown paper. The boilers had been passed by the inspecting engineer ; they had received Mr. Nathan's warmest praises, and the clubs thought so highly of the vessel that she was insured for close on £17,000. Strange to say, Mr. Jonas Landon was the owner of this efficient craft as well as of the *Circe*.

Lennox went home chewing the cud of many reflections. In his dull, slow way, he felt a sense of outrage, of hardness, of meanness, and trickery, such as had never been brought before his mind in his whole simple life.

Next day the workmen were very busy, and a swarm of flitting black figures moved hither and thither on the leaky steamer. Stages were run up, and the riveters plied their trade merrily. In the evening, when Mr. Jonas Landon attended at prayer meeting, he was so fluent his friends considered that the Author of the Universe ought to be very proud of having the patronage of such an eloquent; serene, and moral man.

Within the week the *Circe* bowled over the bar, with a young captain on board who was rather proud of his promotion and of being chosen by the eminently pious firm of Landon and Company. The women watched the streaming column of smoke as the vessel swept into the gloom that brooded over the water by the Ness. They were sad enough,

poor souls, but they would have been sadder if they had
known everything.

The *Circe* did exceedingly well during the first two days
of her run, for the water was like oil, and the propeller had
a splendid grip.   On the third day a snoring breeze came
away from the southward which sent up a short, jerky sea
that made the boat caper a good deal.

" What a deuce of a noise the beggar makes !" said the
new captain to the mate.

" Noise! By the living man, some of us will have to make
a noise before we have done with her.   If it wasn't that I
have my wife and children to consider, and I must run risks,
I would sooner go to Rotterdam in a wheel-barrow.   Just
you wait, sir, till it comes on a bit harder, and then you will
see something."

About dawn the wind was racing in short violent squalls,
and the *Circe* was boring her way into a nasty cross sea.

Everybody was drowned out, and the men who came from
the forecastle could only escape being washed aft in a
smother of foam by timing the lurches of the vessel, and
making struggling rushes for the ladder.

" What on earth is the matter with the old cow ?   Did
you notice, Mr. Brennan, what a tremendous slant she has
from the stern ?   Why, she looks as if she were dragging an
anchor."

Brennan smiled grimly, and said, " If you'll take my
advice, sir, you'll signal some of the smacksmen to stand
by you.   I have watched her like a cat myself for over an
hour, and I have wondered you didn't give orders to sound
the wells."

The captain, who was a plucky enough fellow, said, " But,
good God ! the vessel has just come out of dock.   I should
not have thought that a sea like this could have given her
a shaking."

The man smiled the same grim, sad smile, and said,
" You don't know so much as I do.   Come here in two or
three hours, and then if we can put in anywhere I will tell
you something in confidence.   If you split upon me I shall
never get another ship, but I strongly advise you to go home
and stop with your wife and children until you can get a
chance of a collier.   Eight pounds a month and safety

would be better than eight thousand a year aboard this thing."

The clouds bent low, and hung in dusky wreaths over the labouring steamer. Her stem seemed to rise higher and higher, and she wallowed to port and starboard just as a buoy will do in a swift tideway. The wind swirled her hither and thither, and the captain noticed that whenever the screech of the rigging denoted a blast more than usually powerful his precious craft fell away like the sail of a windmill, and utterly refused to take any notice of her helm.

As the night was sinking, the captain quietly called the carpenter and said, "Now, my man, she is settling down by the stern. I don't want to raise a scare, but you send bo'sun aft with four hands to get the boats out, and then you go forward yourself. Take a flare from the locker, and show it as soon as you hear me whistle twice."

Five minutes after this the chief engineer came up. " I hope you will not think I am funking, sir; but are you aware we are just about done ?"

The poor skipper knew that well enough, and with quiet despair said, "Bring your men away from the fires, and unless we can fetch one of the smacks up we will take to the boats."

The sea was coming very unsteadily, and the unmanagable ship was so cruelly crank that the launching of the boats was a very dangerous task; but the longboat, jollyboat, and the patent lifeboat were got out and manned. Then into the grey of the night the forlorn seamen moved. The desolate storming of the wind and the long angry wash of the waves were the only sounds to be heard save the throb of the labouring oars in the thwarts; and the captain, alert and resolute as he was, thought with bitterness of his professional prospects ruined by such a villainous chance.

Next afternoon a telegram in the evening papers stated that "two boats belonging to the steamship *Circe* were picked up last night by the smack *Jenny Jones.* It appears that the longboat, with seven hands, was capsized by the heavy sea, and nothing could be done to save the men."

As Mr. Jonas Landon read this intelligence he smiled sweetly.

In the course of the evening an official from one of the

principal insurance clubs called at Mr. Landon's residence,
and after a few preliminary words said, "Now, Mr. Landon,
you and I have always been good friends. I hear that you
have lost the *Circe*."

"To my great grief, I have," replied Mr. Landon. "I am
obliged to believe that the unfortunate vessel has foundered.
The captain has not yet telegraphed to me, but the paragraph
in to-day's papers seems quite authentic."

The insurance man went on with curious suddenness,
"You will not think of forwarding your claim, I presume ?"

Mr. Landon's expansive face grew pale.

"Why not ?"

"Well, you see, there is that little affair of the stern-post.
Do you happen to know how the stern-post was bedded ?"

"No, sir, I do not. I know how it was paid for."

"Ah ! but you see," said the smiling club secretary, "you
had two inches of cement and the rest cinders. Now, if you
will take my advice as a friend, do not send in your claim
at all, and, if necessary, make it up to the other shareholders out of your own pocket. I should have stopped the
vessel if I had known in time, but, as it is, we have quite
enough evidence to make things look very ugly for you if it
comes to law business, so once more I advise you to let the
thing slide."

Mr. Landon dropped his pious air, and said, "My dear
sir, I will consider the matter."

And that was the reason why the clubs never paid a
penny on the loss of the *Circe*. Old Captain Lennox had
revenged himself by taking certain workmen who furnished
the club officials with very important information.

There was a great deal of private gossip, and some threats
were used, but, as in all such affairs, the gang principally
concerned managed to hush things up. Oblivion soon falls
on the most startling events that happen in busy places, and
Mr. Jonas Landon knew it.

VIII.

AN OLD PIRATE.

Tom Sinnett was so old that he often said he would have to be shot in the end to prevent him from living for ever. His broad-chested, lean frame seemed made of pin wire, and although the joints of his fingers were a trifle enlarged, his grip was strong, and he could lift a fairly heavy weight. He was not a pleasant-looking person; his brow was low, his eyes were deep set and cunning, and his thin lips were viciously closed. Sometimes he flashed a sudden glance on you which was like a revelation of wickedness, and the hints that dropped out in his talk made you shiver.

When the *Princess Alice* went down in 1878, he heard the men talking about the disaster. He had taken three glasses of rum, and his tongue was loosened a little. "Five hundred gone, is there? Must 'a been a queer sort of sight. I know what it's like well enough. Lor! I've seen 'em wriggling and pitching their hands up one after the other, and squealing when the sharks got hold on 'em. Scr-r-r-raunch! That was it, and then a scoot of blood over twenty yards of water, and a yell. But ours wasn't no collision; they was shied overboard, ours was."

"When was that, Tom? What do you mean?"

"Ah! sonny, that tellin's. Did you ever hear of ebony, my joker? I've done a bit that way."

I guessed what Tom meant, and a few minutes afterwards I hummed the shanty—

> "So where they have gone to, there's no one can tell—
> Brandy and gin and a bottle of rum;
> But I think we shall meet the poor devils in hell,
> Brandy and gin and a bottle of rum."

Tom turned sharp.

"You know it, do you? Many's the time I've heard that for an hour on end when we was having idle time, and the stuff was plenty. Know any more?"

I sang—

> "We went over the bar on the 13th of May,
> Brandy and gin and a bottle of rum;
> The *Galloper* jumped, and the gale came away,
> Oh! brandy and gin and a bottle of rum."

6

" You ain't got it right. You've heerd it aboard a collier, maybe ?"

I had heard the wicked shanty on board a collier brig, as it happened, but my version was corrupt. The gruesome song which Mr. Louis Stevenson lately printed is also corrupt. In fact, Mr. Stevenson's verse is so artistically horrible that I rather fancy he composed it himself. Tom Sinnett knew the real song, and our common possession established a bond between us.

From that time I always drew up to Tom's corner and had his talk to myself. He said very little about his past life at first, but I knew that he must have gone to sea early in the present century. He spoke of having been to the St. Lawrence with a convoy, and I knew that the frigate which he named as being able to go three feet to the merchantmen's two was captured by that old Waggon which lowered the colours of so many of our ships in the war of 1812-14. Then he remembered when the birds sang on the banks of the Tyne near Lizzie Mudie's, and he had belonged to a gang of smugglers who worked to the southward of the Farne Islands during the three years after Waterloo. But it was Tom's talk about life in the tropics that drew my attention most.

The more I saw of Tom Sinnett the more I became convinced that he had been in more than one black business in his time. He spoke so lightly about murder, and he seemed so familiar with the symptoms and movements that precede almost every form of violent death, that I was certain he had been in action. Once he said, " I've seen a man spin round and round like a teetotum after a ball catched him in the temple ; then he lay and dug at the deck with his heel for an hour. He knew all the time he was going, but he couldn't die, and he asked the chaps to club him. A knife wound's a nasty thing. I've seen a lot of that. One chap dabbed his sticker through my arm here. It was like a flash of fire going into you." Then about drowning, he remarked, " I don't think there's much pain there. I've seen them over and over. There's a wriggle for a bit, and then they seem to go sleepy like, and let it come over them. They say there's a flash comes into your eyes at the last, but I don't know about that."

At length I got Tom to tell me something definite about one part of his career, and I now transcribe his story. Of course the man clipped the words which end in "ing," as all sailormen do, but, for the convenience of writing, I put down the participles properly.

"We ran out from Southampton, it's now fifty-nine year since, and I was a stiff young fellow. If it come to fists I wasn't afraid of no one aboard, but some on 'em wasn't partic'lar about sticking to fists. We had two Greeks, and one fellow we called a Turk, but I believe he was Greek as well. Then there was four Italians, and a heavy lot of Englishmen—hot boys, all on 'em. It was a big crew for a schooner, but you see she wasn't a common trading vessel. She was very like that racing yacht that was here the other day, only rather lower, and the way the thing went was past believing. She made no fuss about it, but she'd sneak away from everything that we came across as simple as saying, How are you? One frigate out of Portsmouth tried to do us across the Bay, and the captain was out of his head pretty well, for he reckoned his vessel knew something about speed. We just left him, and our mate, a joky fellow, he says, 'Shall we give you a tow, my lord?' as we went slapping past only about a cable's length to leeward of him. He took the wind from us for a quarter of a minute, but, bless you, after that it was good-night, if you like.

"We was armed. Swivel forrad, and four pretty brass guns as you ever see. Palm oil was what we was on for, or something of that sort. I never rightly knew what the skipper said we was supposed to be after, and it's only since that I heerd it was oil, or ivory. Anyway, no oil ever came aboard of us that I know on.

"We run right to the Bight, and then the gang of us takes our cutlashes, and we divides the sets of wrist-irons, and we has a long steel chain to make the rings fast on, and we soon meets that rotten old king. One-eyed old swine he was—all puffed out with the drink, and knobby with queer carbuncles. He had a fairish lot of black cattle for us, and we took four batches aboard without any mischief at all. Then we waits about and nails some more, and then we lays her away across the Western Ocean.

"That trip we had a lot of them bad with fever, and

6—2

some of the women was very noisy about their babies. Our
boss he pretended to give them medicine, and the poor
beggars sucked it in fast enough. I went round one night
and carried the bottle while the skipper dosed 'em. But it
was laudanum what he give them, and they was soon stiff.
We had to slip about forty over the side next day, and then
the plague seemed to stop.

" All hands did very well out of the run, and there was
two men forrad with the horrors when we came away.
We didn't intend to go back to England again, so we weren't
particular what we did with the two D.T. gents. One on
'em died where we lashed him down, and the way he sung
out was a caution.

" But let me get to my story. Going east, the skipper
turned nasty as nasty could be. He had drink in him sometimes, and he was far too ready with them fists of his. One
of the Greeks cheeked him, so he lets fly at Mr. Antonio
with a pistol. The ball went through the fleshy part of the
man's thigh, and he bled like a pig, so there was plenty of
growling that night among the devils forrad. We were
all pretty well frightened of the skipper, for he was a mad-
blooded rip that cared for nothing, and he would have his
own way if he died for it : but he went just a bit over the
mark this time.

" Next night I was look-out man, and I was trudging,
fisherman's walk like, you know, on the forecastle head. We
were on the starboard tack, and she was going through it
like a dolphin. There was nothing ahead, so when I hears
some one whisper, ' Hist ! come down half a minute !' I
leaves my post, and slips under the shadow of the foresail.

" Then Lips, a big, ugly Yank, says to me. ' Old Hellfire
said he would plug you to-day, didn't he ?' and I says,
' Yes, and he's just the man to do it.' Then Lips he put
his mouth to my ear, and I mind now how his breath
stunk, and he whispers, ' We shan't stand it no longer ;
will you join us ?'

" ' What are you going to be after ?'

" ' Well, we shall settle Hellfire and the mate, and take
the schooner for ourselves. She's just the boat for the
proper business—the real business, you know.'

" ' But how about going back ?'

" 'We shan't go back. We shall go clean round the Cape, and I know a corner where we can lie, safe as Baltimore, and come out when we fancy the job.'

" 'I'm your man. Can we get at the cutlashes ?'

" 'No. We'll knife him, and then we'll have the keys.'

" When the watch turned out at midnight, Jack Jefferson, a rough English boy, whispered to Lips, ' Is he all right ?'

" 'Safe as a star,' says Lips ; and I knew they meant me.

" In the morning we was all very careful not to be seen getting into groups. The skipper gives a bit of drill with the broadside guns, for he managed her just the same as if she was a privateer. We was smart, you can bet, and that Lips could plant a roundshot into a hat at a mile. The mate seemed as if he was uneasy, and he looked at one and another of us, but lor ! we was so quiet he never knew what was on.

" Just as the skipper was going aft, Lips sings out 'Hold him !' Then two of the Greeks jumps at the mate, twisted his hands behind him, and he was fast. Lips would not depend on a knife. He took a small steel marlinspike, then he gives a jump and a growl like a mastiff, and fetches his right hand hard down. The steel went into the captain's back, and ran upwards. He yelled like as if his head would come off, and then he turns round, stares a moment, and drops dead.

" Lips went to the mate, and he says, ' Now, sir, we'll give you a wash, so you'll be clean when you go to Fiddler's Green. Over with him, boys.'

" The poor man says, 'Let me loose, you swines, and give me five minutes with the best two of you—knives only.'

" But they soon stopped his jaw. One on 'em dips a mop in a tar-bucket, and dabs him on the mouth, and then they hoists him over and lets him go ker-whop. He swam for a bit, and one of the English chaps fired an old block at his head. The schooner was sliding away fast, and I guess the mate was done with his job in about ten minutes.

" Not one of us was scared ; we wasn't that sort. We took the skipper's keys, and then we had a blow-out of the spirits, and then we settles our new officers. Lips told us

the new game. He was to be captain, and we all swore on
the sharp edge to stand to him. We was to take no more
ebony, but sneak about for merchant shipping that couldn't
show any teeth. Lips had been in the trade before, and
half a score more of us had been under the crossbones or
in privateers in our time.

"Lips knew of a place where a vessel could lie in thirty
fathoms within twenty yards of the rocks, and the entrance
could be shot in any weather. He had a great notion of
Madagascar, for you could chop up the craft in the Mozam-
bique Channel wonderful, and the devil himself couldn't
find you when you once got into the bay. But we never
got round the Cape, for we catches a vessel as we was
running south, and Lips said it was to be neck or nothing.

"She was Portuguese, and we had hardly any trouble
with her. She tried showing us her heels, but she might
just as well have tried to run away from that there screw
going out. Lips laid the long gun himself, and his third
shot cuts her maintopmast like cheese, and then we raked
her awful as we rounded under her stern, and she wouldn't
steer. When we ranged up alongside of her there was no
fighting to do at all, for the poor beggars did nothing but
pray. I cut one of them down, but I did no more. They
hadn't done me no harm, and bleeding of them makes a
nasty mess fit to turn your stomach. They would have
joined us, some on 'em, but we didn't want 'em, and they
had to go. You must make short work with jobs of that
sort. Business is business, I says, and when your neck is
to be considered, I says, keep to business principles. They
hollered a lot, and didn't go over the side very game, but
we couldn't waste time. One old Jew coming home from
Goa, he shows us a box, and, s'elp me! you can bet there
was a lift. He made signs he would buy his life, but, as
Lips says, the old fool didn't reckon we wasn't there to
bargain. It took an hour to scuttle her properly and clear
everything out, and then, I tell you, we had enough to
make men of us. I don't know the price of stones, but the
old Jew's lot alone was something amazing.

"Lips, he says, 'We'll run for Trinidad,' and sure
enough we goes off without trying any more. I wish we
had gone for the States, got fresh papers, and run home

innocent after the dollars was shared out ; but Lips he was mad on his own way.

"We lay off the south side of the island, and hung by for a long time, till that big, smooth swell eased down a bit. It's a frightful place. There's not a tree nor a grass blade. Mountains sticks up like snags of rotten teeth, and the swell just runs on like a mill-race, so that you have to keep your eyes well skinned to get in any way. Lips he made us pack the stuff in two casks, and we filled up the space with shredded cork, so as to be sure of it floating if anything happened us getting in. Then one moonlight night we took one cask in each boat and aimed for a spring that Mr. Lips knew very well. He steered us right enough, but I was pretty well corpsed as we went sallying in, for my oar catches the rock, and I got a twist on the bellows that made me sing Chissick. The second boat came whack, and stove in her bow above the water-line, but we gets in all right.

"Such a night ! The birds came down in the moonlight, and made as if they would rip our eyes out. The stink of the fish was fit to knock you over, and then the land-crabs, the ugly beasts, was enough to give you the horrors. I once had blue devils, but not a thing that I saw was worse than them awful brutes, chaw, chaw, chawing, and goggling at you with their glass eyes. One of our chaps had been taking double allowance, and he says, 'Tom,' he says, 'have you got 'em on, or have I ? I seen you kick at one of the beggars, but I didn't think he was real : how is it ?' So I comforts him, and lends him my bottle, and then we lugs the stuff up high, and Lips, he swears death to anyone that tells, and we all swears hard enough, and then we buries the casks high up out of the wash of the biggest wave that could come.

"Eh, sir ? it was a bad, bad job. We goes out and tackles a East Indiaman, no less, and he gives us fits. He shot away our rudder, and brings the sticks down about our ears ; and, if he had boarded, some on us would have had a little quadrille party at Execution Docks. We got up a jury mast when the beggar bore away from us, and we makes a run for the West ; but she was hulled so cruel, sir, no mortal men could keep her afloat, and we was thinking of casting lots in the boats when a Yank picked us up, and

the skipper said we looked as if hell had got a short
holiday; but he takes the poor wrecked mariners home
with him, and we goes about our business the best way we
could.

"I've tried every round of the game since, but I never
could muster brass enough to buy even a twenty-tonner, or
by the soul of my father I'd 'a been away to Trinidad. If
I could provision a fishing-smack, I'd be off to-morrow if
two proper boys would join me. Anyway, that stuff is
there now, and it'll lie till kingdom come unless I tell the
spot and the marks."

Then the old scoundrel begged a quartern of rum, and
went home. He was very confidential, and I feel, even
now, as if I were accessory after the fact. Anyway, I am
glad the disciples of Mr. Lips never went to Madagascar.

[Since the above was written (five months ago) I learn
that the barque *Aurea*, of Sunderland, has returned from
the island of Trinidad after a fruitless search for buried
treasure. The difficulties of landing baulked the expedition,
and the men seem to have had no bearings to guide them.
The party should have taken the old captain who saw the
bullion buried, for a sailor would be likely to go direct to
a spot even if he had not seen the landmarks for fifty years.
Berthon collapsible boats are the only kind that could
possibly be used among the rocks.]

IX.

A CHAPTER OF ACCIDENTS.

BETTING men are thought to be the most superstitious
beings on the face of the earth; but anyone who knows
sailors and fishermen will allow that no other class can well
be more given to think of omens and strange traditions.
In one north-country village a fisher would not think of
going to sea directly after a pig had crossed his path; he
would go back home, empty some salt on the floor, and then
set out again. In another village it is counted unlucky to
meet with a woman on the road down to the boats; and in
yet another place a man expects a long spell of ill-fortune
if a hare crosses the road in front of him. Sailors have the

same queer fancies, and men of real intelligence will, when they are at sea, manifest fears which are unmatched for childishness.

Bill Hope was a thoroughbred sailor, and he had more than the ordinary superstition of his class, so he was very dull when he came home on a Thursday night and told his wife that the tug would be ready to take the ship *Bretella* over the bar next morning. "Hoots!" said Polly Hope. "You and your daft nonsense! I have enough to do getting your clothes ready without fashin' myself with you and your old wife's notions. See, here's your needles and thread; here's the bottle of Riga balsam and the rags, in case you get a cut; and here's the new flannels. Better see to your bag and chest than bother about Fridays and Mondays, and mermaids, and that kind of stuff." But Bill was mournful, and his wife's merriment seemed to him put on.

The good woman was stirring at three in the morning, and had a cup of coffee ready for her man when he turned out. She had no time for sentiment, and even if Bill had neglected to kiss her before he went away she would have been less distressed at the omission than she would have been had he forgotten his oilskins or his fur cap. She dismissed him cheerfully, and only said, "If it holds fine we'll come down and give you a wave. Now, don't be thinking of Friday, my bonny man." Polly put so good a face on the matter that Bill strode off quite heartily, and soon forgot all his forebodings in the congenial occupation of swearing at the tug, the forecastle hands, and the nature of things in general.

The *Bretella* was a nice full-rigged vessel, and Bill had been lucky with her for over three years. He once went clean over a hooker in the Channel when the *Bretella* was travelling twelve knots, but no one knew anything of the circumstance, and, as Bill satisfied his conscience by nearly killing the sleepy look-out man who caused the collision, he felt quite virtuous.

The *Bretella* was bound for Boston, and Bill hoped to make a good trip of it, for the ship's bottom had been cleaned, and she looked as smart as a yacht as she went smoothly down the river.

Hope very seldom slept much on the East Coast; but as

the first night was clear, and the vessel was going free, he determined to lie down for a few hours, and he left the mate in charge. He was anxious in his mind as he stretched himself in his cot, but he soon became reassured by the presence of visitors. The rats began to caper along the mouldings, and one or two of the rascals gazed down on him with queer, old-fashioned looks. "Them beggars hasn't left us, any way," muttered the skipper, and he turned over and soon was snoring.

In a short time the boatswain ran below and said, "Can you speak to Mr. Follett a minute, sir?"

Hope at once rushed up and asked, in an agitated way, "What's on now?"

"Well, sir. there's a fellow coming up on us, but the Lord himself can't tell what he means to be at. Guess they're all drunk. He first shows his red, then his green, then his full. It's mad, like, altogether."

Hope took a long, anxious look, and then muttered, "There's his red!"

An instant afterwards he said, "What the h—ll's up? Here's his green! He's fooling round queer ways."

Of course the big ship had to give way, as she was going free, but there was something in the behaviour of the coming vessel which was quite different from that of an ordinary ship that is beating. "Why doesn't he take a long leg off, 'stead of twiddlin' like a —— beetle?" growled the mate. "Is it worth while to give him a flare, do you think, sir?"

"Oh no; we can clear him when we like, and I'm blowed if I don't think I'll stand to the east'ard and not give the lunatic a chance of doing damage. See there, he's ratching away again. Port a bit, and stand by them braces. See whether he'll take a hint."

A demoniac spirit seemed to possess the unhappy vessel that caused such tremors on board the *Bretella*. There was no need for her to get into a mess, yet just as Hope thought all was well the mate yelled, "Holy Moses, he's about again!" The *Bretella* swung sharply on her heels, and only just got clear. As Hope surged by with the vessels red to red, he shouted, "Where's your grandmother, you calf-head? If I had a gun on deck I'd shoot one of you." But the cold sweat stood on him in spite of his loud words, and he muttered, "Friday, by George—Friday! Poll may talk, but I don't half like it."

Bill was too much of a man to lose his nerve over a trifle, but the near shave with the wandering brigantine "waked him up," as he said, and he was much disinclined to go below again till they were clear of the ditches.

In going down Channel he had another fright. A huge steamer stole out of the haze as the *Bretella* was going W. by N.; there was a terrible row on the steamboat, and the captain was still cursing with much fluency as his stern just drew clear of the ship's jibboom. "Third time's catching time," said Bill. "The very deuce is in it. Friday again. Of course, Friday."

It came away very cold while the vessel was stretching across the Western Ocean, and Bill half wished that the owner had kept him in the Mediterranean trade instead of sending him this long roundabout. The days passed quietly for a time, and then an exasperating head wind met the *Bretella*, and the work became desperately hard. The ship could make nothing of it, and night and morning the skipper watched with a groan the rushing array of westerly seas that charged down on him, and kept him thrashing about day after day. Once he said, "I've a good mind to run north, and seek for a wind. It's just like it used to be when we were turning in the coal trade. All hands at their stations, and the cook at the foresheet. I'll commit murder or something if it doesn't blow itself out."

"Won't you run north, sir? We're sure to get a slant in a bit, and it's no good boring away the Lord knows where."

One night Bill was standing right aft, and cursing the obstinacy of the brute that "wouldn't lie no nearer to it nor a coal-waggon," when a vast gloomy hulk hove up on his port bow. "Mercy on us, he's got no lights out!" cried Hope. And sure enough the coming vessel came on like a lowering shadow without one speck of red or green to guide the people on board the labouring *Bretella*.

A dull, cold finger seemed to touch Bill's heart as he once more muttered, "Third time's catching time."

He had not much opportunity for lengthened reflection. The old, old formula, "Where's he going? Where are you

coming to ?   He's into us !" was the only speech proper to
the occasion.   The ship was being navigated with criminal
recklessness on her westerly course ; she plunged over a
travelling sea ; her helm was put hard over, and she went
round to starboard, but she tore away the *Bretella's* mizen
rigging and pulled a lump of the port rail off as if it had
been a hoop-stave.

Hope was dancing mad ; he had been utterly unable to
avoid the catastrophe, and he naturally thought his luck
most cruel.

All hands were turned up to make the best of a bad job,
and Hope had to remain another fourteen hours on deck
before he could make sure that the mast was not in danger
of going.   Happily, sailors can always repair their house in
some fashion or other if anything goes wrong.   Shore-going
folks have to send for the carpenter, or the plumber, or the
mason, but Jack has to be a man of all trades.

Slowly the *Bretella* worked on her weary way, and at last
it seemed as though fortune were about to show favour.
The wind came round, and in one day the ship did 192 miles,
which was far and away her best run since leaving.

But all the time Bill Hope was full of apprehensions, and
his depression of spirits quite alarmed the officers.

" He's got that maggot into his sconce about Friday.   As
if nobody had ever been in for a worse time before in all
the world," said the mate.

Although the young man joked, however, he had confidence in his skipper, and he knew that the "maggot" would
never prevent Bill from showing the utmost resource and
daring if there were need.

On the very night of the long run the breeze increased to
a gale, and the gale grew to a hurricane.   The *Bretella*
could only be kept under storm canvas for half an hour,
and then Hope ran her under bare poles.   One unlucky sea
after another seemed to catch her, as though the send of
the water were directed by some malignant power, and at
length she was pooped by an ugly sea that appeared as
though it would never let her up any more.   Hope blamed
himself for this mishap ; he knew he had no business to try
running, but his evil genius seemed to drive him, and
nothing that he did turned out right.

He was grimly pondering after the bursting sea had rushed away in runnels of rolling foam, when another wave caught her on the quarter with a force that seemed enough to split her. There was a crack, and then the chains rattled; the *Bretella* broached to, and Hope knew that his rudder was gone. From that time the vessel did as she chose until the final disaster overtook her. It snowed hard, and she rolled about in the blinding drifts that gathered round her "thick as pudding," so poor Hope put it. He could tell to a little where he was, and he knew that he must shortly try conclusions with the rocks unless something desperate could be done with success. The gale never slept, and the darkened trouble of the air shut in the forlorn *Bretella* as in some strange prison.

At last, after horrible waiting, the mate came up. "There's something nasty ahead of us, sir."

Hope replied, "I know it. I'm going to try soundings."

Two casts showed that the tortured hulk was getting into shoaling water, and Bill let go both anchors; but all was of no avail. The *Bretella* steadily dragged, and soon she was beating herself with wild crashes on the rocks. It was dark and freezing. The crew took to the rigging, and hung on anyhow; but the cold was agonizing. One sea after another struck like a hammer on the helpless ship, and the wreckage began to surge around her in the boiling spume. One man cried, "I can't hold upright, sir! Won't you lash me to something and let me take my chance of getting ashore?" Bill could only shake his head. The second mate was a fine young chap, and a good seaman, but the trouble unmanned him and he lost his senses. He began to try singing shanties, and his hoarse shrieks were awful to hear in the pauses of the gale. With chattering teeth and contorted face, he yelled:

> "Now, my bully boys, all get ready,
>   We'll be stiff when the sun shall rise;
> And here's to the dead already,
>   And hurrah for the next that dies."

Then they heard him sing:

> "The standards was gone and the chains they was jammed—
>   With a heigh-ho, blow the man down;
> And the skipper, says he, 'Let the weather be damned—
>   Oh, give me some time to blow the man down.'"

It was awful work. To finish all, the young man drew
his knife from the sheath and shouted, "I'll stand it no
more!" Then he cut his throat, threw away the knife, and
sprang right into the mountainous bosom of a big breaker
that hurled itself over the vessel.

Even at that moment Hope's whimsy came into his head,
and he muttered to himself, " Friday.   Oh, Polly, my dear !
And I'll see thee never more."

The first mate was clinging by his chief.   Looking to
windward, he pointed up and shouted, "Good-bye, sir !
This 'un does the trick."

Four or five monster waves seemed combined in the
terrific sea that now came roaring down.   It fell on the
Bretella, and the vessel could stand no more.   She parted
amidships, and in a second Hope found himself far under
greenish depths of water.

He was half-stunned, bleeding, and breathless when he
came up; his left arm got jammed between a spar and a
timber that dashed against each other, and, with agony past
words, he knew that his arm was broken.   Clutching wildly
with his right hand, he managed to get hold of a fragment
of wreckage, and a green sea from the eastward carried him
with railroad speed towards the shallow water.   His feet
grounded, and a short, desperate struggle placed him beyond
the wash of the next sea.

He looked around, but all was quiet save the wide thunder
of wind and breakers.   He staggered further away from the
shore-line, and found that he was on comparatively level
ground.

A faint hail came to him from the darkness, and he summoned all his power to answer ; then two drooping figures
came slowly towards him, and he shook hands, even in that
supreme moment, with the mate and one of the forecastle
hands.

The poor mate's hand was crushed, and the frost hurt
him sorely, but he was plucky through it all, and said,
" Now, sir ; we've only got one life to live.   Let's save ourselves this time.   All the other poor chaps is gone, and I
feel uncommon near done myself.   Come on, sir."

Just at this moment the flying drifts of snow parted for
a little, and a long gleam of light shot through the rift.

The mate gave a wild cheer. "I know where we are, sir. That's Sable Island light for a thousand pound! Never say die. I've marked the direction." And Captain Hope bent forward with a new heart and toiled over the snow.

But the light was not so near as it seemed; the men's clothes froze on them as they walked, and it soon needed a violent exertion of strength to move in garments that had stiffened like boards. The sailorman gave a long sigh, and moaned, "I go no further. I'se been fall sleep, capeetan. You let Giuseppe stay him men self."

"No, no. Come on, Joe," said Hope; but the man had gone down on his face, and he rose no more. The chill had iced the very spring of his pulses, and his heart soon throbbed no longer. Poor Joe! He was born far away, where the grey olives and the tender vines make glad the Sicilian hills. He died that dog's death on the awful shores of Sable Island. Alas!

The creeping cold stole over Bill Hope's numbed limbs, and he reeled to and fro. The mate glared forward, and his lips moved like the lips of a man who is in the midst of an evil dream.

"No go, old man," said Hope; "I think I'm frost-bit."

"Never mind," whispered the mate. "One try more, now, my bully boy. No quarter-deck manners here. Give her more sail, Bill. Out with your stunsels, old man."

This last furious attempt at mirth was too much for the gallant fellow, and he fell on his side. Hope fell beside him.

Presently Bill said, "This is our last trip together. Can you get near enough to kiss me, my boy?"

The mate raised himself on his sound arm, leaned over, and touched Hope's cheek with his icy beard. "It's a cold kiss that, Bill; you'd sooner have had one of Polly's."

The name seemed to send a jerk through Hope. He roared with febrile energy, "I'm damned if I'll die—just to spite them for it's bein' Friday!"

He struggled to his feet, clutched the mate's collar, and hauled at him till it seemed as if the fingers of his right hand must break. The officer got up in turn, and the two brave men reeled on once more.

After three hundred yards or so Bill said, "Can't we

crawl, old tintacks?" The suggestion struck the mate, and the poor souls went forward on hands and knees, thus avoiding the chance of being blown aslant by the savage gusts.

The dark was coming over Bill Hope's eyes when he found himself on a sort of rampart. "The lighthouse!" he cried. "One more yet, my sonny, and the trick's done."

A sharp nasal voice rang out, "What cheer? Shall I come out to you?" and in a few seconds Bill and his officer were lying in front of a fine fire, while the clothes were torn off them by the eager lighthouse-men. After a tremendous rummer of Bourbon whisky, the wrecked mariners were wrapped in hot blankets and put to bed. They slept the clock nearly round, and if a sudden wrench of Bill's broken arm had not waked him with a grinding pang, there is no knowing how long he might have lain.

The two sailors were sent home, and resumed work as if nothing had happened, but Bill always says that he would sooner lose his berth than sail on a Friday again to please the best owner in the world.

PART II.

Alongshore.

I.

A SAILOR FAMILY.

WILLIAM BURNAGE and his wife lived for forty years in a lonely cottage that stood by the seashore a little to the southward of the Tweed. The nearest town was just ten miles away, and Burnage was a very old man before he saw a railway, for his life was not changed in any fashion by the swift movement of invention and progress. The great engines flew across the county day by day, but the line of their passage lay seven miles westward of the cottage, and Burnage never thought about travelling so far inland. Once or twice, when he was walking over the high ground that rose to the northward of his house, he saw a wavering streamer of smoke athwart the sky, and he supposed that the smoke came from the engines that he had heard about, but he never troubled himself to walk to the station ; and when he heard that Darling, the carter's grey mare, had staked herself after being frightened by a train, he said it was just what might have been expected from the fond ways of new-fangled people.

He had been a sailor in his youth, and he used to run in a sloop from the Firth to London in the old days. He went to sea at ten years old, and until he was one-and-twenty he was never ashore in any place excepting his own home and Limehouse. Of London he knew nothing. As soon as his vessel was warped to her place in the Pool, he went ashore and bought a few things at a little chandler's shop in Thames

7

Street, and then he stayed on board till the *Jane and Mary* was discharged. For the little old sloops were generally family concerns, and it happened that the members of Burnage's family were very religious people. His uncle, the skipper, took a good deal of raw whisky in the evenings while the ship was in port, but he would have been grieved if one of his lads had drunk a single glass in a Southron's public-house. It would have disgraced the kirk and the town.

When the sloop dropped anchor in the cove at home, Burnage landed on the jetty, and straightway cleaned himself. In the evening all the lads and lasses strolled up and down the wide street, and they were a gay company. The lads wore blue jackets, white trousers, and elaborate caps ; the girls had scarlet cloaks or bright shawls. Burnage looked very well in his go-ashores, for he was bright-eyed and handsome ; his pale yellow hair fell over his high collar with an attractive wave, and he walked as if all the place belonged to him. The girls called him Bonny Wully, and although they were shy as maidens ought to be, he might have taken his choice among them before he was twenty years old.

In the little port it was not thought wrong for men and girls to meet in the kitchen of a tavern, so at dusk Burnage joined a laughing company that met in a great sanded room which overlooked the harbour. Very little drinking went on. A man who had passed middle age was excused if he got solemnly tipsy on occasion, and he suffered no loss of dignity ; but no young woman would look at a lad who drank too much. The guests in the sanded kitchen were content with twopenny bottles of " yill," and the girls took a glass without shame. Men and women did not dance together save in threesome and foursome reels, and even the reel was not very much practised in the seaports. There was a big, solid table in the room, and when the fiddler came the sailors used to mount this table and perform step dances to please the company. Burnage was a very good dancer, and it was said that he knew eighteen different steps. He was light on his feet, and the airy way in which he did " cover the buckle " always delighted the lasses. The men were not jealous of him, for, as they said, " Wully but to be better at the steps than folk that lairnt the ordinar' gate.

His uncle was well kent te hae sailed norrard' aboot tae Liverpool, and there's aye new things tae be pickit up amang tha far-traivelled yins." So William was in great request whenever he was at home, and his fame spread far down the coast.

When Burnage was two-and-twenty years old he married Jean Lockhart, a tall, yellow-haired girl, who had gone to school with him.

Jean had high notions in her way, for she read books at night, and she did not approve of the dancing and ale-drinking that went on in the Billyboy Inn. She never saw Burnage the worse for liquor, but it struck her that he made himself common by dancing on the big table. One night when the pair were walking home together Burnage sheepishly approached a subject which had been in his mind for a good while. He said, " I've putten my fourth ten pund safe, Jean," and the girl, who could get to her English when she chose, answered, " That's very right and careful, William, and I'm glad you are doing so well." Then Burnage went on, " Ye ken I was aye for ye, Jean. Will you hae me ?" Jean made no hesitation, but she imposed a condition. " I'll take you, William ; you know that. But I won't unless you promise to drop dancing and drinking. It doesn't set you."

The bargain was made, and the noisy, simple wedding came off in a short time. The minister said he had not married such a bonny couple since he came to the town, and indeed both Burnage and his young wife were very good-looking. The man stood six feet high ; he was broad in the shoulders, straight-limbed, small-jointed, and graceful ; the woman was strong, erect, calm, and healthy.

The young folk did not stay long in the town after their marriage, for a great gentleman took a fancy to William, and got him nominated to the coastguard service, so on one spring morning the Burnages took all their belongings on board the revenue cutter and sailed away southward.

William's first appointment was his last ; the cutter stood into the bay, the furniture was landed and placed in the little stone cottage, and the coastguard lived there till the hearse came for him and bore him across the moor to the churchyard.

7—2

When Burnage was first married, he knew no book excepting the Bible and Burns's poems ; but his wife influenced his taste, and he gradually widened his reading. In the loneliness of the dark nights, when he walked on the moor and the sands, he had thoughts about religion, and he forsook the narrow formalism of the church in which he had been brought up. When he was about eight-and-twenty years old, he obtained a copy of Butler's "Analogy," and from that time onward he found complete mental satisfaction. In the course of ten years he learned Butler by heart, and could repeat any page, if the cue was given to him ; but he never ceased to like the sight of the print, and he pored over chapters of which he knew every syllable. From being passively pious, he became an active thinker, and neither poverty nor hardship lessened the eagerness with which he meditated on spiritual problems.

The world and the movements of men were nothing to him ; he never read a newspaper ; never longed to change his lot ; never repined. On roaring winter nights, when the darkness was full of trouble, and the waves crashed in the hollows of the rocks with strange noises, he went his rounds calmly, without heeding the tempest. The spray lashed at him, the crying wind struck chill on his face, and the whole night was quick with warfare ; but Burnage let the wild hours go, and communed constantly with the God whom he believed to be ever near him.

Four sons and two daughters were born to the lonely pair, and Jean Burnage had hard work to support her family on the scanty wages of a boatman ; but she toiled cheerfully, and gained much happiness from seeing her lads and lasses grow up brave and bonny around her.

There was little difficulty about keeping the children well fed, for Burnage converted a broad stretch of the waste into a good garden, and the potatoes that were put into the pits in September served very well until the spring. Then the rabbits were plentiful, and red cod could always be caught with lines laid as the tide flowed into the sandy gullies between the ledges of the rocks. The chief trouble was to provide clothes and to meet the miller's monthly bill.

Burnage had only four pounds a month, and that amount does not go far when six healthy children have to be fed

and clothed out of it. He spent nothing on himself beyond
a few pence monthly for tobacco. He learned to make
shoes, and saved money that way ; and he toiled in the daytime at his garden just as vigorously as if he had no night
work to do. So the household rubbed along roughly. The
children were rosy and beautifully built ; and when the
quiet evening came, and the family knelt around their father
as he prayed before they went to bed, Burnage was quite
sincere in offering solemn thanks for the many blessings
granted to him. He felt himself blessed whenever he looked
at his strong, ruddy youngsters ; and he loved them with
an intensity that was too deep for words.

Great confidence existed between the parents and their
children. When Burnage came over the moor after drawing his month's pay, his sons and daughters awaited him,
and took part in the talk about the disposal of every
shilling. They learned the value of money very early, and
the parents had no reason to be sorry for having dealt so
openly.

Once, when Maggie, the eldest daughter, was only eleven
years old, she thought that her mother was distressed
because young Wilfrid could not be provided with a new
cap that month. Maggie said, "Never you mind, mother,
I'll fettle the cap ; you watch me if I don't." The girl took
a pail down to the rocks, and went straight to a ring of tiny
pools that were only left at extremely low water.

She had always been given to wandering by herself, and
in one of her silent rambles she had noticed that these pools
were thickly studded at the sides with rounded shapes that
looked like heaps of broken shells and fine gravel. She had
examined some of the heaps and found that the fragments
of shells were the disguise of a great fleshy creature, which
put out waving tentacles and made a gentle whirl in the
water. Not long afterwards she had discovered that these
strange objects were in great request among the fishermen
for bait. The glossy anemone is useless, but the firm, solid
crass makes the best possible lure for cod.

Maggie worked hard and filled her pail ; then she
staggered wearily along the sands, and bore her burden into
a kitchen where a group of women were sitting baiting the
lines.

She soon came to the point. "I'll take sixpence for this lot," she said, pursing her mouth and looking severe.

One of the women cried, "Eh! hinny birds! Whatten a job's this! Whummle them into this kit, hinny Ye've getten mair nor aw cud a ploated off the rocks iv a month."

Maggie sternly repeated, "Sixpence for the lot. And I'll fetch you fower pails more if you'll let your Jimmy help me to carry them, and not watch where I go."

Maggie's ring of pools yielded enough to buy the cap, and she forgot her ruffled hands and cut feet when she saw her mother's pleasure. Burnage did not usually fondle his children, but when he heard what his girl had done, he kissed her, and said, "You're a good bairn to your mother, my wee woman, and Wilfrid 'll have to pay you when he's a big fellow."

All the children were alike helpful, and they were in every way a wholesome brood.

The lads were so like each other that when they sat together you could hardly tell (as their father said) "which was Cuddy and which was Bill." Burnage often remarked that he would have to make them wear different coloured earrings when they got to their full height, else he would be miscalling them. Wilfrid was perhaps the most powerful, but the others ran him very near. The girls were handsome, deep-bosomed creatures. They mostly went barefooted, so that their fine limbs worked uncramped; they were swift of foot, muscular, and very strong. They lived on perfectly equal terms with their brothers, and Mrs. Burnage always said that "her bairns were muckle mair like sweethearts than come o' the same father and mother."

All the lads went to sea in time, for they would have thought it beneath the dignity of a man to be anything else but a sailor. Far away north the black colliers bore round to the eastward, and turned into the little port that was the metropolis to which the thoughts of all the Burnages bent. The lads watched the ships dropping slowly in on the flood, and they longed for the time when they might sail toward that dim boundary and move among the wonders of the quays and wharves.

Cuthbert and Bill went together; there was but a year between them, and they were inseparable companions. It

happened that the owner of a fairly large barque wanted
two apprentices, and he agreed to take both the boys and
make out their indentures alike. So on one gurly morning
the rude haycart came, the two little boxes were hoisted up,
and the lads drove away across the moor, accompanied by
their mother, who sat sturdily on a cross-plank, and bore
the wild jolting with composure. The remainder of the
family kept very silent that night, and when Burnage prayed
for the absent ones, the two girls and their mother could
not keep from crying.

Within a week the barque went swaggering past with a
rare nor'-easterly breeze on the quarter. She was plunging
with long swoops into the grey rollers, and Burnage thought,
" Eh, but the bits o' bairns'll be bad."

Wilfrid and Jack were very uneasy after their brothers
went away, and the former often dropped hints about his
own strength and the ease with which he could wrestle Bill.
There was no help for it. Burnage knew that when once
the salt-water craving comes on a boy of the right breed
there is no guiding him, and he must even take his own
way. In those days it was not at all uncommon for
youngsters of ten years old to go on board the coasters and
Baltic traders, so no one in the port thought it strange when
Wilfrid Burnage and poor little Jack came from the southward and went away for their trial trips.

Jack was put on board a schooner that ran to Bergen, and
Wilfrid joined a squat brig that crossed the Bay, and plied
regularly to Cadiz.

The brig looked very ugly as she passed the cottage outward bound, and Burnage told his wife that he wished " the
bairn had gotten a clean ship, instead of that donnart old
barrel." Indeed, the *Beauty* offered a curious spectacle as
she thumped and reeled on her southerly course. She looked
like some dirty profligate who had been long on the spree ;
her patched sails were bent anyhow, and their grimy spots
resembled black eyes ; her topsails were not set, and the
fashion in which they were huddled to the yard with a big
lump like a feather-bed at the bunt was enough to break a
smart skipper's heart. As she swung to the point, she
yawed about as if she wanted the whole North Sea to herself, and the old coaster, who remembered the dandy vessels
from the Firth, sighed at her culpable vagaries.

After a long time—ah, how long it seemed !—the home-comings began.

On a golden evening, just when the yellow moths began to twirl round the ragworts with subtle hummings, and the white owls beat stealthily through the rising mist, two figures topped the northerly hill, and Maggie screamed, "Eh, mother! Jean! run ; here's the lads."

Jean and Maggie ran a race over the moor, and the elder girl won. She tried to hug both her brothers at once; then she changed from one to the other, with sweet, murmured incoherences, until the lads laughed and placed her between them. Then Jean came up, and the four "linked" home-ward.

Both boys were unspeakably sailorly ; they wore thin earrings ; their hair was combed in large curves behind their ears, and their flat caps were rakishly cocked on one side. The walk which each of them assumed was totally indescribable in its peculiar combination of lurch and strut, while, sad to say, Cuthbert showed an ominous swelling in one cheek, which painfully suggested a quid. From the earliest days those old-fashioned sailors carried out a droll system of dandyism ; yet, what fine fellows they were ! No nonsense about My Hearty, and You Swab, and Shiver-my-Timbers ! They were too nautical to use tinsel nautical terms, and their dialect was as straight and strong as their dandyism was ludicrous.

Mrs. Burnage had rushed into bewildering exploits of cookery when she heard Maggie cry out, and she was ready with tea when her stalwart boys came in.

It was a long, happy night, for the sailors told queer stories about their skipper and their shipmates, and the girls asked all kinds of questions, and the old man sat smiling placidly as the merry babble went on. Long after-wards, on blowy nights, when the wild darkness was clamorous with weird sounds, and the vessel crashed among the flickering crests of black seas, the lads recalled that tender firelight, and remembered the low, tremulous tones of their father's prayer. Folks have got much into the way of slurring religion nowadays, and I am no better than the rest ; but I cannot think of the past simple days without a tremble at the heart.

Life became quite eventful at the cottage as the boys settled down to their regular trips, and the visits came with brief intervals. The members of the family grew fonder and fonder of each other as they got older, and when the pinch of poverty was lightened as the sailors' wages increased, there could not have been a pleasanter household.

Jean went out to service, but Maggie stayed at home and busied herself with the garden and the cow which the lads insisted on buying. She employed all her spare hours in reading the sparse handful of old books that stood at the foot of the ladder which led up to the garret; but her work left little time, and her thoughts had to lie deep. She was really made for action, and not for speculation, though she dreamed much, and before she was twenty years old her chance came to show herself strong and faithful even if need be to death.

Maggie's mind had been little employed on great and heroic things beyond the pages of " The Pilgrim's Progress," but she never could picture herself as anything but one of the humble and lowly ones who helped Christian on his way. Her time came, and she rose to the necessity; but I question whether even then she had any idea of placing herself with the Shining Ones.

Let me tell the story of Maggie's doings.

On a grey December day William Burnage travelled southward to meet the captain of the station. He was obliged to cross a stream which ran sluggishly between deep banks, and spread over the sand at a distance of about four miles from his house. Early in the morning a light, steady rain fell; the slight covering of snow that lay on the ground rapidly melted, and the little river began to run in quick freshets. As the sun drooped a wan glare came into the sky, and the woods made hollow moanings. The sea-birds were uneasy, as they always are before bad weather comes away. The kittiwakes came screaming inland and settled upon the ploughed fields, and the curlews sought the innermost depths of the moor. By three o'clock the storm broke with a sudden easterly squall which blew the waves white at first, and then plucked the tops from the trailing seas, and sent the foam inland. The sun went down behind the Cheviots, and threw long swords of light in a wild circle

over the westerly sky. By half-past four in the evening a
ten-foot sea was galloping up to the very foot of the
cliffs below Burnage's house.

Maggie went out on the cliffs and watched the ships trying to run northward. She saw one little fishing-boat running under the jib alone, and making a hard fight to gain
the village, but an ugly cross-sea was running from the south,
and where it met the easterly sea, raised by the sudden
wind, great towers of water shot up in conical hills, and made
the navigation very difficult indeed for small craft. The little
boat was sweeping down the long incline of a southerly wave,
when a sullen black roller from the east caught her on the
starboard bow. She turned over, and the girl soon saw that
the poor fellows on board were swept far away among the
wild drift.

Wilfrid was at home, and the girl begged him to
come out into the open and watch with her. The desolate
ships scurried hither and thither, some trying for the Tyne,
some trying to get under the lee of the Coquet, some
making desperate efforts to haul off the land.

Before the last gleam of light had left the sky, a
ship's red light suddenly appeared round the point. The
vessel was evidently making very heavy weather of it, and
the water seemed to go clean over her, for her light
was only visible at long intervals, and through the driving
haze Wilfrid and his sister could see the long sweeping
strokes made by her masts as the puzzling sea caught
her sometimes to port, sometimes to starboard.

"I can't tell what that fellow means to do," said Wilfrid.
"He is trying to haul off the land, but I doubt the sea will
be too much for him. He is right inside the bend of
the Point. I guess it's a case of cold coffee with the lot of
them unless he can manage to club-haul her. Run in
and fetch the glass, my girl."

The fat old Dollond was brought out, and the young
sailor said, "I can just make her out—it's a barque ; she is
under storm canvas, and he is trying to get away, but he is
making far more leeway than headway."

The vessel threw up a flare, and Wilfrid said, still talking
to himself—"Ah ! he finds he has got into the wrong box ;
I rather guess we will have his company presently."

The red light went on pitching in short, sharp jerks, and Maggie watched, with clasped hands and eager eyes. She drew her breath with relief as she saw the light move eastward, and whenever the tiny red spot seemed to have been flung nearer to the rocks she tightened her hands, and remained rigid as a statue.

Suddenly Wilfrid whistled, for the vessel swung round, and showed both her red and green lights. The sailor said —"She is coming dead on. She will strike about 200 yards from our house. I will lay five to one she jambs her nose on the cliffs close in."

The lights came on with terrible rapidity. "Oh, for God's sake, my boy," exclaimed Maggie, "let us run round and meet her !"

Before they reached the edge of the rock the masts of the vessel loomed beneath them, and they heard a long, grinding crash as she blundered over a low ridge, then planted herself hard and fast at the very foot of a great scarp that the boldest cragsman in the whole country-side dare not have scaled.

Maggie and her brother looked over into the troubled darkness below them, and they heard loud cries. Wilfrid shouted, "Hang on as long as you can ! We can't get round to you. There is nothing for it but a rope."

The voice of a woman answered, but they could not exactly make out what she said, for the hoarse moaning of the wind and the booming of the waves made every other sound indistinct.

"We cannot let them stay there," cried Maggie. "I will go and get the rope from the well, and we'll get mother to come and help us."

Swiftly she unwound the long coil from the windlass of the draw-well, and brought it to her brother. Mrs. Burnage came out, and the three deliberated for a while.

"It's no use to lower the rope," cried Wilfrid; "they would never see it ; and unless we could put some heavy weight at the end the chances are ten to one that the wind would twist the strands among some of the points. One of us must go down. If you two women folk could hold on I don't mind making a try myself."

But Mrs. Burnage objected. "Oh dear, no ! Supposing

our nerve was to fail us for a minute, and we should let go
of you !"

A sudden resolution flashed into Maggie's mind, and she
said, " You are strong, Wilfrid, and I am not very heavy.
If you and mother can hold on I will go down myself."

The sailor saw that there was good sense in the proposition. " All right, old lady ; you are a good plucked one,
anyway. I guess my twelve stone would be too much for
you. Put my jacket round you. You had better be well
wrapped, in case you get a bump. We will stand well back
from the edge, and you must screech as loud as you can if
you want to give us any directions."

He made a clever hitch at the end of the well-rope, and
placed it round his sister; then the girl, with her heart beating furiously, went cautiously over the edge of the rock, and
a moment afterwards was swinging hither and thither in the
grasp of the wind.

The rock rose sheer from the water's edge, and the vessel
had come in so close that her foremasts were within a few
yards of the face of the cliff.

Wilfrid had measured his ground to a nicety. In
less than a minute Maggie had planted her feet on the
forecastlehead of the ship, and, excepting for a bruise on the
forehead, she was quite unhurt, and her nerves were
as steady as though she had been at the fireside at
home.

The men took her out of the bight of the rope. One of
them said, " Lord's sake, captain, why you are twenty miles
out of your reckoning ! This is my sister." And sure
enough it was Cuthbert Burnage and his brother who were
thus caught in the very jaws of death within pistol shot of
the house where they had been born.

The captain's wife was aboard, and she and her baby were
first placed in the bight ; then Cuthbert fitted a guy on
to steady the rope, and a tremendous hail through the
speaking-trumpet told those on the cliff-head when it was
time to haul away. By means of the guy the rope
was easily brought back again, and Maggie made the ascent ;
then Cuthbert Burnage said, "Better send the mate up
next ; he is the biggest and strongest of the lot of us ;
he will be able to help them on the rock-head."

So at half-past eight in the evening the whole crew were safely planted in the little kitchen of the cottage, while the poor barque was distributed in ragged fragments over a mile of the iron coast.

When William Burnage reached home he found his sailor-lads ready to greet him, and, although they had lost everything in the world, they counted the bargain a good one, because, as Cuthbert said, they would "never have known what a *nailer* Mag was if the old hooker hadn't broken her nose on the High Scarr."

Maggie Burnage had no reward, and I don't think she earned as much as a paragraph in the newspapers; but when her brothers kissed her that night before she left them, and spoke rough words of praise to her, she was more than satisfied.

II.

THE SQUIRE'S GRANDSON.

ALL the fishers and sailors were very much surprised when Mary Caseley came back to our village, for they had heard that she was married to a smacksman away down south, and they thought she would settle. She was better dressed than most of the people, and her little boy wore a suit on Sundays that was regarded as quite a credit to the village. Mary never talked much with the womenfolk, and they used to say she was proud; but, as she looked pale and sad, they did not trouble her with unkind remarks.

On Sunday evenings, when all the people lounged on the rock tops and the gossips kept up their shrill babbling, Mary sometimes went out and listened awhile, as the affairs of the village were discussed. Then her father would loiter near her, and when the dusk dropped down, he would say, "Haud thy ways into the house, maw woman, and we'll hev wor cracks." When Mr. Caseley's pipe was lit, Mary took her place on the other side of the room, and talked softly to her gigantic father until it was time for him to roll away into the great box bed. She sat up late, and sometimes she went and leaned over her little lad. Often she made his face wet with tears, and she moaned to him, "Poor bit bairn, thou's fatherless, and

worse than fatherless, but I'll keep to thee, and thou shalt
never want so long as thy mother has fingers to bait a
line."

Mr. Caseley looked strangely at the child at times, but
he was very gentle, and he never let his girl see that he
wished the bairn was not there. Everyone knew well
enough why the boy had such a grand Christian name as
Ellington, but nothing more than whispers passed, for it
was felt that Mary's marriage with the Hull man wiped off
all the previous events of her life.

Little Ellington Ross grew apace, and he was soon noted
as the most "hempy" boy in the whole district. He was
a well-built youngster, with clean round limbs, and a bold
carriage. His face was delicately featured, and there was
an air of good-breeding about him which made people take
great notice when he passed them. His eyes were blue, but
he had thick black eyebrows like his mother, and his fine
skin had a dark flush which burned brightly when he was
enraged or otherwise excited. On moonlight nights, when
the lads turned out for their wild games, he was always the
leader, and he sometimes held his companions breathless by
the mad freaks which he performed. He was sent to school,
but, as the minister remarked, he looked more fit to go with
the gipsies than to sit at a desk. Mary would have liked
to keep her bantling nicely dressed, and she had money
enough to get good clothes, but young Ellington despised
the bonds of boots and stockings, and he was fond of going
bareheaded and barefooted whenever there was a chance.
As soon as he left home for school in the morning, he slipped
the detested footgear off, slung the boots round his neck,
and trotted up the long road with his strange, springy
gait. The schoolmaster always said that the boy would be
hanged, and the minister entirely agreed with this doleful
opinion. Did he not let two large rats loose in the gallery
of the church one Sunday morning, and cause all the ladies
of the choir to jump on the seats in a most irreligious and
indecorous manner? Did he not secretly slip a noose over
the organist's foot, and tie that respected man to the crank
of the organ so that the string was wound in a tight coil
as the handle was turned? We had an organ into which
rollers were slipped, and our musician simply ground out

his tunes as an Italian grinder does. In the middle of the
Hallelujah Chorus, which was our finest piece of music,
Master Ellington s string suddenly became taut, the organist's
leg was drawn up into space, and the expiring shriek of
the instrument, blended with the outburst of improper
language from the musician, formed an interruption which
did not harmonise with the sacred character of the service.

At length a culminating outrage ended Ellington's education. It was customary at certain seasons of the year to
bar the master out of school. The desks were piled against
the door, and the instructor was not permitted to enter
until he had humbly promised to grant a holiday. Ellington took part in this solemn rite with much satisfaction,
and he acted as spokesman for the scholars. All would
have gone well had not the mischievous fellow been tempted
to bombard the master with peas during the parley, and
for this crime he was condemned to be locked in after the
rest of the rebels had gone home. Ellington carefully piled
fuel around the master's great desk, made an excellent bon-
fire, removed half of a window, and escaped homeward.
He was expelled, and the clergyman made such pointed
reference to his incendiarism in the next Sunday's sermon
that Mr. Caseley never went to church again for very
shame.

The wild boy at once began work as a fisher, and for
years he did not resume his studies, so that he could not
even spell through a chapter of the Bible. But this didn't
matter, for we never read anything in our village, and such
a thing as a newspaper had not reached the place within
the memory of man.

Ellington liked the coarse hard life on board the coble
and he soon became very useful. His daily round would
have been monotonous but for the caprices of wind and sea;
but the wild humours of the breezes, the incessant changes
in the perpetual assault of sea upon land, gave him enough
variety. In the evenings he slung his little oilskins over
his arm, and tramped with a very manly swagger down to
the haven, where the gaudy boats swung at their moorings.
The brown sail was run up, the boat curtseyed to the kiss
of the wind, and then, with a long rustle, she laid herself
over and stole far away toward the mystery of the North.

The boy generally sat amidships until the fishing ground
was reached, and then the hard labour began, which made
his hands horny, and tightened his muscles like springs of
steel. All the night through the boat lunged over the liquid
hillocks, the curlews called overhead like voices speaking
doom, and the whistle of the otters pierced the troubled
silence. Then the livid grey of the dawn lit in broad flaws
on the mystic water, and soon the wild misty roses of the
east were reflected in gallant splendour on the swinging
rollers. Ellington liked at such times to lay hold of the
tiller as the hoarse wind from the fields of sleep crisped the
ripples and made the sharp bow of the boat roar through
the cloven sea. He loved the excitement when the coble
lay down to her bearings and rushed past the gnashing
rocks into the still haven, and he loved best of all the walk
up the beach when the pale smoke was curling from the
cottages, and the riot of song raised by the sweet birds filled
all the sloping woods with lovely jargoning. He did not
think, he only felt ; and the delight in his free, toilsome
existence grew into his innermost being, and wedded him
in spirit to the sea. Before he was sixteen you might have
blindfolded him, and he would have taken you as far north
as Berwick quite safely, if you only told him the quality of
the soundings brought up on the tallow of the lead.

On one blowy autumn day, when the seas crashed heavily
over the beach, he and his friend Jimmy Story were the
only effective males left in the village, for all the men were
away south with herring. A small barque was making very
heavy weather of it in the offing, and presently she flew a
signal. Ellington watched her as she hove to, and he saw
that the sea was mauling her pretty badly. He said, "That
fellow wants a pilot, Jimmy ; let's be off to him."

"Got nobody to steer."

" We'll take old Adam."

" He's half deed wi' the pains."

" What's the odds ? He can grip a tiller."

Old Adam was sitting indoors brooding over the fire with
rheumy eyes, and breathing hard as his enemies, the pains,
nipped him here and there, but he brightened up at the
prospect of earning half a sovereign, and hobbled down to
the beach.

Mary Caseley (we never called women by the names they took on marriage) looked anxiously at her swaggering lad as he marched off to the seething beach, but she knew it was useless to curb him, and she only said, "Eh, hinny, be canny. Gan canny. I misdoot me but thou'll droon thysel'. Keep her hard this side o' the rocks as thou runs north, and let Adam keep the tiller all the time."

The boat flew into the wrathful flurry of cross seas, and gallons of water jumped into her as she crashed into the charging waves, but Adam nursed her cleverly, and the balers were kept going, so that she got out alongside of the barque without suffering much.

The skipper of the ship yelled, "I want to get inside the island ! Durst I go ?"

Ellington answered, "Take us aboard and hoist our coble if you can !"

"Can't be done ! We'll tow your boat if you like."

" But you mon stand off, and wait for the tide, and we'll get stove in."

In the end Jimmy and Ellington climbed on board, and old Adam agreed to tow astern in the plunging coble.

" How much do you draw ?" Ellington asked.

" Twelve aft, eleven forrad."

"That'll do. I can doctor you. You're not a frightened man, are you ? becass I'll make you sit up in a minute as we do the Race."

The captain laughed, and said, "Frightened ! no. Only I never was up here before, and they told me I could save the tide by cutting inside."

"All right. Now you catch hold of the wheel yourself, and shove her away till you fetch that black door on the tower and this post on the rocks well in line. Then let her rip."

A savage roaring sound was in the air, and right ahead was a field of rushing whiteness that seemed to fly forward with terrible speed. Ellington was really doing a most risky thing, and not three feet of water divided the whole crew from death as the barque yawed and rolled into the sucking stream that boiled round her with howling noises. The Race was in a bad state, for there was a short sea that jerked up fully six feet. Crack, crack went the bows as the rearguard of the travelling cataract was reached. Crash !

8

and away went the foretopmast in a piteous wreck.   Flap !
and the maintopsail flew.   It was lively work.

Suddenly Ellington shouted, "Hard over!" and he jumped
at the wheel to lend the skipper a hand.   Old Adam, in the
coble, was all but drowned as the barque went staggering
broadside on to the swift stream ; but she plunged through,
and swam gracefully eastward, with her stem dead on, for
the mouth of the little river.   Once Ellington had felt her
bump, but he held his tongue, and no one knew what mortal
danger the scapegrace had put the vessel in.

This was rather a clever bit of piloting to be performed
by a mere boy, and the captain said, " Well, young fellow,
you've started early, and you couldn't do much better if you
were grey-bearded."

This was but one among many of the feats which the
young barbarian achieved.   He seemed to take a fierce
pleasure in looking into the very jaws of death, and his old
grandfather often said, " Eh me ! but he never got his pluck
from his father.   It's all your own, Mary.   He'll be fetched
home in a cart one of these days after they've picked him up
on the beach ; but he'd better die a real man's death that
way than turn up soft."

Besides the exhilarating dangers of his ordinary life,
Ellington had other delights of a more questionable kind.
The sporting instinct was very strong in him, and he recklessly indulged his fancy when he had a night ashore.   He
knew several poaching pitmen, and he joined them in many
a secret excursion.

Matthew Hobson was a sly old fellow, who had not done
a stroke of work for years.   In the afternoons Matthew was
generally seen lounging about in his village with an inno-
cent-looking Spanish pointer at his heels.   He was always
comfortably dressed, and he was never short of money, yet
he did not even handle a spade in his own garden.   In
confidential moments, Matthew would inform privileged
persons that he always earned enough in the pheasant
season to keep him during the year.   In truth, Mr. Hobson
was the most skilful poacher in England.   In all his life he
never was caught, and his depredations were so extensive
that a sporting baronet offered him double wages to take
service as a keeper.

Then there were Joe Pease, the banksman who trained
lurchers up to a supernatural pitch of intelligence, and Billy
Pearson, who had taught some greyhounds to run by scent
at night. People imagined that greyhounds could not be
used in the dark, but Billy's two snaky villains were as keen
as terriers on a trail.

All of these ruffians were glad to have Ellington's aid at
any time, and the boy became skilled in all manner of secret
woodcraft. You may make Game Laws till all eternity, but
you will never stop high-spirited lads from poaching. The
natural disposition will assert itself, and neither policeman,
nor prison, nor gunshot, nor bloodhound will ever deter the
humble sportsmen who imitate their pastors and masters in
a clandestine way. The pleasure is too wild and keen.
You may preach about morality as much as you like, but
where do the moralities fly when the quick thud of the
quarry's feet sounds in the darkness, and the deadly lurchers
glide like dark streaks after their prey? The dancing pulses
caper away with your reason, and your primitive ancestor
asserts his sway over you.

Ellington escaped capture until he was seventeen years
old. He poached everywhere, and he once shot a pheasant
in the coverts within one hundred yards of the Hall. His
mother bemoaned his waywardness, but his will mastered
her, and she ceased to raise her laments when she saw him
chalking his gun-barrels in the dark evenings.

While he was at the very height of industry as a poacher,
however, the Squire came home from abroad.

The Squire had grown very pompous and overbearing
during his long absence. Mary met him on the moor one
day—a stout, well-looking man, with florid cheeks and a
weak, retreating chin. He drew his cob across the path,
and the worn, pale woman saw that his face looked ghastly.

He stammered, "Why on earth! what brings you here?
I thought you would come no more."

In gentle but scornful tones she said, "You mean you
wished it. What was I to do, man? If I'd depended on
thou, and thy fine words, it would have been bad. But the
old man that saved you stuck to me when my good man was
drowned, and we had no need to be beholden to cowards."

"But look here now, Mary. 'Pon my soul, anything in

8—2

reason. I suffered enough, but what could I do? I was nearly out of my mind, and I was tied hand and foot. I'll do what you like now."

"My good lad, I'm grown old, and care for nothing. I'm thinking it's a pity such a fool as thou ever tried to be a scoundrel as well. Go thy ways, poor man! I've nothing but pity for thou. Thy fine lady couldn't bear thou a son, and I have the laugh of her there. Go thy ways—go!" Like all women from our part of the country, Mary used the words "thou" and "you" by turns as she wanted to express shades of meaning, but she leaned to the more impressive word when she was strongly moved.

The Squire was maddened by her quiet gibe at his childless state, but he spoke never a word, and rode sullenly away.

The new-comer soon made his presence felt on the estate, and the marauders from the collieries had a bad time. The staff of keepers was doubled, and half-a-dozen huge mongrel night-dogs were brought from Norfolk to impress the imaginations of ill-doers.

But young Ellington was not in the least daunted by the hulking beasts that stole round the coverts, and he went on with his depredations for a good while. At last the end came. Our hero had noticed that in the early morning the rabbits used to steal away before the dawn to nibble the sweet thymy herbage that grew on a wide stretch of moorland : and he saw that the little creatures left their burrows in the sandhills a long way behind. It struck him that by carrying the dogs round in a boat and creeping up from the beach it would be possible to cut off the retreat of the game. So he named his project to his friends. Accordingly on one clear, starry morning the coble ran on to the sands, and two lurchers, two greyhounds, and a terrier were lifted out. The dogs sneaked silently under the brackens, and waited for orders. Ellington bestowed himself carefully in a sandy hollow. He pointed to the broad flat and whispered, "Go away!" The wicked lurchers wound like snakes through the ferns, and ranged with their long gliding gallop over the shadowy ground. Soon the fun grew fast and furious. Four courses were in progress all at one time, and the doomed victims twirled and scuttled with swift dodging

motions, while the murderous pursuers followed every turn
with quiet ferocity. The flat was alive, and murder grim
and great went on until the last fugitive had rushed to
shelter. Ellington whistled softly, and the dogs came to
the call, trembling with pride as they laid their game down.
The lad bagged the rabbits and turned to go.

A quiet voice said, "Stand where you are. If you stir
I'll empty both barrels through you."

Ellington found himself confronted by a grave man in
velveteens, who covered him accurately with a gun. Presently his arms were seized from behind, and he knew it
was all up. Looking down the beach he saw his companions
running to the boat, and he resigned himself to his captors.
His hands were tied behind him, and he was ignominiously
driven to the Hall, where he was locked up in the harness-
room until the Squire was ready.

Meantime the escaped poachers rowed round to the haven
and went ashore.

Joe Pease entered Mr. Caseley's house and asked for
Mary.

The woman came out looking pale, and she said, "You
needn't tell me what's happened. I dreamed he was a bit
bairn again last night, and he held out his arms for me, and
I took him, so I know what's come to him."

'We couldn't help him. They've ta'en him away to the
Hall."

'What'll he get?"

'Three months if they can manage it."

'Will he be with thieves and bad folk in the lock-up?"

'Aye, will he. I've been in twice myself."

Mary moaned to herself after the men were gone. She
had never taken heart to check her wilful boy, and her
punishment had descended heavily upon her.

At ten o'clock Ellington was taken into the study, and he
found the Squire seated in great majesty. The lad threw
up his head proudly, and stared the great man full in the
face while the under-keeper told the story of crime and
capture. "If you'll ask him to turn out his pockets, sir,
you'll see we caught him in the very act.'

Three rabbits were extracted, and then the Squire said,
"Have you anything to say? You understand, of course,

that I am a magistrate, and my duty is very clear. You need not speak unless you like until you are brought up before the Bench."

"I can't say nothing, except that I was catching rabbits. I've done it before and never was caught. Now you've got me, you must just do as you like. It's a fair game, and I shall do the same thing again when I have the chance."

"You're an impudent scoundrel, I must say."

"You dursn't tell me that if my hands were loose."

"And why, pray?"

"Because I'd knock your teeth down your throat."

The Squire could not speak. He gasped and glared, but the cool young ruffian before him never moved a muscle, and kept his clear eye fixed on his enemy with a steady gleam.

A knock came to the door, and the keeper looked out to see who was there. A servant said, "A woman wants to see Mr. Ellington directly. She says she'll take no denial, and she'll come in without leave if she's ordered away."

The Squire roared, "Tell the woman to leave the grounds at once, or I'll have the dogs loosed."

Presently the servant came again, and asked to be allowed to come in.

'She says, sir, that you'll rue every hair of your head, and she bids me say her name is Caseley."

The Squire meditated for a moment, and then said, "Take this fellow out, and come back again when I ring."

Mary entered the study without making any reverence, and, after calmly looking at the magistrate for an instant, inquired, "You've got a poacher taken last night?"

"What business is that of yours? I have no wish to be unkind, but I ask you, how dare you break your bargain? You were treated fairly, and if you venture to rake up old stories I shall face it out and you will be hardly dealt with."

"I asked you if you had a poacher locked up here by your keepers last night. Answer me, or I may forget myself."

"Well, yes—and now?"

"What'll be done to him?"

"I can't say. He comes before me in the first instance,

but he will meet the magistrates in due course. I presume that he will be imprisoned."

"Do you know his name?"

"It is written down here."

'Take my advice and let him go at once. Keep the thing quiet, or you'll be sorry."

A dim suspicion took shape in the weak man's mind, and he asked, "Do you venture to interfere with the course of justice? Is this a planned insult?"

"Nay, my man; your deeds have come back on you. Did you notice the lad's look? Can you not mind the lass that had cheeks like him? Do you mind the sea walk? Do you mind the bairn that was born to you when I went away with the disgrace on me? Seventeen years, and you've never once thought of your own flesh and blood. And him a man now worth ten of you. When I look at you now, I could burn my eyes out to think I ever broke my heart over you. But broken it is, and I advise you to do no more harm."

"Do you mean to say——"

"That's just it, hinny. I'm telling thou the plain truth. He's your son, and he was my shame; but all that's past and gone. It's little enough trouble thou's had with your lad."

"But, good God! I can't have him about the estate."

"What for not? Where else should he be? Could we tramp on the roads? Could we take the dirty money you had the face to offer us?"

The man grew desperate, and determined to play a bold move. "Unless you promise to send him away to sea at once, out of mischief, I swear you shall do your very worst, and I'll press for severe punishment. If you like to promise, he shall go home with you, and you shall have money to fit him out."

"Your money's not wanted, man. I wanted yourself once; but now I would have neither you nor your money if I was to beg on the road. I want my bairn; and I'll let him away to the sea."

So the Squire called the keeper in, and said, "I think, as this is the boy's first mistake, we may treat it as a mere freak. Let him go, and perhaps the fright may act as a warning."

" As you like, sir. But he's no boy. There isn't a worser hand in the whole country, sir."

Then the keeper went to his prisoner, and gruffly observed, " You're not to go in again. You're let off this once, but mind we don't nail you any more."

" All right, mistor. And now let me tell you something. You've squeezed my arms up pretty tight. Some day I'll meet you on the open road, and you'll have to try who's the best man."

       *   *   *   *   *

Mr. Caseley was a very prosperous fisherman, and he had no difficulty in giving Ellington a good rig-out for the sea. The lad went away quite happily, just patting his mother on the shoulder as he jumped into the cart. The fisher folk never kiss, and never use such words as " love." They are a hard, self-contained breed ; and although our young sea dog felt sore at heart to see his mother looking so pale and anxious, he went off quite jauntily.

He was only bound apprentice for a short term, and he went away in a splendid clipper that sailed for New Orleans. Before the ship had been a week out the captain said, " I can't make you out, my joker. You're not sick ; you pick up your rope without a bungle. I believe you could steer if you were set to it."

" I was a lot aboard ships when I had the chance, sir, and I picked up things very quick. They learned me to steer before I was twelve year old, and I learned my ropes just for fun, and the compass too. I'll take a spell at the wheel, if you'll let me have a try, sir."

And the big apprentice showed that he was a really admirable helmsman. He watched his ship like a cat, met her beautifully, and proved that he had an instinctive understanding of her peculiarities. The rough men in the old port had taken a great deal of pains with him, and a lad who could manage one of our old barrels was good enough for anything, you may be sure. A fisherman has the most lordly contempt for a mere sailor, but when he does take to the business nobody can beat him.

The skipper could not make enough of his youngster. He scarcely ever swore at him, and, although he once aimed a large rhubarb pie at Ellington's head, this disciplinary

measure was adopted during a dead calm, when the mildest
of men might be forgiven if he showed irritation.

On one great day the captain proposed that Ellington
should resume his schooling, and the young fellow went at
his books most ardently. He had plenty of time on his
hands, and he spent long, quiet afternoons in attentive study.
Soon he was able to read very well, and before he was out
of his time he had become a very fair scholar. His appetite
for books was insatiable, for, like many other learners who
begin late, he was so surprised and delighted by his new
experience that it seemed as though he were entering on a
new and beautiful country which he must needs explore
with all his vigour.

* * * * *

Ellington was twenty-two years old before he ever saw
the village again, and by that time he had managed to get a
berth on board of a big liner that ran to New Zealand. He
was in uniform, and his resplendent appearance made the
fishers look on him with awe. Like most harum-scarum
lads, he had become rather staid since he took to steady
labour, and Joe Pease could not tempt him to "try one
more turn at the old game." He walked his mother out on
the Sunday, and Mary was very gay in her green shawl.
His old friends greeted him with gruff but sheepish kindness, and he made a very profound impression on the
girls.

Before he went away he held one brief and strange conversation with his mother.

They were sitting together in the sanded kitchen, and
Mary said, "We'll not have a light, my man. I want to
say something to you, and it's best said when you can't see
me. Maybe I'll be gone before you get back, and I want to
tell you something; though maybe the bairns or the women
folk has told you before. I want you not to put yourself in
the way of that man that was going to send you to gaol.
He's talked to your grandfather about leaving you money,
and father said he could please himself, but we wanted none
of his brass. I've been thinking, maybe we did wrong when
we refused help for you. We hadn't the right to rob you,
for nothing was your fault; and he may as well make it all
up to you, as the saying is, as far as he can."

" Why should he give me money ?"

" He's your father, hinny; and the old Squire, your
grandfather, made him put me out of the place.   And now
go away from me, my son, for my heart's just broken, and I
would sooner died than said a word only for your good."

" But I thought my father was drowned on the Dogger ?"

" Oh, hinny, hinny ! don't say one word more, or I mon
lie down and die.   Get thee ways out till I quiet mysel'."

*   *   *   *   *

Ellington Ross worked his way upward until he became
a captain, and he left the east coast altogether.   He was
accounted the greatest dandy in all Liverpool ; but, although
he was very fastidious about his dress, he was manly withal,
and a more cool and successful daredevil never stood on the
quarter deck.

He once brought a rudderless vessel right across the
Atlantic, and that, too, when she was so badly knocked
about that he had to take his spell with the hands at the
pumps.   The underwriters made him a present of £500,
and the owners gave him £250, so that he had a good lump
of money.   He ran over to the village, and his mother cried
with joy and pride, for he was such a specimen of a man as
you do not see every day.   He had inherited his grandfather's mighty frame, and the strength of him was past
calculation.   His beard fell far down on his breast, and he
looked the very incarnation of luxuriant virility.   He was
an aristocrat, every inch, and his mother was secretly pleased
to watch the proud flash of his cold stern eye.

Before he went away he said, " I've brought £500 for you,
so you'll need to ask no one for help, whatever may come.
Spend it all, and deny yourself nothing."

Then he went away, and his mother never saw him
again.

*   *   *   *   *

Ellington was bound out with a clipper that had to call
at Madeira, and he had two invalids on board.

One was a pallid, soft man, whose face seemed strangely
familiar to him.   He did not appear to be consumptive, but
it seemed as though his blood were thin and poor.   After
taking several long glances, the captain bit his lip and
reddened to the roots of his hair.   The pale man was peevish

and very tiresome during the first days of the run ; but
Ross treated him with much kindness, and the two became
friendly. The Squire had forgotten the name that he wrote
down years before in his study, and he did not know that
he had seen the bearded giant before.

The clipper met fearful weather after crossing the Bay,
and all the passengers were ordered to stay below. The
captain stood to his work day and night, but the sea beat
him, and at last one enormous wave broke over the ship and
crippled her. Her rudderhead went, and she was strained
all to pieces. For two days and two nights the gale lasted,
and the sea took its own way with the wallowing hulk.
She began to settle on the third day, and the most desperate
work at the pumps did no good.

Amid the awful noise and confusion the passengers were
secured in their cabin, and the scene below was cruel to
look on. At length the captain was obliged to say, "Ladies
and gentlemen, there's nothing for it but the boats. Keep
cool, as she won't go down for an hour yet. Obey orders
and take your places as if nothing was the matter."

The pale-faced man rushed up after Ross ; his mouth
gaped, his eyes were red, and every limb of him shook in an
agony of terror. He screamed, "Oh, for God's sake, captain, are we going to be drowned ? Oh ! why could you
not save us ? Save me ! save me ! for mercy's sake, and
I'll give you all I have in the world. But don't, don't let
me die yet."

"I've got work to mind, sir. Be a man. If you don't
care for yourself I must make you care for me. I'm going
to die presently. Do you see me squeaking and shivering ?
If you create any disorder I'll brain you !"

"But why—oh why ?"

"Because you're my father, and you're disgracing me in
my last moments. Down below till you're called ; then I've
got something to give you."

Two boats were lowered—the rest were smashed. Limp,
white, and quaking, Mr. Ellington was dropped over the
side, and hauled on board the long-boat. The boats were
fearfully crowded, yet some thirty men were obliged to
stand by the vessel.

Before the long-boat got clear, Captain Ross leaned over

and said to one calm gentleman, "I'm going down with my ship. When that coward comes to his senses, give him that address, and make him go there if you're saved."

Then Ross resumed his fight with death, but it was of no avail, and he passed away like a brave man, amid the vast music of remorseless winds and the desolate storming of wild waters.

*   *   *   *   *

Mary Caseley was earnestly begged to visit the Hall. She went unwillingly, and was shown into the study where she had faced her betrayer long ago.

A pretty child was sitting on Ellington's knee, and the woman shrieked and turned pale when she saw the face.

" You know what happened to our boy, Mary ?"

" No ; don't say the worst."

" I must.   This is our grandson, and I will bring him up as my own.   I have no one else in the world now, and this was left to me."

III.

THE DESERTED CHILDREN.

THE snow lay heavily on the roof of the Westmoor Farm House, and the clumsy road that led up to the farmyard was frozen into irregular hillocks as hard as iron. On one bitter afternoon the sun had struck the Cheviots into sullen, icy splendour as he sank behind them, and the last lordly swathes of flame were just trembling into dull, neutral violet, when a cart bumped over the terrible road, and two little girls who were swaying on the seat gazed with fear at the looming mountains. It seemed as if the cart were bearing the children into some hideous enchanted country, and they were very glad when the driver pulled up at the gate and lifted them down.

One of the girls said, "Have you got the letter, Dolly ?" and Dolly nodded.

A broad-built and bronzed man came out and shouted, " Hello !   Who's this, I'd like to know ?"

Dolly put her finger in her mouth, and stole timidly up to the questioner.   " Please, it's Dolly Feltham and Winny Feltham from London.   We want our aunt Foreman."

"And what set you here, poor little body? Come in. You're like ice. Aunt! Come down and see these two visitors of yours."

A large and stately dame entered the glowing kitchen. She was erect, deep of bosom, strong limbed, and ruddy. Her pale blue eye had a keen flash, and her mouth looked determined but kindly. She looked for an instant, and then said, "Why, by your looks you should be Amelia's children. What in the name of mercy sent you here?"

"Please, we want Aunt Foreman, and we've got a letter."

"Where have you come from?"

"We were in London, at a place called Commercial Road, and father never came to see us, and mother took ill, and they put her in the coffin, and took her to be buried, and she left a letter and some money, so the neighbours put us into the train, and the man with the bright buttons looked after us, and the man with the cart took us up at the station."

"Where is the letter?"

Mrs. Foreman flushed hotly as she read, and muttered, "The scoundrel! The heartless rascal!" She crumpled the paper up, and said fiercely, "Come and get warmed, and eat something. Then I'll put you to bed for to-night."

The children thought she was angry, and they began to cry piteously, but she sat down in a big chair by the fire, and pressed the little things to her bounteous breast, murmuring endearments all the while. She made ready some warm milk, and her guests were soon glowing in the pleasant firelight. They ate as if they were starved, and Mrs. Foreman was frightened at their eagerness, but she pressed them with more and more food till they were satisfied. Then she put them snugly away in a cosy bedroom.

She was very grave when she came down, and said, "I've got a bad affair to talk over with you, Ned. Here's that wretch, Ralph Feltham, has left the country. He lost his ship through his gambling habits. The owners found out that he was never out of the hells either at Liverpool or London when he was ashore, so they dismissed him. He left the bairns to starve, and Amelia had only six pounds in the world when she wrote this. And now she begs me to care for the bits o' bairns. How can I? I get through,

and that's all. If the bit land wasn't my own, and there
was rent to meet, I couldn't manage."

Ned Shotton knitted his brows and remained brooding
for a good while. At length he said, " It's a queer job ; but
we can't send the bairns off. Feltham has no one belonging
to him, and you and me and Aunt Jane makes all the relations the poor things has got. Aunt Jane might lend us a
hand, and I'm ready to do my best. I've neither chick nor
child, and I can leave three pounds a month for my share.
What do you say ?"

" It's the future, Ned, my man. *Two* pound a month 'll
more than keep them just now ; but it's an awful responsibility."

" Never mind ; we'll take the chance. In fact, we've got
never a smell of a choice. Very likely they'll be a bit
comfort to me when I come from the sea."

So, although Mrs. Foreman shook her head and tapped
dubiously with her foot, she was won over by her nephew's
rough kindness, and she said, " You're a good lad, Ned," before she went out to make the cows comfortable for the night.

Ned Shotton was in command of an East India trader,
and he went away for very long spells at a time. He stayed
with his aunts when he was ashore, and the married woman
and the old maid alike adored him. The great event in the
life of each was his arrival, and his jolly ways gave them
something to talk about from the time he sailed until they
heard his burly roar as he came past the hinds' cottages.
On wild mornings Aunt Jane would say, " Poor Ned, poor
fellow, I doubt he's getting badly knocked about," and Aunt
Foreman would sigh, " Eh ! Weary on the sea ! I wish he
was only ashore for altogether before it takes him away
from us."

Mrs. Foreman had spoken of her lack of means, but in
truth she was very well off. The farm was her own, and it
was well stocked. There was a certain sluttishness about
the appearance of the place, but an air of plenty seemed to
be diffused around, in spite of the confusion in the folds and
stackyards. If old George, the chief hand, had chosen to
tell the secrets of his mistress, he would have named at
least £300 a year as the net profit of the estate when every
claim had been met in its season.

When the young Londoners were dressed in the morning, their childless aunt was drawn to them strangely. They had lost their starved look, and they were a pretty pair of blue-eyed pets. Cousin Ned rather frightened them with his great voice, but when he took them on his knee and said, "Are you going to be my little girls now? Will you stop till you're big women, and be my sweethearts?" they were restored to confidence, and Winny stroked the sailor's beard, and whispered, "Nice man; I like you."

Ned went off to sea, and the children quietly settled down to the life of the farm. They were sternly kept in hand by their aunt, for the fashion of indulging children has not penetrated to that lonely region even now. But they were not unhappy. Their only playmates were Tom and Lancey Hindhaugh, the sons of the coastguard, whose little hut stood on a bleak hill to the east of the farm. Tom was a tall boy of ten, Lancey was a stout rosy lad under nine years of age. On fine days the children went to the sands, and constructed wonderful dens, in which they played at gipsies or wild beasts. Sometimes they gathered purple geraniums, or chased the black and scarlet butterflies on the breezy sand-hills. They fell out, called each other naughty names, got up little jealousies, and made friends again. In winter time they were allowed to go into the warm back kitchen along with Susan, the big servant girl, and they amused themselves with making rabbits on the wall, or propounding the "guessing stories" which are popular in rustic circles. At eight o'clock Aunt Foreman came in and said, "Now, Tom and Lancey, light your lanterns and go home." Then the candles in the horn lanterns were lit, and the boys wound their way over the links, whistling very cheerily, with a view of impressing the imaginations of the bogles who were believed to haunt the eerie hollows.

Tom attached himself to Dolly, and he really liked her, though he often slapped her severely by way of teaching her the true relations of the sexes. Winny made a slave of Lancey as a rule, but sometimes he rebelled, and asked injurious questions, like, "Who made you so fine, then?" "I suppose you think you're master maybe?" "You're not going to make a cuddy of me, I can tell you. Do you think

I'm just a cuddy?" Then Winny would say, "Oh, very
well. We can do nicely without your company, so you
needn't speak to us any more." These dignified passages
of arms were followed by speedy reconciliation, and Lancey
became peculiarly abject in his docility when his revolt had
been more daring than usual.

So the happy time sped until the lads were big enough to
go to sea, as their father had done before them. In the
common fashion of those days both brothers were bound on
board one vessel. Tom was thirteen, Lancey was twelve,
and they were well-grown fellows.

There was very little sentiment about the parting. Dolly
said, "Don't get drowned, and come back when the goose-
berries are ripe." Winny gave Lancey a pincushion, and he
put this appropriate nautical implement into his trousers
pocket, along with a ball of cobbler's wax, two fishing floats,
a bundle of string, and an old pipe (which he fully intended
to smoke as soon as he got his first oilskins).

All of us knew the vessels that bowled away from the
river and faded off to the southward, and Mr. Hindhaugh
brought the girls to the cottage to see him run up the flag
as the lads went past. Of course Mrs. Hindhaugh cried—
that is the way of the women-folk—but the girls merely
danced with delight when the flag was answered by Tom,
who stood in the starboard rigging and waved a pair of
trousers with great emotion. Then the *Brotherly Love*
lumbered to the south, and the matter-of-fact Hindhaugh
went in, expressing a hope that that fond laddie hadn't
dropped the breeches over the side.

*   *   *   *   *

The links were all ablaze with shining flowers ; the larks
were filling the air with notes that fell like a hail of pearls
from the glad sky ; the little stonechats jerked their way
from boulder to boulder, and turned their wise heads
to tantalize the wayfarers. The full-toned symphony of
summer and delight was sounding, and the two tall girls
who walked over the joyous moorland looked happy amid
the colour and music. Dolly had grown tall and powerful.
Her face was strong and regular in every feature, and her
proud head was crowned by a mass of blonde hair that made
her queenly. She was ashamed of her robust build, and

her arms were a continual trouble to her, by reason of their massive contour. Winny was more delicately framed. Her high, aquiline nose was daintily shapen, and her little ears were like lovely shells. Both the girls were rich in colour, and they made a pretty pair. But, alas! they were condemned by Aunt Foreman to wear the garb of the eighteenth century, and, while all the servant-girls from the Chase were gorgeous in expansive crinoline, the two beauties were clad in robes as straight as any æsthetic milliner ever devised.

The bells clamoured, the farmers' gigs converged toward the church, and the stately girls took their place in the straggling procession of gaudy villagers who lounged up the gravel walk to the porch. "I wonder if the lads are here," said Winny. "You shouldn't think of such things," observed the stern Dolly. But I really believe that Dolly looked quite as keenly from under her drooped eyelids as she walked up the aisle. At any rate, she reddened and bridled before she reached her place, and her shoulders moved in a very self-conscious way when she took her seat, and pretended to be engaged in preliminary devotions.

In one of the pews set apart for the rank and file of the populace, two handsome sailor lads were sitting. They stood up when the service began, and gazed forward in a rather vacant and sheepish manner. Their discomfort apparently lasted until the benediction was pronounced, and then the two blue-clad fellows lurched out with the measured roll that is learned by years of sliding and balancing on the decks of labouring vessels. Both lads were very smart. Their yellow hair was cut level, in the style known as "the basin crop," and two waves of shining locks were combed back in a bold swirl behind the ears. Their caps were very finely decorated, their jackets were glossy, the loose trousers fell over the orthodox shoes in baggy folds, and altogether the young men were nautical dandies, rigged out according to the venerable traditions cherished along the coast.

There was much gossip in the churchyard as the folks trooped out, and the sailors had to do a great deal of hand-shaking among their old schoolfellows. Then there were calls to be made in the Row, for it was esteemed very im-

9

polite if a sailor who had just arrived did not make a house-to-house visitation. It was considered right to offer the voyager a nip of raw spirits to give him an appetite, and the time employed in drinking, or refusing to drink, was always somewhat lengthy on the first Sunday.

So it happened that the girls were far away over the moor before Tom Robinson, the eloquent gardener, would allow Lancey and Tom to quit his hospitable kitchen. The two young men would not openly give chase; they slipped down on to the sands, and, after putting the line of hills between themselves and the ladies, they ran with an utter absence of decorum, and, taking a short cut through a gap, sauntered over the moor. Of course, Dolly was excessively surprised, and of course the astonishment exhibited by Tom at such an unexpected encounter was so keen that he panted and sweated with emotion. The couples walked silently homeward, and parted with every appearance of embarrassment. Tom, who used to chastise Dolly so firmly, was quite reverential in his address, and his efforts to begin conversation amused the staid young woman mightily. In the evening, the kindly dusk rather removed the awkwardness, and there is no harm in saying that Mr. Thomas Hindhaugh had his arm round Miss Feltham's waist as they sauntered up from the sands to the farm, while Lancey had got so far as to tell Winny that he wished she was " for " him as he certainly was " for " her.

Our people very much disliked strong manifestations of sentiment, and a young man who was seen to kiss a girl earned the name of " lad-lass," which stuck to him for months, and was shouted after him by the children. But our courtships were most business-like. One meeting served to settle the affair, and there were no delicate gradations, because as soon as a lady declared that she was " for " a man —our euphemism for vows of the tender sort was the single word " for "—the financial question cropped up at once, and the couple considered ways and means with shrewdness and vigour

The girls said, " We've been linking with the Hind-haughs," when they went in, and Aunt Foreman blinked over her spectacles, and remarked, " You ought to be ashamed of yourselves, you sluts. I don't know what the world's coming to, with the bairns walking together. Bring them both here to tea to-morrow." It appeared that Mrs. Foreman was not at all displeased. Indeed, a respectable young sailor, with his prospects of becoming captain, was esteemed quite a good enough match for anybody short of the quality. So with scarcely a word of the sentimental sort the two brothers were tacitly accepted as the sweethearts of the two sisters. They quarrelled amongst themselves, made friends, pretended to harbour jealousies, and were altogether very fond of each other.

When the time came for parting there was a good deal of quiet crying at the farm, but Mrs. Foreman would allow no nonsense, and the lovelorn ladies were sent to milk the cows and feed the calves, so they were soon bustled out of their melancholy. They had no piano-playing to beguile the time; from dawn to dusk they were engaged in healthy work, and they developed into simple, useful women, fit to be companions and helpmates for healthy, homely men.

Ned Shotton whistled when he heard of the philandering that was going on, but he knew that his dependents could do no better, and he said, "I'll ship those fellows with me as soon as they come home." He kept his word, and, after the first voyage, he had some pleasant words to say about the Hindhaughs. "Them's what I call seamen," said Cousin Ned. "Put them alongside of the beasts from Liverpool and London, and you will see which is men and which is mice. There's nothing they don't know about their trade, and so respectable too! They went ashore twice or thrice, but the only money they drew was to buy presents for some people that I think I know. And game! Game isn't the word. The shortest one was wiped off his feet with a big sea, and he was only fetched up by the rigging, and a very lucky catch, too. Yes, you look white, but you'd ha' looked whiter if you'd been there. When he lowered himself he passed me, and I'm blowed if the beggar wasn't singing 'Old Randso.' Singing, mind you! They'll be good men, good men. Far better than picking up with some calf of a farmer."

Ned's judgment was received as final, and Mrs. Foreman condescended to pat the lads on the shoulder when they went away at night.

So the beautiful hours of youth went by, the hours whereof the memory comes to you in sad moments when all illusion is dead, and the heart is cankered with bitterness and venomed regrets. The time came when the lads were free to try for their certificates. A solemn council was held on the links, and it was agreed that one brother should stay at home and work with a tutor, while the other should go to sea and leave his half-pay for the benefit of the student. Such arrangements were quite common, and the girls agreed to "draw cuts" to decide which man should bide at home. Winny won, so Tom went off, and Lancey settled hard down to his navigation, permitting himself just one visit per week to the farm. He passed with ease, and sailed in his turn until his elder brother was ready. Then the paths of the brave fellows diverged, and they were sorrowful at heart to think they could sail together no more.

When Tom went away he said to his brother, "Look here, old friend, you and me never talked much, but you know we go share and share, no matter what luck there is. I'd give my hand right off there to serve you." The men parted with a rough "So long, partner," and neither showed any feeling ; but Lancey was pensive that night, and when he was pressed to take supper he rose quickly, growled, "I'm none for eating, hinny ; I've a bad throat," and then went hurriedly out. He was crying.

The dumb men feel most. I once knew a fellow who was very fond of his shipmate. He was out of a ship, and hadn't a penny for train fare. He heard that his old chum had come in, and he fretted for a week because he could not go to meet him. No one could tell what ailed him, until he got up one night and said, " I'll away for a crack with Wat." He tramped thirty-five miles, had his chat, and came back looking footsore but cheerful.

Lancey lost his sadness in the hard work of the sea, and the brothers henceforth were much apart. In due course, both became captains : Tom was three-and-twenty, and Lancey got his certificate a year after Tom.

Then the great marriage question came up, and the wise Dolly said, "One of you had better speak for both of us. Tom's the best talker, and we can stop out together while he sees her in the parlour."

Tom did not by any means act up to his character as a good talker. True, he boldly asked for an interview with Mrs. Foreman, but he occupied himself during a whole minute in trying to destroy a fan which he had brought home, and he was finally rescued by the lady, who observed, "I know fine what you've come about, Mr. Captain, with your grand buttons, but you must wait. If you please me, I'll see you don't start with empty pockets; but I don't care about these early marriages. You daft lads and lasses never think any at all. You may do well if you wait a few years, but if you get married now you'll be sore held down with children before you're thirty, and it's like to make a man cast up things to his wife when the money's short. Go to sea for a year or two more, and if you show me a few canny hundreds of pounds, I'll put as much as you've saved. Let Dolly keep your money. It'll be practice for her, and I'll tell you when I'm satisfied."

The diplomatist looked rueful, but there was no help for it, and the queer lovers decided to wait. I am not sure that this hard, calculating kind of arrangement does not bring about quite as much happiness as the blind thought-lessness of passionate enthusiasts.

Tom Hindhaugh sailed for Bombay, and Lancey went to Sydney. At Bombay Tom wrote, "I'm away to the Cape from here, so you'll hear nothing for ever so long. Take care of yourself. I send you more money, and I would keep it at home if I was you, for them banks is not safe." The vessel arrived in England after weary months, and the first thing Tom asked was, "Any word of Lancey?" Not a letter nor any news of the ship had been received, and Winny was inclined to be uneasy. Tom took charge of both sisters, and Ned Shotton passed many sly remarks about the rip of a fellow that "couldn't go out without his stunsels set." Ned was understood to refer to the spread of sail which Tom carried when he linked with a girl on each arm. The same sober courtship went on, and then Tom went away to Yokohama, and from thence to San Francisco and round the Horn home.

It was a long, long trip, and the man was changed at the end of it. When he ran into Liverpool a letter was lying for him at the broker's office. Dolly wrote: "I expect

you'll get here about a month or so after this, for Ned looked
you out on the chart after the steamer spoke you. I want
you to let me meet you at Morpeth, and you can drive right
home, for there is something very particular to talk about.
Not a word has come from Lancey, and it's all I can do to
keep you know who from falling ill. We caught her going
out early in the morning with her bag, and she said it
was nothing, but I knew well enough she was off to ask
the owners. And this is it, my man : the owners have
given the *Evening Star* up, and I made away with the *Herald*
that had it in. So come soon, because I've got head enough
for most things, but I cannot do without you just now."

Tom was dazed when he read this letter. Lancey was
part of his very being, though the men had never spoken or
written an affectionate word once in their lives. He was
past tears, and he forgot even to smoke as he went home.

Dolly was waiting for him. She had driven Matchem,
the odd horse of the farm, and she looked a splendid
specimen of a countrywoman as she sat with her elbows
squared and her strong arms moving quietly to meet the
tossing of the horse's head. She nodded cheerily to Tom
as he jumped up, but she did not kiss him—that was not
our fashion.

When the open country was reached, Dolly slowed the
horse down to a walk, and said, " I want to take as long
over the distance as ever I can. I see you're badly put
about, and so am I ; but my poor lass is worse than either
of us, so I want you to know how I'd like you to go on.
You must cheer her up, and make out that it's all right.
Don't give a single hint that the owners have lost hope, and
laugh it off as well as may be. You must try to ship in a
vessel that's going over the same track, and maybe you'll
fall in with some news."

" It's a bad, bad job, Dolly, my woman. I see very little
chance."

" Do you think he could have taken on to the drink any
time ? I've seen so many that way, and they say our father
first went wrong over the whisky."

" Lancey never was a chap for the liquor. I've seen him
sprung, you know, at an odd time, but only twice in my
life, and then it was more accident than anything else."

" Then you must go after him sooner or later. You see, the time you're away Winny may contrive to get her mind easy. Time does a lot."

" But I thought we were to be married this trip."

" So did I, and I would have married you directly. We've waited plenty long enough now, and I'm wanting a home and children of my own, the same as any other woman. But it's not to be this time. You see I'm wrapped up in the poor girl. I like you better than anybody, because that's nature for a woman to like her own man best, but I couldn't go away and get married and leave her till the last hope was gone. That's what I drove out for, so that we could have a good quiet talk before any of them asked you questions."

" Well, it's queerish luck, but I suppose I must do as you say. I'm good enough at my own business, but you seem to know things far better than I do."

This ended the parley, and the strange, matter-of-fact couple drove up the lane, and were met by Winny at the gate. The girl had a wistful, inquiring look in her eye, yet she gave no sign of strong emotion. Her lip "bibbered," as our folk say, when she asked, "Have you heard anything ?" but she never cried. That was left for the silent nights and the dreary dawns. A hard, reticent people are ours ; and even strangers who are not of our breed fall into that repressed, silent way of meeting good and evil fortune. I once saw one of our women watching a small boat that was pitching over the most awful sea that ever I have known. Her husband and her sons were there, and she would have been alone in the world if an unlucky comber had hit the coble ; yet she never made a moan. But, oh me ! the look in her eyes and the convulsive parting of her lips as each fresh wave rushed at her brave fellows ! It is twenty years since I saw you on that rock head, Mary Brown, but your eyes look at me in my sleep sometimes, and the intolerable pity and terror of that supreme moment take hold of my soul. You never spoke, Mary, and you went very coolly to work with the men's breakfast when they fetched the sailors home ; but I know you lived years in those agonized minutes. It is the way of the race, and I wouldn't have it otherwise.

Winny Feltham had learned her lesson, and she kept her
sorrow in her own heart. Before Tom left the moor he
managed to pretend cheerfulness so well that he heartened
the girl up, and when he went away, he shouted from the
cart, " I'll fetch the beggar back, and you take my advice :
comb his hair fine for not sending a word." Then the
routine of the farm went on as usual, and the girls once
more looked out in the morning to read the skies, and
wonder how their lads were faring.

A whole winter wore away, and one letter from Tom
came, but no word of Lancey. In the spring Aunt Foreman failed a good deal, and she died in May. The good
woman faced her end with stern courage, gave minute
directions about her funeral, showed Dolly where to find
every paper, and dictated a letter to Ned Shotton in which
she asked him to stay ashore for a while, and see the girls
settled. She said, " You've pleased me always, Dolly, and
it was a good day for me when I took you. I shall die
about to-morrow, and I haven't one thing to be sorry for,
except that I haven't seen your children."

*   *   *   *   *

The girls were left alone, and their life was blank, for it
seemed as if the sailors would never come back any more.
Tom's last letter was sent by a homeward-bound ship that
spoke him at sea. He was bound for Sydney, and the luck
seemed to have gone against him. Nothing but constant
work kept Dolly from brooding ; she steeled herself to
show serenity, and she treated her sister with a continual
tenderness that was beautiful to see. Every kindly fibre in
the strong woman's soul was touched when she saw the
patient, uncomplaining sister bearing daily her burden of
grief with calm heroism.

Winter came, and an ugly incident broke the long
monotony of life at the farm. The girls were going to
walk on the sands when they were addressed by an old
man. A hideous creature he was ; his shaking chin was
dirty and bristling, his eye was bleared and cunning, and
every limb of him was meanly posed.

He spoke with a drunkard's voice. " I should know you
ladies."

" Perhaps you do," said Dolly. " You're not a very nice

man to know. Go up to the house and ask the girl for some bread and milk, and then get away."

"But you're Miss Feltham."

"Yes, and then ?"

"Well, my name's Feltham. I'm your father."

A flush of anger rose into Dolly's face. She sternly said, "Well ?"

"Oh! I saw that your aunt was dead by the papers, and I knew you wouldn't let your poor father want now that you're well off."

"You poor thing! You mockery of a man! Call yourself father? You poured our living down your throat; you left our mother to hunger herself to death; and you let two infants take their chance in a bad world; and now you have the face—the face——"

The girl choked with passion. She seized the wretch by the shoulders, ran him on to the path, and fairly shouted, "If you come within a mile of the place again I'll send out the man with the dogs to worry you." And this young termagant meant to keep her word.

The man turned round and yelled, "All right, my love. Wait till your ragged old father shows himself in the village, and you'll see what a few nice stories will be going round. I'll make the place too hot to hold you."

"Come away, Winn. Let him do as he likes," said Dolly, and swung away to the shore.

Under the shadow of the hills the girls stopped to talk, and Winny saw that her sister was crying. The strong woman had broken down at last, and she felt the true womanly craving for support, for rest, "If we only had our men, only the lads, we might stand out. But what can two women do? I wish, I wish, I wish my canny Tom was only here."

Winny sighed, and played for once the part of comforter.

When the walk was over a dreary evening followed. The sisters liked to go for an hour or two into the old kitchen, and they each knew well enough what attraction took them there, though they did not talk about it. They remembered the evenings of the sweet old time, and they pondered over the dead days as only women can.

On this evening the dogs in the shepherd's cottage began a great noise, and then old Loup in the yard gave his sonorous bay, and tugged at his chain. Suddenly Loup stopped and whimpered joyously.

"It'll be Ned. I'm so glad," said Winny.

A knock came to the door. Why did Loup continue his joyous whining and barking?

Dolly went trembling through the kitchen and slipped the latch. "Well, hinny, how are you by this time?"

Two men were there, and Dolly seized the shorter and pulled him in. "Oh, Lancey, Lancey! My poor lass is about dead. Go into the room. And where's your arm? Oh, me, Tom, my man, I'm just half-daft with waiting for you."

And then Dolly, for the first and only time in her life, went off into a genuine whooping fit of crying.

Winny Feltham rose up as a stout, one-armed man stepped into the old room. She laid her head on his breast and said, "Don't speak to me for a while." And the shadows flickered merrily, oh so merrily! on the wall. I can't tell you in this chapter how Lancey Hindhaugh came to be there, for it is a very long story.

IV.

LANCELOT HINDHAUGH'S LONG VOYAGE.

WINNY FELTHAM cried a good deal over Lancey's lost arm, but it was better to have the lad back with a limb short than to lose him altogether; and regrets were soon forgotten amid pleasant questioning and joyous talk. The ruddy blaze in the kitchen was kept up till near midnight; and after that there were prolonged partings before the lads went out to face the dreary moor.

Then Dolly Feltham and her sister sat and listened to the rush of the chill wind through the elders, and they heard the low thunder of the waves with quiet delight, for they knew that their men were snug at home in the hut on the bleak hills.

Winny Feltham said, "It was a sin for me to cry about his arm, but I liked him sometimes to put them both around me; it's so weary to think he's a kind of lameter now."

" You should be pleased, my lass, to see him again, never mind if he had both his legs off. I've got a thankful heart. It's a strange story, my woman. Strange it is, far by ower any one of the books. That is it."

And the two meditated over the account of Lancey's long trial. Indeed, it was a very strange story, though it was not more wonderful than hundreds of others that never get into the books or the newspapers.

I give the man's story as nearly as possible in his own style, merely putting in correct form the words which those of his class always clip :

All the mischief came of the crew. If I could have had men from our own place it would have gone right. You never see one of our chaps going away to sea without his chest well filled, and they're warm and comfortable in any weather. They've had their time to serve, and they know what obeying an order means. But our owners want to do things on the cheap, and they pretty near lost their character as well as their ship with it all.

You never saw such a lot of pictures as I went away with. The big ships going out there mostly have tiptop crews, but my lot was just the mangiest that ever went to sail a valuable ship. Some of them had just their oilskins and a few spare rags besides what they stood up in ; and as for looks, mercy ! it was enough to turn you only to glance the gang over. We weren't much troubled with foreigners, but we had about the queerest flock of English and Irish that ever you saw. The mate had picked two or three niceish chaps, but he had no hand in getting the others, for the managing man ashore here breaks all the old rules that we were used to in our early time, and I reckon he has a commission or something of that sort from the fellow that got the advance notes. Anyway, there we were, and I had only two officers and two men that I could put a morsel of trust in. The mate was a young Scotchman they called Donaldson, and the second mate was Tom Weare, out of our own place— both stiff chaps, and Tom especially was strong as a pony. Then there was two very canny North-country sailors, and the rest was tag-rag creatures—the whole lot.

Half the men just rolled into their bunks when they came

aboard, and before the tug left us we had seven of our nice
ship's company snoring like pigs there—no use to anybody.
Next day was worse. They could come out right enough,
but most of them had had a hot time ashore, and they were
shaky as you like. And temper ! Never knew such a
quarrelsome, foul-mouthed lot in my life. I was determined
to be among them to help the mate, so I kept myself handy,
and as soon as I got a chance I tackled the nastiest one.
He answered Donaldson rather disrespectfully, and seemed
to take no heed to my being there, so I shouts at him, and
makes myself seem more in a rage than I really was. He
looked hard at me, and seemed as if he would like to say
something, so I walked up and said rather loud, " No back
sling here, sir, or you'll find yourself in the wrong quarter.
You're not sober yet, but, sober or drunk, if you answer an
officer you'll go in irons right away."

He muttered something, and I saw there was no chance
for me if I didn't scare them at once. I never would lift
my hand to a man in the ordinary run of work, but with
some fellows there's nothing for it but to behave like a
downright brute. I never hold with the driving business,
because even grumbling sailors are often good men, and
you can pretend not to notice their sulks, but this joker
was a bad sort altogether, and I made up my mind very sharp.

I shouted again, " What was that you said ?" and he made
answer, " It's nothing to do with you."

Then I struck him fair and he went over, and I stood over
him making as much row as if I was a regular tiger, though
really I was cool, and I meant no harm to the man or to
any of them. It's only that there must be discipline. Well,
he was cowed for the time, but it was an ugly beginning for
a long trip.

Just before the watch went on at eight o'clock that evening, I was troubled in my mind, so I determined to call the
men aft before they took their stations. I said, " Now,
men, I've had to do something to-day that I haven't done
for these many years, and I didn't like it. But I want you
to know that the same thing 'll happen again if I see any
one of you carrying on as you did this morning. I'm mostly
easy on men that have been on the rampage, so long as
they're civil and do their best, and you'll find me not bad

to deal with if you take the right way. But no nonsense, or I'll make some of you sorry for it."

One or two of them seemed as if they would make faces if they only durst ; but they went away meek enough, and there were no complaints for several days afterwards. All the same, I wasn't happy about things in general, and I had some talk with the mate. He said, " I don't fancy our job, somehow. I believe our lot wouldn't mind doing the same as those beauties in the Liverpool barque."

" What was that ?"

" I mean the fellows that were hung five in a row. They pitched the captain and mate overboard, and pelted the poor souls with champagne bottles that they nailed out of the cabin. If they'd had a man among them that could have navigated a ship they would maybe have got clear. I wonder if any of ours could sail a vessel ?"

" That's hardly our business. We have to save our own skin if any mischief comes on. It won't be much interest for us if we're among the sharks whether the rascals get clear or not. In future, carry your revolver constantly, and be very careful never to let them have a chance of talking among themselves."

I slept with the state-room door locked, and my shooter lying handy under my pillow, and we scrubbed along as well as we could in such a case. They were a bad ship's crew, bad all ways. Very few of them were anything like sailors at all, and there was neither cheerfulness nor cleverness about the work. Twice or thrice I caught the man I struck looking at me, and, if looks could kill, I shouldn't be here now. I don't mind saying that I was frightened, and the constant thinking wore me out, so that I seemed to turn against food, and baccy, and everything. Donaldson would say, " Force yourself to eat, and we'll fight through ;" but it's easier talking than doing. It was like having a wild beast crouched at the foot of your bed waiting for you to move. Never a scoundrel of them all guessed what was in me, but I died a good few deaths in the first forty days, if pain in the heart goes for anything. I'm not one for any sentiment and such-like, but I thought about you often enough, and when she was going quiet and nothing to be attended to, I would think and think till I could see this house

as plain as plain, and your faces would come so near I fancied
I was with you. Then, when I fell asleep, I was often
happy, for my thoughts had been running on you, and I
dreamed about you. Then I would say to myself in my
sleep, " Surely it's all over, and I'm home." And then I
got to be so joyful I waked myself in trying to smile, and
my heart went like lead. I knew there was to be mischief,
for it seemed to be in the air, and one evening one of the
North-countrymen passed me, and gave me a funny look.
He whispers, " Listen to what I sing when I get into the
boat," and I was puzzled. Then he went away forrad,
singing as he walked. I heard him say to one of the chaps,
" That plug's got lost, Mr. Billy ; nice thing if we had to
lower the boat in a hurry, and then whittle a thole-pin to
stop the hole." Then he starts singing again one of the
ordinary capstan songs with a chorus, and you could hear
the hum of his voice all over, for there was no wind to
speak about. He climbs into the boat, and I went by him
careless like, and he says, " Damn the thing ! I can't get it
right. Here, you, tell the carpenter this is his job ;" and
so he gets the only man near out of the way. Then, with
his back to me, he sings rather low :

" Look out to-night in the middle watch—
     Roar, my boys, I like to hear you ;
Oh ! keep your eye on all the lot,
     And, my Way-O, we'll make her ring.'

You would have thought he was only going through a
common shanty, as the men will do at their work ; but I
heard the words plain, and I knew the time was come for
me. Before the man came back from the carpenter, the
sailor went on :

" Keep your eye on Donovan—
     Cheerly, men in the Quebec Line ;
He's got the rope to throw round your arms—
     I-oh, cheerly men, cheerly men.
I'll stand by as long as I can—
     Cheerly men, why don't you sing ?
But there's just me and Jimmy to face the gang—
     I-oh, cheerly men, cheerly men."

Then he jumped smart out of the boat and went away, still
singing, and pretending to stop now and then like as if he
had forgot the song.

By this time, I tell you, my nerve was about gone. I had held the fellows hard down, and never tried to carney round them, because boys of that sort don't understand no kindness, and now I knew they meant paying the scores off nicely. I thought about the *Flowery Land* fellows that swung, if you mind rightly, not so long since, and when I remembered the way the officers was treated you can lay I was a bit feared. I never hold with chaps that say they're not frightened. It isn't nature. You have to pretend not to be frightened, but all the same it's in your heart, and it's best to tell no lies about it.

Well, I had a chat with Donaldson, and we agreed to stick together all the watch. It came in very dark, and about nine it began to sniffle and blow a bit. There was a queer haze hanging round, and every now and then we went smack into a regular field of it, so that you couldn't see your hand in front of you. All the time it blew hard, but the wind took no hold on the haze to drift it away, and it just tumbled round and round, and then round again, the same as you've seen mud rise up in a pond when one of the cows has gone in. Every minute or so, a fireball—one of them queer things like a lamp, you know—would light in the rigging. I'm used enough to them, but on this night they completely scared me.

At last I said, quiet like, " By the Lord, Donaldson, I've a good mind to take you forrad, stand at the forecastle hatch, and have it out with those swines before it's time to call them."

He said, "No ; they might make an ugly rush, and get us both down before we could aim straight."

So we waited on, and at eleven I put more sail on her, so that she went at a rare bat, and she was taking plenty of it over the bows, and making as much noise as you please. Everything was straining, and you know the rigging screeches, like as you were flogging a regiment of women, when there's much wind. It was no good trying to talk, for the row just deaved you, and I had to whisper very low right in Donaldson's ear when I wanted to say a word. At eight bells the watch tumbled out, but I was rather surprised when I found that the fresh hands made no sign of coming aft. I told Tom Weare to bustle his men round, and he staggered away forrad. Presently he came back, and said, "They're all in a clump talking, and one of them told me to get clear before I came to some harm."

This was a facer for us. The wind was freshening, and I had no one to help shorten sail. Then we went clean into a bank of the blinding haze, and of a sudden I heard a kind of whistle over my head. Then Donaldson yelled, "Fire, sir, fire!"—but I couldn't fire, for my hands were made fast to my sides. In the thick weather they had crept up behind us, and we were done. Tom Weare came to me after I was laid on my back. He was free, and it struck me like a shot that he had joined them. Then, strangely enough, I fell asleep, and lay out in that cold like a dead man. Donaldson was tied to the foremast a long way off me, and the two of us got through the time very differently, for he was cut with the cords, but I slept fine, and dreamed about you quite pleasant.

Tom Weare was in command all night, and he put on plenty of airs in the morning when he came to speak to me.

It was beautiful weather after the rough time, and there was no need to be anxious, so Weare amused himself with looking at me, and making as if he was pleased to see me laid out so helpless. Donovan walked aft, and hit me a smack in the face, but Weare would not let him badly use me any more, and he said, "Never mind hitting him, Pat; we can pay him out better than that."

About ten o'clock Tom fetched up five bottles of spirits, and he winked at me as he passed by. I begged for a drink of water, so he set me upright, and I noticed he stopped the other chaps from hitting me all the while. When Weare brought me my drink it was in a deep coffee-canister, and I noticed he sent away the two scoundrels who were watching me before he put the water to my lips. I started a bit when I looked into the round tin, for there at the bottom was the little compass that swung over my head in my state-room. Weare had unscrewed it, and I knew now that he meant no harm. He was play-acting a bit, and I'm dead sure if he hadn't done that I shouldn't be here now.

The fellows were wonderful business-like about their goings-on until the afternoon. They cut our legs clear, and let us have a walk, and they gave us some of the grub that the hands forrad usually have. That was for a joke, you know. But the discipline was gone, you may be sure, and by the time they had divided all the five bottles among them they were ready to go on to anything. Seven of them linked their arms and came rolling along the deck, very jolly like, and one of them shouts, "Here's a game! let's have a trial before we do for these two ——"

Some of the men was keeping an eye on the working of the vessel, but the most were clean idle and drunk ; so there was a roar, and they put up an Irish fellow that could read and write for judge. He had been in a court often enough, and he knew something about the way things are done, and says he, " Put the prisoners into the dock."

Then us two poor bloods were stuck up against the companion aft, and the trial starts. The counsel for the prosecution had made himself a wig out of a bundle of sinnet, and he kicked up a rare lot of antics. There was a lot of swearing in his address, and he made them laugh. I expect they didn't laugh quite so hard at the next trial they attended. Says he, "My lud, these two —— swines is brought up for knocking us about, keeping us on bad grub, and otherwise playing old hell with the privileges of her Majesty's subjects. I say, hang them, or drop them over the side. I call witnesses." He called one or two men, but Donovan had turned nasty with liquor, and he says, "Let's be done with this damned fooling. I say, chuck 'em over ;" and, by the living man, the beggars looked like doing it sharp.

Then Tom Weare came laughing aft, for he was looking smart after the navigation of the ship, and two men stood by him to see he kept about the course they thought the right thing, and says Tom, "If his lordship will permit me, I should like to shove a word in. I have heard proposals to cut the prisoners' throats ; I have also heard proposals to shy them overboard. May I suggest that we give them a little pleasure trip in the longboat? We are now a thousand miles from the nearest land, so, if we give them a little food, and turn them adrift without a compass, they may have a good deal of fun while they are picking out a proper course, and they can study sharks and other wonders of the briny deep so as to improve their minds."

10

There was a regular howl of laughing at this, and Tom said, "Now, my lord and gentlemen, break up the court, and get the pleasure-boat ready." So away they all went, and three of us were left together. Donaldson whispered, "You scorpion, if I could get my hands loose for three minutes, I'd end you." But Weare said, "Don't be a fool, old man. It was my only chance to save you. I've sneaked you within a hundred miles of land, and I'll give you your course. The boat can do it in twelve hours nicely. They think we're going to sell the ship to one of the Germans at the islands, but it's a dead take in. I'll get help for you. Now, no more; the canister's under the bottom boards of the boat."

The way they hustled us and jollied us was cruel, and Donovan gave me one parting kick before my hands were loose. They were just drunk enough to be mischievous, but none of them were mad, and they really enjoyed the game like a lot of boys making a kettle fast to a dog's tail. In their hurry they never even noticed that there were two breakers in the boat, or I guess some of the funny ones would have had us sent off without water if they had thought it over for a moment. Anyway, they dumped us in, and yelled at us rarely as the boat went plash from the falls. We bumped away aft, and they gave us a cheer, and one of them let fly a spare block that shaved me by an inch. Then I heard Tom cry (as if he was speaking to the blackguard at the wheel), "West, half south. Keep her at that," and I knew that he must mean us, for the ship herself was going S.S.E. The man brought her round, and I could see that Tom meant to run for a bit on our course, and then take her away.

So there we were, fixed in a twenty-two foot boat, and bound for nowhere. We watched those fools dancing and shaking their fists at us for a bit, but the big ship soon drew away, and we were left sliding up and down on a long, easy roll. Donaldson pulled out a small flask of brandy, and, says he, "I was lucky to save this. You look whiteish. Try a nip. We'll never be nearer death till we do go for altogether. What a 'mazer that Tom is for cleverness!" and I said, "Yes; but I hope they'll not cut his throat when they find he means to jink them." I didn't know how near a prophet I was.

We found the compass dry and in good order, and I fixed it rare and careful, for our chance depended on that. Then we looked round, and we saw that everything was in order, just as the boat was left when I inspected her on the Sunday before. I like always to cover my boats in forrad with tarred canvas, for it often saves them from shipping water very bad, and under the cover there was a bag of biscuits as dry as a bone. Then we had a small lugsail and a pair of long oars. The rudder had been missed, but I steered quite easy with an oar rested on the nick that you scull from. We got a beautiful breeze after dark, but we made our minds up not to hoist the sail until the moon rose, for we had only two boxes of matches between us in the way of lights, and I wanted to steer her as true as a hair. At eleven the moon came up red and round like a big cheese, and we soon were as good as in daylight. Then we put the lug on her, and she went at it—whissssh! whoosssh! like a good one.

A fast boat that was as ever I saw, and stiff too, I tell you. I was happy then for the first time since many a day. I never would be frightened of any weather in a good small boat, and it was better to be bowling along there all alone than to be going day and night wondering what those scoundrels would do next. I'd done my best for the owners' property, and so there—well, I can't say more.

Donaldson had a plug of tobacco, and we had a rare smoke till the morning, and then the wind was so strong that she scooted over the sea with the sail fairly lifting her. When the sun was high, the breeze fell, and we had a blistering, stewing calm until some clouds rose black astern of us. Then a squall came like a musketry firing, and pretty well buried us, but I shifted the breakers right aft, and I wouldn't take in a single reef, although Donaldson was nervous a little. She certainly did move, and, although we took a good deal over, it was easy enough kept down with constant baling.

At five in the afternoon we saw a low-lying cloud, as I thought, away a bit on our starboard bow, but Donaldson, he says, "There never was a cloud like that, sir. It's land, and not a very small island either, and we'll be there by eight o'clock easy if this holds." Then we both gives a

10—2

good hooray, and, do you know, the very first thing
I thought about was you. I mind now saying, "If Tom
only jinks those coons, we'll see home again," and, there and
then, we finished the flask for luck.

The boat tore at it, and I was determined to beach her
before dark, so I ran every risk, and Donaldson was feared
we would be swamped. She must have gone about eleven,
for we were well in sight of the rocks in two hours, and we
saw that there was just a bit lipper against the foot of them.
I crept close in, and edged away round to look for an opening. As the dusk began to come down, my mate saw
a blink of sky between two high horns of rock, and
he points and shouts, "Take your chance there : I fancy
there'll be quiet water inside."

Well, if you believe me, there was a long smooth sally
of sea running through an opening about as wide as
the mouth of the burn, and we went at it as hard as ever I
saw a coble run for the haven. She was bustled on the top
of a lot of short lumps, and one crest curled clean into her,
and left her half full, but she soon rolled into a broad, winding channel, and we got the thole-pins in and pulled. We
went over four hundred yards, I believe, and then we were
in a biggish basin with a nice shingly beach. Queer it was.
We'd had no adventures, as they call them in the books,
but in coming among those funny short seas I seemed to
have put something wrong with my wrist in holding on so
desperate like to the oar, and, as soon as the flurry was
over and I let go my grip, my hand felt helpless. I thought
nothing about it then, and we got easy ashore, and hauled
up the boat past the tide mark.

Then says I, "We'll go on our knees, mate. It can't do
any harm, and it may do good." And we did, and then we
turned the boat over, and lay down to sleep under her out
of the damp. In the morning we went for a look round,
and we found that on the other side we could have got in
well enough. There was a bay there where five ships could
have laid easy, and a fine shelf of beach for boats to land.
It seemed that the place was known, for right staring us in
the face was a good strong hut, like the one the keepers stop
in at nights. I knew directly where we were, and I
wondered at my own fondness for not knowing where Tom

meant us to steer for. But I was stupefied, you see, and trouble takes it out of a man.

I don't think any ship should go to that bay for water without adding to the provisions in the hut, and I believe most of the captains leave what they can spare. There was two or three good blankets safe from the wet, and there was a barrel of biscuits and a few fishing lines, and a goodish gun and some powder and shot, and a pair of flags, and I think the flags was as sensible as anything—except maybe the pipes and baccy.

The last three men that were there had written their names like this: "william smith, Nils Johnsen, Tom Boag; taken off by her Majestie's ship *Boxer* after six months, somewhere about August, 1861. The spring bears W. from the door, and you can fish off the rocks at high tide, and get plenty while wave is coming in, eggs on the ledge other side but mind you doan't slip, good luck."

So here we were, and no sentiment about it. There was a flint and steel and some oil, so we could send up a smoke if a ship seemed likely to miss our flag, and we just settled down as if nothing was the matter.

I don't believe in them grand stories, where the men talks grand about desolation and misery, and things of that sort. I'm fleyed about death, like anybody else; but if you're in a bad mess, it's no use to use long words. It was dull enough, you can lay your life, and my left hand was bothersome and swelled like a pudding; but we got along, and sometimes I told Donaldson a yarn, and sometimes he told me one, and we had a game at duckstones just to put the time by.

That was about all, till we sees a ship standing dead for us, and then I remember very little more till Tom turned up, and then I cried because he cried, the big soft! and there was Weare too, that shall never want as long as I'm a man.

And I think that's nearly all; and a very good get out, too, don't you think? They could do nothing with my hand, and I suffered very hard; but Tom's is a swell ship, and they had a doctor, and—— Well, that's the way I've only got one arm instead of the pair. And now light my pipe for me, Winny; I'm dry for want of a smoke.

    *   *   *   *   *

Lancey's incoherent ending of the story needs filling up with a few details.

When Tom Weare bore away from the two men whom he liked so much, he felt like a murderer, and yet in his secret heart he knew that he had done a good thing. With men like those on board there is no safety. They are monstrously cruel by nature, and, like all criminals, they seem to have no idea of the future when any strong passion has possession of them. They are always capricious, and their brutal rages are uncertain. They had settled to kill Lancey and the mate, and they would have killed Weare if he had not pretended to throw in his lot with them. They were suspicious of him, but no one of them could sail the ship, and they therefore resolved to make use of him as long as possible, and kill him if he showed any sign of flinching. One rascal had heard that a mutinous crew made a good thing once by selling a smart ship to a Pacific trader, and he played on the vague cupidity of the fellows who had writhed under Lancey's severe discipline.

Tom Weare lived a fearful life for over four weeks. Every day at noon he was required to mark the vessel's place on the chart under the eye of the two guardians chosen for the occasion, and every day he cheated them. The vessel met no bad weather whatever, and she went on with light winds taking her steadily. She made no long runs, and the mutineers lounged and grumbled as she stole slowly toward her destination.

On one day the gentleman who had acted as judge asked Weare, "Can you get out some of the skipper's clothes!"

"What for?"

"Well, you'll have to be the owner that's settled to sell the ship, and I'll be the skipper and talk flash while you make your bargain."

Tom knew that the thing was impossible, but he humoured the stupid rogue, and said nothing about the intricate formalities connected with ships' papers, and suchlike. The criminal—criminal like—missed the essential point, and was quite delighted at his own sharpness.

Now, Tom Weare was a very determined and astute young man. He had resolved to take his vessel to her proper port at any cost, and he was steadily making his way for Sydney. Not a soul on board, beside himself, had even a rudimentary notion of navigation, and he was succeeding in his purpose beyond all his hopes. Like the clever man on board the *Caswell*, he was sailing his troops of rowdies right into the very clutches of their enemies, and all the while he was keeping their suspicions asleep, even at times when they threatened to saw his throat to the bone if he didn't play straight.

His heart beat hard one morning early, for he knew that he must win or lose the whole game that day, and to lose meant losing his life. In the early dawn a vessel bore up astern of him, and in less than an hour he saw that she was gaining, for she seemed to grow out of the water. The *Evening Star* was carrying every stitch that she could show, and her stunsails were on her, but she could not get away from the stranger.

Little by little the *Evening Star* was overhauled, and it soon became evident that the chasing ship must pass within a quarter of a mile on the port side. She was under sail, but as she drew near it was seen that she had a funnel, and her propeller was probably disconnected. Tom could not make her out, and a thousand schemes for speaking her came flying through his head. His guards asked, "What is he?" and Tom said, "He's one of the German company's vessels, I fancy. Bring my glass."

With a quick throb of mingled fear and pleasure the young man caught a glimpse of one flash that came as from a great looking-glass, and he knew that a Queen's vessel was coming fast up to him, for it was a gun that shone.

He affected extreme delight, and shouted, "Here's the very boy we want. Bring me the bag and I'll signal him. He's German, sure enough. Pearl trader."

All the time he was in fear lest the British flag might be flung out, and he hurried on so that he might signal before the ship came alongside and spoke.

In desperation he ran up this : "Mutiny. Don't board. I send a boat."

Then with an air of joy he cried, "Get the stunsails off her ; cant that square mainsail and let him come up." Then he cried, "Now, four of you, take me aboard of him, and I'll get all the news we want."

But Mr. Donovan said, "Ah, no, then! you've let him come here, and we'll keep you."

Weare saw his fate staring him in the face, but he "bluffed" with great skill. Laughing, he asked, "That's pretty; which of you can talk to him right? Let ten of you go, and then you'll have enough to murder his whole crew if there's any mischief."

The lieutenant in command of the man-of-war whistled when he deciphered the signal, and shouted, "Mr. Gainsford, keep your men down. I fancy there's some trick intended. Don't show a cap, and hand me my waterproof."

The boatload of men from the *Evening Star* put out; the man-of-war brailed up both her fore and aft sails, and the boat's crew of indescribables were greeted by a bareheaded man who wore a shiny coat buttoned to the throat. The bareheaded man hailed, "You can easily come alongside," and Mr. Donovan said, "He can speak English very well, and a damned smart trader this is." Then to Weare, "If you've let us in for trouble, I'll drive my knife through you, suppose I drown two minutes after."

Weare was white enough in all conscience, but he laughed and said, "Rubbish! You hear me gammon him," and then he said, 'All my men want to board you, sir." The officer saw the whole situation in an instant, and he courteously let Weare and the gang of ragamuffins get up the ladder.

Then all Tom's weeks of agony came out in one shout: "These are mutineers! Secure them all, and fire on the ship if she tries to get away?" The fellows were stunned, just as the other blackguards on the *Caswell* were. The bluejackets formed a ring; the gun at the bow was laid for the *Evening Star*, and the smart "trader" was taken within fifty yards of the lumbering merchantman. An armed boat's crew was sent out, and in half an hour the whole of the *Evening Star's* company were in very uncomfortable quarters.

"You've done a very smart thing," said the lieutenant. "Where are the other officers?"

"Turned adrift in an open boat; and I've had to diddle these fellows the best way I could."

"Well, we shall see you through, even if I have to tow you. But we can be at the Lights by four this afternoon if this holds up, and then we'll settle these gentry."

*   *   *   *   *

Tom Weare hung about Sydney for long and long till the whole of his ugly business was settled, and the men had been dealt with. Communication was not speedy, and the agents did not see their way clear to letting him try to take the ship home. A fresh crew was shipped, and Tom received his promotion before the vessel was started for England. Weare was eager to call at the island, for he knew that his captain could hardly miss, but it could not be done, and it was not until Tom arrived at home in the nick of time and shipped as mate with Hindhaugh from England that the rescue was managed.

And that was how Lancey Hindhaugh came to be seated in the old kitchen.

V

THE BAIRNS FROM THE ISLAND.

LONG ago the monks lived on the island, and for two hundred years the sound of their chanting mingled with the rustle and boom of the surges. The strange, lonely men left their mark in the northern regions, and the traditions of their presence and their doings endure to this day. On the mainland there are roads and hills and valleys with curious names, which have become corrupted by rustic pronunciation, and the common countrymen will point out to you the spots where the abbot was seized by robbers and where the murdered monk was trailed along by horses. No one can rightly tell how such stories survive, because the people do not know anything about books. It is probable that in the winter evenings generations of hinds and fishers have been entertained with old-fashioned stories, and the legends have descended to us in varied and grotesque forms. An atmosphere of romance surrounds the island, and the thoughts of all who dwell near it are touched by the sight and the abiding memory of the grey ruins which frown on the sea.

The channel between the island and the mainland is

shallow, and it falls dry at low water, so that carts may easily cross if they beware the lines of quicksands. Grisly stories are told of engulfed men who wallowed and shrieked in vain after the treacherous dusk had led them out of the proper path. The children who heard the curlew call in the sonorous darkness believed that the wild, shrill cry of the bird came from the ghost of some wayfarer whom the sands had swallowed, and they would stop their ears to shut out the piercing wail. It is a sad region, and men who dwell in it are given to brooding and melancholy. The influence of old, unhappy, far-off things, and battles long ago, hangs in the air, and meets the heart of the dullest rustic, and all the folks are grave in their ways.

When wind and sea drove in the right direction, and the sands were dry, two boys often went to the mainland and performed various errands. One was a blue-eyed fellow, with light chestnut hair. He always looked dreamy, and when he talked he moved his long slim fingers with subtle gestures. The other was dark, and his singularly foreign appearance was intensified by the earrings which he wore : he looked like one of the swarthy lads who came to the port in Genoese vessels, and he was not at all vexed when the hinds called him " Johnny Frenchman," for his mother was French, and she had taught him to be proud of his mixed parentage.

Henry and Frank Winthrop were the sons of the farmer who held the whole of the island ; and they grew up in very wild fashion on that sorrowful and isolated plot of ground. The lighthouse-keeper and his family lived in a cottage which stood on Mr. Winthrop's land, but there was no other company, and sometimes, when the weather was bad, the Winthrops and the Boltons were exiled as completely as though they had been shipwrecked in the Southern Ocean (for the Race ran terribly high), so that the families were a great deal thrown together.

Henry Winthrop, the fair boy, was reckoned to be rather queer in his ways ; he would settle on the yellow sands and gaze long over the sea until every sign of animation passed from his face, and he never took notice of time when these dreamy fits were on him. The clouds and the trees and the waving expanses of bents on the mainland attracted him in the same way, and he never tired of looking at animals. Once, when he was alone, a beautiful red-and-white cow fixed his attention. He leaned against the gate of the field, and fell into his usual absorption. The morning sped away, the shadows grew longer, and still the odd boy stared at the peaceful creature as she moved lazily over the grass. All the while he scraped the ground with one foot, and his mother used to say that he nearly rubbed the sole of his boot through, but this was probably an exaggeration.

Frank Winthrop was a quick, practical fellow, with ready tongue and nimble fingers. He could not remain still for long at a time, and he was often impatient with his dreamy brother; but he regarded himself as the young poet's champion, and he used to tell the village people that Harry was none such a fool as you might reckon. Frank was very friendly with the fishermen, and he especially liked to go on board of the great French smacks which ran up from Dunkirk and Dieppe to work in the northern waters. When his mother allowed him, he spent many nights at sea, and saw a good deal of rough work, which, however, did not frighten him. His coolness was as remarkable as his precocious capacity for business. On one chill August evening he went out with a herring boat, and his mother insisted on his wearing a huge comforter of the gaudiest hues. The boat was tearing along before the hard breeze that came from the land as the sun drooped, when of a sudden Frank, who was standing on a pile of nets, went clean overboard. The man at the tiller roared, the halliard was let go, and the boat was rowed back just in time to save the boy. After a good deal of sputtering he found his tongue, and the first thing he said was, "Eh, Bob, I've spoiled my good new grahvat." The ruin of his comforter grieved him sorely, but he never spoke of the risk to his life.

The two boys were very fond of the lighthouseman's daughter, and Kitty Bolton played with them, and quarrelled with them, and made them jealous in turn, and they hardly thought of their pretty little companion as belonging to a family other than their own. All three of the children were almost entirely uneducated, for Mr. Winthrop

was their only teacher, and reading was not an accomplish-
ment in which he excelled. In the long evenings he contrived to take his scholars through the easier parts of
Mavor's " Reading-book,' but he never attempted to teach
them writing.

The future was vague to these young exiles, and they
seldom talked about their plans, although the boys, at any
rate, had shadowy visions.

Harry said one day to his brother, " What are you going
to be?"

" Be? Why, I expect I'll be the same as you. Both on
us goes to sea. That's what I think you're so fond for—
sitting and staring as if you were bad, instead of getting
along with the men same as me. You miss all the fun."

" I don't think I'll go to sea."

" But father 'll make you."

" No, he won't. He's not hard on neither of us."

" And what daft notion have you set up now?"

" Oh, I think about all kinds of things. I make them
up in my own head, and I would like to have some paints
and make pictures like them on the back of the almanac.
When I see the men shearing, or anything like that, it
comes in my head again regular plain when my eyes is
closed. Same with a cow, or a cuddy, or anything. If you
give me a keely-vine I could make them on a bit of paper.
What do you think about that?"

" Think ! Why, I think you're just a born fool."

" You needn't say that, Frank. You know I tell you
everything, and I never let out anything you do noways."

" You're straight enough ; but what do you go talking
about cows and almanacs and things for ? We've got to
work the same as the other lads, and I expect we'll have to
go to sea, without father wants us to work on the land.
But he can do all that himself ; so I expect it's the sea, and
nowt else."

This halting conversation sufficiently marks the characters
of the two boys, and they never altered in essentials during
their lives.

When Henry was fourteen and Frank thirteen, their
father had a grave talk with them. He said, " Now, lads,
it's time for you to get your hands to something for a living.

You've had a canny lazy time, and I've fed you well, and now you must help yourselves. By-and-by one of you can work on the land, but there's hardly enough to keep me and your mother going just now."

Frank replied, " I'll go to the sea to-morrow if you like."

Mrs. Winthrop, a dark, fine-looking woman, who spoke English with a strong foreign accent, broke in, " I wish both of you might stay on the shore. All my people at Havre are dead, and, if anything happened your father, I couldn't go stewardess again, and I couldn't manage the farm." Frank set his lips : he meant to go his own way. Harry said, " I'd like to go to the town, and learn a trade ;" and this closed the conference.

So the little household on the dreary island was broken up, and Kitty Bolton was left alone.

Kitty was quite mature compared with the lads when they went away, and she managed the parting more gracefully than her poor clumsy friends. Nothing can be funnier than the way in which these same partings are arranged among our people. Men and women are alike so desperately afraid of showing any soft emotion, that even the action of shaking hands is performed in an apologetic manner. The hand is sidled forward, and the two friends gaze sheepishly on the ground as though they were extremely ashamed of themselves. As soon as the hands are parted, the pair venture to look each other in the face, and there is an end of the matter.

Kitty and Frank achieved the most amazing salute ever seen, and the girl was inclined to laugh at the contortions of her handsome friend, but there was something in his face which touched her with real sorrow, and she said, " Dinnot be dull, lad ; you'll soon be back again."

Speech was out of the question for the boy, and he went away with a droop of the head.

Harry was not much better, and Kitty laughed outright when she saw a suspicious moisture in his eye. " You big fondy ! What for do you not be like Frank, there? You make your face as if you were away off to t'other side o' the world."

So spoke Miss Kitty Bolton, and Harry Winthrop, poor little man, went with a sad heart.

The girl watched the lads trudge over the sand when the
tide was out, and then she went to the foot of the rocks and
lay down on the sand, burying her face in her hands.

At dinner-time her mother said, "Thee face is red, lass.
Has thou been crying ?   Ay, ay, I'se warrand it's the lads !"
and Kitty blushed.

At night she went to Winthrop's house, and found the
father sitting very gloomily in the chimney-corner.   The
girl scarcely spoke a word during her visit, but Mr. Winthrop
knew by instinct that she had come to be near the place
whence her playfellows had gone.   He smoked on quietly
till it was pretty late, and then he said, "Time for you to
go, Kitty.   Your father 'll just be going up to look at the
lantern now.   I'll take care you have every letter that comes,
my lass—never mind, family affairs or whatever it is.   You
shan't be out of it with either of them."

Kitty made no answer appropriate to Winthrop's remarks,
and she went away after merely nodding to the farmer and
his wife.

At home she preserved her calm, and she never let herself frame a thought until she had bidden her parents good-
night and got to her garret.   Then she went through her
prayers in the orthodox form, and put in a supplementary
petition for the two lost ones.   Lost, she counted them, and
she pondered much as to which she should support most
warmly in her prayers, for, like the rest of her class, she
imagined that her addresses to the highest regions must
meet with prompt attention.   As I have said, she was a
woman, but she had only the womanly frame matched with
a child's intellect, and her own account of her deliberations
was one of the saddest and drollest things I ever heard   In
the end she said, "Fetch Frankie round safe, because I
think he's my lad, and the other I just like," and then, with
full confidence in her own impartiality, she cried herself to
sleep.

Harry and Frank parted at a remote station, and the
sailor saw his brother into the train.   He said, "None o'
that loony, fond business, you know.   I'll be seeing you soon,
and we can have our cracks ; and don't you be sitting and
glowering when I'm not there to wake you up, else they'll
think you want taking up.   Good-day, old foggy, and I'll

get away, for fear I start like the women does." Frank always took the mastery, and the fair youth accepted all the lectures meekly, as he had done from the earliest days.

  *   *   *

A tall, swaggering young sailor strode briskly over the miles of moor that lay north of the island. He had a lumpy canvas bag—a dittey-bag they call it—on his shoulders, but the weight seemed to trouble him little. He rolled in his walk, with that curious swelling of the calf and leaning of the knee-joint which became a mechanical habit with men who are used to heavy weather; but he was springy and supple, and he could have run very fast in a sprint, despite his lumbering roll. When he reached the village, he stepped into the dim-lit parlour of the inn.

Whistling Sandy, the fisherman, looked up, and after four solemn whiffs, said, "Ay! ay! Well, it's him, and we all thowt you was ahint yor time, hinny. Sit thee doon, and try a pint to rax yor thropple."

Mat Hobson, the poacher, preserved his usual secretive, aggressive aspect until his pointer came out from under the benches and began twisting around in ecstasies of humiliation before the returned one. Then he whispered hoarsely, in the fashion of men who are out late amid surrounding dangers, "It's thee. The dog kenned thee, so I knawed it was. Where's Ellington Ross, then, naw, bonny lad? Sit thee here, and bring all the beer there is i' the hoose." Mr. Hobson's final order was given with a strident yell, and it created much pleasure among the occupants of the parlour.

The young sailor swung his dittey-bag on to the floor and straightened himself up. A broad-shouldered, brown athlete he was, with swift, keen eyes, and long, sinewy hands that looked full of character, determination, strength, and dexterity. He laughed, and said, "Think I'll get on to the island the night? I heard the grumble on the Murderer's Rock just now, and that means mostly you can't cross."

Mr. Hobson gently remarked, "Drink your stuff. Never mind about the island to-night. Have a turn at the old game. Eh, me; I doubt me Ellington's gone."

But the sailor was stubborn against blandishments. Gladly he put his lips to the cool, frothing mug, and gladly he exchanged tobaccos with the assembled wisdom. Nevertheless, the thought of certain anxious faces came to him, and he resolved to push on. There were no telegraph wires in our countryside in those days, and he knew that several good people were worrying about him; so he said, "I'll leave the bag here, and I'll swim the Race sooner than stop."

One of the quiet listeners broke silence. "We have a boat on the beach. If you like to try we'll run you round to the outside of the island, and shoot you ashore under the rocks. You take some stingo, for fear we have to lie off."

The dark sailor accepted this offer with joy, and soon a coble swept off into the moaning night.

The sea ran very true, and there was not much trouble about landing; the boat's shallow stern ground lightly on the gravel, for those men can plant their craft within a foot of any spot they aim at.

Presently a yell came from the hut at the far side of the lighthouse—"Want any assistance! Surely you've not got aground a night like this?"

The dark sailor soon answered the inquiry by jumping ashore and shouting, "Kitty—Way-oh!"

Bolton slipped out with a lantern, and went off into raptures when he had focussed his new visitor's face. "Come on, come on, mother! Here's that lad got round again."

Mrs. Bolton came down in unconventional attire, and took both the sailor's hands : "We thought you were done, and Kitty sends, A-darrsay, every other day to know; and they've not lost you."

The good woman was sadly fluttered, and her joy drove her into the untranslatable idiom of the district.

The sailor stammered, "Kitty sends? What's up? Isn't Kitty here?"

"No, hinny, she's away, but not far. There was a party of the quality come off to see the eider ducks and the rest of the things, and Mrs. Peddie, the housekeeper away at Witherington Hall, was there to look after the lunch, as they call it, for she's never sick now, and she says, 'What an active girl!' she says, and says she, 'I could find room for her at the Hall, if you could spare her,' and that was how it was. So Kitty's up there, still-room maid now, and a good job for her."

The sailor blurted, " Damned if my wife's going to be a servant!" and then he stopped, and looked very silly under the wise, piercing glance of the woman.

"Your wife!" said Mrs. Bolton. She laughed loudly, and chuckled, " Eigh, weigh ! You're first there, anyway. Get thee ways up to see her the morn."

The dark, handsome young man went on to his father's house, and was received with tremulous rejoicings by his mother. There is no need to speak about the talk that went on. I remember it all in the old days, and I like to sit in my dark corner and listen with secret rapture to the lads who have come from the sea.

It is enough to say that Frank bargained to be called early, and that he went over the dry channel attired in the most approved style of nautical splendour. He was dusty before he reached Witherington, but nevertheless he looked so fine that Mrs. Peddie, the housekeeper, to whom he was presented, gazed on him with kindly patronage.

Mrs. Peddie modelled her manner on that of the great lady whom she served, and she was magnificently lofty in her dealings with the middle and lower classes.

"You're a very nice sailor. Pray be seated," said the great dame. "And you wish to see Bolton? Well, in the whole course of my experience I never knew a follower come in this way, and I think, Sailor, you're decidedly bold. But I presume that your period on shore is distinctly limited, and I therefore feel inclined to stretch a point."

Poor Frank did not understand the long words; he bowed his haughty head and touched his plume of jetty hair. Alas, how humble he felt; and he muttered, "Well, mum, we've got to move middling sharp, and if you think it's no freedom, why, I'd like to see Kitty when you've done with her."

"Then the odd man shall take you to the beach in the trap, and Bolton must come back with him. And, understand, I expect her to be no more than two hours away. Under the circumstances I make a distinction, but it's a thing never done before, and you must earn your privilege by strict care. Good-day, Sailor." Then, with a superb sweep, the ruler departed, and soon Kitty came down.

11

The girl frowned shyly, and reddened as she said, "Surely you didn't tell Mrs. Peddie we linked together, did you? Because it isn't true, you know, Frank."

"I only told her I wanted to see you before we move, and if you like to link with anybody else you can, but I'll always like to see you, anyway."

The sight of the proud-looking fellow humbling himself in this way mollified Kitty, and she said, "Eh, well, I may just get my cloak on and be with you."

Kitty Bolton was splendid to see. Her dark, rich face was regular in feature, and her eye was brilliant. Like a good many of our girls, she resembled the Spanish type, and the resemblance ran even to the delicate down which fringed her upper lip like a shadow. Her figure was exactly what you might expect to see in the case of a girl who had never been cramped in any way. She avoided the slouch which the fisherwomen sometimes contract through carrying the heavy creel, and she bore herself upright as a dart—a wholesome, powerful, lovely girl was Kitty. The æsthetic division in London would have raved about her. Indeed, as she comes before my mind's eye now—vivid, almost startling in fulness of colour, perfect in rosy health—I am inclined to say that I have only seen two women who could compare with her.

Frank was oppressed by the very splendour of this opulent beauty. He had never seen or dreamed of anything like it, and the commonplace slip of a girl with whom he used to argue and wrangle became his queen of a sudden. Frank made very sorry attempts at conversation as the trap rattled through the lanes. He hazarded an observation to the effect that Bob Staveley's cow was getting old, but he felt that this was not a brilliant or amorous remark. With subtle feminine tact the girl drew him out as they neared the sea. She daintily alluded to his long absence, and to their droll parting when they were bairns; she led him on to speak on his own topics, and, before the cart drew up, he was quite at ease, and Kitty thought he was a very bonny lad as he smilingly stood waiting to lift her down.

The inexorable Peddie could not be forgotten, however, and the time of grace soon expired.

"You'll let me come and see you again when we're in, won't you, Kitty?" said the sailor. "It doesn't matter if we don't link together."

"You know nicely I'm glad enough to see you, Frank, hinny, ever since we were little. It made me look daft for you to come ram-stam in that way and ask for me; but I was pleased all the same."

"Very well. Then I'll keep my mind on you wherever we are, if it's at t'other side of the world; and if you're not for me by the time I'm master, I'll never look at anybody else, and I'll let no one come near you without he hears a word or two from me."

This was equivalent to a declaration, and Frank departed with a wild fluttering of the pulses. The lad was transformed.

During his long spell of absence he had picked up much knowledge of men, and even of books, for his master insisted on his reading, and grimly superintended his afternoon studies. His vocabulary had become enlarged with his power of thinking, and he could put into words ideas which in boyhood only floated vaguely before him. The image of the pretty child whom he had left was always in his sight, and the dreamy fondness burst into sudden passion under the light of that beauty which amazed him when he first saw Kitty in her womanhood.

Frank was at home for a fortnight, and Henry Winthrop stayed with his brother during the whole time. The lads were passionately fond of each other, and they were perfectly content to lounge and wander together all day, talking with strong sense about the subjects which interested them. So it is with many of those rude provincials. Alas! do I not remember the immortal nights on the darkling moor, when we talked for hours in perfect simplicity and earnestness? Do I not remember our first Tennyson and our first Shelley—ineffable possessions to be learned by heart and talked over. Yet we were but sailor folk, and we should make game of our own selves now. Alas!

Here is one chat that passed between the brothers. They were standing among the ruins; Henry was bareheaded, and he had shaken his curls back; Frank was frowning, and evidently in deep thought.

11—2

Henry said, "Do you notice any difference in my way of speaking, Frank?"

"Yes. You're getting very fine. I've seen it ever since I came down. Some words you say just like the quality folk."

"Shall I tell you how it is?"

"Go on."

"Well, I hardly liked to speak about it before, because I was afraid you might think I was growing proud; but you know I'm too fond of you to keep anything from you, so I'll tell you everything. The fact is, I'm a great deal out in the evenings among well-to-do people, and I've caught their ways. You've seen none of my pictures, but I do lots of little ones now. I lodged with a young fellow that colours photographs for a living, and he taught me how to use paints. I seemed to work with colour without knowing how I did it; the knack came to me, and I couldn't help myself. Then I went to a drawing-class, and worked right on to the life-school, where you draw real men and women, and I got a medal. The chief said that art was my proper trade, but of course I couldn't break my indentures. Well, at last I began working out of doors on Sundays, and once I painted a sunset. It was a bitter evening, and the red light made some fir-trees shine very brightly, and the shadows among the brushwood made me feel sad. I did it, and it was shoved into a local exhibition. Well, one morning I got a letter, asking me to call at Lockhart's, the great soap-boiler's place, and I did. The old man saw me in his library, and he said, 'You are aware that I bought your picture, Mr. Winthrop?' Well, I wasn't aware of anything of the kind, and I was ready to drop; but he went on very kindly, and asked me to do him a good lot of pictures. Then he said, 'What are you by trade?' and I told him. He insisted on my knocking off, and so I shall when my indentures are out. I shan't tell the old folks till it's done. And, let me tell *you*, I've saved fifty pounds out of picture money alone, so I want you to take half, and that will help to pay your schooling."

Frank hardly understood the situation, but he gathered that his brother had been lucky, and he was far too sweet of temper to feel a twinge of jealousy about anyone breathing, much less his gentle friend.

Before Frank sailed he asked, "Can you remember Kitty Bolton's face, Harry ?"

"Oh yes, I could paint it now."

"Do me a little one of her for fun."

So Harry produced a portrait on the sly, and his miniature resembled the child whom he had known to a miraculous degree. At least so Frank thought, and when the good sailor went away for his long Australian trip he wore the little picture round his neck. Before going he sent a letter to Kitty—a quaint and unutterably touching production, ending in the orthodox form observed on the coast, "Your faithfull friend till death, F. Winthrop." Many of those strange sailors' letters have passed through my hands, and some of them are heart-breaking.

Frank kept to his work like a man, and it never entered his simple mind to think of what might pass in his absence. The big ship rolled away south, Harry Winthrop mounted the ruins to wave good-bye, and the life of the island went on placidly once more.

*   *   *   *   *

A pretty girl was swaggering down the coach-walk from the Hall, when she saw a man seated on a camp-stool and engaged in painting a long mysterious glade that stretched deeply among the fir-trees.

The sound of the girl's foot startled the man ; he turned, blushed, and said, "Why, Kitty !"

His hat was off, and Kitty thought his blush became his perfectly handsome face. He was dressed carelessly, but like a gentleman, and the girl noticed his white, long fingers and dainty nails. She said, "I thought you were working in the town."

He did not hear her. He appeared to be dreaming, and she felt a shock of surprise when he said, "How beautiful you have grown !"

She could not even scold—she was so thunderstruck, for a phrase like that completely transcended her actual experience. How long the couple stood awkwardly together Harry never knew, but before they parted the young artist passionately begged for another meeting with this servant girl.

It was noticed after this that Harry Winthrop came from

the town every Saturday, and that he contrived to meet Kitty Bolton every Sunday night. With Machiavellian skill he had managed to captivate Mrs. Peddie, and the housekeeper, like all good women, took pleasure in the brightness and freshness of young men, so that an alliance was struck, and soon it was rumoured that Kitty Bolton was leaving her place.

The rumour was true enough. Winthrop was infatuated with a beauty who could barely read and write. He was cultured in his way ; but no thought of incongruity struck him, and he was keen for speedy marriage—he did not like the notion of leaving his treasure in any risk, and he plunged headlong into his new enterprise. Once he said, "I wish, Kitty, we could have waited till Frank came home," and he wondered why the deep crimson rushed up to the girl's very forehead.

Kitty had always been fond of the brave sailor ; but the dainty gentleman with the white hands was irresistible. Kitty was but a woman after all.

  *   *   *   *   *

Frank Winthrop returned to the north after two years' absence, and went to his old inn to wait as usual for the tide.

In the course of conversation one of the men said, "You're just in time."

"For what ?"

"How long is it since you heard from home ?"

"Six months and more."

"Well, Harry's going to be married."

"Who to ?"

"Kitty Bolton. What ails you ?"

"Good-night ;" and Frank strode off into the dark.

He muttered to himself, "What a fool ! What a baby ! But I won't disturb old Harry. I wonder he never spoke. No ; I'll go to the other end of the earth."

Harry received a letter which ran thus : "I thought I wouldn't come home this time. I'm going out to New York, and if I can ship in a Yankee vessel I will. Good-bye."

Then Harry remembered that tell-tale flush.

  *   *   *   *   *

Henry Winthrop is esteemed as a man of genius by the

community of St. John's Wood, and his wife is accounted a charming wild creature. The lonely Captain Winthrop now commands a liner. He is always sad, and he is never known to speak to a woman.

VI.

IN THE GOOD OLD TIMES.

JUST now there is deal of sentimental talk going on concerning the decay of English manhood, and about the good days long ago. I never can get any one of the sentimentalists to fix the date of the Golden Age for me, and even Mr. Ruskin, who is the chief of the lot, can only speak eloquently to you about Scott's novels and their pure heroes, and about the general delightfulness of life in England at the early part of this century. To hear these folks chatter anybody would say that everything had gone to ruin since we had the honour of being ruled by King George III. and plundered by the gang of shameful patricians who fed themselves and their brood at the nation's cost.

I should like to speak with all modesty, yet I cannot help saying that the moony, poetic babble regarding the past is neither more nor less than poisonous falsehood. I was brought up among very poor men, who lived far away from cities, and who preserved the manners and the habits of a bygone century. My boyhood was really passed amid an eighteenth-century environment, and, in our own house, the traditions of six generations of seamen were around me. Only ten years ago my father, who was then an aged man, had a long, long talk in my presence with my great-uncle, who was close on one hundred years old. This tough veteran was a strapping lad of five-and-twenty when this century began, and his memory of the palmy days was singularly clear. He knew what used to be the fate of the lower classes in the blessed times of pressgangs and imperial grandeur, and I fancy Mr. Ruskin would have been a little bit shocked at his report. He remembered only too well the hideous evenings when the women sat shivering at home waiting for the bold sailors who had to skulk like thieves in the byways when the prowling ruffians from the men-of-

war were hunting for prey. Many a lass lingered on hoping
that her lad might come back to her, while he, poor fellow,
had long ago been smashed by a French roundshot and
pitched overboard. We are so free now, and the claws of
the powerful caste are so effectively clipped, that we can
hardly call up a vision of the times when harmless British
citizens could be dragged from their shelter, knocked on
the head, and packed off to a fate worse than penal
servitude.

A whipper-snapper of a lieutenant might come into a
village with his gang of armed rowdies, burst open any
house where he fancied seamen were hid, and clap the
handcuffs on men who had never known shame. If a
sailor stooped to cringe he might get on pretty well until he
was released or killed, but it was not always easy for a
proud man to make himself behave like a serf. A look of
ill-nature, a sign of discontent, led to his being hauled up
before the captain, and his fate was pretty certain unless he
sacrificed his manhood. Those precious captains about
whom the praisers of bygone days write slavering rubbish
were a set of disgraceful tyrants, pampered into insane pride
by constant sycophancy, and disdainful of the commonest
rights of humanity. To me it is simply awful to think that
a brainless despot, who gained his rank by back-stairs in-
trigue among the supporters of a corrupt bureaucracy,
should have had the power to tie up a grown man and lash
the skin off his back. On board some vessels it was considered a mark of extreme smartness to have plenty of
punishments. Daily the boatswain's call was winded,
daily the silent crews fell into lines. The naked wretch
was seized up with his feet off the ground, and the "gallant"
officer told the stalwart executioners to begin. Then the
heavy strands of whipcord, weighted with knots of lead,
whistled in the air, and fell with their sickening plash on
the bare, delicate skin; and one of God's creatures was
kept enduring agonies worse than many deaths till his
"gallant" master let him off to go and shiver and groan
in the cockpit.

Let it be remembered that this monstrous cruelty was
inflicted, in the romantic days, on decent fellows who had
been kidnapped away from home and from honest labour.

Many an honest lad crept back to his village bearing the frightful criss-cross gashes left by the torture, and bearing, too, the sense of the inexpiable wrong, the unutterable shame, that poisons the very soul.

Truly I think that the good old times should not, for very decency, be mentioned by rational Englishmen. If Mr. Ruskin and the rest would only trouble themselves to form a vivid idea of the state of society in our seaports during the years of the great war they might be tempted to hold their tongues and incense us no more with jeremiads. Both of my grandfathers fought at the battle of the Nile, and both of them were pressed men. They were respectable sailors, earning good money, and living in the religious, harmless fashion so common among the matchless fellows who commanded the old Scotch coasters. But they were kidnapped in defiance of law, and placed in a service where they could not hope to rise beyond a certain low grade. One of them rose to be sailing master, and he was under command of an aristocratic cub who, of course, could not navigate a vessel. The two men got home at last, but their lives were broken up by the peculiar customs which prevailed in the good old times. No wonder, then, that those of us who know something about the matter listen with scorn to the stuff which certain of our instructors try to thrust upon us. We are content to do without thieving bureaucrats, pig-headed monarchs, " gallant " floggers, fetid guardships, rowdy pressgangs, and all other ancient agencies of happiness ; and now here is a pressgang story which is true in all essentials.

In 1797, Henry Lanyer was nineteen years old, but he already commanded a sloop, which ran from the port of Cambus. He held no certificate, but he knew every inch of the coast, and was a good sailor all round.

It was the fashion in those simple places to marry early, so Henry Lanyer was engaged to a pretty girl who was a farmer's daughter. His father had retired from the sea, and was living in Cambus on the interest of his savings. The old man was still hearty ; in fact, it is hardly correct to call him old, for he was not more than forty-six years of age. He had picked up his money in the quiet times, and he determined to have a long rest.

On one memorable night Henry had brought his sloop in and placed her nicely on the hard. He arrayed himself in the pretty fashion of the port, and in his blue coat, white duck trousers, and smart cap he looked very handsome. He walked out to see his sweetheart, and returned in the evening.

When he entered the kitchen, and took his seat by the side of the great fire, he found his father in deep thought.

"I have just had an offer, Henry," the elder man said, "which has tempted me a great deal. Old Mr. Simpson has been here, and has made a proposal to me that will give us a good bit more money, and will let me have more to leave you when I am done with it. You know, of course, that young Simpson has gone to the drink. Well, now he's in command of the big barque, and his father wants me to stay at the sea at any rate until the lad has settled down. Now, the barque's going to Genoa, along with the convoy, I suppose, and Mr. Simpson is very much afraid that the young fellow will break out again. He said to me, 'Lanyer, I hope you won't be offended if I offer you a mate's berth. You know that I want my son to remain skipper of the *Halicore.* Well, I can't trust him with strangers, and it has come to this—that he must leave the sea, and do nothing at all except drink about the town, or else he must have a steady man that will watch him. Now, if you will go as mate of the *Halicore,* I will give you captain's wages, and if you will undertake to carry the ship about for a couple of years, I will give you £100 over and above your pay.' Now," said Captain Lanyer, "I am just thinking whether I shall take it or not."

The young man replied, "Well, I would rather have you here; but still, I know it's a big temptation. Wages are £12 a month in Simpson's employ, and that means a lot for us."

So the end of it was that old Lanyer shipped aboard the *Halicore* as mate. Young Lanyer sailed for Leith, and when he came back he heard that his father had run round to Hull in the vessel.

Young Simpson, the captain of the *Halicore,* did not by any means impress favourably the man who had been put in charge of him. He was an insolent fellow, with a puffy face and an extravagant swagger. He esteemed himself an athlete (without very much grounds for the belief), and he was still more possessed with the idea that he was a lady-killer. When he was on shore he spent most of his time drinking, and he got into more mischief with the girls of the town than any other man of his age. Lanyer found that he was no seaman. On the very first morning after the vessel had weighed, he came on board with his hands shaking and his teeth chattering. At breakfast he could eat nothing, but turned with an oath to the cupboard in the cabin. He then drew out a bottle of whisky, and, filling half a tumbler, placed it to his lips. His hands shook so that the glass rattled against his teeth ; but, when he had swallowed the dram, he grew a little more steady, and straightened himself up. All that day Lanyer dared not leave the deck. The vessel had to beat every yard of the road, and rather an ugly head sea was running, so that a man of nerve and judgment was needed to handle her. The night came on thick and dark, and Lanyer still remained on deck, while the vessel thrashed her way through the short waves. Suddenly he heard a voice at his elbow, " Look here, Mr. Lanyer, I'm not going to permit this any longer. Do you still persist in letting these men chase me and sing about me ? Listen to them ! There's a woman as well ! Whoop ! There goes the girl's voice ! Did you ever hear a woman sing like that ? She draws music out of every nerve in my body, but I can't allow it. Now, listen again ! That brute's been whispering to me all day, ' Smash 'em, Simpson,' he says ; ' smash 'em. Make their blood and brains fly.' Now, if you, as mate of this ship, don't stop it right away, I'll unship you as soon as we get into the Humber."

Lanyer's blood turned cold. He called one of the hands aft, and told him to bring a lantern. He then saw the captain standing rubbing his hands and glaring into the dark. As the light shone on his savage face he looked demoniac. At last he stood still and stared fixedly. " For heaven's sake, Lanyer, get behind me and pull this man away. I dare not look over my shoulder. He's grinning at me. I feel him grinning through my back. If he's not gone in two minutes I must die. I cannot move."

Lanyer turned to the imaginary man, and roared out,
"Down, you scoundrel!" and the drunkard said, "Ah!
that was a splendid wipe you gave him. Now let us go
below and polish off these singers. You lay hold of the
tenor, and I'll run my knife through the bass. Then we'll
lock the man up in your berth, and when we get ashore
we'll have an action for libel. I'll let them know whether
they shall come aboard my vessel and sing about me."

Suddenly a bright light shone over the water from a point
about a quarter of a mile to leeward of the *Halicore.* Side
lights were not used in those days, and vessels simply beat
their way in the dark, taking care to keep a sharp look-out.

If one ship was seen coming up astern, the foremost
vessel hung a lantern over the side.

When Simpson saw the lantern his intention of destroying the singers faded away, and he began to dance with a
wild ferocity. "Look here, Lanyer, here's some fun. We
can sail three feet to that fellow's two. Ram the topsails
on to her. Now, then, drive her nose under. What a
spree it will be! We'll be up to him in an hour. Drive
the bowsprit right into his cabin window, and you'll see
them all tumble up."

He then straddled across the companion, and yelled,
"Now, then, go it again! Let's have our bowsprit through
him! Let's see the skipper dance, and see how the men
look in their shirts!"

Lanyer said to the man at the wheel, "Put your helm up
a little," when Simpson turned upon him: "Did I hear you
say, 'Put the helm up'? Did I not tell you to bear
straight on for that fellow's stern? And you take my ship's
head round four points! We shall go half a mile to the
northward of him! What is the meaning of it? Look
here, I'll murder you before I begin with those in the
cabin."

Then Lanyer saw the flash of a knife in the dark, as the
mad brute sprang at him.

For a moment the old man was mastered. Simpson got
his hand on the mate's throat, and made a blind stroke with
the right arm. He did not take good aim, and only tore
Lanyer's cap off. In another second he was on his back
the knife was flung over the side, and the old man knelt

upon him. Lanyer called the second mate, and the two carried the struggling wretch down below. They locked up the spirit cupboard, and fastened Simpson in his bunk. For a while the man screamed, and called out that things were crawling over him. Ever and anon he would declare that the woman must be murdered instantly, and he would wait with his finger poised in attention to the sounds of ridicule that his diseased nerves had conjured up. Presently he fell over into sleep, and lay until the vessel was in smooth water.

The *Halicore* brought up close by the quay, and in the morning Simpson said to his mate, "Lanyer, I was a little queer last night, was I not? I was not very well, you see. Of course, you'll not mention the circumstance. I seem to have lost the key, by the way, and I think I have got a fit of the ague. I cannot keep myself still. Would you mind letting me have your bunch?"

Lanyer replied: "Captain Simpson, I have the key of the spirit cupboard, and I am willing to let you have it."

The fellow drank off one or two glasses of raw spirit in rapid succession, and recovered himself so far that he was able, with that cunning so often displayed by men in the extremes of alcoholic debility, to go ashore and transact his business without showing more than a slight occasional thickness of accent.

All day long Lanyer stayed aboard. In the afternoon one of the able seamen, who had been sent ashore, returned, and stepped up to Lanyer.

"You'll excuse me speaking to you, sir, but I don't quite like the look of things. There's the crew of a man-of-war's boat ashore. They came from the frigate out there as soon as it was dark, and I rather fancy they mean mischief."

"Oh, don't trouble yourself about that, my lad. As long as you are not away from your vessel they cannot touch you, and if they catch us at sea we must just take our chance."

At eleven o'clock a heavy and unsteady step thundered along the deck. Lanyer was sitting at the cabin table reading his Bible for a few minutes before turning in. He was very peaceful, and would have been entirely happy if the memory of the terrible scene that he had gone through the night before had not come to him at intervals. Simpson entered the cabin, and glared with that glassy appearance of the eye which marks a certain stage of drunkenness. He was surly and ill-conditioned.

"Now then, you old pig, why haven't you gone to your sty?"

"Captain Simpson, you are your father's son, and I will take a good deal from you, but I must ask you not to be insolent. You are touched with liquor, but you ought to have sense enough to be responsible for your actions."

"And who do you think cares for you, Methuselah? You are an old cheat! You've come aboard here, and I suppose that you'll let everybody see how exemplary you are, and how sober you are, and what a nice old gentleman you are to take care of wicked young men. Then you'll go back, and my father will say, 'We can't trust the ship with that ruffian any more'; and then you'll be quietly put in her, my excellent old image. You go crawling about rich men, do you? And you want to turn a man's affections away from his children? Of course, your son is virtuous, is he not? but I could tell you something of the things that go on when he goes to see Fanny Greaves. I could make you open your eyes if I liked, old Hymn-book."

"Captain Simpson, you may insult me, if you like, to a certain extent; but you are not to say another word against my son. If you do, I will resent it."

"You will do what? You old mutineer, are you aware that I can put your name in the log-book and stop your pay? I won't do that, but I'll see if your old skin won't be better for a basting," and he hit out smartly with his left hand before Lanyer had time to rise.

A white mark appeared on the old man's cheek where the blow had landed. He rose up and delivered a tremendous right-handed blow full in Simpson's face. The bully was lifted off his feet as though a ball had hit him, and he fell against the cabin door, crashing one of the panels out. The blow took away his senses for a few seconds, and partially sobered him. He rose, wiped the blood from his mouth, and growled, "That's the ugliest day's work ever you did in your life." Presently Lanyer heard him say, "Boy, scull me ashore."

Half an hour later the lieutenant of the frigate was told
that a man wanted to see him—the captain of the barque
that was lying in the basin. The officer got scent of business,
and very politely welcomed the fellow who entered.

" I want you to go aboard my vessel to-night, sir. Take
your boat's crew, because you'll have a very strong man to
master. My mate's been insubordinate, and the best thing
you can do is to press him."

The officer said, " What is the nature of his insubordina-
tion ?"

" Look at my face, and you will see. Look at this cut in
my mouth. I might have swallowed that tooth. The
scoundrel was in liquor and assaulted me unawares, and I
think a trifle of man-o'-war discipline will do him good."

Just as the first low ripple of the dawn swirled up into the
sky Lanyer was on deck. He had determined that he would
take the vessel out and back again, but that he would never
more sail with a madman. Presently he heard a whisper
under the ship's quarter. Then Simpson climbed over the
bulwark ; then came the officer, and half-a-dozen bluejackets
and a marine quickly followed.

Simpson pointed. " There's your man ;" and the officer
smilingly said, " Now, are you coming quietly ?"

The whole situation flashed upon Lanyer at once. He
sprang aside and seized a wooden handspike.

" Over the side with you ! You have no right here. I'll
brain the first man that makes a step forward !"

The officer drew a pistol and presented it, observing
quietly, " I think I should make no fuss if I were you. You
dare us to move. Now, if you lift a finger I'll put an ounce
of lead through you."

The words were hardly uttered when the handspike
struck him on the fore-arm—his right hand dropped to his
side, and the pistol fell on the deck.

" Don't harm him !" the lieutenant shouted ; "club him,
and pitch him aboard the boat."

The six men made a rush all together, and a blow with the
flat of a heavy cutlass knocked Lanyer down. When he
came to himself he was in the dark, and round him were
huddled some dozen more men.

" Where am I ?"

" You are aboard the guardship, my sonny. All of us were hooked in here last night."

" The guardship ? What do you mean ?"

" Well, you are going to serve George—that's what I mean—and if you had had as much of it as I've had, I rather think you would not enjoy the prospect."

The bruised and battered man lay back on his plank bed, closed his eyes, and groaned.

That very night young Lanyer brought his sloop in once more, and once more arrayed himself in his bravery. He trod very lightly as he went up the lanes, for the rumour of spring was in the air, and the light breeze seemed to bear joy and youth on its scented wings. He reached Farmer Greaves's cottage, and knocked at the door. A tall and pretty girl opened it for him. She was a commonplace, rosy lass, with bright lips and a lively smile. She put her arms round Lanyer's neck quite simply, and said, " I am glad you are back. I don't know how I shall do afterwards when you have to be going away to the sea."

" All the trips are not long. Bless my soul, you'll have all the pleasure of waiting for five or six days, and then you'll have the pleasure of seeing me again, and there's only the partings to be counted on the bad side. How long is it now ?"

" What do you mean—till we are married ?" She did not blush or perform any of the evolutions which are supposed to be appropriate during conversations of the kind. She merely said, " Let me see, you take out your next cargo. Then you'll come back with grindstones. Is not that right ? Then you'll go up the Forth again and fetch grindstones again, and then that will bring us nearly to Saturday morning, and on the Monday morning we'll be married."

So the two young people strolled out, and returned towards nine o'clock.

Harry lay in harbour for three days, and at the end of that time the mainsail was slung ready for an afternoon tide. A small lugger came in, slid over the bar, and lowered her sails close by the jetty. Harry was on the quay when a man stepped up to him and said, " Do you happen to know one Captain Lanyer, the youngster that commands the sloop out of this port ?"

"That's me, my son ; what do you want ?"

"Well, I'm glad we have found you. You may think yourself lucky that we got here. I see you're just ready to go to sea. We've had the wind on the quarter all the way, and we've done the run in ten hours easy. I've got something for you."

He handed a dirty letter. Lanyer read it, and stepped back with a kind of stagger. The note was from one of the men on board the *Halicore*, and contained these words :

"Your father has been nabbed by the pressgang. They broke his head for him, I hear. He is aboard the guardship. There will not be any delivery for three or four days. Come you down as smartly as you can.—Yours very faithfully, JOHN REA."

Lanyer said to the master of the lugger, "God bless you. I must pay you, and go." The fisherman made answer, "I'm sorry to take money from you, my man ; I know what the job's about, and I took my chance. If I could have done it for nothing I would. But you know we must live, and there's always two mates to pay. If you can pay us for our time I'll not ask another farthing."

Lanyer handed over the money, and then turned and walked smartly through the lanes to the farmhouse. Fanny was busy in the dairy, and she turned with a little scream when she saw her sweetheart's face.

"I have come to bid you good-bye, my dear. We cannot be married. I am going away for a long time. Don't blame me for this. My father has been taken by the pressgang, and God knows what may come of it."

The girl quavered out, "But where is he ?"

"That's not the question, my woman. He is not very far off, but I am afraid that it's me will have to be far away for a long time."

The poor girl trusted her sweetheart so absolutely that she did not ask another question. She laid her face on his breast, and sobbed for a while. Then she spoke to him : "Go, my boy, and if it's fifty years I'll think about you all the time until you come back." She was quite enough acquainted with the villainous system to know what Lanyer would be likely to do. She knew—none better—that when

12

she next saw him he might be maimed, he might be in the
prime of manhood. She also knew that there was a chance
of her never seeing him any more.

Lanyer went to the quay and asked a friend to sail his
ship round to Leith for him. He then took the road.
Sometimes he walked; once he got a lift with the coach;
and sometimes kindly waggoners set him on for a mile or
two. After fifty hours of almost incessant travelling he
arrived at Hull.

A wherryman put him on board the guardship, and when
the sentry asked his business, he replied that he wished to
see the officer in charge. He was shown into a smart cabin,
and a stern face looked at him.

"What do you want?"

"You have got a man called Lanyer aboard here, have
you not?"

"Supposing we have, what has that to do with you?"

"I am his son, sir, and I have come a many miles to see
him."

"Hum! Well, he ought to be proud of you. I see you
are a sailor by your hands. I should not have thought such
a young-looking fellow could be father to such a slasher as
you."

"Can I see my father, sir?"

"Well, no; I am afraid that cannot be done. He is to
be drafted on board the *Minotaur* to-morrow."

"That can never be, sir. My father should never have
been at the sea. He was settled down quietly, and could
live on his means, and I'm not going to have him stolen
like that if there's law to be got in the country."

"Well, now, my fine fellow, quiet a moment. If I chose
I could have you put ashore at once, but I rather like your
looks, so I had better tell you that anything you can do in
the legal way will not help your father. We have got him,
and we will keep him. Take my advice, and make no
trouble about the matter."

"Could we not get a substitute?"

"If you like, certainly."

"Well, then, I'll volunteer. Now let me see my father."

"Well, you certainly shall have your way, and I wish you
were going to serve under me. I would like to have two

hundred like you. Just wait till we swear you in, and then you can do as you choose, and I'll let your father go ashore this very evening."

The young man went down in the wretched cockpit, and found his father sitting with his head bound up. At first the old man could hardly believe his sight, but he sprang up and folded his son in his arms, as he had done when the lad was young.

"I have come to take you ashore, father; and I want you to take the coach back to-morrow morning to Branspath. I have volunteered in your place, and I want you to go and look after Fanny till I come back. I'll give you a little note for her, and you must go up every day and just keep her in mind of me. To-morrow I have to go aboard the *Minotaur*, forty-four. A ketch is going to run us round."

"God treat you as you have treated me, my son! I won't refuse your offer, because I know it would be no use. You will have your way. I cannot say a word, only that I am proud to be your father."

So Henry Lanyer went with Nelson and fought at the Nile. He pleased the officers with his smartness and bright intelligence, and as the sailing master was bowled over by a chain shot in the course of that terrible fight, Lanyer was allowed to bring the ship home. His captain was very loth to part with him; but as soon as they touched English ground again, and the ship was paid off, Harry left by coach for the North.

Branspath was twenty miles from his home, and he had to walk every foot of the way. It was in the course of these twenty miles that the most remarkable event of his whole life befel him.

He had reached a place within three miles of home, when an old woman stepped out from a cottage and stopped him.

"Oh, sailor man, sailor man, do you see what yon is coming down the hill?"

Harry looked up the road, which sloped along by the sea, and saw a gang of men travelling down. They were armed sailors, and he knew that the pressgang were prowling in the fashion that was permitted by the statesmen of King George.

"Can you hide me in the cottage?"

12—2

"No, my bonny lad ; you must run for it."

Lanyer cleared the hedge, but the middy in charge of the gang had caught sight of him.

"There's a bluejacket, boys ; after him !" and the sailors, who were delighted with man-hunting, started as keenly as a pack of dogs. Lanyer dared not run straight home. He saw the roof of Greaves's cottage, and his heart gave a bound of delight. He gathered himself together, and whispered, "I will be with you, my girl, to-night, or I shall be dead." And then he struck away inland. He knew that if he could gain the limit he would be safe. He sprang over a hedge into the turnpike, and ran until his breath came heavily. Four men were gaining upon him very fast, and he felt, with a chilly despair, that his strength would only last him for a minute or two longer, and then the thought of the long dark nights at sea came to him, and he dreaded the slow months that he would pass in pining for a sight of his love.

A turn of the road took him out of sight of his pursuers. An old man was breaking stones at the corner, and when he saw this distressed creature, with the sweat pouring down his white face, and saw also the broad collar of Harry's pilot-cloth coat, he knew exactly what was happening.

"Through the hedge here, sailor; there's a deep sludge at the other side. Jump over that, and cut into the wood."

When Lanyer had got through the gap in the hedge his strength failed him. He knew that if he sat on the bank the sailors would see him, and he actually heard their footsteps. With sudden desperation he lay down at full length in the muddy ditch, and drew the weeds over his face. He was afraid his breathing might be heard, and the deathly cold of the mud made him feel as though he had been suddenly paralyzed. Presently he heard the old stone-breaker say, "He is up the hill there ; I expect you will catch him in the public-house :" and then the thunder of feet passed up the road. Next he heard the old man say, "You swines! He has done you this time."

He lay in the ditch until dark, and then struck off across he fields.

Late at night a tap came to Farmer Greaves's door. The girl had been waiting all day with a strange sense of expectancy. She did not know where her sweetheart was, but, as she said to her father, she "felt him in the air" all day. When she opened the door and saw the dripping figure, the memory of the old ballads came to her with a sudden shock, and she screamed : "Oh, father ! oh, my bonny lad ! He's drowned—he's drowned !" She thought that Lanyer had come back to her as Sandy came back to his love in the old rhyme. But the ghost quietly stepped into the kitchen and shook himself. Old Farmer Greaves's pipe fell in fifty pieces. The situation was utterly beyond his intelligence. When at last he was able to attain a conception of what had really happened, it struck him that the only legitimate thing to be done was to call for incredible supplies of food and drink. Lanyer asked for dry clothes, and he was equipped with a very extensive suit belonging to the farmer.

If I could tell you the numberless witty ideas that presented themselves to Mr. Greaves's mind when Lanyer appeared, lost in an enormous suit of baggy garments, you would feel that literature has no proper record of a very great humourist. I shall say nothing about that pleasant evening. Those who have known what joy is at its highest, those who have felt the keen delight of youth and love, will understand what was experienced by those three simple country folk, who have passed away so long, long ago. Greaves relieved his feelings at intervals by letting loose a laugh of the most gigantic order, but Harry Lanyer was silent.

In a month from that time the young man was once more at sea, and after two voyages he and his father and Fanny Greaves went to live together in one of the little houses that look from the Cambus cliffs out seaward.

Before old Captain Lanyer died he was one night accosted by a dissipated-looking man, who seemed worn by sickness. Lanyer said, " What is your business, sir ?"

"I've come to ask your pardon. You never told my father how I served you, or I should not have had another penny. You are a straight man, and I've never done a day's good since I harmed you." He was speaking with difficulty. Presently he protruded his tongue, and Lanyer shuddered. "That's for my lie. I've got cancer in the tongue, and I'm going to London for an operation next week. Will you forgive me before I die ?"

The old captain looked down at the supplicant and said, " I forgive you, my man, as I hope to be forgiven."

And Simpson burst into tears.

VII.

A SAILOR'S EDUCATION.

THIS is a plain account of the way in which one sailor was trained.

Tom Bassett parted from his mother at the gates of the great naval school, and he cried bitterly, for he was a very little fellow, and he had never been away from home before. On first coming to London the stir and stress of the swarming city impressed him, and he was eagerly interested in all things that he saw. The high houses amazed him, because he had never seen any building larger than a two-storied farmhouse. The endless procession of people that passed over the bridges ; the tramp of the stately great horses, the solemn rush of the brown Thames, the wide forests of masts, the shrill Cockney accents of the street boys—everything around made a new wonder to the tiny country-bred boy, and he kept up his spirits at first, though the shadow of imminent parting loomed over him. But when the good-bye had to be said the sense of utter loneliness descended on the poor little man with a sense of doom, and his heart was full of a dim, childish sorrow. People talk of happy childhood, but few of them ever give themselves the trouble to remember the hours of blank, hopeless sadness and misery that children endure.

When Tom saw his mother's tall figure pass away amid the hurrying crowd he felt as if the light of his life had gone out, and he sat him down by the side of a big cannon that stood in the grounds, and sobbed hard.

A loud, strident voice called him to himself. "New boy ! Crying over your mother, eh ? You'll soon stop that. I never knew one that cried after his mother that didn't turn out a bad lot."

Tom looked up and saw a huge man dressed in naval

uniform gazing down on him, and he shrank with fear from
the scowl that darkened the heavy face of the looming
giant.

The person who spoke to Tom was a man named Blobb,
who had been a sergeant of Marines. When he was
pensioned off, he became an officer in the school, and he
had excellent chances of indulging certain caprices which
had been restrained in the service. He liked to see suffering of any kind, and he liked, above all things, to watch the
sufferings which he inflicted with his own hand or tongue.
When he flogged a boy, he made the operation a protracted
luxury for himself. As soon as the victim was slung up
between the stanchions, Blobb loved to spend a little time
in making whistling noises with the instrument of torture.
The sight of the pale, agonized face turned sideways over
the shoulder of the crucified wretch seemed to stimulate
Blobb's wit, and he often indulged in sarcasms which varied
the rhythmic swish of the lashes. If a boy writhed and
yelled, then Blobb would take a little walk between the
strokes, and smile at his own humorous thoughts while the
child shrieked and begged for mercy. Sometimes a resolute
youngster was made fast to the horrible stanchions. When
the first lash whistled down, and left its bleeding marks,
the game youth gripped his teeth together, and never
vented a groan. Blobb always took such silence as an
outrage of his own tenderest feelings ; he swung his huge
shoulders in an ecstasy of effort, and, if the hardened sinner
still bore the ordeal in silence, Blobb was certain to leave a
big, raw patch where the skin had been torn off by the
cruel lashes.

If a master in a Board school were to give a boy only
one stroke with the weapon which Blobb wielded, he would
certainly be heavily fined, and very probably the Bench
would commit him for trial ; yet this big ruffian was
permitted to cut the skin off children in ribbons. If the
big scabs which Mr. Blobb left on the sufferers who received
his attentions had been shown in open court, the people
would have lynched the gallant officer ; but the palm of
publicity was denied him, and he had the privilege of
revelling in his peculiar enjoyments for many a year.

One narrow escape Mr. Blobb had. A child had been

found with a dirty head—the big lads often appropriated the soap in the lavatory, and little fellows found it hard to keep themselves clean—so Blobb, in his comic mood, resolved to inflict exemplary punishment. He made the barber shave the boy's head, and he then waited until night before completing his corrective work. At ten o'clock the shaven youngster was awakened, and his head was held under the tap in the dormitory until he became unconscious and could struggle no longer. This boy died of brain fever within a week. Probably the disease was due to dirty habits.

Mr. Blobb fully meant what he said when he spoke to Tom Bassett; he really did cherish a strong feeling of malignity to boys who cried when first they were left alone, and the odd thing was that the tender-hearted little fellows had a way of getting into trouble. The very sensitive feelings which make a lad sorrowful when he leaves those he loves are usually allied with genuine lightheartedness, and a lighthearted boy is always abhorred by creatures of the Blobb species.

After a long glare, the giant strode away, and left little Tom alone with his misery.

A bugle sounded, and converging lines of boys marched to a corner of the grounds, where they fell into columns, and remained standing at ease till a hoarse roar from a drill-master set the deep columns moving, and, like monstrous winding snakes, the companies filed into the tall building.

Tom remained by the gun-carriage until a smart-looking youth, who wore silver badges on each arm, touched him on the shoulder, and said, " Look here, Mr. New Jack, you'll get sent to drill after tea if you don't turn up sharp. Mr. Blobb's in a rare paddy about you."

Mechanically the little fellow went after the " captain," and soon stood amid the tremendous din of the dining-hall. About eight hundred boys were talking mostly at the top of their voices, and Tom felt as if he had been turned loose in a kennel of hounds.

Blobb addressed him : " Well, Mr. Mammysick ; you didn't fall in with your company. If you're a second out of your lines again I'll put something on you that you won't rub off in a fortnight."

The boy sat down in his proper mess, and tried to drink some of the dreadful mixture which was called tea, but he could not get it over, for it tasted like soup. The washing of crockery was loosely managed in the school, and the tea and cocoa usually had a powerful flavour of onions.

After tea the boys broke off in the grounds, and Tom was at liberty to shrink away into a secluded spot until the night came, and the long lines of chattering youngsters thundered up the iron stairs into the dormitories.

A shrill-voiced captain repeated collects from the Church Prayer-Book, and then the whole company chanted the Lord's Prayer. Tom noticed the funny way in which the words "for ever and ever" were rolled out; the Portsmouth accent prevailed in the school, and, no matter what dialect a lad spoke when he first entered, he soon fell into the Portsmouth twang. Dead silence was now enforced; the lads undressed by word of command, and climbed into their hammocks.

Tom was shot over on to the floor by a treacherous lurch of the hammock when he made his first attempt to get in, and it was not until he had struggled for ten minutes, amid the smothered laughter of his mates, that he contrived to lie down safely. The lights were turned low, the last whisper echoed furtively among the rafters, and Tom went off to sleep.

In the grey of the dawn, the clangour of a large handbell resounded, and instantly the whole place was alive. Only five minutes were allowed before the companies stood to attention, and in that time each lad had to turn out, dress, make his hammock, and sling it afresh. If any hammock looked baggy, or if the "knittles" were not hauled taut, the owner received a caning on the spot, and there was a good deal of squeaking as the sergeant went round.

Every step in the daily life of this school was carried on to an accompaniment of pain. From morning to night it was flog, flog, flog, and Tom Bassett looked forward with terror to the time when he also would be set dancing by the writhing lash of the long canes.

The companies next marched into a wide shed, where a thick iron pipe supported by tripods stood over a broad trough. The pipe was pierced with small holes, from which streams of water squirted. The boys, stripped to the waist, knelt down by the edge of the trough and washed themselves under the trickling runlets; then, shivering and stamping, they went forth into the open air to complete their toilette.

Happy lads who have a warm room to dress in can hardly imagine what it is like to comb one's hair on an icy morning in the open. The frost catches the damp locks, and sticky ice glues the hairs together, so that it is almost impossible to achieve a neat parting. The fingers are numb, and the comb plays exasperating tricks owing to the shivering of the hands. Yet the naval schoolboys in winter and summer dressed their hair and cleaned their shoes in any odd corner that happened to offer shelter from the scathing wind. On bright mornings it was all very well, but when the sleet fell and the hard breezes of January roared over the iron ground the performance was no joke.

Tom Bassett was somewhat surprised by what he saw at breakfast time. The companies were divided into messes or "ends," each of which contained six members. One loaf was put down for division among the six hungry mortals, and little Tom thought his share would be quite enough for him. He was mistaken. The biggest boy cut off the whole bottom crust of the loaf, and threw it across the table to another lad. The second young gentleman appropriated the top crust; the third took one half the middle of the loaf, and the remainder was left for the three juniors. Tom soon finished his tiny dry scrap, and was about to take a mouthful of cocoa, when he noticed that neither of the two juniors, who fared equally with him, had ventured to touch their pots. He soon found out the reason for this abstinence. The big bully, who had taken the first helping of bread, reached across, and said, "Here, New Jack, empty half your cocoa in there." Tom obeyed, and saw the precious warm drink disappear. He was about to take the poor remainder of his allowance, when the second boy shouted, "Easy there, Skug; wait till I give you leave." Tom waited, and just before the signal for rising was given he had to hand over his pot to the second of the young tax-gatherers.

That was a very hungry morning for the boy, and he felt

quite an unwonted sensation like a gnawing at the pit of the stomach.

The same proceedings went on at dinner. The lean meat and gravy were divided between the big boys, and a few scraps of fat were thrown to the little ones. The stout youth who was "wissey" of the mess cut off far more than he could eat, but he was a provident individual, and, after wrapping half of his share in paper, he flung the parcel to his fag, saying, "Bring up that for my supper."

At all meals this light-handed mode of sharing the food was lawlessly observed, and the younger boys were starved. In truth, the school offered an example of society relapsed into its primitive elements. Only the law of the strongest held, and the weak went to the wall. Each company of one hundred had its champion, who fought his way up until his supremacy as a fighter was placed beyond dispute ; then he became a chief, and the food, the liberty, even the money of those beneath him were all at his mercy. One commercially minded young man forced the whole of his company to hand over the bottom crusts of their loaves to him. The tribute was secretly collected by one of his slaves, and the barbarian chieftain sold the pieces of bread for twopence apiece, thus making a very comfortable amount of pocket-money. Another powerful fighter used to annex from twenty to thirty allowances of duff every Sunday. In the evening when the boys were hungry a little fag walked round the play-room crying like a costermonger, "Who wants to buy any duff?" The slabs of pudding were sold for a penny, and the lord and master spent the money in luxuries.

To all intents and purposes the boys formed a barbarian community, and their laws were quite independent of the stern discipline to which all submitted when once the bugle sounded, and the companies fell into column. The sections of the strange little nation had their tribal customs. Company No. 8 wore their hair long, and the personal appearance of one of the braves was not esteemed as correct until he could take the ends of his hair in his mouth. Company 4 wore belts, and allowed the shirt to be seen below the waistcoat. Company 3 modelled their gait on that of a famous pugilist, who was wont to lean forward with a

peculiar curve of the back. This company parted their
hair in the centre, and combed it behind the ears in huge
greasy waves. No boy was considered to be completely
adorned unless his head was clammy with oil, and the
ceremony of confirmation must have been very trying for
the officiating bishop when a row of the oleaginous tribes
knelt before him.

The strongest rivalry existed between the boys occupying
the east and west wings of the school ; fierce snowballing
matches came off in the winter, and these matches were
always followed by set fights in which the champions of
the sides took part, amid the roar of clustering hundreds.
From generation to generation fragments of slang were
handed down, and the ordinary language of the boys was
quite incomprehensible to the outside public. Cruelty of
the most brutal kind was the rule. Some pretty little boys
were pampered and petted by big louts who became the
slaves of their tiny henchmen, but the ordinary juniors led
dogs' lives. No one ever complained. When once a lad
took his place in the ranks he was bound to take care of
himself, and, until he could fight his way up in the queer
hierarchy, his only resource was to cringe. A few daring
spirits resented every blow, and fought each new aggressor
as long as they could stand or see ; but a high-spirited lad
was soon taught to know his place, for the whole society of
bullies made a mark of him and rendered his life a long
trouble.

Tom Bassett suffered a good deal in many ways. He was
nearly always hungry, and when he went out into the town
he used to stare into the bakers' shops with a watery mouth
when he had no money. The few postage-stamps which
his mother sent him he invariably spent in buying bread,
and the best moments of his life came when he could pay
for a few thick slices in a warm coffee-house.

Then he had to endure a good deal at the hands of
Blobb. He was in that worthy's company, and his legs
were seldom free from weals inflicted by the big sergeant's
cane. The cuffs and kicks that he received in the bear-
garden of a playroom were hardly counted in face of the
more acute miseries of starvation and cold.

The winter became very hard towards the end of January,

and the young boys fared much like the poorer classes in the hideous deserts of East London. The winter clothing was quite insufficient. The thin trousers and thin, wide-necked shirt offered no protection against the bitter winds, and Tom's legs were red raw, so that oftentimes he could hardly walk. Then there was the terrible affliction of chilblains. The fingers swelled to a great size, the skin was strained to bursting point, and the useless, aching hands at last broke into gruesome sores. Half the lads in the place were disabled, and poor Tom's hands were mere sickening masses of festers and scabs. It was so difficult, too, for a boy to keep clean in that dismal weather, and troops of the children went to the infirmary with ringworm, sore legs, and other ailments which arose simply from dirt.

Truly Tom Bassett served a hard apprenticeship. As the winter wore on he grew dogged and stoical in his puny way, and he would have got through without any failure of health if Mr. Blobb had only let him alone. But it happened that on one night Tom was tempted, after the company had turned into their hammocks, to chat with his neighbour. Blobb caught the two little gossips, and gave one of them a few ringing weals on the naked legs. He then shouted to Tom, "Downstairs you go."

The boy turned out and picked up his trousers.

"No, go as you are," growled Mr. Blobb.

"What? Into the grounds, sir?" faltered Tom.

"Yes, into the grounds. And look sharp, or I'll help you."

It was the 5th of March, the snow had fallen all day; but in the evening a kind of sleet fell which turned the surface of the grounds into slush. Little Tom felt inclined to cry out when the icy mud flowed over his bare feet, but he bit his lips and stood it out. For half an hour he endured that murderous cold, and he could not mount the stairs by himself when Mr. Blobb called him in.

Next morning Tom was taken into the infirmary, where he stayed for three months. When he came out his frame was lathy and his muscles faded; but his spirit was stead-fast, and he never said one word to incriminate the brute who brought him to the very doors of death.

Through cold, and hunger, and ill-usage, Tom Bassett

lived, until he joined the big lads in his turn, and became a champion, after one heavy fight with a boy from the west wing. Then things went well with him, for he was able to appropriate the food of the unhappy little ones; his limbs filled out; his strength was kept up by ample rations; and he became a long-haired, muscular, ruthless tyrant, like the youths who had kicked and beaten him at the beginning of his time.

A boy is naturally the cruellest of animals, but there are degrees. The home-bred lad resembles those gentle islanders whom the missionaries have tamed; the naval schoolboy resembled those remorseless North American Indians who rather enjoyed seeing a foe fastened to the stake. The curse of places like the naval school lies in the fact that a boy, in order to hold his own, must act in all ways like a savage; and his early training is apt to remain with him.

Tom Bassett began as a gentle, petted child, who cried on leaving his mother; he ended his school life as a swaggering, overbearing bully, who kept slaves like any other savage potentate, stole his subjects' food, and cared for nothing except securing a big share of good things for himself in the struggle for existence.

I may have something to say about his future, but for the present I may leave him at the point when he passed from a great training ground of ruffiandom and went out to take his place in the merchant navy. He had a good knowledge of navigation and nautical astronomy; he could knot and splice well, he could swim, run, and box like a trained athlete, and he was, take him for all in all, the most unmitigated young rough that ever was turned out by any process of miseducation.

If the gentle mothers who sent their lads to Tom Bassett's school could only have known what would be made of their bantlings they would have kept them at their apron-strings.

Our friend Tom began the world with three aspirations. He meant to smoke as soon as possible, he meant to command a vessel (a pirate schooner for choice), and he meant to return some day and thrash Mr. Blobb to a jelly.

VIII.

THE AMATEUR SHELLBACK.

THE incidents related in the following narrative formed a
source of great amusement to the hero's friends, but the
comic side of the matter was by no means so vividly apparent
to the hero himself.

A sailor-like man stood in the dock of a frowsy police-
court. The stains of his trade were very visible on his face
and hands and clothes; his fingers were smooth enough,
but the tar had become so thoroughly engrained that his
fist was like the paw of a Lascar. His face was unwashed,
and a stubble of many days' growth adorned his chin. But
for a certain air of distinction, conveyed by the carriage of
his head, he would have looked a very unpromising subject,
and the careful policemen who 'guarded him held themselves in readiness for violent action. A bulbous and beery
man who sat on the Bench remarked, with a fat smile of
triumph, "This is the most desprit ruffon we ever had
before us !"

Let us see how the "desprit ruffon" happened to get
there.

Clever young men generally begin their career with the
intention of "revolutionizing" something; a few go further,
and resolve to revolutionize everything. William Tressell
was clever, but he knew his own measure, so he resolved
to be content with revolutionizing literature, and he began
his great task when he was two-and-twenty years of age. In
his opinion the professors of the Art of Fiction stood most
in need of an inspiring example. He was grieved at the lack
of conscience shown by gentlemen who describe things that
they have never seen, and who spin out long chapters dealing with experiences which the writers cannot possibly have
undergone. In conversation with his friends Tressell would
say, "What business had Shakespeare to write about
Antioch and Tyre, and old Romans, and that sort of
thing ? Coriolanus is only Essex with a candidate's robe
on. Falstaff is alive, Dame Quickly is alive, the carters
at Gadshill are alive ; but the Greeks and the Volscians, and

the rest, are frauds. No one has a right to go beyond his own vision and his own experience; in fact, it cannot be done, and anybody who tries only perpetrates an annoying deception. I shall illustrate my principle in my own works as soon as I am ready to found a School."

Tressell was severely conscientious. When he wanted to describe the dawn he stayed out all night and took elaborate notes from the time when the first swirl and ripple of grey flowed upward in the east until the superb rosy mists were dispersed by the level volley of light from the sun.

One of his characters was represented as having escaped from the pursuit of certain marauders by swimming across a river on a dark autumn night. Tressell went to the Thames and rowed over to an eyot; he made his boat fast to a tree, and proceeded to consider the situation. His hero would creep stealthily through the osiers and plunge into the murmuring tide. Should the fugitive swim with boots on? That was a grave question, which Tressell decided to answer in the negative. A picturesque hero should not be hampered with too many wraps, either; so the novelist took off his coat and waistcoat. Then it occurred to him that trousers, however little they might trouble a shadowy hero, would be apt to embarrass a flesh-and-blood composer of fiction; and he was brought face to face with another difficulty. In the end he sprang over the side in very light attire; the water roared past his ears as he lunged forward with his long stroke, and he soon reached the other bank, for he was a powerful fellow and a crack swimmer.

A voice from the eyot called, "Say, old man, your boat's gone adrift."

Certain very mischievous young men were camping out in the centre of the island, and they had watched, with suppressed laughter, the preparations and the attitudes of the Reformer. One of them said, "What fun to let go his painter! The boat would go down to the lock, and he would have to walk home." Then these heartless persons pushed the boat into the current, and Tressell saw a dim shape twirling away towards Teddington.

He set off down the tow-path, but at Kingston he was compelled to follow the ordinary road, and pass through the market-place. A black lurcher came out from an archway and smelt cautiously around the wanderer. A policeman said, " Easy there, you," and began a most untimely cross-examination. Then some loiterers who stood in the porch of a low lodging-house scented fun, and came up to hear the stern constable and his victim. These ribald individuals followed Tressell to the waterside, and made most trying remarks all the way, so that his memories of a really strong " situation " were confused.

The martyr to literature was nearly apprehended for larceny when he was seen to borrow a dinghy that hung at the counter of a barge ; but he convinced the policeman by sheer native eloquence, and was allowed to recover his own boat. His passage to his inn was chilly, but triumphant, and he was convinced that his account of the hero's wild feat would mark an epoch in the history of letters.

In the pursuit of truth William Tressell was often brought into unpleasant contact with the police. On one occasion he made up his mind to visit the scene of a great country fair and commune familiarly with the nomads who camped on the common. At one in the morning he dressed himself roughly, and came downstairs bearing a candle.

He had scarcely had time to close the door when a man sprang at him and seized his throat.

" A fair cop, this time, matey. You don't do me no more," said this sudden assailant, and whistled shrilly.

Tressell struggled hard for a moment, and the man quietly remarked, " Don't let me have to use my truncheon, matey, or I'll scobe yer mug for yer."

A grim sergeant came up, and the plain-clothes constable said, " Ketch hold t' other side. I seen him going about with a light, and I copped him."

Tressell had presence of mind enough to hold his tongue till the first excitement of capture was over, and then he easily obtained release. The two guardians were quite affable as they emptied Tressell's flask, and the Realist agreed with the constable when the latter gentleman said, " Been a queer start if I'd caved yer nut in, captain. I made for sure I'd nailed one o' them rum 'uns off the Fairfield."

The indomitable Reformer pursued his researches in spite

13

of much hostile criticism. His friends had an unpleasant way of suggesting enterprises of a totally impracticable kind, with the evident intention of turning his zeal to ridicule ; but he did not care. It happened, however, that a very exciting experience caused him to reconsider his whole position with regard to Art and Letters.

He was about to send one of his heroes away to sea in a subordinate capacity, and he went to work on his preliminary studies with much thoroughness. First of all he spent three weeks in that awful locality round about Shadwell. He could speak the dialect of the waterside characters with faultless blackguardism, and he stayed till closing time in various drinking-shops night after night without ever being suspected by the fellows whose filthy liquor he shared. But he was vastly puzzled about his "discharges," for he had never been to sea excepting as a passenger.

He was staying at a boarding-house kept by a crimp, and he mentioned his trouble to his host. Mr. Olsen, the crimp, was a very well-known character. At an hour's notice he would guarantee to find a crew for any vessel going, or he would fill up vacancies within ten minutes. He always had a stock of completely useless men on hand, and he mixed up his efficient and non-efficient dependents with extreme skill. He owned a small steamer which ran regularly to Norway, and Mr. Olsen used to bring over cargoes of farmers and fishermen who had never been on board an English vessel in their lives. He also picked up wastrels from the English streets, and palmed them off on ships that were pressed to make up their complement.

Mr. Olsen's collection of discharges was very extensive and varied. He could fit out a man as A.B., cook, or ordinary at an instant's warning, and he was the cause of much astonishment among many captains whom he accommodated. A seaman would go on board a sailing ship bearing discharges which showed that he had served with success in half-a-dozen British ships. Half an hour after the vessel met the sea, this experienced mariner might perchance be found groaning in unspeakable torment. Some of Olsen's able seamen, when asked to haul on a rope, cheerfully replied, "No speak Inglis." It often happened that a ship went to sea bearing three or four men who signed articles

without ever having served before in their lives. In bad
weather they were utterly useless, and the labour fell on
the seaworthy men, who had to toil till they were worn to
the bone.

There is a lot of noise made about seaworthy ships.
Pity it is that something is not said about seaworthy sailors.
Many and many a vessel has gone to the bottom because
there were not enough hands to work her at a critical time.
There are moments when the mere fact that a man has to
run ten yards forward or aft makes all the difference between
life and death.

Gentlemen like Mr. Olsen have much to answer for.
They carry out an enormous system of fraud; they flood
the market with cheap and useless men, and they are
actually destroying our race of sailors. A wretched foreign
landsman, with his false discharges, is willing to ship for
half the wages of an Englishman; he pays no rates or taxes;
he has none of an Englishman's burdens of citizenship, and
he beats our countrymen out of the field. The owners do
not much mind, as a rule, for they calculate on their vessels
getting through somehow or other, and so the ugly business
sways on.

Mr. Olsen said to Tressell, " Are you going A.B. ?"

" Yes."

"Oh, then, here you are." And after fumbling awhile in
a drawer the obliging Olsen handed out a certificate, observing as he made it over, " You tip me your advance and
I'll give you oilskins. I'm going to send you up the Baltic
after you've called at the Tyne for cargo."

So Tressell found himself shipped on the *Maria*, collier,
under the name of John Jackson.

He had a terrible time, for the weather was cold and the
work very hard. Like all vessels of her class, the *Maria*
was undermanned, and often there were only four men on
deck during the night watches. The mate on the bridge
made one, a hand at the helm was the second, the deck
hand third, and the look-out man made up the fourth. The
clumsy mass of five thousand tons or more blundered along
at eight knots; and sometimes there was no look-out at all,
for the man had to jump down from the forecastle head to
lend a hand on deck. There is hardly a collier running

13—2

that does not stand a strong chance of causing a tragedy
through the scandalous cupidity that reduces the crews to
the extreme verge of shortness.

At night William Tressell had high moments when he
tramped on the look-out. The cold was ill to bear, but then
all round was the morning gloom, the ineffable mystery of
marching the waves, the hoarse undersong from the dim
distance. In his solitary marching his thoughts ran on
solemn things, and the mystic, immortal hours planted
their influence on his soul for life. The ghostly ships that
slid by like phantoms were as friends to him, and the keen
biting of the salt gale struck health through blood and brain.
His food was coarse, and the mate's mode of driving the
men was rather offensive, but when Tressell got into the
reeking forecastle and thawed his benumbed limbs between
the blankets he felt almost happy, and he grumbled out his
few sentences of commonplace talk with all the acrimony
and satisfaction of an old hand.

During the day he went about his rough labour with a
muscular vigour that very much amazed the other hands.
The mate ceased to discharge missiles at him, and on one
memorable occasion Tressell had the immense satisfaction
of accepting a chew of tobacco from his officer. He did not
read at all during the voyage, and he aped the North-
country dialect so well that he was generally taken for a
rough, genuine Blyth man. Of course his mind was active,
and he had sources of enjoyment which are denied to the
poor drudges who fare so hardly on the sea in order that
millionnaire coalowners may continue to live in profuse
luxury and make our laws in Parliament. The fate of the
ill-used seaman roused him to boiling indignation, and he
resolved to shake all England some day with his story of
the life that our mariners endure. Among other things, he
decided to write some *real* sailor songs, that should tell
something about the thoughts of the great dumb multitude
who work harder than navvies, fare harder than convicts,
and bear cold, exposure, drenching rain, iron frosts, and
sleepless hours to enrich the fine persons who spend their
money at Torquay and Harrogate and Belgravia.

When the vessel reached her English port after her long
knocking about in the North Sea, the Realist left her. He

rowed about the harbour, drank with the foreign seamen in
the low public-houses, danced in the saloons where Jack is
poisoned by bad drink and rooked by harpies, and, in short,
learned a great deal about the place.

He had settled that his hero should depart at about
midnight from the port, and that the heroine should stand
in a pathetic and statuesque way on the jetty as the ship
surged outward to the bar. This noble scene was fully
arranged ; but Tressell resolved to be strictly accurate, and
he therefore waited till two o'clock one morning, and strode
forth in his seaman's garb to catch the aspects of the
witching hour.

Decidedly Tressell was in luck. He tramped up and
down on the lonely quay, making rapid notes of the strange
and beautiful effects ; he fancied his hero at the helm, he
pictured the gentle heroine on the jetty, and he dramatised
the last scene—the sad waving of the humble but lovely
heroine's hand, the passage of the barque into the haze, and
the wild gesture of despair with which the girl turned homeward.

In his excitement Tressell quite forgot that he was
making a fool of himself until he was rudely recalled to the
world of facts. A hand was roughly laid on his collar, and
he received a shove which sent him reeling towards the
quay wall. Then a stern voice said, "Get home, you
drunken fool ! We'll be having you raising the neighbour-
hood next."

This sad interruption was brought about by a curious
train of circumstances. Tressell had ventured one evening to enter an inn which was frequented by smart captains
and mates, who mixed freely with the townsmen. Two
young men sat at one of the tables, and Tressell took his
place beside them. One of the men was a squat-nosed and
pimply person, who occupied himself in telling unpleasant
stories in a greasy undertone ; the other was a rather handsome fellow, with a shifty eye and a general air of cheap
flashiness.

The possessor of the squat nose said to the Realist,
" Hadn't you better get to another table ?" and Tressell re-
plied by a quiet and inquiring look. The bully said,
" Here's a shilling. Go and get your face washed, or I'll

sling you through the door ;" whereupon Tressell slowly
answered, "I don't want to create any disturbance. Dare
you repeat that outside in a quiet place ?"

The squat-nosed gentleman was an utter coward. He
changed colour, and muttered something about calling the
landlord. Tressell's blood was up, and he said, " I'll do
that for you."

The landlord, a stout, beery person of choleric tempera-
ment, came up. Tressell pointed to the two cads.

" These persons have insulted me. I don't think it can
be to your interest to have a respectable sailor insulted in
your house. I give you notice that if either of those men
addresses me again I shall use very strong measures."

He forgot his dress, and spoke in the tone of a cultured
man.

The landlord growled, " Don't interfere with no customers
here, mister ; we're all alike if we pay our shot."

Tressell stared the squat-nosed one out of countenance,
and then retired, abusing himself for having risked a
brawl.

Alas ! it happened that the two exclusive young men
were returning from a prolonged gambling bout on the very
morning when Tressell was studying his great scene. They
crept into a narrow passage, and watched the Reformer's
innocent fooling.

Presently the squat-nosed gentleman whispered, " He's
drunk ; wouldn't it be a lark to set the bobbies on to
him ?"

The youth with the shifty eye received the proposition
with rapture, and the precious pair stole up a flight of steps
into the main street, and engaged in converse with a policeman. Said the squat-nosed youth, " We've been annoyed
by a drunken fellow down on the quay here. He's throwing stones, and playing all sorts of games. You had better
give him a word before he does more mischief."

Then the worthies watched what followed with much
glee, and the fun was so good that they did not grudge the
half-crown with which they had stimulated the policeman
to vigilance.

Thus was the assault on the innocent literary man brought
about.

Tressell assumed as lordly an air as possible when he had ceased staggering, but the sudden attack of the policeman had shaken his mental balance, and he spoke with a kind of stutter.

"What is the meaning of this assault?" he inquired.

"I'll meaning you, if you don't skedaddle sharp. Can't let decent gentlemen come home in peace! Out of that, you scamp!"

Tressell quietly said, "I shall go to the station and inform your superiors, my man."

Something in the voice persuaded the policeman that he had made a mistake, but he rose to the situation with a promptitude which distinguishes certain members of his admirable force.

"You're drunk and disorderly, sir. Come on with me." And in a moment Tressell was hustled along a narrow street, and conducted to the police-station. A burly sergeant, of most truculent aspect, produced the charge-sheet.

"Dangerous customer you've got there, Tipper. State the charge."

The policeman improvised a very romantic account of the struggle which he had supported single-handed against the desperate ruffian.

The truculent sergeant asked for the name and profession of the delinquent, and Tressell said, "I am a gentleman. You may telegraph to my club in London, or I will refer you to three noblemen who know me. This charge is utterly false, and I will make you suffer for it."

"Gentleman, eh? You've got rayther tarry hands for a gentleman Jack, my boy."

Tressell looked up, but the humorous aspect of the situation remained with him, and he said, "Come, my lad, you are quite mistaken."

"None of your familiarity here, sir. My lad, indeed! Put him in the second cell, and handcuff him if he is violent."

Tressell was at bay. He said, "I demand to see two surgeons."

"Surgeons be damned! Get in with you, or we'll strap you on a shutter."

But the unfortunate Reformer persisted, and in about an hour a fat and untidy man arrived, who said, "Trot him out."

Tressell was duly trotted out, and the sagacious surgeon saw a well-looking fellow, roughly dressed in a guernsey frock and a rough pilot jacket.

"Well, Jack. Paid off? The old game, you see. You will do it, all of you, and you land here safe at the finish."

"You are absolutely in error, sir. Put any mental test to me that you like, and I'll prove my sobriety."

"Ah, a real sea lawyer! What do you call yourself?"

"I'm a gentleman, sir, and I live on my means, as people say."

The doctor winked compassionately to the policeman and whispered, "Poor devil!" Then, aloud, the intelligent medical man said coaxingly, "Come now, Jack; what were you after on the quay, now, at this time of night."

"I was studying the effect of the moon on the water."

The doctor gasped, "Oh! this is sad. He's got delirium tremens badly. Put him in a darkened cell, and take care he has no weapon about him. Good-morning. Moonlight on the water! Lord, Lord!"

The doctor went off, and resolved to tell this joke all over the town next day. Then the sergeant observed, "Now, Mr. Cocky, we'll make you snug for the night."

Tressell had no very pleasing reflections during the hours that passed before the court opened. He had seen much of life during his conscientious researches, but this was a phase which somewhat surprised him. He was still more surprised when he was marched out at noon and placed in the dock.

The presiding magistrate was a stout and red-nosed person, who blinked with severity, and gaped as the more important items of evidence came out.

The policemen gave their testimony glibly, and, in spite of Tressell's close cross-examination, the careful officers succeeded in representing him as a singularly violent drunkard.

Then the squat-nosed youth stepped into the box, and reeled forth a most consistent story.

"You declare that I was drunk?" asked Tressell.

"Yes. Raving mad with drink. You wanted to fight me, and your language wasn't fit to be repeated."

The doctor then appeared, and declared solemnly that, judging from the eccentric ravings of the prisoner, he had believed him to be threatened with delirium tremens.

The toils were closing round Tressell. One question addressed to the surgeon settled the case. Tressell politely asked, "Did I not request you to set me any intellectual test in reason?"

The fat magistrate woke up to a sense of his own position. He had been tipsy the night before, and he was very sleepy, but the strange words of the prisoner roused him.

"Intellectual test! Intellectual test! What's intellectual test got to do with a man being drunk? The Bench are of opinion the case is proved. We can't waste the time of the court any longer. Seven days, without the option of a fine."

The squat-nosed and pimpled youth murmured, "Tit for tat, mister," as Tressell was dragged away.

This narrative proves two things: First, that an enthusiast may go too thoroughly to work; second, that you should not offend the police.

*   *   *   *   *

Tressell continues to produce works of fiction which he ranks very high in the scale of merit; but he is less comprehensive and minute in his search after material.

He goes to sea still, but when he comes ashore he is very careful to dress well.

Long after the squat-nosed young man and the flash youth with the shifty eye played their trick on him, he was much amused on meeting the policeman who knocked him about. Tressell was in yachting costume, and the graceful way in which the policeman touched his hat supplied a social lesson which was cheaply bought at the price of seven days in prison.

Tressell has completed a remarkable romance in which the squat-nosed young man figures as comic villain.

PART III.

Saltings.

I.

THE CAPTAIN'S WIFE.

THE money-making dulness of our town was sometimes broken in the winter time by concerts which were given in the great hall of the Institute, and on these occasions we flattered ourselves that our amateurs made a very respectable show. Mr. Spall, the bass singer from the choir at St. Christopher's, used to sing "The Wolf" in a way that made your skin creep ; and nothing could be finer than the duet of the "Gipsy Countess" as rendered by Mr. Morrow, the schoolmaster, and his daughter. Morrow had been disappointed in his youth, and thus his nature had acquired a romantic quality which made him sing as though he had never seen a cane in his life. Many young ladies told him that he was quite poetic, and he knew enough of his own complicated mind to make him believe their statement. Then we had young Mr. Dodds, the shipbroker, who could sing comic songs so well that you might have fancied yourself in a London music-hall. No wonder we were proud of our native talent. When country visitors came at convenient seasons they were taken to these entertainments, and they always went away much impressed by our advance in the direction of pure culture.

But our singer of singers was Cissy Halkett, and when her name appeared on the bills the young men of the place went to great expense in the matters of new ties and hair-oil. Cissy was very pleasant to look at as she flashed down the main street with her swift walk; but what was a mere glance in the street? You saw her approach; you caught a confused gleam of bright cheeks and violet eyes, and before you had time to raise your hat in the proper London manner the swish of her dress had gone past you, and you were gazing forward on a populous desolation. Many youths would have gladly looked round after her, but ours was a well-bred town, and this breach of fine manners was rarely committed. Young Thomas Watkins, the tobacconist, was much envied, for he had a corner shop, and he could not only see Cissy coming, but could watch her right away till she turned the corner. Peter Laverock, the romantic hairdresser, said that Watkins was a prying fellow, without a soul capable of understanding the behaviour of a true gentleman; but we thought that this severity was due to the fact that Peter hadn't a corner shop.

The concerts gave us all a fair chance. For five pleasant minutes Cissy stood on the platform, and her adorers tried not to look self-conscious. Her voice was not very well trained, but it was strong and sweet, and when she finished her song everybody applauded, from the hoarse skippers who came in charge of their wives to the shiny young persons who had offered up hair-oil on the altar of affection. Cissy was very pretty indeed. Critical ladies sometimes called her a barnyard beauty because her cheeks were so brilliant, but there was really nothing coarse about her radiance. Her eyes, as I have said, were violet in colour, and she had a wonderful way of letting her long curved lashes droop for a moment till their crescent lay like a delicate shadow on her clear skin; then she would raise her eyelids and make your very heart tremble (if you were youthful and sus-ceptible) with a steady dark glance. Mr. Traill, the banker's son (a fashionable person who often mentioned the fact that he drank champagne), once paid Cissy a patronising com-pliment. He was a very fascinating fellow was Traill, and he used to say he really must get out of the town, for the girls made up to him so that he never felt safe; but he looked foolish under Cissy's glance. The girl was really too stupid to have any satiric intention, but her look always seemed to say a hundred times more than she was capable

of thinking. Then she was majestic too, and her height
and solidity gave her a great advantage over individuals
like Traill. She awed them by the suggestion of strength
and calm that was conveyed by the lines of her magnificent
figure. For the rest, Cissy was very pure, very healthful,
and very commonplace. She did not like lads to send her
what she called " potery and rubbish," and she had a good
eye for manliness in men. Had she been educated she
would have been very clever at picking up second-hand
ideas ; as it was, she only received a kind of loose training
which did not enable her even to spell properly, and her
accent in speaking was sometimes deplorable. But extreme
refinement would perhaps have been lost in the town,
although we did certainly think a good deal of ourselves ;
and thus Miss Halkett was as much admired as though her
manners and accent had been perfect. The males of the
populace were content with believing that there wasn't a
handsomer girl anywhere, and with this belief I am disposed to agree, for I have never seen anybody quite so
beautiful.
    Cissy could have taken her choice of men had she
wanted to marry some one with money, but she didn't like
the well-off folk, with their caricature of south-country
ways, and thus the passionate shipbrokers wooed in vain.
She chose her lad when he was third officer, kept faith with
him till he passed the Board for master, and married him
when he came back from his first voyage. This fortunate
man was named Henry Halcrow. He was a slashing fellow,
with a rare pair of shoulders and a fine carriage of the
head. Cissy used to say she liked him because he "looked
like being master-man anywhere," and she was not very far
wrong.
    Halcrow had been brought up in a rough school. On
board ship he was not very fluent with his tongue, excepting
when he felt that discipline required him to be profane ;
but he made up for his slackness of speech by being always
extremely ready with fist and belaying-pin and rope's-end.
In the pleasing service where his youthful time was passed
the rule of conduct was—"The blow first, and jaw afterwards." This chaste and simple motto guided Halcrow,
and he was considered to be a real smart skipper. After

he met Cissy, Halcrow's ways changed in many respects.
He had, like nearly all high-spirited sailors, been used to a
coarse and violent life when ashore—what else can be expected after the long monotony of a voyage ?—but he took
up a new way of living when he first saw that he had a
chance of the girl whom all the men talked about. It was
rather touching to see how the big, boisterous young reprobate tried to go straight after Cissy first took pointed notice
of him. He tried to smooth himself down, and he felt
positively gentle whenever he thought of her.

If the truth must be told she did not think much about
reforming his morals. She liked him to be " decent," and
she would have spoken gravely to him had she seen him
going into a public-house ; but his powerful aquiline face
and his tall figure were far more in her mind than were
any reflections about his moral reformation. The couple
went through the courtship usual in such cases. When
Halcrow came home he walked out every afternoon with
his sweetheart to the pier. The wind raced over the dappled
sea and brought the flush to Cissy's face ; the light hand of
the breeze plucked at her hair and set the rippling tresses
flying (for the girls wore their hair loose over the shoulders
in those days), and she looked the picture of health and
hopefulness and strength. Then the two went home to
tea. Old Captain Halkett explained to the young sailor
the precise causes of the decay of manly spirit and nautical
ability among modern men. Then Halcrow smoked a pipe
with the old skipper, and then came the time for saying
good-night.

So the days passed till the wedding came off, and soon
after that memorable morning Henry Halcrow went over
the bar in tow of a remorseless little tug. Cissy was inclined to cry when the tug came alongside, and the barque
began to draw slowly ahead under the weight of the topsails. But the old mate's wife comforted her by saying,
" Never thou mind, my woman. Ye'll easy get used to
them gannin' away. It sune gets ower, and then you can
coont the days till she's signalled at the Downs comin' back
agyen. Eh, hinny, ye hev little to freet aboot. There's
wor Mary's man was droonded his second voyage eftor they
wor married, and her left wi' the bit bairn. Ye'll hev ne

sic luck as that, maw bonny." So with these comforting
remarks the good soul kept on till the ladies were landed.
Then Cissy went to the pier, and pleased herself with
thinking that she could still see the wake of the barque
trailing sinuously over the quiet sea from the pier to the
long, low Point. She stayed listening to the gurgle of the
little waves until the pink flush reflected from the west
told her that the sun had gone. Then the first long sigh
of the night-wind came, and the grey catspaws crept over
the chilly bay. Cissy sighed in echo to the wind and went
home.

Halcrow came back more bronzed than ever, and his wife
was exceedingly proud when she was able to show him off
at church. He did not understand much about religious
affairs, and I am sorry to say that he would have given
anything for a smoke while the sermon was going on ; but
he turned out every Sunday evening during his stay at
home, and he learned to like the long cool stroll on the
swarming pier when church was over. Cissy was quite
happy. She said, "I would like to live on like this till
I'm old ;" and Halcrow approved the saying.

One morning the Captain came in from the owner's office,
and said, "It's a bad job this time, Ciss. We're fixed for
Callao." And sure enough the barque left within ten days,
bound round the Horn. Halcrow declared he would have
taken his wife, but she wasn't fit to go to sea, and she
didn't even go over the bar with him. Cissy was very low-
spirited for a long time after the barque's dusky tower of
canvas swept into the gloom of the gathering night. Harry
had kissed her at the dock-edge before the tug took hold of
the ship, and she dreamed strangely of that kiss night after
night.

One morning early she woke up, and called out loudly
with fear. She had dreamed that she had seen Halcrow.
His hair was streaming wet, and his oilskins looked as
though he had been overboard. She told the old Captain
about her dream, and he laughed. "You'll get right
presently, my woman. I bet he's home in time for the
christening," said the old man, and then he roared at his
own slyness. Cissy waited a long time before she got news
of her husband. Then some one enclosed her a slip from

a newspaper, and she learned that the barque had been spoken at sea. She pressed the paper to her breast, and said, "Oh, my dear, my dear, don't be long!"

She often used to sing to herself as she went about the house, and I will repeat the song she was fondest of, because I think it the most beautiful of all songs, and I like it for her sake now that she will never sing it any more. There are not three people living who know all the words, for those who used to sing it long ago are dead and cold now. I hope the words will never be made too common, but they are too pretty for their life to be trusted to one man's memory :

> "Oh ! Amble is a fine town, with ships in the bay,
> And I wish with my heart I was only there to-day.
> I wish with my heart I was far away from here,
> A-sitting in my parlour and talking to my dear,
> And it's Home, dearie, Home, oh ! it's Home I want to be.
> My topsails are hoisted and I must out to sea,
> For the oak, and the ash, and the bonny birchen tree,
> They're all a-growing green in the North Countree,
>   Oh, it's Home, dearie, Home !
>
> " In Baltimore a-walking a girl I chanced to meet,
> With her baby on her arm as she came down the street ;
> And I thought how I sailed when the cradle it stood ready,
> For the pretty little babe that has never seen its daddy.
>   And it's Home, dearie, Home !
>
> " And if it be a lass she shall wear a golden ring,
> And if it be a lad he shall live to serve his king,
> With his buckles and his boots and his little jacket blue,
> He shall walk the quarter-deck as his daddy used to do.
>   And it's Home, dearie, Home !
>
> "Oh ! there's a wind that blows, and it's blowing from the west,
> And of all the winds that blow 'tis the one I like the best ;
> For it blows at our backs and it shakes the pennon free,
> And it soon will blow us home to the North Countree.
> And it's Home, dearie, Home, oh ! it's Home I want to be.
> My topsails are hoisted and I must out to sea,
> For the oak, and the ash, and the bonny birchen tree,
> They're all a-growing green in the North Countree."

Cissy felt a kind of companionship for this song. It made the world feel friendly and hopeful to her, so she sang it when she was sure the neighbours couldn't hear.

Henry Halcrow got round the Horn on his way back not very long after Cissy's baby was born. No one at home

knew his whereabouts, but the feats of decoration wrought
upon that infant in anticipation of the father's return were
very surprising and recklessly premature. Cissy quite forgot
her dignified stature and her majestic ways, and she
chattered to the young fetish in a very odd and playful
fashion. When news of the ship came from the Start the
girl felt much inclined to camp out on the pier and wait all
the time until the barque got round.

The weather was very ugly after Halcrow passed the
Goodwins, and the volunteers had to stay up night after
night on the pier. One bad morning Cissy looked out from
the garret window after she had lain long awake listening
to the vast roar of the wind and the sullen boom of the
sea. There was nothing to be seen but a mad conflict of
white water that twisted and spurted, and lashed up great
columns of fierce spray. Sometimes a charging host of
waves swept sonorously from the north; then came an
aimless cross drift from the south; the ranks met in thunder,
and the rearmost waves seemed as though they tried savagely
to climb over and throttle the opposing legions. A little
Danish schooner lurched through the awful hurly-burly, and
the men got the rockets ready in case she took a wrong
turn. The flying seas flowed over her, and she staggered
again and again; but her captain kept his nerve, and presently she shot into the fairway. Then the people cheered,
and the captain waved his sou'-wester. Cissy gasped, "Oh,
Lord, have mercy!" Then she wrapped a shawl round
her head, and fought her way down to the brigade-house.
The men were very kind to her, and she tried to smile in
return for their attentions, but her face was drawn and
rigid, and her eyes looked as though she were dreaming.
The mastheads of a ship appeared to the southwards, and
the vessel seemed to be rolling heavily. The fellows on
the pier could see that the captain was trying to claw off
from the land, but he could not gain an inch. The old
father of the brigade said gruffly, "I wonder who *he* is,
then." Cissy could have told him, for she knew in her
heart that the hour had come, and that vision of the man
with the streaming hair crossed her and touched her pulses
like ice. The barque hove up her port side as she rolled
over the bulge of a great sea, and a sailorman said, "Blowed

if it isn't Harry Halcrow. He'll get fits, I doubt." Peter Laverock touched the man sharply, and whispered, "Hush! Don't you see the girl?" The barque might have come round to the westward, but as soon as her helm was put up a succession of seas hit her, and her scrap of sail was of no use to her. Her head slewed round to the south, and she came like a bolt right on to the stones. "Matchwood she'll be," said a pilot. Cissy tried to get out, but friendly hands held her, and she sat down and clenched her hands. The men did their best, but the ship was beaten to bits in ten minutes.

The old chief said, "Come thy ways, my bonny; we'll bring you news if anything comes." Cissy was still staring forward, and her eyes seemed to have an inward gaze. She moaned, "Oh, the stones! the stones! They'll bruise his face, and I won't know him. And the bairn! Oh, the bairn!" They led her home, and the men who were coming down lifted their hats as she passed, for they saw by her face what had happened.

That evening Peter Laverock plunged in up to the waist and brought in the Captain's body. Peter said, "I'm glad his face isn't spoiled. She'll get her last look at him."

So Captain Halcrow never saw the baby, and he didn't know that Cissy's arms were round him, although she knelt all night by the bed where the drowned man lay.

This is just the kind of luck that befalls some people on the weary coast.

II.

THE ROCK SCORPIONS.

THE screw steamer *Jenny Jones* was lying alongside a coal-hulk at Gibraltar one October afternoon. By three o'clock her bunkers were nearly filled, and the captain was getting ready for casting off, when one of the natives came aboard. Captain Hindhaugh looked about for something to throw at the visitor, and only the difficulty of selecting an efficient missile from a large and varied assortment prevented him from letting fly at once.

The "Scorpion" said: "Ah, no, no, Capeetan! No been

14

throw nothing at myself. Beesiness!—I'se been com' for beesiness. Big thing, Capeetan!"

The last phrase was spoken with such a profound wink that Hindhaugh held his hand, and, addressing the man as one would an ill-conditioned dog, said: "Don't keep bowing and scraping there, you tastrel. Get it out, sharp!"

The "Scorpion" whispered : "No been talk up here. Keep ship one hour, two hour, three hour. You'se been com' with me, and I speak you somethin' myself."

Like many of his tribe, this interesting native spoke a kind of English which is not heard anywhere else on the Mediterranean shore. A few of the people on the Rock learn to talk very well to our men, but most of those who come about the ships use a picturesque lingo in which "myself" takes the place of quite a variety of parts of speech.

Hindhaugh invited the man below, and asked him to explain himself. The fellow leaned over the table and chattered on, throwing quick side glances at every few words.

"This been big thing, Capeetan. You get away a little; drop your anchor a little. Then three felucca com' alongside, and you'se been hoist bales. Then you'se go where agent say you. Very big thing. Five thousand sovereign."

"What is it? Tobacco?"

"That been it."

"Where for?"

"Huelva."

"I'm not going out of Portuguese waters at no price."

"Ah, no, no, Cheesu, Capeetan—no? Five mile. We have felucca there ready. I'se been see him myself."

"What's the figure? What's the money?"

"You com' shore and see agent with myself."

Hindhaugh put a revolver in his pocket and went on deck ; the Scorpion got ashore and hung about with an air of innocence. The Captain was about to follow, when the man in charge of the hulk called out, "Do you intend to keep bumping us like this all night? Why don't you cast off? You're knocking us to flinders."

Hindhaugh beckoned. "Look here, my good chap, it won't matter to you for a couple of hours ; let us lie till dusk, and then I'll get away. I've got important business ashore."

"That's very well, Captain. But look here; if there's anything on, I'm in it. You understand—I'm in it."

"You understand that, do you? Well, then, I'll tell you to keep your mouth shut just now, or never another ton of coal will you put aboard of us as long as I run here."

"All right, Captain. No need to be nasty. You'll do the square thing, I bet."

Then Hindhaugh went ashore, and the Scorpion walked on ahead, gazing on architectural beauties with easy interest. Presently the two men came to a narrow stairway, and the Englishman gripped his revolver. A dark-eyed Spaniard was waiting on a landing, and held up two fingers when the guide passed. The Scorpion knocked at a greasy door, and an ugly fellow, with a cowl on, looked out and nodded. Hindhaugh stepped into a room that reeked of garlic and decay. Two men sat in the steamy dusk at the far side. An oily gentleman rose and bowed. "I'm the interpreter, Captain. You and this merchant must do business through me. What'll you take to drink?"

"Get through your business, mister. I'm not wanting any drink."

In brief jerky sentences the interpreter explained what was wanted.

"You steam slowly till you're near the Fleet. Then put all your men on, and get the stuff up. This man goes with you, and he'll tell you where to go. Lie five miles off Huelva."

"I shan't go except to Portuguese waters."

"Good. Then the lighters will come and the men will discharge you."

"And now," said the Captain, "what about me? How much?"

"One hundred and twenty pounds."

"Can't be done. Make it two hundred and fifty."

After some haggling a bargain was made for two hundred and twenty. Then Hindhaugh went further: "I want one hundred and ten down before we start, and the balance before you take an ounce of tobacco out of us."

This was settled; the merchant bowed, and the skipper

went away, still keeping his hand on the revolver. Every
cranny in the walls seemed fit to hide a murderer—seemed
made for nothing else; and Hindhaugh thought what a
fool he must have been to venture under that foul arch.

On getting aboard, the captain sent for his brother, who
sailed as mate with him. He said, "Now, Jack, I'm going
to run some risk. You take this pistol, and get her oiled
and put right. When you see three feluccas coming alongside, get all the chaps on deck—the *Dora's* crew as well as
ours" (Hindhaugh was taking home a shipwrecked crew,
and he was very grateful just then for that accession of
force)—"whack on everything you know, and get the bales
up sharp. Tell the engineers to stand by for driving her,
and leave the rest to me. If we're nailed, we'll be detained,
and I don't know what may happen, so you'll have to look
slippy."

Jack replied, "All right, sir!" Quarterdeck manners
were punctiliously observed by one of the brothers.

The shadows fell low, and the crown of the Rock grew
dim. The creeping wind stole over the Pearl Rock, and
set the sinister ripples dancing; the bugles sang mysteriously through the gloom, and the mystery of the night was
in the air. The *Jenny Jones* stole quietly toward the broad
sheet of water where the vessels of the Fleet heaved up their
shadowy bulk above the lapping flood. All the English
sailors were stripped to the shirt, and a low hum of excited
talk came from amidships. Suddenly the raking yard of a
felucca started out from amid the haze; then came another,
and another. A sailor slipped a cork fender over the side,
and there was a muffled bump and a slight scrape. Jack,
the mate, whispered, "Now you cripples!" and a brief
scene of wild hurry and violent labour ensued. Bale after
bale was whisked aboard; the Englishmen worked as only
English sailors can : and the Scorpions excelled themselves
under the influence of fear and black wine. When the
last bale was up, Hindhaugh said to the man who first
boarded him, "Who's got the money?"

"Me, Capeetan. All right. Honest man myself. You'se
been have every dollar."

"Well then, it's neck or nothing. We have half an hour
to clear out into the Gut. Come below and shell out."

The Scorpion counted out one hundred pounds in gold, and then asked, " That be enough ? Other money all right other end."

" Deuce a bit. Down with the other ten, or I'll sliver you."

The Scorpion did not know what sliver meant, but the gleam of the skipper's cold eye was enough for him. He paid up and went on deck.

Hindhaugh had just said to the engineer, " Now, rive the soul out of her," when a low, panting sound was heard, and a white shape appeared gliding over the water. The captain had let the feluccas go, and the *Jenny Jones* was moving. He waved for the mate. " It's all up. Here's a mess. You must go home overland—suppose you swim ashore. Steady the men down."

Jack performed one or two steps of a dance, and placed his finger against his nose. He rather enjoyed a scrape, did this frivolous chief officer. The white shape came nearer, and a sharp whistle sounded. Hindhaugh had known well enough that it was a steam launch that made the panting noise, and he got ready for the worst. The launch drew right across the bows of the steamer, and then the throbbing of the little engines ceased. Again the whistle sounded ; the launch gave a bound forward ; then she struck away into the darkness, and Hindhaugh drew a long breath.

In an instant every possible ounce of steam was put on, and the *Jenny Jones* went away at eleven knots toward the Gut. All night long the firemen were kept hard at it, and before morning the Rock was far astern of the driving steamboat.

Three of the Scorpions had stayed aboard, and Captain Hindhaugh noticed that they carried their knives. He noticed, too, that the cringing manner which the fellows had shown before the Rock was cleared had given place to a sort of subdued swagger.

About noon the engines were slowed down almost to nothing, and the *Jenny Jones* crept gently on toward the shore. By four o'clock the vessel was well into Portuguese waters, and Hindhaugh was prepared to defy any quantity of Spanish coastguards. When the sun had dipped low the

Scorpion-in-chief came aft, and pointed mysteriously to the north east.

"You'se been look where I point myself.   Feluccas! You'se follow them in, and drop anchor."

Hindbaugh smiled.   "Do you think you're talking to a fool ?   Come you below there, and let me have that other money, sharp."

"Ah, Capeetan. Wait till agent's man come with felucca. I'se been have no money myself."

Hindhaugh was not a person to be trifled with.   He quietly took out his revolver.   "Now, do you see that pretty thing ?   First shot for you.   Look at that block forrad, and see how much chance you'll have if I fire at you." The pop of the revolver sounded, and then Hindhaugh went forward, pulling the Scorpion with him.   "Do you see that hole, you image ?   How would you like if that was your gizzard ?   Now, no games, my joker."

The Scorpion begged for time, and Hindhaugh was so sure of his man that he made no further objection.   He had another conference with Jack, and, to that worthy man's great delight, he expressed certain forebodings.

"We're going to have a fight over this job," said the skipper.   "I'm dead sure of it.   Go down and load the two muskets, and give them to the safest men.   When the lighters *do* come, borrow the firemen's iron rods.   I've lent the steward my bowie that I got at Charleston, and you can try and hold that old bull-dog straight.   We mustn't show the least sign of funking."

Then Hindhaugh and his brother called for tea and fed solidly.

The Scorpion whispered down the companion, "They'se been com'," and the captain went on deck.   Two large felucca-rigged lighters hove up slowly through the dusk, and the chief Scorpion's signal was answered.   Hindhaugh saw both lighters draw near, he felt the usual scraping bump, and then he heard a sudden thunder of many feet. The second mate sung out, "Here's half a hundred of these devils, sir.   They're all armed to the teeth."   And sure enough a set of ferocious-looking rapscallions had boarded the steamer.   They looked like low-class Irishmen, browned with walnut-juice.   Each man had a heavy array of pistols in his sash, and all of them carried ugly knives. The Scorpion waved to the gang, and they arranged themselves around the pile of bales that stuck out through the after-hatch. Hindhaugh had fully discounted all the chances, and had made up his mind to one thing—he wouldn't be "done."

The Scorpion imperiously observed, "Come below, Capeetan," and Hindhaugh went. Then the defiant native of the Rock put his back against the cabin door, heaved out his chest in a manly way, and said, "Now, Capeetan, you no have more money. You speak much and I'se been get your throat cut myself."

"You've got no money?"

"No; not a damn dollar."

"You won't keep to your bargain?"

"No. You come shore for your money, if you want him."

Hindhaugh made up his mind in a flash. In spite of his habit of wearing a frock-coat and tall hat, he was more than half a pirate, and he would have ruffled it, like his red-bearded ancestors, had fighting been still the usual employment of Norsemen. He marked his man's throat, and saw that the insolent hands could not get a knife quickly. Then he sprang at the Scorpion, gripped him by the wind-pipe, and swung him down. The fellow gurgled, but he couldn't cry out. Hindhaugh called the steward, and that functionary came out of his den with the long bowie. "Sit on him," said the captain. "If he stirs cut his throat. Now you; if you move a finger you're done." The steward straddled across the Scorpion, and held the knife up in a sarcastic way.

Hindhaugh went swiftly on deck, and stepped right among the jabbering Spaniards. He smiled as though nothing had happened, but when he saw one man lay hold of a bale, he pulled him back. "Tell them I'll shoot the first man that tries to lift a bale till I'm ready."

This message brought on a torrent of talk, which gave the captain time. He whispered to Jack, "Sneak you round through the engine-room. That lighter's made fast forrad; the second one's fast here. Get a hatchet from the carpenter, and set him alongside of the second rope. When

I whistle twice both of you nick the ropes, and we'll jink these swindling swine." The engineer also received orders to go full speed ahead on the instant that the whistle sounded.

Hindhaugh kept up his air of good humour, although the full sense of the risk he ran was in his mind. His threat of shooting had made the Spaniards suspicious, although they were used to big talk of the kind. One peep into the cabin would have brought on a collision, and although the Englishmen might have fought, there was nothing to gain by a fight. Everything depended on swiftness of action, and Hindhaugh determined grimly that if rapidity could do anything he would teach the "furriners" a lesson for trying to swindle him.

He said, very politely, "We're all ready now. You get your men aboard the lighters, and we'll soon rush your cargo over the side." This was transmitted to the smugglers, and immediately they swarmed aboard their own boats. They had rather expected a quarrel, and this pacific solution pleased them. As Jack afterwards said, "They blethered like a lot o' wild geese."

All the foreigners were gone but three. Hindhaugh stepped quietly up to the interpreter, and said, very low, " I'm covering you with my revolver from inside my pocket. Don't you stir. Is that other money going to be paid ?"

The interpreter had been innocent of all knowledge of the wild work in the cabin. He stammered, "I thought by your way it was all right. Where's our man ?"

"I've got him safe enough. Ask those fellows in the lighters if any of them can pay the freight for the job. If you tell them to fire they may miss me, and I can't miss you."

No one, not even the consignee's man, had any money ; the smugglers meant to trick the Revenue and the English captain as well. Hindhaugh whistled ; and then roared out, "Lie down all of you. Ram her ahead." The hatchets went crack, crack ; the steamer shuddered and plunged forward ; and the lighters bumped swiftly astern.

"Over the side, you animals, or I'll take you out to sea and drown you."

The three Spaniards rushed to the side, and took flying

leaps into the lighters ; Hindhaugh stooped low and ran to
the companion. " Let that beggar up," he shouted. The
Scorpion scuttled on deck. " Now, mister, I'll let you see
if you'll take me in. Over you go. Over the stern with
you, and mind the propeller doesn't carve you." Two
shots were fired, but they went wild. The Scorpion saw
the whole situation ; he poised for a second on the rail and
then jumped for it, and Hindhaugh laughed loudly as his
enemy came up blowing. Jack performed a triumphal
war-dance on the steamer's bridge, and the *Jenny Jones* was
soon far out of pistol range.

All that night Captain Hindhaugh did not sleep a wink.
He was quite persuaded that he had acted the part of an
exemplary Briton. What is the use of belonging to the
ruling race if a mere foreigner is to do as he likes with you ?
But the adventurous skipper had landed himself in a pretty
mess, and the full extent of his entanglement grew on him
every minute. At twelve o'clock, when the watch was relieved, Jack came aft in a state of exultation that words
cannot describe. He chuckled out, " Well, sir, we've made
our fortunes this time." Hindhaugh damped his spirits by
saying slowly, "Not too fast, that baccy's got to go overboard, my boy." Jack's mental processes became confused.
He had been measuring the cubic content of the smuggled
goods, and the thought of wasting such a gift of the gods
fairly stunned him. Had it been cotton his imagination
would not have been touched. But baccy ! and overboard !
It was too much, and he groaned. He was ready with
expedients at once.

" Why not run it to Holland ?"

"Can't be done ; where's our Bill of Lading ?"

"Make one up yourself ; you have plenty of forms."

" And suppose the luck goes the wrong way. What's to
happen to me—and to you too, for that matter ?"

" Run to a tobacco port and warehouse the stuff in your
own name."

" We're not bound for a tobacco port. What's to be done
about the cargo of ore that we're carrying ? No, John ; the
whole five thousand pounds must go over the side."

Next morning broke joyously. The sea looked merry
with miles of brisk foam, and the little Portuguese schooners

flew like butterflies hither and thither. Every cloud of
spray plucked from the dancing crests flashed like white
fire under the clear sun ; it was one of the mornings when
one cannot speak for gladness. But Hindhaugh's thoughts
were fixed on material things. The rich bales lay there,
and their presence affected him like a sarcasm. The men
were called aft, and the shovels used for trimming grain
were brought up. Then the captain said, "Now each
of you take a pound or two of this tobacco, and then break
the bales and shovel the rest overboard." The precious
packages were burst, and the sight of the beautiful leaf, the
richness of the tender aroma, affected the sailors with
remorse. It was like offering up a sacrifice. But the
captain's orders were definite, so until near noon the shovels
were plied smartly, and one hundredweight after another of
admirable tobacco drifted away on the careless sea.

Hindhaugh watched grimly until at last his emotions
overcame him. He growled, "Confound it, I can't do it.
Belay there, men, I'll have another think over this job."
And think he did with business-like solemnity all day long.
He saw that he might make a small fortune by risking his
liberty, and the curious morality of the British sailor
prevented him from seeing shades of right or wrong where
contraband business was concerned. Had you told him
that the tobacco was stolen he would have pitched you
overboard ; he felt his morality to be unimpeachable ; it
was only the question of expediency that troubled him.
For three days it was almost unsafe to go near him, so
intently did he ponder and plan. On the fifth day he had
worked his way through his perplexities, and was ready
with a plan. A pilot cutter came in sight, and Hindhaugh
signalled her. The pilot's boat was rowed alongside, and
the bronzed and dignified chief swaggered up to the captain
with much cordiality. No one is so cordial as a pilot who
has secured a good ship. The two men exchanged news,
and gradually slid into desultory talk. Suddenly Hindhaugh said, "Are you game for a bit of work ? Do you
ever do anything ?" The pilot was virtuously agitated.
He drew himself up and, taking care that the mate should
hear, answered, "Me ! Not for the wurr-rld, Cap'n. I've
got a wife and children, sir."

"All right, Pilot, never mind; come down and have some tea."

Then Hindhaugh gradually drew his man out, until the pilot was absolutely confidential. The captain knew by the very excess of purity expressed in the pilot's first answer that he was not dealing with a simpleton, but he carefully kept away from the main subject which was in his (and the pilot's) mind. At last the man leaned over and gave a masonic sign. "What was that job you was speaking about, Cap'n ? We're near home now, you know. Better not go too near."

Hindhaugh played a large card. He said carelessly, "Fact is, I've just told the fellows to shy the stuff overboard ; I shall risk no more."

"Mercy me, Cap'n. You're mad. How did I know who you were ? I see all about it now, but I did not know what game you might have on with me. I'm in it, you know, if the dimes is right ?"

"How ?"

"Why, if the job's big enough ; you stand off for a day. Go down to the Sleeve, and hang round, and I'll find you a customer."

"If you do, I pay you three hundred pounds as soon as his money's down."

"Done then. My boat's not gone far. Whistle her and I'll go slap for Bristol. Never you mind for a day or two. How's your coals ?"

"They're all right. You scoot now and fetch your man over this way. I'll go half-speed to the sou'-west for twelve hours, another twelve hours half-speed back. You'll find us."

In thirty-six hours the pilot-cutter came back, and a Hebrew gentleman boarded the *Jenny Jones* from her. After a long inspection the visitor said, "Now look here, I must have a hundred per cent. margin out of this. What's your figure ?"

"Two thousand five hundred."

"Won't do. Say two thousand, and you pay the jackal out of that."

"Done. And how do you manage ?"

"I'll split the lot up among three trawlers. You wait off

and give the jackal an extra fifty for bringing the boats
down. I risk the rest."

Another night passed, and the dawn was breaking coldly
when the dirty sails of the trawlers came in sight. Ship
after ship had hailed Hindhaugh, and offered to tow him if
anything had happened his engines. He knew he would
be reported as lying off, apparently disabled, and he was in
a feverish state of excitement. The Hebrew speculator
watched the last bale down the side, and then handed over
the money, had a glass of brandy with the pilot, and
departed—whither, Hindhaugh neither knew nor cared.
The *Jenny Jones* ran for her port. She had just slowed
down, and the great waves of smoke from the town were
pouring over her, when two large boats, heavily laden with
men, came off to her. The men swarmed up the side, and
the officer in command shouted, "Bring up the pickaxes,
and go to work." The hatches were pulled off before the
steamer had taken up her moorings, and the men went
violently to work among the ore. Hindhaugh looked innocent and inquired, "What's all this about, officer?"

"Fact is, captain, we've got a telegram from Gibraltar
to say you have contraband aboard. You may save all
trouble if you make a clean breast."

"Contraband? Who told you that?"

"Oh, we should have known without the wire. That
gentleman on the quay there came overland, and he put us
up to you."

Hindhaugh looked ashore, and saw a dark face that he
knew well. He whistled and smiled. Then he said to the
officer, "You may just as well stop those poor beggars from
blistering their hands. You won't find anything here
except what the men have in the forecastle. You're done
this journey fairly. Come away down and liquor, and I'll
tell you all about it." Then Hindhaugh gave an artistic
account of the whole transaction, and put the matter in such
a light that the Custom-house officer cordially congratulated
him on having escaped without a slit weasand.

The *Jenny Jones* went back to Gibraltar, and Captain Hindhaugh was very careful never to go ashore without a
companion. One day he was passing a chandler's shop
when a sunken glitter of dark eyes met him. His old

acquaintance, the chief Scorpion, was looking stilettoes and poison at him. But Hindhaugh went by in his big, burly way, and contented himself with setting on three watchmen every night during his stay. To this day he is pleased with himself for having given the foreigners a lesson in the elements of morality, and he does not fear their knives one whit.

III.

MISS ANN.

YOUNG SQUIRE LONGHIRST was walking up and down over a path that led through the woods. Every pose of his body and every change of his face betokened deficient self-control. He was a handsome fellow, but his loose mouth and the insolent lines of his nostrils gave an unpleasant impression. As he clinched his fist, and ground with his sharp step on the gravel, he looked like a wild creature. Presently he said, "I must speak ;" and then, with the forlorn inconsequence of men whose faculties have been grievously stunned, he repeated, "I must speak, I must speak." His walk lasted till the night had nearly gone, and the pale grey of the dawn quivered coldly up over the far-away hills. He went silently into the house, and flung himself down on a bed without undressing. He seemed unable to sleep ; his hands twitched ; and at last he sprang to the bell and rang. When the servant appeared the Squire said, " Bring breakfast here. I will see no one to-day. Tell Rodgers to saddle the brown horse, and bring him round to the Sea Walk." Longhirst rode moodily down the path, with his hands still maintaining their nervous motion. Presently the figure of a girl appeared under the trees, on the left side of the broad path.

The morning was bright, and she herself seemed like the very spirit of brightness and joy. Her fair hair fell over her shoulders in the curious ringlets that were fashionable long ago. She carried her head erect, and under the quaint gipsy bonnet her brown eyes looked with a quiet expression. Longhirst's twitching hands clinched again when he saw her, and he drew his horse straight across the path and sat looking upon her, while she trembled and waited to be allowed to pass. By a sudden movement the man sprang from his horse and stepped forward, holding out his hands with a kind of appeal which was in touching contrast with the savage fixity of his face. The girl said, " Mr. Long-hirst, may I go on ?"

He caught his breath, and answered, "Give me your hand, Ann. This cannot be. Look at me. I cannot sleep all night for thinking of what you have said, and I have come this morning to ask you once more."

"You pain me, Mr. Longhirst. What you wish might have been, but you know best my reason now for asking you not to meet me again."

He started once more, with the strange convulsive move-ment that shows when a man has lost control of nerve and temper alike. "Good God! Do you want me to kill my-self? You know what I am. You know what I dare do."

"I know too well what you dare do and what you are, Mr. Longhirst. I ask you as an honourable gentleman to force yourself upon me no more. Surely you must see that there is something gross in carrying on a pursuit which I am bound to discourage."

"My dear, I must die if I am out of your sight. Why should you listen to what is said? Suppose that every story is true. Suppose that I have been bad. Has the sight of you not made me better? You are cool and calm. Oh! you are very virtuous. You thrust me from you like a dog. Where am I to go if I am out of your sight? On the one side of my life there is your face ; and on the other side there is death."

This outburst did not affect the girl. Her nerves were steady now, and she said, "All this is unseemly. If I were a man I would not lower myself to speak such childish things as that, and it is just because you are not more of a man that I gave you my answer yesterday. For the last time : It cannot be. You tire too quickly of things, and I cannot trust my life with you."

He placed his hand on the horse's mane, and set the spurs hard in. The horse shuddered and plunged, and then struck into a mad gallop that led in the direction of the sands. The fierce rider sat steadily until the heavy sand completely tired the startled animal.

The young girl's name was Ann Braithwaite, and she had refused Squire Longhirst, although certain gallant qualities in the vain and foolish young man had drawn her to him. Perhaps in time she would have forgiven him for excesses of a venial kind, but a miserable scandal that had come to light during the last month had made his name the talk of the whole country-side. She only knew vaguely what the scandal had been; but her aunt's look of gravity and the hints that constantly recurred were sufficient to scare her.

On the morning after Longhirst had set off on his gallop across the sands Miss Ann's aunt entered the breakfast-room and said, "This is a terrible business. Do you know what has happened Squire Longhirst? He hung himself last night in his own barn."

A spot of red burnt on each of Miss Ann's cheeks; but the rest of her face was pale, and she rose and went out of the room. All that day she sat looking over the hills, and spoke to no one. When the night came she knelt down, and as she arose her face seemed to have taken a new expression—an expression that never left it. Week after week she went about her ordinary pursuits, but her aunt noticed that she was a little strange. She was very kind to dumb animals, and she showed an exaggerated fondness for children. When a year had passed over she said to her aunt one day, "Aunt dear, I wish we could go away from here." It made very little difference to the older lady where she stayed, and, sure enough, within six months the Braithwaites had moved to a little village twenty miles further down the coast.

Forty years passed over, and I then became acquainted with a certain delightful old maid who lived in an old-fashioned farmhouse about five miles over the moor. Nobody in the village thought much of her second name, for she was generally mentioned as Miss Ann. I got my first sight of her one bright morning. A prim little lady was walking up and down amongst the flower-beds in front of the farmhouse. She bent over her flowers tenderly now and then, as though she loved them. Her perfect figure was dressed in a style that had long been forgotten. She wore a narrow gown, very high at the waist, and her shoulders were covered by a curious cape. Her head was bare, and I could see that she had not merely traces of good looks but considerable beauty. Her mouth had a humorous cast, and her eyes twinkled kindly under delicate brows. Her hands were long and white, and I shall never forget the dainty movements of her fingers as she tied up the drooping roses and lifted the heads of the heavy peonies. Two fat old spaniels walked about with an air of dignity over the paths, and some four or five tortoiseshell cats disposed themselves in sunny positions. When Miss Ann had seen that all her flowers were rightly placed to take their joy of the sun she went indoors, and proceeded to move briskly about from room to room. She belonged to the era when culture was not thought necessary for young ladies ; but all the work of the household she could superintend with a tact and vivacity which made the place delightful to enter. In the afternoon she put on a strange old bonnet, from which her dainty face appeared as from a cavern, and sallied forth with a little basket. She went first to old Betty's house, and entered without knocking. The old woman looked up and said, " Miss Ann, come thy ways here and sit down."

Miss Ann said, " Oh ! Betty, you have been smoking again. I wish I could cure you of that habit. You know you are sure to shorten your life with it, and I am told by very good authorities that it stops the growth."

Betty looked sympathetic. " Ah ! well ; I am seventy-six gone April, and if it does shorten my life a bit, Miss Ann, there will be nobody very much the worse."

" Well, and pray why should you not live till ninety ? But I am not going to scold, for I have something in my basket for you ;" and then Miss Ann took out a very neat parcel of tobacco.

She then went on to Mrs. Turnbull's, where a swarm of children insisted upon forming around her. She proceeded to address them according to their deserts.

Mrs. Turnbull stood by and smiled approvingly, and the youngsters smiled with still more approval when a number of little packets came out of the basket. Then Miss Ann turned to go home. On her way she met Big Bill, the fisherman, and that giant gazed at her kindly. He took off his sou'-wester, and, in spite of the somewhat critical air which his height gave him, managed to put on an appearance of extreme respect.

"It's a brave mornin', Miss Ann. I've got the finest turbot there, down at the boat, that ever you saw in your life ; and I says to Mary, I says, this mornin', you take that over to Miss Ann ; and now I'll walk down with you and see if it's there, and if it's not I'll go and fetch him myself."

One after another of the villagers met Miss Ann, and each showed the same curious respect, mingled with familiarity. She was given to making the most stringent inquiries into the antecedents of scores of men and women who asked for help, but the sternness of the cross-examination was always followed by a gift of one kind or other. Ferocious moralists declared that Miss Ann demoralized the beggars ; but it was a very odd thing that, although her hen roost was always unlocked, and although the chickens wandered over the hills and the moor, she was never troubled by theft of any kind.

It was a strange and solitary life for a woman to lead, but somehow or other she seemed to have her consolations. Every Sunday her quaint figure could be seen in church, and although she knew the Rector's sermons all by heart, the sound of the music and the quiet drone of her old friend the preacher seemed to give her constant gratification. Her life had flowed on for so many years that it seemed as though nothing, save the interruption of death, could ever cause any change in the beautiful passage of her days.

But there is no spot in the world that is safe from turmoil. One morning a neighbouring farmer, who was also the local preacher of the district, came to Miss Ann as she was tending her flowers, and asked to speak with her for a few minutes. He said, "There's a queer kind of a tramp fellow along at my house. He seems to have had a little too much to drink, but he wants to see you very particularly, and so I'll keep him quiet until he is fit to meet you. I never met such a man on the road before. He has been entertaining my lads with showing off his scholarship. He read a chapter of the Greek Testament with the book held upside down, and he can translate my boy's ' Virgil '

15

and some French poetry as well. He is very ragged and
very much done with the drink, so I'll try and make him
presentable before he shows himself here."

Miss Ann said, "Had not you better come with him?"
and the farmer at once consented. Next day a strange,
shambling creature trailed his feet over Miss Ann's trim
garden path, and found his way into her pretty sitting-
room. The canaries were briskly moving in their cages,
fresh flowers were placed all about the room, and everything looked bright and wholesome. In the midst of it all
a sodden and bleary creature sat staring sulkily on the
ground. The fellow had a high, white forehead, but his
hair was ragged and dead, and his mouth looked cruel and
sensual. The ugly blotches on his cheeks told the tale of
long excesses, and his hands trembled as though he had
not had his accustomed stimulus to begin the day with.
When Miss Ann entered he looked at her and said, "I
would not let Harrison come in with me. I wanted to see
you alone. Do you know me?"

Miss Ann said sharply, "May I inform you that you do
not speak in a respectful manner? If you have anything
to say, say it and begone. If I can help you, tell me how
I can do so. I have learned something about your habits,
and although you have fallen so low I should not like to
turn you away. But please to remember that I allow
insults from no one."

"Stop a minute, my lady, stop a minute. I've got something that will perhaps bring you to your senses."

He took out a ragged purse and produced a dirty scrap
of folded paper. He then looked up with his bleared eyes
and said, "Did you know Jack Longhirst?"

Miss Ann sat down, and clasped her hands without
answering.

He said, "I see that touches you up. Now, look here,
if I happen to show this bit of paper round the village it
will make things look very awkward for you. I have got
my price, and I will keep out of your way if you pay
You may fancy that affair is altogether forgotten, but Jack
left something for me before he killed himself, and I know
that you of all others would not like it to be seen."

Miss Ann said, "You are wicked. I trust your heart

may be softened. You have hurt me, who never did you harm. I suppose you are the man that I once knew as Mr. Paulin. Do you think a threat will touch me? I am past sorrow. I live my life mechanically, and when I am dead I will leave no one to grieve for me excepting the poor. How could your exposure, whatever it may be, hurt me? My reputation is dear to no one. If you take it away, what good can it do to you? Show me how I can keep you from living wickedly. Show me how I can make you less like a remnant of manhood, and I will do it for the sake of the times when you were strong and pure, and for the sake of the man whose name you have just spoken."

Paulin was sorry. He looked shamefaced, and began to apologize. "I didn't mean any harm, but the drink's in me now, and I'm cankered and miserable."

Miss Ann said, "Can you work?"

"Well, I never was very good at that."

"But would you not rather work than starve?"

"Yes, if you'll tell me what kind of work it is."

"Then you shall stay in this house. There are many things you can do, and you must consent to forget what you have been; but remember that if you threaten again, or if you mention our dead friend's name again, you part from me, and I will let you do the worst you choose."

Then the resolute little woman stood up and faced the miserable creature. He said, "I will do my best," and so the strange bargain was completed in few words. Miss Ann sent Paulin, under the care of a friend, to the market town, and he came back clothed and looking something like a respectable servant. Within a few months Miss Braithwaite had completely mastered the drunkard. Once or twice he broke away when he managed to get a few pence, and, after drinking himself stupid, returned to be forgiven and to make abject promises. At last circumstances arose that made a great change in him. Miss Ann was a strict Churchwoman. She believed there could be no salvation out of the Prayer Book, but, at the same time, she could not shut her eyes to the marvellous improvement that had been wrought in the village by the Revivalists. One Sunday evening a strange whim took her. She walked

15—2

out into the kitchen, where Paulin was moodily preparing to make his round of the gardens and stables, and said, "You can get George to do that for to-night, and you come with me."

A little while after the congregation of fishermen, who had met for their ordinary worship, were greatly startled and flattered by the appearance of Miss Ann's quaint figure. She sat down amongst the women and motioned Paulin to a seat by the side of her friend, Big Bill. When the hymn had been sung and the prayer finished the sermon began. Had one of the rude fishermen been preaching, Paulin would not have been touched ; but his gentlemanly instinct still survived in him, despite all the degradation through which he had come, and the unconscious refinement of the preacher's speech was grateful to him. Presently the good man grew animated, and exerted the magic that always drew his hearers together and caused them to forget themselves. He had finished a passionate appeal, delivered with magnificent gestures and complete self-abandonment, when the drunkard stood up and burst into hysterical crying. The fishermen were not much surprised, for they had seen the same thing take place with much stronger men than Paulin. Two of them took him out into the open air and soothed him. When the sermon was over Miss Ann nervously followed. She felt that she had done a strange thing in coming to the conventicle at all, and the sudden outburst of her curious hanger-on had affected her even more than the extraordinary eloquence of the Revivalist. Paulin followed the lady home, and remained silent all the rest of the evening. Next morning he asked if he might have the whole day free, and, when consent was given, he walked over the Moor to the preacher's cottage, and found the good man sitting outside. What his thoughts were no one knew. Probably he did not know himself. He started with pleasure as Paulin shuffled towards him. Miss Ann's servant said, "I have come all this way to shake your hand, and then I am going away again. I shall never forget —never—and you will see that I will not be a child any more."

From that day forth Miss Ann was astonished at the extraordinary industry displayed by the man whom she had saved. Nothing was too hard for him, and he seemed to take a delight in exerting himself about trifles which might easily have been left undone. Had he spoken much, and made many professions, she would have feared that another bout of drunkenness might soon come. It so strangely happens that as soon as we have expressed a resolution aloud the very power of keeping to our resolve seems to be lessened ; but Paulin became positively saturnine. He tried to anticipate his mistress's wishes. He did little things with a delicacy and foresight that showed pathetic memories of high breeding. He had been a sot, but he never could become ill-mannered. Perhaps on the face of the earth no stranger thing could have been seen than this companionship between a rich lady and a man who had bowed to her, who had met her on equal terms, who had made pretty speeches to her, nearly half a century before. With her rigorous notions, Miss Ann hardly cared to grant that this change had been wrought outside the orthodox fold, and she used to hold comic little arguments with certain villagers on the question. But she was quite contented with results. Every Sunday she walked in her rich brocade and her old head-gear, while Paulin followed her, respectfully bearing the one tiny hymn-book which served the fishermen to sing from. The rough men and women of the village made much of the convert, and his appearance under the influence of temperance and regularity began to grow more and more refined as his hair grew more and more grey. They never tempted him with drink of any kind, for indeed the practice of drinking had completely died away during the long revival. Some of them who had a shrewd guess as to his antecedents spoke about him among themselves, but they never reminded him that they knew him for anything but a man-servant, and they sometimes made fun of him about his luck in having fallen across an eccentric like Miss Ann. One bitter winter night, when Paulin had taken his accustomed seat in the kitchen after chapel, he shivered a little. The cook suggested that he should take some spirits and get to sleep, but he shook his hands violently, and said, "No, no ; not now, of all times. I have kept clear all these years, and now I know that my time is over."

In the morning he was ill, and during the day he asked to see Miss Ann. He was laid out on a settle in the kitchen, and she came in and seated herself in her proud, erect attitude close by him. He was dressed, and fumbled in his pocket for a little. After looking at his mistress with that odd look of almost canine fidelity which had lately come over his face, he took from his purse the ragged slip of paper which he had first shown to Miss Ann in his desperation. He raised himself uneasily, and said, "See you. I am going to send that on to Jack Longhirst now. When he gets it he will know I am not far off." He held the paper slowly against the bars until it was burnt to ashes. He then waved his hands, and said, "There ! Jack will be pleased to see that." And then Miss Ann saw that he was wandering. There was something in his look and something in his feebleness that alarmed her, and the curious madness of his action in burning the paper touched her superstition. She left orders that he should be tended, and when she went back to her sitting-room she sat down and burst into tears.

Everybody says that truth is stranger than fiction, but the saying is one of the commonplaces that are not sufficiently believed. Those who have followed my little story will fancy that I am now about to tell them of the death of Paulin. But that is not so. Miss Ann was strangely restless all day, and it was only when the doctor assured her that nothing serious ailed the man that she settled into calm. At night the wind began to rise, and the sea roared hoarsely in the hollows of the rocks. She could not sit in one place, and finally, with a movement as of desperation, she went to her room and opened an old writing-case which always lay on a table by her bedside. She said, "I wonder if it is still there ;" and presently, with her long trembling fingers, she loosed her dress and took out a pretty locket which contained a portrait. She dared not look at it until she reached the brightness of the sitting-room ; but there, with the companionship of the fire and her birds, she gained courage to look at the face. Her hand grew steady, and her face seemed suddenly to be touched with the beauty of youth. She murmured, "Oh ! John Longhirst, how ill I used you ; but I have suffered, my dear, oh ! I have suffered. Fifty-seven years now—fifty-seven years I have lived away from you, and all because of foolish talk. And they said you were bad, my dear; but I shall know the truth about you very soon. You could not think I had kept this, and I could hardly think it myself. Fifty-seven years since I looked at it. Fifty-seven years I have borne the world. You shall stay on my heart to-night, my own love."

When she had finished talking low to herself her face and her forehead were flushed. Paulin's sudden madness had startled her out of herself. She wrote a few words on a sheet of paper, and the servants saw her no more that night. In the morning she was long in rising, and the maids grew alarmed, for they had been used to hear her quick step before the dawn, even in the winter time. At last one girl suggested that the Preacher should be sent for. He came with a friend, and waited until noon. Then, finding that the lady still did not stir, he removed the shutters and broke in the window. Ann Braithwaite was lying with her eyes closed. The few wrinkles on her face were emphasized by her grey pallor, but her beautiful hair, which had never changed colour, seemed to surround her dead face with a lovely suggestion of youth. When they opened her right hand they found a miniature clasped in the stiffened fingers, and they saw that the portrait was that of a truculent and handsome young man, whose long hair flowed downwards in the fashion of the gentlemen of another generation. They buried her, and all the village followed her to the grave, although the churchyard was far enough away to tire the old people. Her house was closed, but she had left provision for all her servants, and they scattered themselves in various places. The strangest being of her household struggled passionately, and besought his nurses to let him follow her coffin, because he said he would be quite content to die; but they forbade him, and he grew well again. For six months after her death a bowed and shuffling figure would steal into the churchyard day by day. One cold night some men of another village were passing among the graves on their way from the public-house. A collie who accompanied one of them stopped, howling dismally, and refused to come on. One of the men said,

"See what ails the dog, Ned." A shout called the whole company back, and there they saw the dog still howling, by the side of a man who was stretched on Miss Ann's grave. They turned him over, and one of them said, "That is Miss Braithwaite's daft servant." Another lifted his arm, and let it go. The arm fell with a thud, and the countryman said, "Well, he will never be daft any more."

IV

THE TWO CAPTAINS.

Two lads were brought up together in one of those pretty villages that lie to the northward of the Tyne. The place where the boys lived consisted of a few white sandstone houses which straggled along a low cliff. The back doors of the cottages all opened toward the sea, and you could have jumped right into the cove from the roof of one of the coal-houses if you had cared to try. Away to the west-ward were deep woods, and to the north and south the rolling links stretched away for mile upon mile. It was a wild, healthy place, and most of the children born there grew up to be fine, powerful folks. There was so much to tempt a lad out of doors. When the tide came up and began to roll into the little pools among the rocks there were always flounders and crabs, and pretty sea-minnows to be caught if you took the trouble to wade. Then, in summer there were scores of copses and hedgerows where the swarm-ing birds built their nests, and you could festoon your rooms with strings of blown eggs if your fancy lay that way. At night the rabbits crept from their deep holes in the great sandhills, and sidled through the ferns till they reached the rich grass on the westerly side of the pathway. By walking along the beach, and leading a terrier quietly over the hills, you could cut the rabbits off from their refuge, and you had all the fierce joy of the chase when your dog skimmed over the green and the white tails went bobbing about with frantic speed. No wonder the freckled children looked hard and healthy. Certainly there was no lack of open-air fun for them.

Tom Weatherburn and Jack Winter lived near each other,

and they were constant companions. Every morning they set off to school together, with their white wallets tied over their shoulders, for the distance was too great to allow of their coming home to dinner, and they carried a bottle of milk and some bread and meat with them. They seldom fought more than once on the road, so it will be seen that they were very friendly indeed. In the evening they slung their shoes and stockings round their necks and raced home over the hard road without appearing to mind the chance of hitting their toes against the broken whinstone. They caught the fishermen just going off for the night, and sometimes they were allowed to go in the trouting-boats for an hour or two. While the coble lay inside the nets the lads would watch the vessels scudding north and south, and they soon learned to know the rig of every ship that passed. They never heard any talk that did not refer in some way or other to the sea, and the thoughts of the boys continually dwelt on the mystery that lay beyond the ring of the horizon. They sometimes saw the fishing-boats fade away in the east when the evening shadows fell, and they often spoke of the time when they would sail out there and see strange countries. The possibility of living permanently on shore was not conceivable to these two wild young people. They were of nearly the same age, and when their twelfth birthdays drew near they began to fidget a good deal, and spoke much to their parents about their wish to go away south. So one spring morning the miller's mare was harnessed to the market-cart, and old Adam Weatherburn and his friend Jack Winter drove with their sons to the black little port that lay eight miles southward of the village. The boys came back rather repentant from their trial voyages, but Jack didn't want to seem sheepish in Tom's eyes, and Tom had the same thoughts about Jack, so they signed their indentures gallantly, and fixed themselves for five years on board two Baltic traders. In a year's time both the lads landed home, and they were already beginning to look like men so far as sailorly swagger was concerned. Then came a second long spell of the sea and of lodgings, and the youngsters paid yet another visit together. They were smart sailors by that time, and the girls turned round to look at them. They wore flat caps with low peaks, blue trousers, which were very wide over the boots, and rough blue jackets. A sarcastic gardener said that they walked " as if they wanted to let a pig run through their legs ;" but this was only his comic way of describing the orthodox sailorly roll. They were really two fine young fellows, and though their long hair would not have suited a naval officer's notions of trimness, the thick, hanging locks somehow seemed quite in keeping with the pretty, old-fashioned sailor's dress. There are no sailorly fashions nowadays ; the men go ashore anyhow, and I have met shellbacks who outraged my better nature by wearing billycock hats. If I met an able seaman who wore a frock coat in the very face of day, I should not be surprised.

Jack got through his apprenticeship without any mishap ; but Tom's career was interrupted for a short while. The old *Arethusa*, in which he sailed, made a southerly trip for a change. She got into bad weather at Flamborough, and the wind and sea grew stronger as she worked south. It fell thick, and the old brig blundered along through it till she suddenly ran her nose against Yarmouth Sands. She broke her back in half-an-hour, and the crew had to be taken off by the lifeboat. Tom came home dressed in a pair of old trousers and a sleeved waistcoat. These articles of attire constituted his whole worldly possessions ; but his mother was only too glad to see him safe in any rig whatever. He laughed at her when she cried about his danger, and clapped her heavily on the back, which salutation was his substitute for kissing. In a fortnight he shipped on board another vessel in the same employ, and finished his time there.

While Weatherburn and Winter were able seamen they often came home. They never would ship unless the skipper would take both of them ; and most captains were only too glad to have such a pair of seamen. When they came off a voyage they kept the whole place alive, and the servants up at the Hall nearly always took a fancy for the sea air when the two bronzed sailor-men had been seen about the village. The woods are very lonely, and if the girls sometimes needed to be escorted homeward it was only natural in the sailors to volunteer. The dark arches of the trees were enough to frighten anybody, and very often the young ladies grew so nervous that they had to be reassured and comforted. Then there would be some giggling, and Martha, the still-room maid, used to say, "I never did see anything like the forwardness of them sailors." But Martha and the other girls were not altogether displeased, and all the young people had a very pleasant time of it.

As Jack and his friend grew older they became ambitious and serious. When the two years which they were required to serve as able seamen had expired they had some grave talk together. One night Jack said, "Look here, old 'un, do you know neither of us has got any money ?"

Tom soberly replied, "I stood the beers at Shields out of my last sovereign."

Jack considered, and finally proposed a plan. "We can't go on before the mast, my boy. Now look here, we've got to learn some navigation, and we can't do it in the blowed forecastle. Let's toss up and see who's to go to sea. If you win, then I go, and you stop at home. I'll leave you my half-pay, and you go to school and scuffle on the best way you can. If I win, you go to sea and leave me *your* half-pay."

"Right you are. It's all one to me, my son."

So a penny was spun, and by this mystic test it was decided that Jack must go. And go he did for a long while, and all the time Weatherburn drew the half-pay, and toiled painfully on at book-work until he was almost fit to pass for captain. He got his mate's ticket very easily, and soon afterwards Jack came home. Then Tom went away as mate with £5 a month, and his friend stayed on shore and stuck over his big navigation slate all day for nearly three months. The two good fellows did not need to share in this way when their time came to pass for master. Five pounds a month was fair money in those days, and a man could save out of it. They got their masters' certificates, and Jack went away with a big barque to New Orleans, while Tom ran to Sulina in a smart brig. They seldom met for several years, but they remained fond of each other. Weatherburn used to say, "Winter's the best sailor between here and Shanghai, and I'll back him ;" Winter often said, " Eh, man, if Tom didn't try so much to pull the masts out of them, he would be the smartest chap I know."

By-and-by Weatherburn got command of a steamer and drew £16 a month, but his chum didn't envy him at all. He said, " Ay, the beggar won't have the chance to carry away no more suits of sails ;" and with this grim expression of admiration Jack's comment ended. Weatherburn grew quite genteel in his habits. When he walked down the main street in Shields you never saw such a swell in your life. Winter met him once, and Tom was wearing buff gloves, a grey tie, and a silk hat. Jack quietly observed, " Man, I feel as if I was walking alongside of a sunflower. What a gay bird you've turned." But nothing shook the quiet, mutual affection of the two men, and they admired each other more than ever. Once when Winter had taken dinner with Weatherburn, Tom blushed and said, " I say, Jack, do you know it isn't proper to put peas into your mouth with a knife ? I only learned that with seein' the swell fellows you know, so I'm not puttin' airs on." Jack was not vexed. He only replied, " Hoots, man. It looks so hungry-like to ram them into your mouth with a spoon." Tom explained that a fork was the orthodox weapon, and Winter was puzzled. In short, the two captains could say almost anything without fear of breaking their friendship, and they had no secrets between themselves, excepting about one thing.

There was a girl in the village who was liked by both of the men. She treated them much like brothers, and neither of them had ever said any word to her excepting what passed in ordinary chat.

Jenny was hardly the kind of girl whom you would have selected as being likely to please sailors, for she had none of the very pronounced charms that the simple fellows usually admire. She was slim, and her hands were long and white. Her face was rather pale, and only her mischievous eyes saved her from looking a little insipid. Insipid she certainly was not. Her father, a chief boatmen in the coastguard, had educated her fairly well, and besides book knowledge she had wit enough to set up two or three of the town dames. She could keep the two young fellows laughing for an hour together when they called to see her, and she could draw them out until they talked as only sailors can talk. When Weatherburn first wore a silk hat she teased him so delightfully that he put it on every time he went, only to set her joking again. While they were still mates she insisted on teaching them both to dance, and she brought the school-master's daughter down to help her. When Jack carried away two flower-pots from the inner window-sill, and said, " Hard a-starboard, Miss Jenny ; we've done damage," she sat down and laughed till the tears came into her eyes. Jack brought her two new flower-pots of a gaudiness un-paralleled in history after his next run from Bordeaux, and she said, " You *are* a kind boy." Then she put the new ornaments on the sill, and said "Hard-a-starboard" with such a pretty burlesque accent that Jack nearly lost his head on the spot.

Somehow the men never talked about the girl when they were away. Weatherburn brought her scent-bottles and Maltese lace ; Jack brought her a pretty pair of furred slippers and an elaborate cloak from Cronstadt, but the gifts were handed over in the most brotherly way. Poor Jack was really very hard hit, but he said to himself, " I believe Tom's going to hang up his hat there, and she likes him best ;" and Tom thought, " I'll wait and see what old Jack means to be up to."

The girl had hardly allowed herself to think definitely about the matter at all, although she and her father had both taken it for granted that she must marry one of the friends some day.

The two simpletons most concerned went on in their stupid way, always hovering on the verge of an explanation, and yet never explaining. Had they not been two straight, good-hearted men, the affair might have developed a quarrel ; but they were too large in nature and too essentially delicate to do anything petty. Both of them could swear hard, and drink hard when they chose, and neither of them was more spotless than sailors usually are ; but they had something of what people call " the gentleman " in them, and their perceptions in certain respects were fine. So they went on, living amid a perpetual crisis, and at last the crisis grew acute.

The captains had not seen each other for a good while. Jack was in a nice full-rigged ship, and Tom still commanded a steamer.

Tom's boat came out from Rouen one bad February day, and ran for Cardiff. She was light, and her rails were a tremendous distance out of the water. The weather became worse, and the steamer was almost unmanageable. The wind was northerly, and the ship showed such a side that it was barely possible to steer her. High as her rails were, she rolled them under, and the men aboard could not lie in their bunks. They had to squat on the floor to take their meals, and no one on board could wash, for a bucket wouldn't stand, and a basin simply emptied itself. The great, clumsy steamer knocked herself about for forty-eight hours, and Weatherburn bitterly repented having come out with nothing but his water-ballast; he made sure of losing the vessel. All the ships at the Foreland had slipped their anchors and run round, and the Channel was in about as ugly a humour as it well could be. The steamer decided to take her own way in the matter of steering, and the men grew sullen and almost hopeless. When things were nearly at their worst Weatherburn's mate came stumbling below and said, "Big vessel away on our starboard bow, sir. She's swept, by the look of it. Seems foundering." Weatherburn ran up with his glass and took a look. The ship was plunging anyhow, and was badly down by the stern; she could not lift herself, and she lunged like a mere floating hencoop. Weatherburn was in a nasty fix. It was all he could do to hold his own; if he went up to windward of the ship, his exasperating steamer might go off at any moment, and sink both herself and the distressed vessel; all he could do was to try somehow to get near. It was heart-breaking work. Again and again he struggled and dodged to fetch the boat's head to the north, and again and again she blew around like a cork. The engines were of scarcely any use, and Tom's heart sunk as he thought of leaving the men to drown. A slight lull gave him a chance, and he rammed his boat full speed ahead till he almost got within hail. As he got a good sight of the sailing-ship, he said, "Thank God for that, anyway! Damned if it isn't Jack!" He got hold of his trumpet, although he might have known it was of no use, and roared, "Hang on, old Tintacks. I'll stand by you till this old swine drowns us."

Hour after hour he strove, but the sea and the gale were too much for him. The engineer came up.

"Do you intend to keep on trying, sir? Mr. Toulmin thought the coals we had would serve us to Cardiff. We're short now."

Weatherburn turned grimly and said, "Look here. mister. If you were out there with them chaps and waving your shirt because your sticks was gone, how would you like for us to leave you?"

"I only asked if you would keep on trying, sir."

"Yes. I'll try and I'll try and I'll try all night, and start in the morning again. You go down and make them fire up, sir. Time enough for you to come up when we're going down."

By incessant effort and patient skill the steamer got within three hundred yards of the sinking vessel. Luckily, it is almost impossible to capsize a screw, let her be ever so light, or Tom's boat would certainly have turned turtle; certainly "she had enough temptations," as her master afterwards remarked. She lay and wallowed within easy distance of Jack's ship, and Weatherburn saw that he wasn't a minute too soon. He sung out, "You'll have to leave her, hinny. Drift down on us with your boat." And sure enough the ship's longboat was got out, and presently the whole crew were dangerously near the plunging steamer. It was neck or nothing, however, and something must be risked. Every man had to be hauled up that immense iron steep; sometimes the boat was completely under the tremendous sweep of the steamer's side; sometimes she was pitched right away among the smoking wreaths that crowned the swift seas. But the crew were brought on board, and Jack came last of all. Tom said, "Well, Boss. Did you think you would have your breakfast to-morrow? She pretty near did you. Look at her now." Jack smiled sadly and said, "All right, partner, I'll be even with you before we die. You'll have all you can do to save your own bacon now. Lord, Lord! to think I chaffed about you losin' your sails, and me to lose my masts with the same games. Get her away, old man."

Weatherburn did save his bacon, and that was all. The two friends went home together, but Jack only went once to see the girl. After a fortnight he called one night to see Tom, and the two lit their pipes.

At last Jack spoke. He said, "I'm off on Thursday, Tom."

"Where to? What the deuce? Why you haven't had time to get your clothes yet."

"I'm off. That West India chap's going to try a new lay. He's going to run the *Saghaline* between Shanghai and Hong Kong. Local trade, you know. I've taken her, and I'm away for five years."

"But I say, mister, what am I going to do? When you were up the Black Sea I always felt as if I could clap my hand on you, but Shanghai's a large order."

"It's better so, old man. You come over the bar with us, and I'll find you a bit o' baccy if you're good."

The friends parted soon after, and Jenny cried so much that Tom had a lot of trouble in consoling her.

Jack had bribed a Newcastle photographer to get a portrait of the girl, and he wore it round his neck. Every night he blushed at his own softness when he saw the thin chain on his breast, but he kept it there all the same. After poor Jack had been grilling out in China for two years he got a letter from Tom. The letter said, "I knew by your going away that you didn't care for her. I thought you did, and that's what made me hang off, for you know I would die for you like a shot. The affair comes off in a month, and I stop ashore a bit."

Jack went on deck that night and dropped his miniature overboard. "Can't be carryin' another chap's wife about," he growled. Then he said softly, "I'm glad old Tom didn't guess what I took this berth for. I swore I'd be evens with him. But, Lord! what a mess a girl can make of a fellow. I thought I should die. Good-bye, my woman."

Jack got home just in time to be godfather to Jenny's second son.

V.

THE SALVATIONIST.

THE pale curve of the pier looked ghostly and unsubstantial under the transforming moonbeams. The iron grimness of the daytime was gone, and the sweeping white road seemed like some strange pathway stretching far away toward the dreamy East. A great steady wind flowed over the bosom of the sea, and the winds and the waters, and the sailing clouds, and the silent ships formed one mystic procession, that seemed fleeting, fleeting, with soundless impalpable march, ever eastward. High over the silvered harbour the Castle ruins showed their stately delicacy against the clear hollow of the sky, and the swelling slopes were checkered where the shadows lay like dark pansies amid trembling motes of light.

The sordid and vulgar hills on the south were touched into beauty by the cold gleam, and every large sigh of the wind that breathed across the solemn flood struck the ripples into splendour, as though a sleet of diamonds had fallen. The houses looked asleep, the tender ripples inshore seemed murmuring in sleep, the dim expanse of the southerly bay swam before the gaze like a place seen in dreams. All things appeared to slumber under the lull of the magnetic night—all save the red eye of the lighthouse and that soundless procession of clouds and waters that went fleeting, fleeting, ever eastward.

A large barque glided softly down over the ebb, and the yelp of a Norwegian seaman who was hauling on a rope came over the water with its sharpness toned down to music; but this man's voice and the muffled clank of a winch were the only sounds that could be heard over the sleepy plash of ripples.

Thomas Lyell, second mate of the screw steamer *Starfire*, stood alone in the midst of that still glory, and he was wakeful enough in all conscience, for he had passed on that night through one of the experiences that change men's lives for ever.

Lyell was little more than an ordinary rough sailorman.

16

He had a fair schoolboy knowledge of books, and he could do his navigation according to approved rule of thumb methods ; but he knew nothing of finer emotions, and I rather fancy that he was even a trifle brutal. His life had been passed amid rude work and rude pleasures, and he behaved himself just as sailormen usually do. When the ship reached a foreign part he stuck to his duty all day, made himself abominably grimy, and used very bad language at the labourers, and at the order of the universe in general. When the time came for knocking off he washed himself, put on his cheesecutter cap, and went ashore without any intention of getting drunk. He usually half broke his virtuous resolution, and came up the ladder towards midnight in a friendly and garrulous humour ; but he never was silly enough to imitate the ill-balanced revellers who get into such a state that they have to sleep on the quay all night. He never believed in making himself so drunk that he couldn't scull the ship's boat off if necessary. At home he passed his evenings in the simple sailor fashion. If he had not drawn too much of his pay during the voyage he had one vigorous spree with his chums, and by the time his repentance was half completed the vessel was ready for sea again. He was a handsome, red-faced fellow, with strong, unrefined features, tangled beard, and deep chest. His hands were covered with cracks and horny excrescences, and when he was scrubbing decks with the men he showed a hairy, brown arm, on which the strenuous muscles rose like bulbs of steel. His morals were defective in purity, and his ordinary language had certain emphatic qualities which can only be acquired in full beauty by a long apprenticeship in the merchant service. I love sailors far too well to give any fancy portraits of them, so I have placed Lyell before you just as he was—fierce, brutal in some things, proud, dauntless to the last degree, lustful, heavy-handed— a man all over, with a man's sins, and a man's kindness.

And now we must see why this shaggy, healthful Titan was mooning about on the pier and muttering to himself at that irregular hour of night.

Lyell had been strolling about from bar to bar, taking whisky with one friend after another, when he happened to pass a long building like a tall shed. A great clamour came to his ears. He heard shouts, groans, blurred and inarticulate yells, and women's voices sounding with notes of pain. High over all the muffled tumult one clear, full cry rose again and again with sonorous triumph.

Lyell said, "Come in here, Jimmy. There's some fun on ;" and the two friends entered. A beetle-browed ruffian, dressed in a crimson jersey, stood at the door, and motioned the sailors forward.

Then Lyell saw a great, dimly lit room, where the shadows lurched heavily in the corners, and an unpleasant haze hung in the air. The enthusiasm was at full height. Some people were kneeling and tossing their arms with agonized gestures ; one rough fellow glared upwards and raised his arms with convulsive stiffness ; a woman danced and swayed her body in wild abandonment ; hoarse cries for mercy rang through the building with throttled sounds ; sharp shrieks pierced the deep chorus of male voices, and shattered the night.

One huge fellow with hairy throat and heavy shoulders knelt on the floor in a conspicuous place. The poor soul was writhing in an agony of penitence, the thick sweat stood on his forehead, and as he rocked himself furiously to and fro he burst into mere howling. His bull-voice broke in his throat sometimes, and his lips slavered as he vented a terrible gurgling groan ; his hands gripped at the air ; and it seemed as though the swollen column of his neck were too straitened a pipe for the mad blood that flushed his brain.

A light-built man with a humorous face danced a genuine music-hall step, and shrieked " Hallelujah !" as if he were applauding a comic singer, and he went from one to another of the convulsed and kneeling figures, and shouted encouragement. Hard by the rim of the crowd a girl sprawled across the seat, and turned a bloated face up to the bleared light of the gas. Gin and nameless debauch had worked havoc on her face ; her blue lips were parted, and over her blotched cheeks the tears made slimy streaks. She groaned low, and her fingers sometimes tore weakly at her trailing hair that had fallen in clumsy coils from its net. A decent woman of the working class sprang up and chattered something with a long shrill ripple of sound ; when she sat down

16—2

the bull-voiced man uttered a hoarse roar, and hugged himself with inarticulate ecstasy, and then beat his face on the floor.

From the gloom of the far corner two red jerseys shone with a sombre gleam, and these two spots were the only signs of colour in the whole weird scene, so the general effect was dark, grimy, ghastly.

Presently a merry hymn tune was started, and the worshippers sang confusedly, while some women clapped their hands to the rhythm. The coarse voices had gone on for a little while, when, of a sudden, a clear contralto note soared over the tumult. Pure, full, resonant, the note took possession of ear and nerve alike, and sank on the soul. The voice sang on, and Lyell had no sense of any other sound, for it seemed to draw music out of every nerve in his body. He looked to see where the marvellous chant came from, and he soon knew. A tall woman dressed in black mounted the platform, singing. Her head was bent back, and the royal column of her throat showed white through the haze. She was large-limbed and powerful, and from her deep chest the miraculous mellow song came without effort.

When the magnificent farewell of an "Amen" sung by Antoinette Sterling has died away I have felt the tears in my eyes; but the great singer could not equal the profound musical effect produced by this enthusiast.

When the strange, irreverent hymn ceased, the woman knelt, and lifted her arms up with a strong gesture. Then she seemed taken with some inspiration. She did not pray, but only cried, "Have mercy! Have mercy!" The voice thrilled through the air, and its subtle inflections spoke ineffably of agony, pity, divine tenderness, passionate supplication. It struck the heart with arrows of sound, and the rough men and women fell to sobbing. This woman was a great tragedian out of place, and had she sent that deep cry through any theatre in London the audience would have risen at her.

Poor Lyell was not classical enough to know that a genuine Pythoness was before him; but I know now what kind of women were priestesses of the Delphic temple.

The sailor tried to keep down the lump in his throat, and swore to himself very volubly; but he had to give way at last, and the tears ran softly through his hardened fingers. The lady came down from the platform, and walked softly about among the people. She bent caressingly down to some of the women, and when she came to the dishevelled prostitute she stooped over her with a gesture in which there was no repugnance, no patronage, nothing but pity. Her face was calm, and she carried herself with an air of good breeding. As she neared the sailors she fixed her eyes calmly on Lyell's face, and Tom remembered with regret that he stank of whisky, and that she would smell him when he answered her. He put his handkerchief up, not, I fear, to conceal his emotion, but to prevent the fumes from being wafted abroad. The Salvation Captain said softly, "Will you come forward? The Lord has room for you with us;" and Thomas Lyell replied, "No, ma'am. I've been crying while you were hollerin' so bad, and I think I've had enough of this tomfool's game for one journey. Excuse me speaking plain, ma'am, but I'm not used to crying."

"Cry over your sin, dear friend. Weep over your sin, and the Lord will hold your tears blessed."

Lyell felt like a fool; he made a clumsy bow, and said, "It isn't my line at all, ma'am. I came in for fun; and I'm damned sorry I ever looked nigh hand."

Then he slouched out with his sailorly roll much exaggerated, and forgot to put on his cheesecutter till the waft of the wind blew cool on his brow. As soon as he was well clear he said, "Let's away to Jimmy Mather's. By the living man, I can drink a pint of Scotch to my own cheek."

Jimmy laughed heartily, and said, "Who'd have thought of seeing us two squinnying? Blowed if I didn't cry harder than you the time the beggar was squealin'."

And then the two worthy and profane young men crossed the silvered river. But the most mellifluous "Scotch" that the renowned Jimmy could supply had little charm for Lyell, and the barmaids could not stimulate him to a single witticism. All the sailors were there talking that fresh, jolly nonsense that I like so well to hear. Even the atmosphere of a dark and odorous bar seems to be cleared by their hearty fooleries as by the pure breath of the sea wind.

Tom Lyell paid no heed to the chaff of the bronzed fellows, and he did not contribute a single improper expression to the fund of conversation. Which was very remarkable for him.

At midnight he strolled down the long, blank road, and the travelling glitter of the sea drew him mechanically forward, as a shining glass draws a wild bird down. He glared fiercely over to the Castle, but the unutterable pathos of the shadowy ruin had no attraction for him, and the passing ships were merely swimming shapes.

I might tell you a pretty story about his meditations, but the story wouldn't be in the least true. Men of his sort do not meditate coherently, or even incoherently. Their supply of words and mental images is scanty; they are men of action, prompt and ready; but they never enter on set trains of thought. I have lived much on equal terms with them, shared their amusements, listened to their talk in every mood of which they are capable, so that their ways and their habits of mind are as familiar to me as my own. Therefore I am able to say that Thomas Lyell did not soliloquise to any great extent—he only felt that he had received what he called " a smack."

As he stood there aimlessly grinding out odds and ends of profanity from between his teeth, two dark figures moved down the white pier. He stepped back into the shade made by some waggons, and the Salvation Captain and her friend came on and halted close by him. Then Lyell heard the deep contralto voice once more.

"It was a good gathering, but it wears me. I dare not go home yet to risk another sleepless time. My forehead seems on fire; yet we must suffer. Did you see the sailors? I liked the strong man who cried. His heart is touched, and we shall gain him. It was so strange and blessed a sight to see the handsome fellow with tears on his face."

The lady's companion was narrower in sympathy than the artist. She primmed her lips in a way that was not unkindly, and said, " We mustn't think about looks, sister. Not looks. We have only their souls to care for. Their unhappy souls. I wish the burden hadn't been laid on me."

"I couldn't help seeing the sailor was handsome. If we could gain him, he would bring many more."

From which it appears that ladies who have effectually found grace do not part with feminine prejudices all on a sudden.

At this point of the conversation Lyell stepped forward, and the shorter of the ladies started violently. The Pythoness turned calmly, and faced the sailor without a tremor.

Lyell stammered, "I had no business listening to you talking, but I couldn't help it like, ma'am. I stood in there to get out of your way."

The Captain replied, "We hope in future you will not be afraid of us. You must come to our meetings very often, and we shall be proud to welcome you."

Lyell was not much used to high-bred people, but he knew that he was speaking to some one whose manners were out of the common. And indeed he was right. Jane Langley was a lady, and her sudden resolve to join a sect of convulsionists had caused much sorrow in a precise and respectable family. Her father went to one meeting, and when he heard frantic roughs shouting to his daughter, "Wire in, Captain Jinny! Give the devil one in the eye! Double him up!" with other devotional expressions, he was about as much disturbed as a respectable British merchant could very well be. The coarseness, the gross familiarity, the riotous emotion of the meetings set Jane Langley's nerves on edge at first; but she chose her road, and she was ready to place herself under the orders of the acute commercial genius who organized the Army. She saw that jumping and convulsions must inevitably pall; but the men who had learned to lead decent lives would not all relapse to the mire from which the excitements of the Army had tempted them. Then, if the truth must be told, she had the artist's instinct for the stage, and she unconsciously satisfied her craving for dramatic expression by the very performances which her relations thought unspeakably vulgar and distressing.

Miss Langley treated Lyell on equal terms, and her face took a very sweet expression as she spoke to him. He said, "I'm completely turned over. I'm sure I don't know what's happened exactly, but I've not been my own man since you started that praying affair."

"I know what has happened. Come to-morrow. Come every day while you are on shore, and you will take a joyous heart to sea with you."

Lyell would have liked to swear, but he had committed himself once in that way, and he felt that his conduct had not been quite decent. He bowed again and turned to go, when the thrilling voice said, " You will come. *I* want you there. Come to please *me*."

So poor Lyell went night after night, and I am afraid to say how much he had to put up with from his friends. He bore it all with quietness, although he was about as far as possible from being regenerate ; but it was possible to try him too far. He had gone aboard his boat one day to see what the chippers were doing, when a friend came up in a sculler-boat to see him. Lyell was rather moody, and spoke little. In the course of a rambling chat his friend, a brisk little man, said, "I say, Tommy. Is it true you're spooning a blazing Salvationist ? You artful old rat. What'll Polly Crow at the 'Compasses' say ?"

The big sailor's face reddened with a sudden gust of rage, and he said, "Blast you. Shut your mouth. I'll snap your backbone across my knee if you meg half a second more."

Assuredly the Christian virtues had not taken complete hold of Thomas Lyell's soul, so I am not going to claim undeserved credit for him.

His friend said huffily, " Well, come now. You were always a good hand at chaffing about girls. You needn't eat a fellow right away."

But Lyell was not to be appeased, and I am afraid that his merry acquaintance had hit the truth rather too nearly.

The *Starfire* lay a long while in the repairers' hands, and Lyell hung on, because he knew he would start on full pay as soon as the ship was ready for sea. He went every night to see his strange goddess, and every night she spoke to him prettily, and tried to bring him forward among the ring of converts who cried and writhed near the platform. But he had little taste for demonstrations, and although the Captain's voice set all his nerves vibrating, he could not pretend to any religious excitement.

One evening it fell cold and dark. As Lyell was passing

along the dismal street that led to the ferry, a sharp step behind him made him turn, and he saw the tall, dark figure that he knew so well. He said roughly, "This isn't a place for you. Characters about here would interfere with anybody. I'll see you safe home."

And Jane Langley did not refuse him. Perhaps she liked to hear his heavy, decided step, and to catch side glances of his powerful face? I do not know, but I know that women of all sorts admire manly men. For several nights the lady went homewards with the same escort, and she often tried to draw him into talk about religion. Although she was terribly in earnest, the bluff decision of his answers touched her sense of humour, and she sometimes ventured on a smile. Once, while she was trying to lead him on, he struck in sharply and said, "It was you that fetched me. It was your voice, and then what I saw of you when you tidied that drunken randy's hair. It wasn't conversion, I tell you ; it was you."

She felt that it was dangerous to pursue the line of her inclinations.

When Lyell's last night on shore came he managed to snatch an hour amid all the bustle, and presented himself like a faithful dog at the end of the street. On parting he had intended to say something that was on his mind, but his lips seemed to dry whenever he tried to speak, and it was not until the end of the journey that he managed to get out a word. "I'm off to-morrow. Sorry I shan't see you home any more."

"Going ! And going without any change in your soul ? You that I have prayed for ?"

"Can't help it. I've done nothing out of the way since I saw you but those whiskies that night. I'll keep straight till I see you again. You've made a soft of me."

Then Lyell put out his hand with a kind of grace that the lady found very pathetic. She laid her long white fingers on his rough palm, and never winced when his hand closed tightly. Then she went swiftly indoors and burst into hysterical crying.

I don't think she cried about losing a possible convert.

Lyell did his work just as usual on the voyage. In bad weather he sometimes used his ordinary persuasive methods when the men were not lively, but he always said (strictly to himself), " God forgive me !" when he had been peculiarly eloquent, and silenced his conscience by the old sailor's subterfuge. A lot of his friends were ashore when he got to Cronstadt, and they tried hard to tempt him away for a jaunt to Petersburg ; but he settled the matter in his own decisive way.

" If I go with you loons, you'll get drunk. I'll get drunk too, or anyway half slewed. I don't want to get drunk, and I shan't go."

He sat down and wrote a letter instead. Here is part of the letter :—" I shall be glad to see you again, and if I can please you about the convarsion, I will try. But it is no good for a man to say a thing that he does not mean. I wanted to pray when I heard you pray, but it soon wore off, and I thought more of you than your praying, if you will excuse me being so bold as say so. I think always about you, and I shall not go on any rough carrys-on that you don't like, and when I come back we can see how I get through. I have tried praying, but I don't seem cut out for that sort of thing, and I don't want to be caught on a sham. I shall come first to see you when we come ashore, and I am very greatful to you for your kindness, and I wish you very happy, and not to get stopping up so late on these cold nights. I shall think about you to-night and always, and I hope you will remember me, for I think more of you than anyone I ever saw.—Yours respectfully, T. Lyell.

" P.S.—You will not mind if I have one drink, not to hurt me, but just to keep the men from chaffing, for I don't care much, but it's bad to put up with."

When the *Starfire* reached the mouth of the river all was well ; but when she had got up, the captain suddenly shouted, " Where are you coming to ? Hard a-starboard. Are you all drunk ?" In a second the towering bow of a steamer struck Lyell's vessel amidships with a slow, heavy scraunch, and as the *Starfire* drove slowly ahead Thomas Lyell was dragged away in the tangled wreck of the bridge. Something had gone wrong with the other ship's steering gear, and there was only time to run the *Starfire* on to the hard before she was ready to sink.

The Salvationists were all busy with " Knee-drill " and

other forms of devotional pastime when a waterman came in and called the Captain. "Second mate of the *Starfire* wants you, ma'am, bad. You'll look pretty slippy or he'll miss seeing you." Lyell was stretched out on a bed when the Captain arrived. A dull pallor seemed to gleam under the deep bronze of his face, and his forehead was smeared with a red streak. His eyes spoke when Jane Langley entered, but his hands seemed paralyzed. She looked at the surgeon, and the mute glance that she received in reply satisfied her. She knelt down, took Lyell's hand, and bent over him. She said, "Time is short. Oh, are you safe? My friend, my brother, my dear! Are you safe?"

Lyell asked, "How?"

"Your soul! You are passing. Your soul! Your soul!"

Lyell spoke with a gasp.

"I shan't tell a lie. I don't know. I'm not converted, if that's it. If I lie to please you, God'll meet me wrong. Do one thing for me."

"Anything."

He whispered, and she stooped her sweet face and kissed him twice. Lyell's grim mouth softened, and he said, "All right. Stop here till the thing's over. You're the best company to see the last of me." Then he closed his eyes.

A few minutes afterwards the surgeon said, "You had better rise now, madam. We can do no more." She looked up, and her one deep cry broke the quiet of the grim, bare room. It was like that awful note that was launched through the darkness when Thomas Lyell went into the hall for his bit of fun. Rizpah might have wailed so for the lost children.

So that was the end of Tom Lyell, and many kind words were spoken about him by the rough men who gathered in the drinking-places. They knew he was a man all over, and they mourned him in their way. But the sincerest of all his mourners was the lady whom he had been so fond of, and I think she will never forget him.

VI.

THE DISAPPOINTED CAPTAIN.

THE village of Callaley was not within sight of the sea, but when the wind blew from the sea there was a kind of sigh in the air mingled with sounds like the beat of a far-off drum. The sighing was made by the many waves that followed each other over the great sandy floor of Druid's Bay, and the hollow boom that sounded at intervals of about forty seconds was caused by the rush of water into the narrow gaps of the rocks to the south. The villagers were very incurious about the sea. When the day's work was over the older men went into their gardens and spent their time quietly till the dusk fell ; the youngsters played quoits and cricket, or carried their hazel rods down to the burn and fished there. Sometimes when a boy was high up in a tree after a nest he caught a glimpse of black sails gliding mysteriously behind the low swell of the links, and he would call, "Aw can see a ship ;" but neither boys nor men cared to pass beyond the woods to look at the open water. There was so much to do in that quiet place, and life was so smooth to the poorest there, that they thought very little of anything that lay beyond the cross-roads. The pilgrimage of the average native was marked out by long usage. When he left school he went to work in the fields, or in the squire's gardens, or at the blacksmith's shop. Then came the time when he looked sheepishly at the girls as they came out of church, and had accidental meetings with them in the long tangled lanes ; then the queer merriment of the wedding, when all comers drank raw spirits at eleven in the morning, and the singer of the day obliged the company with " Barbara Bell," and " Watty the Shaver flank floower o' my hair ;" then the long after-noon of life that lasted till the old man could only sit in the kitchen and gaze dimly forward. Then the time came for the corpse to rest outside the front door while the guttural voices wailed a hymn ; and, last of all, there was the lounging procession, in which the mourners, dressed in their creased Sunday clothes, chatted of cows and potatoes and apple-trees as the hearse moved toward the mossy church. Barring accidents, such as fever or diphtheria, that was the course of the villagers.

Henry Widdrington, the wheelwright's son, seldom thought about such a thing as the future, but he often used to wonder whether he would ever see anything of the world where lived the beautiful ladies and heroic men that he read about in his books. When Henry was twelve years old a young university man had come to the village as tutor to the squire's son. Up to that day the boy had passed his time just as the other lads in the place did, but after he fell in with the tutor his way of life changed, and he could never quite imagine himself as standing over the anvil. The meeting with the tutor came about in this way. Harry was sitting by the burn side watching his float, when a tall young fellow waded through the rank grass and began whipping the water just where the ripples twirled and poppled at the outlet of a pool. The boy said, "Ye can switch away theyorr a' the day, sir. The wund's i' the wrang airt for that place."

The young man turned a dark, kindly look upon Harry, and inquired, "How is that, my man? Where shall I go?"

Harry was pleased to show off as a naturalist, so he hauled his own line out of the sullen pool, and said, "Come alang wi' me."

As they wandered round a bend of the stream the boy chattered on, "That place is varry canny when the wettor's drumly, but thor's been ne rain te stir the clarts up. Noo just theyorr see'st thou, the wund blaws clean doon that hollow, and the wettor's rough on the top. Ye can fish fower hundred yards doon, and the troots rises becas the wund blaws the fly off them hazel bushes when it's this way."

The gentleman said, "Well, you keep your eyes open, I must say. Here, my man."

Harry reddened. "If aw'd thowt ye'd offer us owt, aw wadn't a-comed wi' you."

The tutor begged pardon very gracefully, and cast a queer sidelong glance at the youthful incorruptible. He hurried into conversation, for he felt that the boy had asserted a kind of superiority.

"Do they ever fish by torchlight here?"

"Yes, sir, they did once last year, and the awd squire gat whummled into the Divvel's Hole, and when he com' oot he looked like wor scarecraw, and the cheps had to myek as if they warn't laughin'"

Something in the turn of this phrase attracted the young man. He asked, "Then are you not afraid to be down here at night?"

"No. Aw's not fleyed o' bogles. But aw divvn't like to hear the foxes yowl on the hill."

"Ah! Why?"

"Oh! it minds me o' somethin' wrang. It's like as if ye wor gan to dee and get putten away wi' the deed folk."

"Do you read books, my man?"

"Whiles. Awd Bill Adams, that's wor maistor, says aw lairned faster nor Mr. Gilbert, that's the squire's lad. Aw can read aboot Christian and Sir William Wallace."

"Do you like reading the Bible?"

"No; not elways. At schule we read about kings and things, and it's nowt but he did evil in the sight o' the Lord. If aw'd been the Lord, aw wadn't a-been fashed wi' nyen o' them."

The Oxford man showed a humorous little twitching about the corners of the mouth.

"And whom do you like in the Bible, then?"

"Not monny o' them. Aw like Saul and Esau and David. Not elways David. Esau aw like best. Aw hate Jael and Jacob, and them kings. We had to larn the kings."

"Then would you like some books to read?"

"We hev seven byuks i' the hoose that's a wor awn." (This was a declaration of independence.) "But aw'd like to try some mair."

"Then meet me at the Hall this evening—the lodge, you know—and I'll see what I can do for you." Mr. Landon amused himself with the lad all the afternoon, and at night he sent him home with a heavy bundle of books.

Harry slept in a garret which was reached by means of a ladder, and he was in perfect solitude when once the trap-door was put down. That night he took a book with him, and, as soon as he had fixed his candle, he settled himself to read. The first line, "The stag at eve had drank his fill," struck him with a strange feeling, and he went on and on with growing delight until the candle guttered low. Then he rolled himself up, and fairly shivered with pleasure.

The Oxford man's instinct was right. He had detected the boy's disposition from the very turn of his talk, and he hit upon the one gift that Harry needed more than all others.

From that day the tutor found it very hard to keep his favourite supplied with books. The boy read as though he absorbed the meaning through his pores. When he crept away into the garden, and sat down behind the beehives, he assumed a sort of tranced attitude as he opened his book ; and he would remain for two hours at a stretch without moving, save to turn the pages. Above all things he liked to read about the sea. The brave, jolly stories of Peter Simple and Jack Easy, the brilliant romance of Cleveland, even the melodrama of the "Flying Dutchman," set his pulses dancing, and he wondered whether he should ever see such heroes and such ladies.

Mr. Landon was much tickled by the various affectations put on by his bright little companion. The boy used "book" phrases of the most lordly kind, and his cultured, keen patron often found it hard to keep the twitching of the mouth from developing into a broad laugh. During one of the excursions made by the pair the tutor inquired, "Now which of all the books do you really like most ?"

"Nothin' but the boundin' brine, sir. Aw like the warlike deeds of sailors."

"Good. But you know you mustn't say 'warlike deeds.' All those words are only employed in books. And I heard you just now say that 'a painter might have depicted the scene.' You mustn't say that. And never talk about the 'raving blast.' You understand me ?"

Harry was rather proud of those forms of speech, but his sense of humour taught him that Mr. Landon was right.

"And now," pursued the tutor, "what are you going to be ?"

"Aw hardly know. Maybe a wheelright. But not till aw've seen the sea and some ships."

Landon was amazed to hear that the youngster had never gone to the seaside, but he wisely said nothing, and waited.

After a happy summer, the autumn came, and on one golden September morning the wheelwright's son went out to the burn side, after he had cleaned the knives, and brought the yeast, and performed other tasks for his mother. The brackens were red under the sun, and the whole of the deep dell carved out by the stream shone in a riot of colour. Harry went to a place where the elms darkened the path of the burn, and the hazels made a thick undergrowth. He sat down on the rock under the root of a great tree, and, for once, let his book stay in his pocket. The trout darted like flying shuttles, and a great sullen pike lay with its head up stream. Harry thought, " None of them go downwards. They're like me, maybe, and never saw the sea." When once his thoughts had taken a turn seaward he could not stop himself from longing, and at last he jumped up and determined to follow the burn right to the very sands.

There was not much of a path, so the boy had to clamber round roots, and jump from stone to stone in the shallow places, and dive under the fronds of the bracken for a very long time before he came to any open space. The rabbits sat up to look at him, and once he saw the wicked smile of a fox, as the red thief looked out from his earth in the crag. (The fox's smile supplied the model for the stage Mephistopheles.) After a couple of miles the stream poured through the squire's grounds, and then Harry had easy work to follow it, for the daughters of the house had caused a pretty pathway to be made, and this little thread of a road wound through the leafy darkness of the great dell like the guiding clue of the old story. The hoarse whisper of the sea sounded very plainly now, and the boy was just bracing himself for the shock of a new sight, when a flash of colour came on the path in front of him, and a pretty little girl ran up and spoke, " You, Harry Widdrington, what are you doing here, you wild boy ?"

" Gan to the sea, Miss Conny."

Harry would have given the world if he had been able to muster one of the gallant speeches used by knights in the good greenwood ; bu tthe smile of the servant who accom-

panied the child took all the romance out of him, and he
stumbled into his native tongue.

Little Miss Constance was the clergyman's daughter, and
in dealing with the village children she imitated her
mother's manner with much accuracy. She turned to the
maid and said, "Oh, do let us go, too, there's a dear
Richards, and then you can see this naughty boy home, and
he won't get lost."

Richards replied in a manner modelled on that of the
housekeeper, "We may go for a very short while, Miss
Constance; but you mustn't be picking up every lost boy
you meet. If we didn't know Henry's father I couldn't
consent to your going."

So the three cleared the woods, and then—a broad, grey
floor, with flights of silver sea-birds streaming north, and the
wind dappling the great expanse with swift, dark patches
that flew towards the sharp horizon.

The boy gasped. Many things from the books he had
read came into his mind. How the *Rattlesnake*, with O'Brien
on board, would have foamed along before that breeze!
How the low, black schooner, with her fierce crew, could
have lurked under those rocks till the captain gave the
word, "Up anchor and away!" The sails of a ship stood
up like dim towers far away south, and Harry's heart beat
fast as he thought of the freedom that those sailors must
be enjoying out there.

The boy's fate was decided. His mind had suffered a
sea change, and nothing but force would ever keep him from
that glorious place. So he said to himself, as the whole
spirit of hope and adventure and wild curiosity took possession of his soul. When he had gazed for a long while
the little girl said, "What a queer boy you are, Henry
Widdrington! Don't you see the fishermen down there
waving?" But "Henry" took no notice of the little
tyrant; he only said, "I'm going home."

Richards patronized him graciously, and offered to show
him a short road back, unless he chose to ride behind the
dog-cart with them; but Miss Constance assumed airs of
proprietorship, and took the matter out of the hands of
Harry and Richards alike. She insisted on treating the
boy as a waif, and when she went right up to his home and

17

told Mrs. Widdrington that "This wild boy was going away I don't know where, so I *felt* I *must* bring him back to you," the good woman laughed respectfully, and thanked her.

Before the child left she offered her hand to the boy, and looked as though she would have kissed him had not social considerations prevailed.

From that time onward Henry Widdrington read as much as ever, but he cared for no books excepting those that spoke of the sea. He liked the knights and the fair ladies, but he knew that they could never be met unless he sailed beyond seas to find them. His father gave in to the lad's fancy, so on one proud and memorable day a clean cart came to the door, and Harry drove away with his chest and hammock, and all the other things that were thought necessary for a north-country sailor in the old days.

Old Widdrington was a shrewd fellow in his way; he did not want his son to be a collier captain, so he apprenticed him to a great Newcastle firm, whose vessels went on long voyages. The apprentices in this line were treated well, and dressed in a smart uniform; so that when Henry Widdrington came back, after nearly three years of absence, he looked quite as well as a midshipman from a man-of-war. The glitter of his buttons in our street was a strange sight, and his alert carriage of the head was very different from the slight slouch that most of our men cultivated. He was in no way proud, and on the Saturday evening he stopped at the blacksmith's corner, and chatted with his old schoolfellows for more than an hour. He had to go to tea at almost every house in the place, for the womenfolk would not let him away, and had he not had a very strong digestion he must have been seriously injured by the quantities of girdlecake which were specially made for him. On Sunday afternoon his mother put on her best shawl with the cucumber pattern, and he "linked" down to church with her, which was thought to be an admirable sight by everyone who saw the pair. When Harry stood up and squared his shoulders as the hymn was sung, you could see the muscles move like coils under his coat, and the set of his feet was as firm as a wrestler's. A finer-looking lad never stepped.

While he was away he had undergone constant exercise, and lived the splendid open-air life of a sailor. He was so strong that he could go hand over hand up a backstay without giving one twist with his body, and, with his canvas shoes on, he could clear a ropeyarn held four feet ten above the deck.

But although he was so powerful of body he had not neglected his mind, for besides working hard at navigation he had read as many novels as ever he could afford to buy, and I take it that there is no better reading than novels for a man who is not required to enter on severe study for a living.

Young Widdrington's forehead had a thoughtful look, and his eye was full of meaning. During his furlough he walked about a great deal on the roads and by the burn-side, and the strangers who happened to be staying at the Hall often glanced aside at him as he passed with his bold stride. His face drew the eye, and women liked to watch him.

During one of his walks he met Miss Constance, who had grown into quite a young lady. The girl greeted him very prettily, and said, " We were so glad to see you at church, and, do you know, it was I who arranged for the choir to sing ' For those in peril '? I hope you liked it, and we all wish you well."

"I hope I shan't do you any discredit, Miss Constance." Then Widdrington lifted his cap, and walked away.

On his road through the market town, as he went to the station when his leave was over, he bought a photograph—one of the shadowy things that used to be done in country places years ago—and he made a frame for this picture, so that he could hang it up in his berth. He had seen the name of the artist on the back of Miss Constance's portrait in the miller's book, and he insisted on buying the specimen from the show set.

At nights, when the vessel was going easily and the wind held up well, he often thought of the girl. Miss Constance's father would have been much surprised had he known what aspirations were passing through the young sailor's mind, and so would the lady herself.

After a long spell of coast trading, Widdrington's ship was sent round the Horn to San Francisco. When she let

17—2

go her anchor in the bay all the men were keen to get ashore, and Harry was as eager as any of them. The second mate went with him, and the two men went to a dancing-saloon. Widdrington liked the wine well enough, just as he had liked the porter-house steak which they had on first landing; but the glare, the abandonment, the cursing of the women who had drunk too much, and all the tawdry flashness of the place, were repellent to him. He went to his friend, and whispered, " This isn't my line of rails, old man. If you're on the drift stop your time out, and if you don't get too drunk to hail us I'll come ashore for you myself."

" It's too far to hail, man. What are you thinking about ? Stand by the boat, if you like ; I shan't keep you long. But, dash it, we must have one spree surely after coming round the Horn."

Then Harry went out, and walked about in the strange new city until his chum reeled out, and the two went aboard before the skipper was astir. During all the time that my young friend spent among the crew of mad folk at the dancing-house he had been thinking, " I shouldn't like her to catch me in this shanty;" and he looked long at the photograph before he turned in.

Before Henry Widdrington came home to pass his examination for master he was so long abroad that old Dolly Widdrington used to say, " Eigh ! hinny bords. Aw'll be putten away and happed up amang the mouls afore maw bonny lad comes hyem ony mair." But one fine autumn evening she saw a gleam of brass at the door, and there stood her son—bronzed, bearded, tall—a gentleman every inch. She could not speak, but she wailed so piercingly that the neighbours came in to see if anything was wrong, and they found Dolly crying like an hysterical girl. The sailor soothed his mother, and patted her broad shoulders as though she had been a pet child, until at last she held him at arm's length, and quavered, " Eh ! but thoo's brave and bonny, bonny and brave, maw canny bairn. An aw thowt thoo would a hadden to come and see where they barried us and aw would nivvor a kissed thoo ne mair. And, eh ! but yor bonny, and a' the lasses 'll be pullin yen another's hair for thoo."

The nature of the meal that Mrs. Widdrington got ready cannot be described. It would make you feel dyspeptic only to hear how many different sorts of food she put on the table, and she felt grieved that Henry couldn't try everything. When she went to bed she said to her silent husband, "They can put us away noo as syun as they like, hinny; but aw wadn't a-stopped quiet i' me coffin if he hadn't a-com."

Widdrington easily passed the Board of Trade test, and a fine full-rigged ship was ready for him on the very day after he secured his certificate. Before his vessel was loaded down he had a pleasant spell of leisure, and he kept up his practice of walking daily. He was passing by the very place where he had first seen the sea, when he once more met Miss Constance. She was riding a smart pony this time, but no groom accompanied her; she liked to go over the moor by herself. Her hair had broken loose, and the flaxen locks fell in confusion over her shoulders; her cheeks were bright; and her eyes glittered with the excitement of her swift gallop. She was a joyous creature, and it made one joyous to look at her.

Widdrington thought, " Her or no woman," as he stepped up and lifted his braided cap. "So we must call you Captain now, and never Harry any more. We are all so proud of you, and yet it seems only a day since you came here with Richards." She didn't say, "with me."

Poor Harry's manners were really very good, for he was used to meeting well-bred passengers, and his quick, imitative intelligence had enabled him to copy the reticence and calm which he had begun by merely admiring. But his self-possession failed him here, and his heart beat so fast and hard that he almost feared she would hear and detect him. He blundered out, "Greatest pride of my life, Miss Constance, if you're proud of me." If he only had dared to accent the " you." As the young lady gathered her reins before moving off, she said, " We may see you at the ball when Mr. Osbert comes of age. Shall we not? Papa said he must ensure your being there, and you know how he likes to show his boys off."

" I'll be there for certain, Miss Constance." And the Captain walked thoughtfully home by the woods.

Condescension of the most feudal order was the rule at
the ball. The Squire led off with a very stout lady, who
was the wife of his principal tenant; Mr. Osbert danced
with a selection of farmers' daughters, and everything spoke
of regular rents and kindly relations between landlord and
tenant. Somehow or other there was no poverty on the
Squire's estate, and bad times have not been known there
yet for anybody, so that there was a good deal of reality
in the merriment and obtrusive goodwill.

Henry Widdrington danced twice with Miss Constance,
and acquitted himself admirably. Excepting guardsmen
and hussars and other persons who are specially trained to
the industries of the London season, I do not think that
any class of men dance so well as sailors—especially
merchant seamen. Why it should be so I do not know.
Perhaps it is because the men are much given to practising
if there happens to be an accordion or a fiddle in the forecastle. At any rate a travelled lady who saw Widdrington
waltzing remarked, "The sailor dances like an Austrian;"
yet he had learned mostly on board ship. The young fellow
exchanged very few words with his partner, but her instinct
told her something of his thoughts, and she suddenly ceased
to show that kind of playful patronage which she had
bestowed on him ever since he sat in the desks at the
village school.

Before Henry Widdrington took his ship away for her
New Orleans voyage he met Miss Constance several times,
sometimes in company with her father, sometimes when she
was alone; and she always contrived to set up a kind of
barrier that could neither be seen nor defined. Harry only
knew it was there. He went away with a heavy heart, and
he spent a great deal of money on a frame for his bleached
old photograph. In coming back across the Western
Ocean he carried away his topsails through cramming sail
on the vessel; but his run out had been so brilliant that his
firm ordered him to stay ashore and wait for a new steamer
that they were finishing. He was on full pay all the time,
and of course he must needs go home and put himself in the
way of danger. Had his ambition been even guessed,
it would have been a bad day for the lady and for him;
but the possibility of conceiving such an idea was beyond

the power of the Rector's faculties. He called his old favourite 'Harry,' and treated him as if he were thirteen years old.

But this high way of thinking was very dangerous when a romantic young man, nurtured on novels and poetry, was in the case. Assuredly the Rector would have been sadly put out could he have heard a conversation which took place while the young Captain was waiting for the big liner to take her cargo.

The Captain and Miss Constance met in the old place by the links (it was very odd to see how persistently the two haunted that patch of moorland). After a few common-places Widdrington moved as if to go; but he poised him-self a moment on one foot and prepared to make a diplo-matic speech. "My mother would be glad if we might have one of your portraits, Miss Constance. We have the Squire and your father, and everybody but you. The one I have on board ship is faded entirely."

He had blundered into it, and there was nothing for it but to plunge on. The young lady's eye hardened, and he could see that she was vexed. How could she be other-wise? She liked him; she admired his way of treating his humble parents; she liked the tact with which he avoided giving offence to his old companions by his acquired manners and his easy bearing. Then again she was used to talking with all the men in the parish, young and old, and when she taught in the evening school she was accustomed to domineer over big fellows of all ages, and to call them by their Christian names. She had acted the part of juvenile patriarch for so long that she could not quite manage to separate Widdrington in her mind from the rest of her flock. And now she must change towards him. He was too handsome, too manly, to be snubbed; but she must do something. Her kindness drew her one way, her awakened dignity drew her the other way; and she broke through the difficulty by simply saying, "Of course we mustn't leave you out; I'll see to that."

Widdrington could not get gracefully away. He saw that Constance knew everything, and he took his risk. "It will always be the same, Miss Constance. I never change. I know I have dared too much, but when a man has carried it in his heart so many years—twice or thrice half round the world—it isn't easy to kill it. I'm not one to die of a broken heart, but I think I'd like to die if you didn't forgive me ; though I won't say I have done wrong. Could anyone have done other? But I only think of you, and I'll never come again here if you say no."

"It would be better so. I am to blame. Good-bye."

The young people had to all intents and purposes been exchanging signs ; but the whole story was plain enough. Constance tried to persuade herself that she was very angry, but she was not ; she was only resolute.

Next day an envelope was brought addressed to Mrs. Widdrington, and when Henry saw the portrait that his mother took out, he said, " I think I'd like to have that, mother."

The old woman looked at him, and then went and put her hand on his shoulder. " Aw kenned how it was a' the time, maw man. It wus a fond notion, but thoo's good eneugh for onybody, hinny. Dinnot think ne mair, maw bairn. They'd only say ye'd gyen daft, and geck and gibe at yor fethor and your mother. She gan to be married on yon fond priest over at the East Moor."

Widdrington took his portrait away with him to sea, and as the steamer bowled down the river and surged over the Bar he almost wished that he might not see those banks again. He was always quiet, always keen at duty ; but in the dark nights, when the ship was swooping quietly over the black waves, he had many sad thoughts.

When he had been out more than a month the Rector called out one morning at breakfast, "This is splendid, really splendid ! And one of my boys, too. Listen, my dear. Listen, Conny. ' The screw steamer *Oceola*, Captain Widdrington, arrived here, having in tow the liner *Barrington*. Captain Widdrington picked up the *Barrington* in lat. 35° 18' N., long. 66° 12' W., during the gale of the 20th, with propeller shaft snapped and port bulwark gone. The vessel was in the trough of the sea, and it was only by running great risk that a towline was made fast. Towline parted three times, and Widdrington stood by until bunker coals threatened to give out. Captain Widdrington was offered and refused a purse of 400 sovereigns, subscribed by

the passengers. He was on the bridge for fifty-six hours at
a stretch, and suffered severely from exposure. The lady
passengers presented Widdrington with a silk flag at a
banquet given in his honour.' "

" Now I call that very fine."

" I like his refusal of the money."

" Well, that was rather like posturing, was it not ?"
This last came from a pale clergyman, who sat next Constance at table. The pale man went on, " Who is this
hero ?"

" Oh ! Do you not remember the tall sailor who was so
much about here a little while ago ? A boy of mine. Your
friend Landon made a great pet of him."

" Ah ! Yes. Athletic youth, with romantic hair and
eyes. Carried his head as if it were the portrait of an
ancestor."

There was one person who reddened at this speech, but
she bit her lips and said nothing.

Widdrington came to England, and sent £500 to his
parents—the owners had presented him with £600 from the
salvage money—and he would have liked to bring the whole
sum home to cover the kitchen-table with sovereigns. But
he restrained himself, and went resolutely away for a trip
through the Canal. At Bombay he was ordered on to
China, and he stayed running from Shanghai during two
years. When he came home he had aged sadly, but he still
looked handsome, for his eyes never lost their youthful
light. He came to the village once more, and found his
parents comfortable—the old man had never worked since
the £500 reached them. His mother was feeble to the last
degree, but she brightened when she saw him, just as she
had done when she fancied years before that she was going
to die.

She knew what he wanted most to hear, and she satisfied
him :

" She's mairried the yen aw telled ye on, hinny. Thor's
a bairn."

" And how is she all ways ?"

" Eh, maw mon, she's deed an gyen, and thor's ne use
keepin' owt back. He wus a sair trial tiv her wiv his daft
gyens, and starvin' thorsels like Romans yence a week."

The old woman prattled on to prevent him from thinking; but he was past thought. He smoked a long time that night, and in the morning he went out without ever having been to bed.

At ten o'clock he had reached the East Moor Rectory, and walked past rapidly. A nurse girl was coming across the paddock, and he saluted her. " Good-day, Mary. I didn't know you had taken service here."

"I came with Miss Constance, but I'm going soon. It's like stoppin' in a 'icehouse here."

" And this is the boy, is it ?"

" It's a girl, Captain."

" How have they christened it, then ? I wonder if it would howl, now, if I kissed it?"

"It's called Constance. But you needn't be jokin' and laughin', Captain. It's a bad job. Vincent was just sayin' yesterday she'd far better had you. *He* saw you often and often, when you didn't see him ; but he liked you ower well to tell."

Captain Widdrington shook hands with the girl, and went back home. In two hours he left, after holding his mother a long time in his arms.

He was not a man to pine, and sailors like him are not easily drowned if shipbuilders give them fair play. Before he was forty-two years old he married a pretty and well-bred American, and, in his grave, sad way his life goes on well enough. He often goes to the village, but he never takes his wife, and he likes to stand in the churchyard. Some time ago little Constance Featherstone told her step-mother that a gentleman with bright buttons kissed her, and "cried very funny ;" but he seldom lets memories influence him outwardly.

VII.

OUR CHAPEL.

THERE was no lukewarm worship in our Primitive Methodist Chapel. Our preachers took their turn as they were marked on the plan, and sometimes we got a countryman who had no spirit in him at all ; but when the time came for prayer we were able to display our native resources. We were quite independent of the preacher then, and the visitors from the pit places said that there wasn't a colliery for miles round that could beat us at praying. It was not that the petitions offered were more eloquent than those composed by the pitmen, but our running accompaniment was so good that the folks who lived inshore were obliged to own themselves inferior to us. Sally Routledge led the chorus that followed the clauses of each prayer with approving groans. Sally was an old, old woman who remembered seeing John Wesley, and this fact caused her to be considered as an authority until she died in her ninety-eighth year. She sat in a front seat, and no one ventured even to say "Hallelujah," no matter how much his heart might be stirred, until Sally had spoken. When the prayer reached an acute stage Sally would say, "Eh! Send to glory," with a shrill quaver. Then Big Adam would strike in from the far corner with a crashing "Hallelujah!" that sounded like a signal-gun; then Colin Thompson, the oily fish-curer, cried, "Lord, come amang us;" and after, the rest of the congregation sighed, or said, "Eh! Grace aboundin'," according to their fancy. Last of all, Tommy Blaikie, the cautious draper, who always waited for a lull, murmured, "Oh! bless this day to us," as though he believed that the moderate request of a business man would meet with prompt attention. After the ice was broken the congregation felt more free, and sometimes Big Adam's huge bass note jarred with old Sally's lofty quaver; but the general effect was good, and our people exerted themselves with such zeal that many of them had to wipe their foreheads when the prayer was over. Joe, the gamekeeper, was very useful for swelling the volume of sound, but none of us liked him to ejaculate by himself, for he had been a reprobate in his day, and he sometimes used the wrong kind of words when he got very much exalted. On the whole we were very successful, and we accepted the admiration of strangers as only our due. After our service came the love-feast, and we heard from Big Adam how, before he found peace, he used to hammer the wife, and bring "hyem three gallons o' beer every Settorday neet;" then we broke up, and some of us went over the moor, while others strolled

down the broad, sprawling street of the village. It was
then that business subjects were approached—not in the
keen and secular manner that suited the week-days, but
with mild hints and modest reticence. As soon as Monday
came our chapel members would try to get the better of each
other in business just as readily as though they had spent
the Sabbath in careless living; but during the evening stroll
on Sunday we were apparently as communistic as the early
Christians.

One fine summer night John Featherstone, Tommy
Blaikie, and Captain Robb were walking softly along the
beach. The misguided people from the church were just
leaving that unhappy place where religion was profaned by
genteel mummeries, so John, Tommy, and the Captain
were able to assume that superior air with which you regard
your neighbour when you feel that your chance of salvation
is better than his.

John Featherstone kept a shop in the village, and the
chapel was very proud of him. He was among us a long
while before we suspected the amount of his ability; but
when it was proposed to bring a harmonium into the chapel
he made a speech against the project, and his demolition
of the arguments advanced by the innovators was so complete that we were all amazed. We felt that he was fit to
speak at Morpeth, or even at Newcastle, his flow of language
was so striking.

After that he wrote an essay called, "The Bible our
Guide," and this work was positively printed. The *Morpeth
Banner* said, "Our talented neighbour, Mr. John Featherstone, has enrolled himself among the splendid galaxy of
English authors that began to glitter with the Bard of Avon,
and has shone through the ages until now. His eloquent exposure of Atheism (which may be procured for the sum of twopence at the shop of our townsman, Mr. Rendall) seems to us to
have many points in common with the noble bursts of thought
which emanated from the pens of Edmund Burke and the Great
Lexicographer. We trust that our friend will continue to
soar, and that early success may lead him to fruitful and profit-
able expenditure of the talents with which he is endowed."

We used to show this paragraph to people, and say,
"That man goes to our chapel."

Featherstone had several shares in sailing ships, and his management of one barque of which he was part-owner was considered to be consummately dexterous.

Tommy Blaikie did a large business among the country folks for miles round. He left his shop to his wife, and travelled from village to village and from farm to farm. No one ever saw him hurry, and no one ever heard him speak loudly. He used to walk at the rate of two miles an hour, and he always trod as though he were afraid of disturbing the grass-blades. He muttered as he went along, and people said that he was learning his accounts by heart, for he never seemed to keep any books. If you passed him on the road, he reddened like a bashful maiden, and fixed his gaze more tightly than ever on the ground; but he neither quickened nor slackened his pace for anybody. On gurly winter days, when the sleet flogged the grey waves, and the bents moaned with many voices, Tommy plodded along just as steadily as he did when the ragworts blazed in the sun and the music of the larks fell like a hail of immaterial pearls through the joyous air. When he reached a village the wives would say, "Here's Tommy Blaikie. Why, wor awd clock's gyen half an 'oor fast since his last roond." The people pretended to set their clocks by him. Tommy would knock lightly, and the rough women (if they were not too much in debt to him) would screech, "Had away in, ye awd fox; what d'ye want the day?" Then Tommy would whisper in a sad tone, "What'll be yor orders, hinny, this time?" A dozen words settled all the business, and Tommy went on. So his round progressed until the sun drooped; then he crept like a cat over the moor, and went back home. Tommy could have driven a carriage if he had chosen, but as the villagers said, "He grudged hissel' his meat."

Captain Robb was a jovial old gentleman, with a face like an Easter egg and an eye that suggested whisky. He had a reassuring laugh and an insinuating Scotch accent. His morality was often publicly described by himself, and, from his own description, it appeared that there wasn't a superior morality on the whole coast. He was a managing owner, and he regarded shareholders as a kind of amiable Canaanites who might be permitted to live among the chosen people, but who must be made to recognise the real masters of the land.

These three worthy men walked down the street in all the glory of Sunday black and Sunday shirt-fronts. They looked very devout and very well off, and they felt their own importance.

Presently John Featherstone remarked, "Andrew was grand upon Faith to-night." Captain Robb said, "Ay, was he. And that second prayer was a real good one. Eh! but he can pray fine." Tommy Blaikie softly murmured, "He's bowt Jemmy Nicholson's share in the *Raglan*, they were sayin'."

"Well," said Mr. Featherstone, "if it was any other day I would say that we're all fools if we don't get hold of that new steamer that Dodson and Graves are finishing. They're bound to sell. Some of the Shields chaps 'll be running over and taking her. I believe she's to be had for £8,000 down, and the balance at six months."

Again Tommy murmured, "Could you get the whole sixty-fower placed amang wor awn cheps?" Captain Robb struck in, "Well, I can take twelve if I'm manager. John here can manage another ten; he'll help me. We'll have a double management. Eh? Tommy, there. How many can you manage?"

"Eh! dear, dear, aw wadn't like to say on a Sunday neet. Could we not see Mr. Dodson the morn—the morn mornin'?"—"Right, and we can speak to the others after the prayer-meeting on Tuesday night."

So next day Tommy and John and the Captain plodded over the south moor and took a look at the new boat. In the evening they decided to get a company together, and things would have gone very nicely if, as Captain Robb said, "that Jack Featherstone wasn't always wanting the whole pie, crust and dish, and all away together."

On the Tuesday the prayer-meeting drew a good many of our people together, for the weather was nasty and the boats did not go off. Everybody was much comforted, and John Featherstone touched several hearts by the eloquence with which he besought deliverance from the evils of covetousness. Captain Robb in his devotional utterance bewailed the tendency of men to seek only after material blessings, and he expressed such passionate indifference for the things of the world that it seemed wonderful to find him wearing a gold watch.

After our exercises were over, John Featherstone said, "You go down with David and Old Adam; I'll walk up with Joe and the two Layburns; Tommy's not good at business. He can go home, and we'll tell him in the morning."

Then John took Joe and the Layburns in tow, and speedily opened the subject. Joe, the keeper, was not always a desirable visitor, for the old Adam in him occasionally broke out to the extent of tempting him with a fourth glass of whisky. We used cane-bottomed chairs, and that was why the women did not like Joe to pay a visit after he had passed his third tumbler. He was a very heavy man, who never sat down with proper deliberation when he had drink in him, and it was very awkward work to get him out of a chair when he had gone through the bottom. Nevertheless, Joe was invited into Mr. Featherstone's back shop, and the distinction gratified him. The interviews were most satisfactory, and next day almost everyone in the congregation who had any money was eager to be in the new speculation. The steamer was soon got ready, and went off on her first trip. The way in which John Featherstone and Captain Robb managed her was neither more nor less than a miracle of judgment and dash. Tommy Blaikie, who acted as auditor, was quite amazed by the accounts which were laid before him. Sometimes he was so very much amazed, and so very hard worked, that the two managers made him really handsome presents to encourage him, and these presents were never allowed to distress the shareholders.

All the fishermen and shopkeepers who held shares were completely satisfied. The *Gwendolen* was very fast, and her captain was one of the best business hands that ever wore a sou'-wester. He had a knack of dealing smartly with merchants, and for two years the vessel was never idle, never had a mishap, and never failed to leave over fifty per cent. No wonder that John Featherstone's prayers were admired in the chapel; the gracious powers had evidently taken the *Gwendolen's* shareholders into their keeping, and undoubtedly John had something to do with the luck. All went on pleasantly and smoothly for a long time. The ship was such a splendid speculation that Robb and Featherstone often wished they had borrowed money and bought her between them.

At last one of those little accidents that fret the current of mortal life came to sow dissension in our happy band. One morning John Featherstone was placidly engaged in composing a paper on " The Danger of Little Sins," when a telegram was handed in to him. It came from a southern port, and contained the following information : " *Gwendolen* touched heavily in coming in. Believe plates started. Have put her on ground for the present." John deliberated a little, and then went out. In the street he met Robb, and that worthy old person looked grave, for he also had received a telegram. The Captain had been determined to catch one of them, at all events. Said Robb, "Shall you go or me ?" "Oh, neither of us. Let's wait till Johnson notifies us further. There's time enough."

That evening at nine o'clock John Featherstone was seated in a second-class carriage at Newcastle Station. He was bound south, and he was reading Law's " Call to the Unconverted," to beguile the time until the train started. Suddenly he saw Captain Robb on the platform. The Captain had a woollen cap on, and was evidently going by the same train as Featherstone. Law's " Call " was forgotten for the time, and until York was reached the excellent manager remained in deep thought. " That artful old Robb has some move on." When the two gentlemen met at King's Cross they were so surprised and delighted that they could hardly express themselves. Robb said, with his jolly chuckle, " Lor, John, my boy ! Who would have thought of you being so careful ?" And John replied, " I thought I would save you trouble. I know how ardent you are, and you're not so young as you used to be. We young men must bear the burden and the heat of the day now until the going down of the sun."

Then Robb said, " We'll go together. It's a bad job, but perhaps it'll be blessed to us."

" I trust the best," solemnly observed Mr. Featherstone.

When they reached the vessel they found the skipper

disconsolate. Robb asked how things were, and the sailor said, " Bad, I doubt." " Have you had the divers down ?" said Captain Robb. " No, sir." " Then send ashore and get the divers off. Don't let them go down till we come back." Featherstone and the intelligent Robb went ashore, and the latter remarked in a questioning way, " She can't have very much the matter with her, can she ? Johnson's frightened about nothing."

" Oh ! Captain Robb, I fear that the calamity is not an ordinary one."

Mr. Featherstone's friends said he always used big words when he was going to do anything particularly sharp. He went on, " Had we not better telegraph to the papers at home ? That'll be the quickest way of letting all the share-holders know."

" All right. I'll go with you." It was curious to see how carefully the plants of grace watched each other. Next morning the village was fairly roused by Tommy Blaikie, who went about in a frantic way waving a newspaper. He fairly shouted with excitement, and people who heard his unwonted speech felt all the astonishment experienced by Balaam on a memorable occasion. By noon the whole village knew that the *Gwendolen* was badly knocked about, and anxious visits were paid to John Featherstone and Captain Robb. John had left word that he would be back in the evening ; Mr. Robb had left word that he had busi-ness in Newcastle, and it may here be said that the southerly journey of the two managers was never mentioned by the *Gwendolen's* skipper. A private interview in the cabin had something to do with this circumstance. Next day Robb and Featherstone were about the village as usual ; the *Gwendolen* was still in harbour. Tommy Blaikie met Feather-stone and moaned, " Eh ! what a bad, bad job ;" and Mr. Featherstone tried (with obvious effort) to cheer him. " Eh ! dear, dear. If aw could only get shot of my shares. You'll be goin' to the ship. Can you manage nowt for me at Newcastle ?"

" Well, Tommy, I own it's a bad job, but I'm not down-hearted. I'll give you ninety a piece for your shares now."

" Eh ! then you're on."

Mr. Robb and Mr. Featherstone ended by getting a very

18

large fraction of the *Gwendolen* between them, and the sellers
of shares were really grateful to the two wealthy men for
coming so gallantly forward and standing the risk.

When Mr. Robb and Mr. Featherstone were quite safe a
very marvellous thing occurred. The *Gwendolen* was docked,
and it was found that only one plate was a little bent.   In
spite of the newspapers (which are always believed by true
villagers) the damage was nothing, and the ship paid fifty-
six per cent. on her capital for three years after the sad
accident.   The grief of Tommy Blaikie and the other timid
shareholders was unappeasable, but Mr. Robb and Mr.
Featherstone showed no sorrow at all.   They even offered
to sell shares at 210, and they redoubled their vigour at
chapel, in spite of Mr. Blaikie's quarrelsome remarks.   I
wonder what the divers told the two managers?

VIII.

THE OLD MAIDS.

ON May evenings, before the sun on the high hills had
melted completely, the most southerly bulge of the Cheviots
looked like the bloom of some great flower as the westering
sun touched its gleaming sides, and against the sheet of pale
rose-colour the outline of a farmhouse was sharply defined,
as though it had been stamped out as one cuts a pattern.
Sometimes the image of the house wavered amid a silken
mist, and the smoke from the chimneys seemed to mix with
the shadows in the hollows of the far-off hill.   At three
miles' distance the picture was like a glimpse into some fairy
country, but when you got near enough to see details there
was nothing very delicate or beautiful about the house.   It
was a solid, square stone building, much overgrown with
honeysuckle and the other useless creepers which our
ancestors seem to have loved.

A great garden, with high walls, that fenced away the
blast from the Cheviots, stretched for a long way to the
rear of the building ; and in this garden there were mossy
walks, on which the gnarled apple-trees threw a dreamy
darkness.   On the ledges the wallflowers grew in careles

clumps, and when the dewfall began the odour of the flowers sank down and touched my nerves like music.

But outside the garden all the romance was gone. A very ugly and evil-smelling pond lay close to the house, and the ducks and geese kept up their commonplace chatter and screaming on its oily surface. I tried once to teach a hen to swim in this pond, for I thought the bird's education had been neglected. The circumstance which followed the failure of my attempt have something to do with my unpleasant memories of the pond.

In the big stockyard the pigs grunted luxuriously from their straw, and the comfortable poultry walked around with an air of sleepy happiness. Everything suggested plenty and peacefulness; the very maids who whirled the churn in the long, cool dairy looked as if they never hurried themselves; and old Joe, the steward, walked about the place as though he were the Wandering Jew, and knew he had all eternity to finish his journey in. Fifty years ago such places were common enough. They had a settled air, and you could see that the successive inhabitants had lived on in the same way for many generations—perhaps for centuries.

In the farmhouse lived four old ladies, who divided the property between them. Their land ran down to the sea, and they had rights on the warren that fringed the sand, and also on the foreshore. They and their pets dwelt very amicably together; they never fell out about anything unless it was when Miss Phœbe wanted to keep more than one of a litter of tortoiseshells, or when Miss Frances took a fancy to a new spaniel. In those cases Miss Phœbe thought Miss Frances carried her fondness for dogs a little too far; while Miss Frances thought Miss Phœbe was almost culpably sentimental about the maternal feelings of cats.

Miss Phœbe was a dainty lady, who dressed in the fashion of George II.'s time. She spoke with a sharp kind of twitter, and her voice was refined and very sweet. She loved children, and knew a great deal about their ways; and she was particularly indulgent towards the freaks of bad boys. Her brown eyes twinkled with tears when she heard of some childish trouble, and she had the prettiest little

18—2

ways of giving comfort. Her very voice was like a caress,
and when I made my attempt at the extended tuition of
poultry, and was afflicted for my trespass, I would have
cheerfully drowned another hen only to have the pretty old
dame lay her cheek, with its faded roses, against mine once
more. She would have been the best of mothers, but she
had reasons of her own for remaining unmarried. Her
affections were spent on other people's children and on her
sleek collection of tortoiseshell cats.

Miss Frances was not so refined as Miss Phœbe, for she
had not been away to the South. She was a sturdy old
lady, who spoke with a guttural accent, and never minced
her words very much. Her mode of dealing with risky
subjects was quite Shakespearian—or Biblical—in its directness, for she brought her manners from a bygone time ; but
she was healthy of mind, and far more pure than many
people who would have reddened had they heard her. She
liked manliness in men, and I believe in her youth she
would have married anyone who had pluck enough to run
away with her. But somehow she refused offer after offer
until her strong and beautiful face showed signs of age, and
then she resigned herself to loneliness. After she had
settled her fate she rather liked to speak of her own
marriage as a theoretic subject. She was great on the
bringing up of children, and displayed much fondness of
giving matrons advice. When she was past eighty years
old she would say, with a thoughtful air :—" Now when *I*
have bairns I'll not bring them up in that way. They shall
be learned to be handy—not like these creeturs that's no
more use than a laylock bush. Good bringing up's better
than goold." This showed her hopeful disposition. She
liked dogs, and her black spaniels were the most fat and
absurd creatures of their race.

Miss Hannah was a broad and powerful woman, with
bright cheeks and a pleasant smile. She was very deep-
chested, and when she rolled her sleeves ready to do some
work about the dairy she showed a massive white arm that
infected my youthful mind with apprehension. There was
no saying what such an arm might do if it were employed
in chastising one. Miss Hannah was as kind and tender as
her sisters, and she wou¹ i spend a whole winter evening in

devising amusements for children. She was good to everyone on the farm, but nobody dared disobey her, for her pale blue eyes seemed to strike fire when she had any call to be vexed, and even the Irishmen who came for the reaping were as sheepish in her presence as if she were the priest.

Miss Barbara had less character than the other three ladies. She was very silent, and shrinking in her ways; but everyone was fond of her, for her silence was not due to faulty temper or to secretive shyness. Children and animals, who are the best judges of personal character, always drew up to her and made friends.

These four good women led their calm lives from day to day with hardly a variation save the changes compelled by the seasons. On Sundays they took turns in going to church, and their queer bonnets and rich, quaint silks looked very pretty as they walked up the chill aisle. They were all very devout, and the couple who happened to have attended church according to the recognised rotation were expected to furnish a good account of all that the clergyman had said. This was not very hard to do, for the good man made one set of sermons serve him for forty years, and thus his arguments grew familiar to the more dutiful of his parishioners.

On week-days there was much bustling about the house and the dairy during the morning, but the afternoon was given over to leisure. The sea was close by, and the ladies liked to stroll over the broad sands of the Bay, and gather shells when the weather was fine. When light breezes blew, and the water curled on the beach with soft, purring noises, Miss Phœbe would say, "This is pleasant for the boys;" and when the breakers boomed on the rocks with heavy thunder, the four sisters wondered, with many tender little phrases, where the boys could be in this wild time. Sometimes the masts of a ship could be seen above the sandhills on stormy mornings, and the ladies could soon tell whether she had impaled herself on the low rocks or not. If it happened to be a wreck I am afraid that Miss Phœbe and Miss Hannah thought more about the "boys" than about the sailors, though they were always lavishly kind to shipwrecked men.

These boys, whose names so often came up in the little household, were the nephews of the Old Maids. All the affection that might have been given to husband and children was bestowed on the fortunate pair, and the two young fellows had a pleasant time when they came to the farm together. Henry and Lancelot Bamborough were both sailors, and you could not have seen much finer young people anywhere. Henry was a straight, dark lad, with a keen, bronzed face and resolute mouth. He was as fond of field sports as any landsman, and he never went out without the gun when he was staying at home. Lancelot was a merry fellow, who kept the house lively all the time he was in it. The maids used to retire to the sideboard, and giggle in a most ill-trained manner, when he began with his nonsense at lunch-time, and Miss Hannah had to remind him several times a day that he would be the death of her. Both the young men were in East Indiamen at a time when that position meant a great deal. They had been quarter-deck apprentices in the same vessel, and although they usually had several fights during each voyage in their younger days, an occasional exchange of black eyes did not cause any lengthy breach of friendship. When they grew up and went into different ships they were seldom at home together ; but when they did meet, no two friends could have been more cordial.

Their visits formed the great events in the Old Maids' lives. When one of the youngsters had announced his arrival the whole house was put in commotion, and the most amazing efforts were made with a view to producing a variety of pastry : you might have thought the pantry was stocked for a siege.

As the rattle of the cart came nearer and nearer, the old ladies moved by degrees to the front door, and when they saw the expected bright face, and the gloss of the pretty uniform, they could hardly keep up their stiff, old-fashioned reticence. The young men were never bored, and never asked to sacrifice their amusements. The house was their own, and all the farm people were their devoted servitors.

If Harry came in very late from snipe-shooting, there was more anxiety about his wet feet than about the dinner he had kept waiting; and even if he had let the big black spaniel get smothered in the treacherous moss he would not have been scolded. It would only be tiresome to tell of the long pleasant evenings spent in the old parlour, but I may say that the rattling gossip of the sailors sometimes kept Miss Phœbe and Miss Frances up till after ten o'clock ; the other two ladies would not have been guilty of such profligacy had the whole of his Majesty's Court paid them a visit.

The proudest moments for the Old Maids came when they took their handsome favourites to church. The hushed and admiring gossip of the loungers among the gravestones ; the benevolent and well-bred stare from Sir John's pew by the chancel, and the kindly simple chatter of friends when church was over, all made the morning pleasant in extreme. Miss Phœbe was a born matchmaker, and when Lancelot shook his plume of fair hair and poised his head proudly, she was always certain that Sir John's daughter must admire the boy, and pine for him. The good ladies made all the arrangements for the match by means of dark hints among themselves, but I am sorry to say that nothing ever came of their diplomacy.

Amid all this it was curious to see that none of the Old Maids showed any preference for either of their nephews, and the two young men never felt the least jealousy. I do not believe that the sailors gave much thought to the money that might come to them. Harry and Lancelot met once when their vessels were brought up at Singapore, and they naturally chatted about home. In the course of the conversation Harry said, "Our skipper retires next trip. He's made his lot. I suppose if we had the Moor between us we might retire, too ;" and Lancelot answered, "Plenty of time for that; I'd sooner have the old girls than their money." So one happy furlough after another went by, the pile of merry, good-hearted letters from the sailors accumulated at the Moor Farm (the latest epistles were shown as a great favour to certain selected neighbours), and the Old Maids grew more and more grey.

By-and-by Lancelot and Harry obtained commands, and then a great change took place in the beautiful family life that had lasted so long. Lancelot came home from a very long voyage, and his aunts were overjoyed when the cart went off to the station for him. As he came up between the hedgerows to the house his voice sounded very loudly, and when he came to the door he lurched from the shaft of the cart and staggered clumsily. Then he began to talk, " Hello ! Aunt Phœbe. Well, Aunt Hannah. In fighting trim as usual. Give us a kiss, old girl, any one of you," and as he laid his hands on Miss Phœbe's shoulders a waft of his breath made her wince and shrink away. He turned to Miss Hannah, but that majestic dame froze into an image of displeasure.

"Lancelot ! Nephew ! We've not see anything of this kind in the house for a long time. Are you going the same road as your father ?"

Miss Barbara timidly interposed. " Lancey's been driving fast, Hannah ; he's excited a little. He must come in and have some tea, and then he can lie on the sofa till he's quiet. Silly boy. Come in directly "

The silly boy, who stood over six feet, and had a beard down to his second coat button, lurched into the parlour, blundered heavily over Dash the spaniel, who waddled to meet him, and fell into a cane chair, nearly wrecking it.

Old Joe explained this memorable catastrophe. " Seven whiskies Mr. Lancey had at that infernal station, and he was gay and full when he gat on the platform. He spent a sovereign in ten minutes, treatin' the whole parlour. His fethor ower again. I misdooted but he would tyek the wrang turn one o' these days."

Miss Hannah said, "Go up to your room, Phœbe Bamborough, and take Frances with you. Leave me to see to this silly boy. Silly boy, Barbara calls him. Did I ever think !"

Then Miss Hannah turned sternly to the blinkard, who was rolling on her pretty chair, and bade him lie down at once. She pulled off his boots with her own hand, and when he had fallen asleep, she stood by him a long time, looking sternly at his face. His fine features were just a little puffed, and the sharpness of their outline was gone. Under his eyes two unhealthy prominences rose, and she saw that his forehead had lost its clearness. " The curse, the curse," the old lady muttered. " If I thought he would be like his father I would stab him where he lies."

Miss Phœbe beckoned Miss Barbara into her room, and the old women held each other's hands. " Let us kneel down and pray for the boy, Barbara dear," said Miss Phœbe, and the two ladies knelt sobbing for a few minutes.

In the morning Lancelot's eyes were red, for all the delicate vessels were charged with foul blood. He pushed his plate aside with a sudden movement as of nausea, and said, "For God's sake, aunt, don't put an egg in front of me." Then he drank tea in huge mouthfuls, and crumbled a piece of toast with his shaky and undecided fingers. It was a sorrowful breakfast-table. In the old times he would have been laughing mightily at the dismal show of egg-shells, and his aunts would have been prophesying their own speedy ruin while coaxing him to try some fresh extravagance. But drink is the end of merriment. An ugly ghost of joy haunts a drinker over night; but it is only a nightmare that grins through a mask of gladness. In the morning the mask is thrown away, and the nightmare unseasonably remains to blot the daylight.

Lancelot's fit of penitence and bile lasted for three days, and during that time his manners were subdued and his old charm seemed to return. On the fourth day he took his rod out and went to the burn. Nine o'clock came, then ten, and the Old Maids sat silently, not daring to look in each other's eyes.

Lancelot was the hero at an inn about three miles off. His jolly roaring laugh sounded through the red curtains, and the drunken tailor, who was the oracle of the company, declared that "there nivvor was siccan a chep for good company."

At eleven Miss Hannah said, "If I were ten years younger I'd put the side-saddle on Daisy and go up to the place myself. I know where he is."

At twelve o'clock a jolting was heard in the lane; then the slipping of hoofs sounded in the yard, and a thick voice roared a drunken song:

> "So up came the cook of our gallant ship,
>   And a jolly old cook was he,
> And he didn't care a damn for the kettle nor the pan,
>   Nor yet for the bottom of the sea."

Then there was a prolonged rumbling chorus that sounded as if the singer were slavering. The bright gentleman, the well-bred boy with his frank and charming manners, had come thus far. A man led him in, and Lancelot cried, "Starboard a bit!" as he sank in a heap on the floor.

At midday he came shivering downstairs, and begged a jug of ale from the servant-girl. The mug rattled on his teeth, and he sucked more than a pint before the dry foulness of his mouth was slaked. Then he went into the breakfast-room, and found Miss Hannah sitting at the table upright, stern, and pale.

"We won't make any more delays, Lancelot Bamborough. Your aunts have gone out, and they have asked me to speak for them. We think little of our own convenience, for we love you too dearly to mind any trouble. But you must not ruin your body and soul. We cannot allow you—at least, not here. We shall always love you, and do the best for you; but you shall not come near us again unless you alter. Your father went that way and ruined himself, and you are far down the evil road. Stay with us a little, darling, and try to be better. If you don't, you must go and never come near us any more."

Lancelot remained quite sober for a week, and the pale tints came back to Miss Phœbe's withered cheeks. Her handsome boy walked out with her once or twice, and, although he was too morbidly self-conscious to go to church, he talked with something of his old bright abandonment. When he went away, Miss Barbara sidled softly to the cart and whispered, "Be good, my man; and we'll pray for you all the time."

Then the foolish Old Maids went to their parlour, and did no more work that day.

Nine months afterwards Henry Bamborough came home. He had become a fine fellow, a typical sailor of the splendid old school. There was nothing of the dandy about him, and he showed a fist that had never been used to a glove; but you could not mistake him for anything but a gentleman. He did not look lively, and when delicate questions regarding Lancelot were put to him, he shifted his ground uneasily. At last Miss Frances said quite roughly:

"Tell us plain about Lancey. Has anything happened him? We haven't had a word for months now."

Harry was in an awkward position, but, as he was challenged, he answered:

"Well, if you must know, aunt, Lancelot was unshipped three months ago. The passengers made the chief officer put him ashore at Madeira."

As a matter of fact Lancelot had been taken with delirium tremens, and he was the first man who disgraced the great Company which he served.

"Then where is he now?"

"Well, I heard that he was off to Australia. He can do no more good here, and I'm sorry for it. He was as good a fellow as ever I knew, and I'll share to my last crown with him if he'll keep clear of brandy. If I could have been about with him this would never have happened."

The Old Maids felt that another great change had come upon their lives, and it was the more sorrowful to them since the very youngest of them was nearing the dark verge beyond which the certainties lie. But Miss Phœbe said:

"We must save him. You said just now you were going an Australian voyage in your new employ, Henry. Can you not seek him out and make him come home? *Make* him. We would rather fasten him up here and bar the door than we would let him go out to ruin himself."

"But Australia's a biggish place, aunt."

"Never mind; I'm sure you'd find him, and bring him home before any of us die."

Henry Bamborough stayed for awhile, and amused himself among the rushes and over the moor. But he felt strangely now that he knew Lancelot was gone, for he had been very fond of him, and he was a man of tenacious habits. His liking for Lancelot had become a habit with him, and he held it closely.

So Henry sailed from Liverpool in his new vessel, and the last note he wrote before going aboard said, "My dear aunts, I will rout Lancey up and fetch him home, if I can; but I am bound for Sydney, and heaven only knows where he may be."

All that winter the Old Maids waited for news, but none came. They got up a game at whist sometimes, and played with much severity; but their scientific and rigid play did not give them nearly so much fun as the harumscarum method of the "boys." One evening the snow drifted halfway up the parlour window. Miss Frances looked out,

and saw the blinding whirl blown over the desolate fields.
The sparrows under the eaves huddled together and chirped
faintly. Miss Frances said, "They tell me there's no snow
on the other side of the world. The lads cannot be ill off
if that's so ;" and this consideration made them all rather
happy, for indeed the sea looked deadly cold under the
dropping wreaths. Spring wore away and summer. Then
came the autumn, and the crowd of Irish reapers came over
to break our quiet life with their piggish habits and their
dangerous ways. Miss Hannah often thought : "Eh me !
if they were only here what laughing we should have !
How they used to tease Big Terence and Curly Jack ! I
mind the time when they wrapped the herd's donkey in a
sheet and sent it to meet Terence coming home. And how
he prayed. Eh me ! And I'm old, old, and some of us
must go soon." Poor Miss Hannah's prophecy was not
long in coming true. That winter Miss Barbara grew very
weak and could not leave her room. She would not make
any will, and she died quietly in the night, after whispering, " I wonder when the boys will be down."

Miss Phœbe only lasted a year after Barbara, and by that
time the Old Maids had given up all hope of seeing their
idol again. Poor Miss Phœbe often wandered in her illness,
and once she said, "I should have had a boy like Lancelot,
with the fair, bonny hair, but it's all in the grave now."
There was a portrait of a very good-looking young fellow in
Phœbe's desk, and round it was a strip of paper with " For
Ever " written on it. The young man was rather like
Lancelot in the face.

Miss Hannah and Miss Frances were left to play double
dummy in the evenings. Frances used to say, "The one
of us that's left 'll have a dull time. I'm in hopes it'll not
be me." The sharp, decided woman shared the passion of
her sisters for the two sailors ; she took a fancy now to look
over the sea day by day from a high window, and she came
down quite jocular—sometimes distressingly jocular—when
the ships appeared to be sliding smoothly by. About this
time she began her habit of attending to her own prospec-
tive family, which habit often caused young people to feel
awkwardly inclined to smile. But the poor lady was very
serious indeed about it, and nothing but an allusion to her

adored nephews could draw her from her favourite topic. Miss Hannah had resolutely resolved to think no more of her loss; time was passing; death was nearing, and even her great frame was shaken, although she was much younger than her frail sister. But on some nights when the hoarse roar of the sea filled the air, and the bents whistled as the wind flew over, she could not keep her thoughts from her children—the children that had filled the void in her own life. Miss Frances passed away in her turn. In her last days she used to say, "I thought I would have nursed their bairns. They should have had some fine ones if looks went for anything. But the Lord cheated me of my own and theirs too." Miss Hannah went about such work as she could do, like a hard old stoic as she was. She grew so feeble that a chair had to be placed for her outside the dairy, where she could just see all that was going on. One hot day, when the place was even more sleepy than usual, a tramp toiled into the yard, wiping his face as he passed the wicket. When the dogs were called off, the man walked straight up to Miss Hannah, and said, "Aunt!" The old lady made no sign of surprise. "Where's Harry?" she said sharply.

"Poor fellow! he's gone long since. Ship took all hands down with her, and I wish I had been there."

When Lancelot had been made fit for the parlour, Miss Hannah came in to look at him. She raised herself by a great effort and put her arms round his neck, and rested silently.

She made just as much of the broken ne'er-do-well as she would have made of the brave fellow who was under the sea. But then that is just like the perversity of women, and some of us have reason to be glad that their perversity is so invariable.

IX.

THE FOUR SAILORS.

ON the face of a rolling bluff, caused by a bend of a low stream that worked its way through loamy soil, John Bewick's cottage stood. Great woods waved and rustled on the deep sides of the burn, and on windy nights when I sat by the kitchen fire in John's house the whole air seemed full of a solemn roar that rose and deepened and died away with strange rhythmic intervals. I liked to sit there and listen to this solemn music. Sometimes there would be a long interval of low sighing, as though the tired branches would fain sleep. Then the cool airs would make one effort in unison, and the boughs would bend together with one whistling rush, and recover themselves, panting and trembling, once more. I learned to recognise the different sounds made by various species of trees. The firs always seemed shrewish. The birch made me think of tears, but in the deep, hoarse notes of the elm there always seemed a kind of sombre triumph. The sluggish stream never was flooded, and winter and summer its sullen current rolled down to the sands, where it broke into hundreds of rivulets and straggled away over the bay into the sea. A little way beyond John Bewick's house a narrow footboard crossed the river, and I liked to look down into the brown depths of the water. Everybody who came to our village had to cross this stream, and John Bewick could tell half a mile off which of the residents was coming or going when he saw a figure sharply defined against the grey moor. John was a very quiet and deliberate man who seldom spoke. His massive face was full of thought, and in the strong pose of his hands and feet and in all his gestures there was an indescribable suggestion of manliness and reserved power. If you met him going across the moor, his shaggy brows bent and his head occasionally nodding as he seemed to follow the stages of an intricate argument, you would certainly have been tempted to look round at him. Mrs. Bewick was an uneducated woman, but, like her husband, she had a great deal of natural sense. I liked the couple for their homely ways, and I was also very fond of the four lads who were born to them. John Bewick had been a sailor, but he had managed to lay by as much money as brought him in about £40 per year; and this, with a little farm which had come to him by marriage, enabled him to live very comfortably indeed. The four lads were very near each other in age. Stephen was fifteen, Harry fourteen, John twelve, and Thorncliffe ten, when I first knew them. The old man's talk mostly ran upon nautical matters, and on

winter evenings, when the horses had been foddered and all
the buildings were carefully locked, he would talk for an
hour in his quiet, jerking way about the many adventures
of his seafaring years. You cannot find a sailor of ordinary
intelligence whose talk is not vivid and interesting by sheer
weight of experience; but John had a certain dramatic
quality which made every one of his stories remain in the
memory for long, and nothing pleased the boys more than
to coax a yarn out of their father. They were living by the
sea, and indeed you might easily have thrown a stone from
the door of the cottage into the water when the tide was
high. The ships glided past northward and southward,
and, like all the village children, the young Bewicks had a
never-failing delight in talking about the various vessels.
One of their favourite games on holidays was to sit in the
hollow among the brackens and take turns in regarding the
passing ships as their property. A steamer counted for five,
a barque four, a brig three, a schooner two, and a billyboy
one; and at the end of a given time the boys would count
up to see who had gained the most marks in this queer
competition. As I have said before, no boys living on the
coast were able to conceive any life excepting that of a
sailor. They allowed the existence of landsmen, and they
were even willing to admit that bakers, butchers, and
farmers are not without their ultimate uses, but the only real
manly employment was that of a sailor; and as soon as a
boy reached thirteen he was as impatient as a young sea-
bird to take to the water. Stephen Bewick stayed at
school until he was past fifteen because his father wished
him to have a good knowledge of theoretical navigation.
He could do questions in plane sailing when he was twelve
years old, and before he went away he was capable of working a longitude by chronometer according to the old-fashioned
naval method. At last Stephen was bound apprentice, and
on one dreary morning his mother watched him stride across
the bridge on his way to the little black seaport. She had
shown very little emotion as the boy went away, because
she did not want to distress him, but her lips trembled
when he was fairly across the stream; and when at last his
smart figure disappeared behind the curve of a sandhill she
turned hastily into the kitchen and hid her face in her

hands. When John came in he patted his wife on the
shoulder, and said, "Never thou mind, hinny; he had to go
away some time, and, after all, 'tis only a three months
voyage, and you will be rare and proud of him when he
comes home."

Then Mrs. Bewick said, "It is the first of them that has
gone, and I was just thinking I shall never hear the wind at
night now without fretting about my bonny bairn. Oh,
dear, dear! if we could only persuade them to stop ashore
and take to some job up in the town, why, they could come
home once a week to see us, and not be going away on the
weary, weary sea. I've seen a drowned man on the sand,
John. Do you mind that young Dane when he was drifted
ashore at the Star letch! Eh me! but the slavers was
running out by his poor bit mouth, and his bonny hair was
all tangled and wild like. An' maybe his mother was waiting for him in his own country, and him just pitched ashore
like a lump of seaweed; and I thought it might be one of
mine. The young foreigner wasn't so bonny as Stephen,
but still his mother would be fond of him, and that's
what's on my heart this day." Then the good woman sat
beating the floor with her foot, and making little ejaculations. When the supper was laid and the three younger
boys gathered round, Mrs. Bewick was suddenly struck with
the sight of the empty chair, so she rose and said, "Oh,
Johnny, give the bairns their supper thyself. I will just
away to bed, and maybe I'll forget before the morning."

Some very bad weather came away in a week or two after
this. The wind rushed down the great hollow of the river with
angry noises; and when the smoke was driven down the
chimney and the swift rain-drops flogged the panes, John
Bewick and his wife sometimes exchanged a look that
meant a great deal. At last on one blessed morning a letter
with a strange-looking stamp was brought from the town
by young Thorncliffe, who had been sent every day to the
post-office by his mother; and the good woman hardly dared
open the envelope, the choking in her throat came so suddenly
upon her. Stephen said:—"Dear Father and Mother,—
We arrived here yesterday, after a very bad passage. After
we got over the Bar I turned a little sick, and then I
thought about you a great deal, and wished you could only

come and fetch me back home again. But it soon got over, and although I think about you every night, still, my dear parents, we have to part some time, and I shall soon be making my own living, and then when you get old I shall be able to help you a good deal. The captain is not very rough with his hands, but he swears a good deal now and then, and I wish he would take his meat not quite so dirty. I have to wait on them just as though I was a servant girl, and I don't like to see him throwing bits of onions and splashes of soup all over his coat-breast. It is not like what we were used to at home. I don't like these foreigners much, from what I have seen of them. We have got a lot of fellows on board discharging us, and they look as though they wanted washing very badly. I don't get quite so much soap and water as I should like here, and my hands have been very bad with salt-water cracks; but I think I shall get on very well, for I have helped the captain every day when he has taken the sun. You must tell father that our skipper does not do navigation the same as Mr. Barum taught me. After he has taken the sun he runs to the bulwarks and rubs out the figures he made the day before. Then, if it is dry weather, he just sends me down to look at the declination, and then he gets his latitude out with a sum of two lines. I fancy he must be often miles wrong, but still he makes his ports all right. I miss you most just after the dog-watches, for then I think how nice and warm you all are round the fire; but I have to take my turn with the men, and it is very cold work when the ship is beating. I hope that my brothers and old Teazer are all right. I shall bring you home some wooden bowls for the drawer tops. Give my respects to the minister and all friends. I don't know when we shall sail from here, but it will be a very pleasant day for me when I am able to come across the bridge once more and see you. And now, my dear parents, I must stop, because the letters have to go ashore. So no more at present from your affectionate son, STEPHEN BEWICK."

I like these queer old letters, and I have many of them in my possession. The sailors do not write so well as they talk. Their letters are not demonstrative, but there is something in their simple clumsy phrases that always

19

touches me deeply; and I read the yellow old sheets with just as much pleasure as ever I got from any high-class literature. Long after this there came a brightish afternoon, and Mrs. Bewick had gone down the garden to look after the bees. She looked across the stream and saw something that caused her to fling her arms up in the air, and then, with a total disregard of dignity, she ran to the house and said, " Oh! bairns, hinny, here's Stephen coming down the bridge." Then she ran down the path with her cap strings streaming behind her, and when she got up to her boy she cried and laughed together, and patted him on the back, as though he had been merely a little fellow He put his arm round his mother's waist, and took her into the house, where she proceeded to flourish about in a perfect bewilderment of joy. When John came in to supper there was some brave talk, and Stephen sat up until nearly twelve o'clock, telling his kindly commonplace stories about the voyage. Of course he had to be shown in church on Sunday. That was an essential part of a sailor's duty when he came home to the village. And there was a great deal of hand-shaking and pleasant questioning after the sermon was over. When Stephen went to sea again his mother was just as bad as though she had no previous experience, although when her husband used to go away she got over her dulness after the first day or two; but she never reconciled herself to parting with the lad. In a year after Stephen's first voyage had ended Harry declared he would go to sea, and John Bewick and his wife had to submit to the youngster's inclination, as though it were inevitable that he must be a sailor. They felt it hard to part with their children, but it would have seemed almost unnatural to the old man if any one of his lads had stayed ashore. Mrs. Bewick was quite patient, but always on stormy nights she liked to sit up and take occasional looks from the front door to see if the " white horses " were trampling and rearing out in the bay. Every morning when her husband got up she would say, " Ah ! John, hinny, just tell me what airt the wind is blowing."

John never spoke about north or east, nor'-east or south-west, for he knew his wife cared little about the points of the compass. When he made his report he would say,

" Stephen has got a fair wind, I think he will be about the Sleeve now; and Harry, I fancy, will be getting it warm somewhere down the Channel. If poor Jack's got through the Gut he will have the wind right astern ; but I doubt it will be awkward if they are running down the coast."

The woman liked to have sailors about the house, and the good fellows knew perfectly well what she aimed at when she put leading questions about the weather. They would cheer her in their rough way, and they very often invented fictions of a daring kind to prevent her from worrying.

In due time Stephen passed for mate, and when he came home Thorncliffe's imagination was excited by his brother's smartness. Stephen was rattling on in his loud, jolly way one night, and his mother was looking at him with childish delight. The young man was as powerful as his father, and his face had a kind of mobile delicacy which came from the mother's side. His hair was long, and fell in heavy curving masses behind his ears, for the old sailormen considered long hair to be a proper male adornment; his dark eye and his habit of wearing earrings gave him an out-of-the-way look, and he was very pleasant to see as he talked his jolly nonsense at the head of the big oak table. Suddenly Stephen said, " Thornie should go with me. We'll make a slasher of him in a little bit."

Thorncliffe's eye flashed eagerly, but the mother turned pale, and trembled. " Nay, nay, my man. Nay, nay. Oh! if you're all away I'll never sleep sound no more. The wind's awful at nights now, and eh ! when the froth comes into the garden it makes my heart sore to see. What would I do if all the four of you were gone ?"

Thorncliffe was silent, for he did not like to distress his mother, and he stroked her hair when he kissed her at bed-time ; but when the lads got to their bedroom the youngster said, " Keep that up, Steve. Coax the old lady round, and let me be away soon. I hate staying ashore, and I can't learn anything more at school."

That night Mrs. Bewick said to John, " What was that they were saying about two of a family sailing together, hinny ?"

" Never would do. Don't like it, my woman. Shouldn't

19—2

have too many eggs in one basket. If the ship goes, then
two of your bairns go. If they're in different ships you
have two chances. I never knew much luck come of
brothers sailing together. Tom Ramsden and Bill went
away with the *Peacock*. Never heard of, and the old woman
had no other support. Bill Bowers took his son to sea.
Came away bad weather off the Head, and he goes ashore.
The youngster cried, and old Bill cried too. He wasn't
caring about himself, but, as he said, the old girl would
think him a useless creetur for losing the bairn. Only the
cook was saved out of the whole ship's company. Don't
like brothers going, nor fathers and sons."

"Then, John, hinny, don't let Stephen persuade Thorncliffe away. Let me keep just the one. I try to bear up,
but I think I'll just lie down and die if we're left with an
empty house. And the boy's so bonny and fine-like. His
hands was never made for tar."

Bewick promised to do his best, and a compromise was
arranged. Thornie declared for the sea, but he agreed not
to go with his brother, although he laughed at his mother's
reasons.

When Thorncliffe Bewick's sea-chest had to be got ready
his mother shed many tears over the things as she packed
them. She knew every article that a sailor needed, and
she carefully showed her boy where to find everything.
"Here's your needles and thread, in this side till; and
there's the beeswax with them. And here's a skin cap for
snowy weather. It's better than a sou'-wester. And I've
putten your Bible under the sea-boots, my man, and you'll
look at it on Sundays whiles, will you not? I've put
a place-keeper in there, where I want you to read. It's
about Jesus and the sea, hinny, and 'Peace, be still;' and
you'll think of me when you look at it, and trust in
the Lord to bring you to us again."

So the poor soul talked on, and every little thing that
she put into the box drew fresh admonitions and fresh tears
from her. When the cart came for Thornie the mother
said, "I'm going myself to see the last of the bairns away.
I never could bear it with the others, but I'll try now," and
she jolted across the ford, and went away over the moor
with her darling.

When the train clanked away southward, and Thornie waved brightly from his window, Mrs. Bewick sat down in the station and moaned as she rocked herself to and fro. An old woman offered comfort. "Maw Tom's away i' the syem train, hinny. Eh! weary on the sea. Aw divvn't knaw what for God didn't myek nowt but dry land. Fower o' mine's away, forbye the awd man, but it's elways somethin' when they come back. It's like when the bairn's born—ye forget a' the trubble, mistress."

But Mrs. Bewick was too sad, and a weight seemed to hang on her heart. She fretted about the house when she got home, and her kind husband tried all means to keep her from mourning. He remarked in his odd way, "Why, I always thought you were the best man of the two, but I think I'm the top hand now. Brighten up. You'll be like a young sweetheart when the lad comes back; and here's Harry arrives on Saturday if the wind holds up, and very likely Steve 'll be in. Tuts, tuts! There'll be grand fun yet, bless you."

A month after this Mrs. Bewick was mournfully setting out the tea-things, when a man from the town tapped at the door. Her eyes dilated and her lips parted as she looked at the visitor's face. The kind sailor shuffled a little, and then asked, "John in?"

Mrs. Bewick stared steadily at him. "What are you wanting John for?" Then she said rapidly, "Tell me. Tell me directly. Which is it? Is it Harry or Stephen? You haven't had time to hear of John. And, oh me! is it Thornie?" The woman had caught the man's arm, and the mark of her grip was there next day. The sailor tried to approach the matter cautiously, but the mother's compressed vehemence was too much for his reserve. "Tell me the worst. It's Thornie?"

"Yes."

"Where? Will I ever see him?"

"In heaven. The ship went ashore by Finisterre. All hands gone."

Then Mrs. Bewick said quietly, "You'll wait till John comes in, and he'll get you some tea. I think something has broken in my heart. We must try to keep John from taking on, poor fellow. He liked Thornie best."

When John Bewick came in his wife went up to him, put her hands on his shoulders, and then kissed him. He glanced quickly aside, and as soon as he saw the sailor he knew something was wrong. He tried to say, " Which is it ?" but his voice died in his throat ; and when the mother said, " It's the bairn. It's Thornie," he sat down in a vague kind of way, and repeated her words after her. A little blood ran on to his beard, and he stared stupidly at the red stain on his fingers when he had wiped the drops away.

It was a sad year for the Bewicks after Thornie was drowned, and the mother often spent hours upstairs turning over the drawers and looking at relics. The curl of the lad's hair, the smart red shoes that his father brought from Cronstadt, his schoolbooks—all the forlorn trivialities that mothers preserve—kept the poor soul busy for whole after-noons. There is nothing lamentable at last in the universe, but that dumb sorrow of the mother's lacerates my heart. It is so helpless, so far past phrases. I know so many and many whose children have been drowned, and their silent weakness, the quiet patience with which they wait for the end, and the piercing pathos of their commonplace talk, move me deeply. I have sometimes wondered whether any-thing can ever make up for that helpless suffering inflicted by the random blows that fate strikes from the dark. I doubt it.

Stephen got married about a year after Thorncliffe was lost, and it happened that all the lads were at home together. When the bride and bridegroom came home from the church, the blacksmith's apprentices fired the old cannon off again and again, and the men got very tipsy in the morning, Mrs. Bewick was almost cheerful. After Stephen had sailed she kept the girl a long time at the farm, and talked much with her. One day she said, " When you have bairns, hinny, never let them take to the sea. You'll wish you never had borne them. My lads are good and kind, but I am always letting my mind run on about my poor Thornie that's under the water. You'll not like to think that the bairn you travailed for had his eyes picked out by the gulls. His bonny eyes——" And then Mrs. Bewick fell into many meditations.

But the world is a hard place to understand, and this simple countrywoman had much to bear before her release came. Within a year from that time she came home from the town and found some of the neighbours from the village attending to Stephen's wife. Bad news had come, and the poor girl's baby was born just a fortnight after its father's vessel went down with all hands in the Bay.

Mrs. Bewick grew quite grey after Stephen died, and she ceased to speak about her loss. There was the drowned man's wife and child to keep, and the good woman was passionately fond of the little lad. He reminded her of Thornie. John and Harry grew into slashing fellows, and they were very fond of each other. They liked to be at home together, and the place was made merry by their presence, in spite of the memories that neither John Bewick nor his wife could keep from rising at unthought-of times.

The lads persuaded their mother not to fret when they decided to sail in the same ship, and they were quite joyous when they set off together. Mrs. Bewick was talking softly at supper-time on the night before the boys went on their first voyage in company, and she said, "Now, my sons, I'm going right to the river with you to-morrow, and so is your father. We're going to the pier-end, and we'll see the very last of you, so mind you'll look out and wave when the tug leaves you."

"What's your notion for that, mother ?"

"Why, you see, I let Thornie go, and I never went further than the station, and I mind how he waved, and I can see the way his bonny eyes shone now. And then Stephen went, and I never saw him ; and we've just got the two of you, and so we'll see you for as many minutes as we can. If I could only persuade one of you to stop and help with the farm !"

So John Bewick put on his best black coat and his beaver hat (which was usually brushed very carefully the wrong way), and the old couple went into the great town with their boys.

The ship moved with stately quietness through the churning backwash of the fussy tug ; then the topsails were set ; then the dignified owner got over the side, trying to look as though he had not tasted the captain's brandy ; and then the vessel sank into the southerly shadows. Harry and his brother had both run up into the shrouds, and they waved to John Bewick and his wife until the boatswain began to use bad language.

Twice more the old couple took their trip to the south; once they waved their good-byes from the pier, and once the owner invited them to join the merry party that crossed the Bar. They had begun to think their evil fortune would vex them no longer, but it was not to be. There is no need to draw out a sad story longer, and indeed I hate sentiment too much to be inclined to use many words. The dumb pain, the random tragedy of life, may be thought about with sternness; but phrases are useless. Sometimes I hear a chord of music, a thought of Beethoven's that seems to say what I should like to say about the searing agony of parting, the bitterness of death; but words fail.

Henry and John Bewick died; but they did not meet their fate amid the stress of wild weather, where the roar of great winds and the mad confusion of the water prevent one from thinking of death. Some poet or other has said—

> " 'Twill be like fighting, when the spray
>   Whirls its sharp arrows through the blast ;
> And the long waves, in huge array,
>   March with their heavy thunder past."

But the lads had not the luck to find their doom in the rush of despairing excitement. They went to New Orleans at the bad time of year, and they both died there. Their mother shed no tears, and John Bewick only said, "God has queer ways of doing things. He's taken my lads, and I'll pray never more."

Mrs. Bewick sometimes would say, "All the other folks can go round the churchyard on Sunday and see where their bairns lie, and put flowers down; but all my bonny lads, that had such bonny hair, they're all away, and I can never see their graves."

She lived a good life, and I think she was glad when the time came for her to die. Almost her last words were addressed to Stephen's wife. She said, "Don't let little Steve go to sea, my dear." The people pitied the old couple; but then everyone who has to do with the cruel sea learns to know much of suffering, and there are plenty of others who need pity just as much as did John and Jane Bewick.

X.

THE MODERN SMUGGLER.

THE smuggler about whom we used to read in boyhood was a creature given to secret and desperate ways. His low black lugger was always having hair-breadth escapes from those sharks of Revenue men; and when he got ashore and caroused with his mates in a romantic cave he held his bumper of brandy in one hand and an enormous horse-pistol in the other. Dangers compassed him round about, and he was always under the necessity of making heroic speeches expressive of his contempt for death. If he was caught on board his lugger he invariably destroyed several of his Majesty's Coastguards in the course of the conflict, and when he did succumb he usually expired while making an heroic attempt to reach the powder-magazine in order to blow friends and enemies to destruction together. There was hardly an old abbey on the coast which was not utilized in some way or other by the acute outlaws, and the crooked passages which the monks carved out long ago were employed for the most secular purposes by the men who cheated the Revenue. Down on the Romney Marshes the smugglers were mere cut-throats, who depended greatly upon force; but away to the North the process of dodging the Revenue was more artistic. The East Coast smuggler was not only a good sailor who could feel his way blindfold into his own bay, and who knew the set of the tides over every mile from The Spurn to Harwich, from Flamborough to Dunbar; he was obliged to have some skill in organization, and a great deal of business ability into the bargain. The trade was reduced to a science, and the losses were calculated and allowed for with all the skill of a modern underwriter.

After the cobles came back in a morning one of the fisherwives would carry her creel from farm-house to farm-house. After she and the farmer's people had screeched and argued in the usual way for some time, the fisher would lift her hand in a careless manner and march on. The sign was understood, and at night, when the time for foddering the horses came, the farmer would say, "You'll not need to lock the styebble the neet;" and so, after the horses had been made to move hither and thither while their bedding was tossed up, the stable-door was left on the jar.

If the hoofs rattled on the cobble-stones as the horses slipped and stumbled out of the yard the farmer was not troubled. He simply said, "That'll be the lads. The *Sarah's* in the bay;" and then he turned away quite contentedly when the dull thud of hoofs grew softer and softer as Billy and Beauty and Boxer cantered down to the sea. In the morning he had only to stick a fork into the straw-heap or the midden to find something that paid for the hire of the horses.

Down by the bay and along the sandhills there was much activity. Girls and women were out strangely late, and on dark nights they held up their horn lanterns to take a look at the passers-by. As soon as the flood set inward all the watchers kept a sharp eye to the southward. When a light flared for an instant out at sea a curlew whistled from the southernmost point, and the shrill wail was answered. The birds do pass their signals from cove to cove in that way. Within a little while the thunder of hoofs sounded on the turf of the links, and then the creeping shadow of the low lugger stole away softly to eastward. The farmer could tell very well which of the horses must be eased in their work next day; but he did not lose much by sparing his beasts, for he always had a glass of unusually good brandy in the house from year's end to year's end.

The black luggers have sailed away for ever; the curlew's cry sounds no more at midnight from knoll to knoll, and the rough customers who were so handy with their big pistols will never be seen again. But smuggling goes merrily on, and the secret history of certain vessels that glide peaceably up the Tyne would form an odd chapter. The low lugger, with her keen bow and her tapering run, was very romantic, but the big, ugly cargo-boat is more business-like. There are men who wear frock-coats and go to chapel quite regularly, who could enlighten a smuggler of the old school if they had any talk with him. It is about one of these men that I am now going to tell you.

The screw-steamer *Phryne* loaded wheat at Odessa, and on signing the bill of lading she was ordered to Gibraltar. Everything went well until the vessel reached Matapan, and the captain was in very good spirits. He and the mate held many private consultations, and the talk always ended by one of the men saying, " We shall do it in the time."

Fifty miles westward of the Cape a hard gale came away from the west, and a powerful head sea rose. There was nothing in the weather to be alarmed about, but as the ship smashed into the seas and sent the white water flying aft Captain Winstanley got into a very fidgety condition. He was ill-tempered with the engineers, and he often said, " The brute only averaged four for the last four hours. We're going to be done." The steamer scuffled forward against the quick, angry sea, and the life went on that is usual in such weather. As the men came out of the fore-castle they waited until they got the chance of a downward slant, and then scrambled aft before the crash of the falling water came ; the sooty firemen halted by the shoot, and made their rush when the vessel took her upward swoop ; and the officers as they left the bridge slipped and swore till they reached the companion. The *Phryne* could manage eleven knots when she could set her square sails, but against a head wind she was the most awkward creation of the builder's genius. Winstanley took his meals as though he did not know what he was eating, and he and the mate often exchanged looks. For the sake of keeping up a conversation the mate sometimes said, " It's all over ;" and the burly skipper answered with a groan.

At night, when the dark came down, and the enormous hurly-burly roared around like a battle of armoured giants, Winstanley stood on the bridge and watched every swoop of the ship as though he were on board a mere racing yacht, and he fatigued himself far more than was in any way necessary.

After five days of monotonous drubbing through the exasperating sea, the *Phryne* reached Malta, and Winstanley had the boat out before the vessel took her place at the hulk. He scribbled a telegram in these terms, "I try to do it, but close thing. Hold on till last minute."

When the bunker coals had been taken in the steamer was hurried off, and the captain took the chance of getting his first good nap. When he woke he found the loose articles in his state-room performing in a very lively way, and he knew at once that the luck was against him once more.

The mate came down stamping and streaming with wet.

"Didn't care to call you, sir. There's nothing very bad, but it's come away hard from the nor'-west."

"We'll give the job up."

"No fear, sir. We'll keep her boring away, and take our luck as it comes."

The gale increased, and after four days of incessant mauling the *Phryne* began to make terribly bad weather of it. Off Galita Island the sea came from the north clean out of the Gulf of Lyons, and the ship did not seem able to rise at it. She flooded the decks fore and aft, and smashed things quite gaily. After one sharp bout with a roaring procession of swift seas, a big wave took her on the port side and she recovered very deliberately indeed. Winstanley was hanging on to the rail in front of the wheel-house, and when he had shaken the spray from his face after this last rally he noticed the ship had a heavy list to starboard. She had shifted her cargo badly, and things looked almost dangerous. The mate had not turned in, and he asked rather anxiously, "What's to be done, now, sir?"

Winstanley growled, "Get her there as soon as we can. Blowed if she won't drown us all if we don't watch it. I'm going to put her head on to the sea, and you get the top-masts and square yards down. We must have the top weight off her. This infernal breeze has lost me £300."

When the top weight was taken off the steamer behaved a little better, but there was very little comfort for anybody, and the hands never had a dry stitch. Winstanley had been looking to making what he called a rattling good thing this trip, but he was now inclined to think only of saving his ship.

When the *Phryne* at length reached Gibraltar she was swept pretty clean, and the people on board of her had anything but a holiday look. The Rock hove up like a gigantic apparition in the chill of a grey January morning ; the great guns winked from their sinister casemates as though they wondered at the wide commotion that was going on all round ; but the grey greatcoats and English faces looked very friendly as the *Phryne* worked her way in. She was admitted to free pratique, and went up to hulk to get a further supply of coal for her bunkers.

Some hours after the ship was laid safely an effusive little Levantine came on board. He blinked around cheerfully, and then made a rush for the Captain, holding out both hands as though he were welcoming a long-lost relative.

"Ah, Captain ! This is indeed a pleasure. Dear, dear ! Swept, too ? What a passage ! Oh, dear me, what a passage !"

"Never mind. We're through this time."

"Ah, my good friend ! my dear friend ! Every night when the wind has made a noise, and the sand flew, I think I have thought, 'Poor Winstanley ; my good Winstanley. He is having a bad time—a very bad, bad time.' We are all the same as when you were before here. Calliphronas is still as big a thief as ever. He wants to cut my throat. And yours. How is your health ? You still take what you call 'Eno' ?—the Fruit Salt ? How is the liver ?"

"Devil take my liver, and you too ! Come to the point, you dancing baboon !"

"Oh, Captain ! When have I used bad words to you ? When have I——?"

"Shut up, you image ! Did you get my telegram ?"

The Levantine pretended to be exercising his memory. His face grew suddenly sharp, and his hands ceased their affectionate gestures.

"Ah ! Telegram ! Oh ! to be sure. I got him."

"Well, what then ?"

"Oh, my boy, I thought—why, I thought now my good friend Winstanley has come to great harm. He is behind his time very, very much. He is perhaps drowned."

"You thought nothing of the sort."

"Oh ! good Heaven, Captain ! You give the lie to a

gentleman. I did think that. So I went to our good friend Heather, and I spoke to him."

"Yes. Go on."

"Well, I've partly arranged with him—with our good friend—to give him the job."

"Oh! Have you? Then you just won't."

"Ah! But, Captain, he is much more moderate than you are. I do not love him like you, I do not respect him, but he is—oh! moderate, very!"

"How?"

"Well, he gives me a larger share of the commission, you know, Captain."

"Oh! that's the way the cat jumps, is it? Well then, my beauty, don't you try to back and fill with me. You show a sign of a wriggle, you beggar, and I'll make you wish you never were born. If you mean business, it must be *at once.* Not another wriggle, now, you Greek spawn of old Nick! Have you anything on like what you wired about to me?"

"Yes. Oh, my dear good friend, yes. But you are very hard. I'll tell you all, but don't be so hard. I have your craft up the bay. Each of them has 180 tons aboard. I'll give you one hundred and fifty to tow them to Trafalgar."

"But you said it was a three hundred pound job, you snipe."

"Ah! I did say. But that was just speaking, you know. I mean one fifty."

"Say two hundred?"

"Ah, Captain! That's the way with you. Always wanting more than everybody. I go ashore and see our friend Heather."

"Come you here, mister. Now drop the gas. I have information that the cargo must be run directly. Come now. My information was straight enough, and I'll bet you're nailed if you wait after to-morrow night. Besides, you talk about Heather. Why, you know there isn't a man here bar myself that dare take the risk."

The Levantine turned very white, and became apologetic. "Oh, that villain cut-throat Calliphronas! He has served me this turn, the villain thief! He wanted a nibble him-

self, and he has been to spoil me with you. He sent fifty
ton away to Cadiz, and she was copped, and he thinks I did
it ; but I'll have my turn with him."

"Well, mister, I don't want to hear of any row between
a pair of Greeks. Am I to have the craft or not ?"

"Good, you take them."

"Money down, mind."

"Oh ! There you go again, you're always that way.
Take half down, and half at the other end."

"You want to be dropped over the side, my young man.
I'm not a Greek, and I don't go back when I've said
a thing."

The countryman of Pericles sighed deeply, as though he
were bewailing the hard nature of these cruel northern
men ; but the scamp knew that he had made a tolerable
bargain, and he said (still sighing), "I must. I suppose I
must. You'll give me your conditions in writing though,
will you not ? Just for a friendly little guide, you
know ?"

"No fear, my friend. No fear. I don't sign death-
warrants so freely as that. Get away ashore with you.
I've got some rough work before me, and I must get
ready."

"Then at dark shift your berth nearer the craft, and I
bring them down to you."

"Right. Mind the money."

Then Captain Winstanley went below, and sat for a time
pondering grimly. At dusk the Levantine came aboard in
a state of high excitement. His dusky face was beady
with sweat, and his eyes glittered unsteadily. The merchant
skipper regarded him with the same cool contempt which
he had shown throughout their conversation, and when the
heavy craft were at length seen drifting down through the
misty gloom the Englishman smiled queerly.

Suddenly the light current caught the smuggling vessels
at the exact point where Winstanley had thought it would,
and he muttered, "Now, my gentleman, I've got you hard
and fast."

The Greek spluttered up to the bridge. "Captain,
Captain ! Oh, here's a thing ! Move up. Hurry up, sharp.
Get nearer, or we're ruined."

Winstanley turned, with the same quiet smile, and asked, "What's up? The craft were bound to drift out west a little bit."

"Yes, but they're in Spanish waters now. The Coastguards come off almost directly. Oh, mercy! Give them a pull."

"You stump up, my joker, or I'll let them drift. Come down below, and put down your sovereigns — English sovereigns, mind."

"We lose time. Look north, there! Oh, we're ruined. Pull them out, and the money will be right."

"It doesn't matter sixpence to me. If they're caught I go on. That's all. You had better pay, and be done with it. I shan't move till you do."

Winstanley knew that if he once put the lighters in safety he would be obliged to fight for his money, and he saw an excellent chance now of getting what he wanted without any fighting at all, so he took things coolly, and watched the Greek twisting like a worm on a hook. There is always a good deal of fencing between the agents at the Rock and the Captains, and nine times out of ten the skipper gets very badly bitten. The smuggling agents come quite up to the Yankee definition of the gentleman "who would steal the Lord's supper if he had a chance," and very hard dealing is required with them.

The moon rose and sailed through a rift in the clouds, touching all the haze with cold light, and glancing delicately on the ripples. The light gained power, and the outlines of the shadowy craft gradually became defined with sharpness. The Rock loomed through the brightening night, and the long, mysterious reaches of the Spanish shore showed with soft curves of sparkling spray. It looked as though there would be an hour of brightness, although away to the westward the sky looked weird, and the clouds were rolling with troubled swiftness.

The chief officer stepped upon the bridge, and his whisper made Winstanley start. "That craft coming this way's a Coastguard, sir."

The Levantine had guessed as much before. He caught at Winstanley's arm, and gripped him convulsively. "For God's sake, Captain, tow! Tow like anything!"

"Bring the money, my friend. And now, as the risk has considerably increased, I'll take an extra twenty, my joker! Decide now, or I'm off. Stand by there. You ring. Stand by, Mr. Brown."

"Oh, Captain! Look! I'm on my knees. You won't do this dreadful thing, will you?"

"Won't I, Mister Cute? You were going to have me, were you?"

The excellent agent was taken into the chart-room, and he told down the money on the table. As each coin fell he winced as though he had a twinge of gout, but the grim Englishman stood by smiling the same quiet smile. Just as the last chink sounded on the table the chief officer again whispered, "He's close on us, sir. I've got the rope fast, but it's going to take us all our time. Clear you out, mister, or we'll take you home with us."

The Greek made a rush for the side. When he was safe in his boat he ground his teeth, and with a kind of strangled scream, said, "You dog of an English captain, I give you fits one day!"

Winstanley laughed brightly, and then telegraphed, "Full speed ahead."

The steamer creaked uneasily. Then the foremost lighter surged forward, and then the whole procession glided slowly away. But before the steamer was fairly set going the Coastguard boat had got well up. Winstanley jumped down, and yelled, "Lie down, all of you."

The chief officer whispered, "There's two in the bow and two astern ready to fire. I saw the barrels flash. Whoop! Here it comes."

"All right, sonny. I didn't hear that shot whistle. It fell short. Two minutes more and we're away from them."

A crash of broken glass came, and the steamer yawed as though she were a sailing ship before the wind.

"Joe's down. Jump you into the wheel-house and lay hold."

The man at the wheel was shot.

"Creep aft here, three of you. Batten up that side of the wheel-house," said Winstanley sharply. He exposed himself freely until a pile of thick deals made the chief

20

officer secure. The mate had sprung to the wheel when the boatswain fell, and the escape of the ship depended on keeping the helmsman's skin safe. The Spaniards were using their carbines and making excellent practice, but only Winstanley was exposed, and the steamer was drawing fast away. The captain felt a thud on his fore-arm, and then something warm trickled on his fingers. He tried to lift his hand, but the effort hurt him. "Got it at last," he growled. "I should have hopped into the wheel-house with Brown."

The *Phryne* soon got well away from her pursuers, and Winstanley had time to have his arm bound up. But his troubles were not over. The baffled Coastguards signalled to Tarifa, and when the steamer drew up several craft were seen creeping out from that direction. The captain and mate held a consultation. Said Winstanley, "We can't pass 'em, I doubt. The luck seems all against us."

Brown, the mate, was a ready young fellow. He said, "Those beggars get paid heavy for every capture. Let's slip one of the lighters, and they'll all go for her like dogs for a bone. You take my word, sir, they won't mind us much if one of these helpless boats goes adrift Shall I run aft and slip?"

"Good; and I'll take the bridge till we're in range again."

When the unhappy felucca was slipped Winstanley heard a distant sound of shouting from the Spaniards. He shouted to the engineers to put on every ounce, and the *Phryne* pulled the remaining craft along nearly bows under. All this time the sea had been growing worse, but Winstanley rammed his boat ahead until everything shivered again as the plunging lighters caught at their tow-ropes. Twenty miles north-west of Spartel the weather was terrible. The low sky shut the *Phryne* in like a grim prison, and the sea came clean over her, just as it had done during the run from Malta. At last the steamer reared fairly on end and gave one long plunge. She recovered from this, and she would have served for a swimming bath had you closed her scuppers and set her level; then she took one more wild swoop; the sea overlapped her, and the towing craft were smothered in wreaths of roaring water. Winstanley would not cast them off, but the hands ou board grew frightened and finally slipped their tow-ropes. The *Phryne* was relieved, but the poor feluccas had a bad time. They ran for Cadiz, and when last seen they were scudding under storm-sails. Winstanley muttered, "Well, it wasn't my fault. I'd have held on till all was blue if the beggars had had the pluck. They're done, any way, and now we must look out or it'll be cold coffee with us."

That night the gale grew to a hurricane, and the *Phryne* could just hold her own, and no more. On her way home she was very badly knocked about, and her captain was almost inclined to be superstitious. He said to his mate, in a laughing way, "There's a judgment on us, my boy. Nothing but head winds all the way, ever since we left Matapan astern of us, and here's my arm plugged through. I shan't be on for any more of those games." But ou getting into Falmouth the skipper was himself again, and when he read that four feluccas laden with tobacco had been towed through the Gut and afterwards captured, he only said, "Never mind. I suppose they're in for penal servitude. But better luck next time."

It will be seen that smuggling is still an exciting pursuit.

THE END.

BILLING AND SONS, PRINTERS, GUILDFORD.

A LIST OF BOOKS

PUBLISHED BY

CHATTO & WINDUS,

214, PICCADILLY, LONDON, W.

Sold by all Booksellers, or sent post-free for the published price by the Publishers.

About.—The Fellah: An Egyptian Novel. By EDMOND ABOUT. Translated by Sir RANDAL ROBERTS. Post 8vo, illustrated boards, 2s. ; cloth limp, 2s. 6d.

Adams (W. Davenport), Works by:

A Dictionary of the Drama. Being a comprehensive Guide to the Plays, Playwrights, Players, and Playhouses of the United Kingdom and America, from the Earliest to the Present Times. Crown 8vo, half-bound, 12s. 6d. [*Preparing.*

Latter Day Lyrics. Edited by W. DAVENPORT ADAMS. Post 8vo, cloth limp, 2s. 6d.

Quips and Quiddities. Selected by W. DAVENPORT ADAMS. Post 8vo, cloth limp, 2s. 6d.

Advertising, A History of, from the Earliest Times. Illustrated by Anecdotes, Curious Specimens, and Notices of Successful Advertisers. By HENRY SAMPSON. Crown 8vo, with Coloured Frontispiece and Illustrations, cloth gilt, 7s. 6d.

Agony Column (The) of "The Times," from 1800 to 1870. Edited, with an Introduction, by ALICE CLAY. Post 8vo, cloth limp, 2s. 6d.

Aïdé (Hamilton), Works by:
Post 8vo, illustrated boards, 2s. each.
Carr of Carrlyon.
Confidences.

Alexander (Mrs.), Novels by:
Crown 8vo, cloth extra, 3s. 6d. each; post 8vo, illustrated boards, 2s. each.
Maid, Wife, or Widow ?
Valerie's Fate.

Allen (Grant), Works by:
Crown 8vo, cloth extra, 6s. each.
The Evolutionist at Large. Second Edition, revised.
Vignettes from Nature.
Colin Clout's Calendar.
Strange Stories. With a Frontispiece by GEORGE DU MAURIER.
Philistia : A Novel. New and Cheaper Edit. Crown 8vo, cloth extra, 3s. 6d.
Babylon: A Novel. 12 Illusts. by P. MACNAB. New and Cheaper Edition. Cr. 8vo, cl. ex., 3s. 6d. [*In the press.*
For Maimie's Sake: A Tale of Love and Dynamite. Crown 8vo, cloth extra, 6s. [*Immediately.*

Architectural Styles, A Handbook of. Translated from the German of A. ROSENGARTEN, by W. COLLETT-SANDARS. Crown 8vo, cloth extra, with 639 Illustrations, 7s. 6d.

Artemus Ward :
Artemus Ward's Works: The Works of CHARLES FARRER BROWNE, better known as ARTEMUS WARD. With Portrait and Facsimile. Crown 8vo, cloth extra, 7s. 6d.
Artemus Ward's Lecture on the Mormons. With 32 Illustrations. Edited, with Preface, by EDWARD P. HINGSTON. Crown 8vo, 6d.
The Genial Showman: Life and Adventures of Artemus Ward. By EDWARD P. HINGSTON. With a Frontispiece. Cr. 8vo, cl. extra, 3s. 6d.

Art (The) of Amusing: A Collection of Graceful Arts, Games, Tricks, Puzzles, and Charades. By FRANK BELLEW. With 300 Illustrations. Cr. 8vo, cloth extra, 4s. 6d.

Ashton (John), Works by:
Crown 8vo, cloth extra, 7s. 6d each.
A History of the Chap-Books of the Eighteenth Century. With nearly 400 Illustrations, engraved in facsimile of the originals.
Social Life in the Reign of Queen Anne. From Original Sources. With nearly 100 Illustrations.
Humour, Wit, and Satire of the Seventeenth Century. With nearly 100 Illustrations.

English Caricature and Satire on Napoleon the First. With 120 Illustrations from Originals. Two Vols., demy 8vo, cloth extra, 28s.

Bacteria.—A Synopsis of the Bacteria and Yeast Fungi and Allied Species. By W. B. GROVE, B.A. With 87 Illusts. Crown 8vo, cl. extra, 3s. 6d.

Balzac's "Comedie Humaine" and its Author. With Translations by H. H. WALKER. Post 8vo, cloth limp, 2s. 6d.

Bankers, A Handbook of London; together with Lists of Bankers from 1677. By F. G. HILTON PRICE. Crown 8vo, cloth extra, 7s. 6d.

Bardsley (Rev. C.W.), Works by:
Crown 8vo, cloth extra, 7s. 6d. each.
English Surnames: Their Sources and Significations. Third Ed., revised.
Curiosities of Puritan Nomenclature.

Bartholomew Fair, Memoirs of. By HENRY MORLEY. With 100 Illusts. Crown 8vo, cloth extra, 7s. 6d.

Basil. Novels by:
Crown 8vo., cloth extra, 2s. 6d. each.
A Drawn Game.
"The Wearing of the Green."

Beaconsfield, Lord: A Biography. By T. P. O'CONNOR, M.P. Sixth Edition, with a New Preface. Crown 8vo, cloth extra, 7s. 6d.

Beauchamp. — Grantley Grange: A Novel. By SHELSLEY BEAUCHAMP. Post 8vo, illust. bds, 2s.

Beautiful Pictures by British Artists: A Gathering of Favourites from our Picture Galleries. In Two Series. All engraved on Steel in the highest style of Art. Edited, with Notices of the Artists, by SYDNEY ARMYTAGE, M.A. Imperial 4to, cloth extra, gilt and gilt edges, 21s. per Vol.

Bechstein. — As Pretty as Seven, and other German Stories. Collected by LUDWIG BECHSTEIN. With Additional Tales by the Brothers GRIMM, and 100 Illusts. by RICHTER. Small 4to, green and gold, 6s. 6d.; gilt edges, 7s. 6d.

Beerbohm. — Wanderings in Patagonia; or, Life among the Ostrich Hunters. By JULIUS BEERBOHM. With Illusts. Crown 8vo, cloth extra, 3s. 6d.

Belgravia for 1886. — One Shilling Monthly, Illustrated by P. MACNAB.—The first Chapters of Mohawks, a New Novel by M. E. BRADDON, Author of "Lady Audley's Secret," appear in the JANUARY Number, and the Story will be continued throughout the year. This Number contains also the Opening Chapters of a New Novel entitled That other Person; and several of those short stories for which *Belgravia* is so famous.
. *Now ready, the Volume for* JULY *to* OCTOBER, 1885, *cloth extra, gilt edges,* 7s. 6d.; *Cases for binding Vols.,* 2s. *each.*

Belgravia Annual for Christmas, 1885. With Stories by F. W. ROBINSON, Mrs. LYNN LINTON, GRANT ALLEN, 'BASIL,' B. MONTGOMERIE RANKING, and others. Demy 8vo, with Illustrations, 1s.

Bennett (W.C., LL.D.), Works by:
Post 8vo, cloth limp, 2s. each.
A Ballad History of England.
Songs for Sailors.

Besant (Walter) and James Rice. Novels by. Crown 8vo cloth extra, 3s. 6d. each; post 8vo, illust. boards 2s. each; cloth limp, 2s 6d. each.

Ready-Money Mortiboy.
With Harp and Crown.
This Son of Vulcan.
My Little Girl.
The Case of Mr. Lucraft.
The Golden Butterfly.
By Celia's Arbour.
The Monks of Thelema.
'Twas in Trafalgar's Bay.
The Seamy Side.
The Ten Years' Tenant.
The Chaplain of the Fleet

Besant (Walter), Novels by: Crown 8vo, cloth extra, 3s. 6d. each; post 8vo, illust. boards, 2s. each; cloth limp, 2s. 6d. each.

All Sorts and Conditions of Men: An Impossible Story. With Illustrations by FRED. BARNARD.

The Captains' Room, &c. With Frontispiece by E. J. WHEELER.

All in a Garden Fair. With 6 Illusts. by H. FURNISS.

Crown 8vo, cloth extra, 3s. 6d. each.

Dorothy Forster. With Frontispiece by CHARLES GREEN.

Uncle Jack, and other Stories.

The Art of Fiction. Demy 8vo, 1s.

Betham-Edwards (M.), Novels by. Crown 8vo, cloth extra, 3s. 6d. each.; post 8vo, illust. bds., 2s. each.

Felicia. | Kitty.

Bewick (Thos.) and his Pupils. By AUSTIN DOBSON. With 95 Illustrations. Square 8vo, cloth extra, 10s. 6d.

Birthday Books:—

The Starry Heavens: A Poetical Birthday Book. Square 8vo, handsomely bound in cloth, 2s. 6d.

Birthday Flowers: Their Language and Legends. By W. J. GORDON. Beautifully Illustrated in Colours by VIOLA BOUGHTON. In illuminated cover, crown 4to, 6s.

The Lowell Birthday Book. With Illusts. Small 8vo, cloth extra, 4s. 6d.

Blackburn's (Henry) Art Handbooks. Demy 8vo, Illustrated, uniform in size for binding.

Academy Notes, separate years, from 1875 to 1884, each 1s.

Academy Notes, 1885. With 142 Illustrations. 1s.

Academy Notes, 1875-79. Complete in One Vol., with nearly 600 Illusts. in Facsimile. Demy 8vo, cloth limp, 6s.

Academy Notes, 1880-84. Complete in One Volume, with about 700 Facsimile Illustrations. Cloth limp, 6s.

Grosvenor Notes, 1877. 6d.

Grosvenor Notes, separate years, from 1878 to 1884, each 1s.

Grosvenor Notes, 1885. With 75 Illustrations. 1s.

Grosvenor Notes, 1877-82. With upwards of 300 Illustrations. Demy 8vo, cloth limp, 6s.

Pictures at South Kensington. With 70 Illusts. 1s. [*New Edit. preparing.*

ART HANDBOOKS, *continued—*

The English Pictures at the National Gallery. 114 Illustrations. 1s.

The Old Masters at the National Gallery. 128 Illustrations. 1s. 6d.

A Complete Illustrated Catalogue to the National Gallery. With Notes by H. BLACKBURN, and 242 Illusts. Demy 8vo, cloth limp, 3s.

Illustrated Catalogue of the Luxembourg Gallery. Containing about 250 Reproductions after the Original Drawings of the Artists. Edited by F. G. DUMAS. Demy 8vo, 3s. 6d.

The Paris Salon, 1884. With over 300 Illusts. Edited by F. G. DUMAS. Demy 8vo, 3s.

The Paris Salon, 1885. With about 300 Facsimile Sketches. Edited by F. G. DUMAS. Demy 8vo, 3s.

The Art Annual, 1883-4. Edited by F. G. DUMAS. With 300 full-page Illustrations. Demy 8vo, 5s.

Blake (William): Etchings from his Works. By W. B. SCOTT. With descriptive Text. Folio, half-bound boards, India Proofs, 21s.

Boccaccio's Decameron; or, Ten Days' Entertainment. Translated into English, with an Introduction by THOMAS WRIGHT, F.S.A. With Portrait, and STOTHARD's beautiful Copperplates. Cr. 8vo, cloth extra, gilt, 7s. 6d.

Bowers' (G.) Hunting Sketches: Oblong 4to, half-bound boards, 21s. each.

Canters in Crampshire.

Leaves from a Hunting Journal. Coloured in facsimile of the originals.

Boyle (Frederick), Works by: Crown 8vo, cloth extra, 3s. 6d. each; post 8vo, illustrated boards, 2s. each.

Camp Notes: Stories of Sport and Adventure in Asia, Africa, and America.

Savage Life: Adventures of a Globe-Trotter.

Chronicles of No-Man's Land. Post 8vo, illust. boards, 2s.

Braddon (M. E.)—Mohawks, a Novel, by Miss BRADDON, Author of "Lady Audley's Secret," is begun in BELGRAVIA for JANUARY, and will be continued throughout the year. Illustrated by P. MACNAB. 1s. Monthly.

Brand's Observations on Popular Antiquities, chiefly illustrating the Origin of our Vulgar Customs, Ceremonies, and Superstitions. With the Additions of Sir HENRY ELLIS. Crown 8vo, cloth extra, gilt, with numerous illustrations, 7s. 6d.

BOOKS PUBLISHED BY

4

Bret Harte, Works by:

Bret Harte's Collected Works. Arranged and Revised by the Author. Complete in Five Vols., crown 8vo, cloth extra, 6s. each.

Vol. I. COMPLETE POETICAL AND DRAMATIC WORKS. With Steel Portrait, and Introduction by Author.

Vol. II. EARLIER PAPERS—LUCK OF ROARING CAMP, and other Sketches —BOHEMIAN PAPERS — SPANISH AND AMERICAN LEGENDS.

Vol. III. TALES OF THE ARGONAUTS —EASTERN SKETCHES.

Vol. IV. GABRIEL CONROY.

Vol. V. STORIES — CONDENSED NOVELS, &c.

The Select Works of Bret Harte, in Prose and Poetry. With Introductory Essay by J. M. BELLEW, Portrait of the Author, and 50 Illustrations. Crown 8vo, cloth extra, 7s. 6d.

Gabriel Conroy: A Novel. Post 8vo, illustrated boards, 2s.

An Heiress of Red Dog, and other Stories. Post 8vo, illustrated boards, 2s.

The Twins of Table Mountain. Fcap. 8vo, picture cover, 1s.

Luck of Roaring Camp, and other Sketches. Post 8vo, illust. bds., 2s.

Jeff Briggs's Love Story. Fcap. 8vo, picture cover, 1s.

Flip. Post 8vo, illustrated boards, 2s.; cloth limp, 2s. 6d.

Californian Stories (including THE TWINS OF TABLE MOUNTAIN, JEFF BRIGGS'S LOVE STORY, &c.) Post 8vo, illustrated boards, 2s.

Maruja: A Novel. Post 8vo, illust. boards, 2s.; cloth limp, 2s. 6d.

Brewer (Rev. Dr.), Works by:

The Reader's Handbook of Allusions, References, Plots, and Stories. Fifth Edition, revised throughout, with a New Appendix, containing a COMPLETE ENGLISH BIBLIOGRAPHY. Cr. 8vo, 1,400 pp., cloth extra, 7s. 6d.

Authors and their Works, with the Dates: Being the Appendices to "The Reader's Handbook," separately printed. Cr. 8vo, cloth limp, 2s.

A Dictionary of Miracles: Imitative, Realistic, and Dogmatic. Crown 8vo, cloth extra, 7s. 6d.; half-bound, 9s.

Brewster (Sir David), Works by:

More Worlds than One: The Creed of the Philosopher and the Hope of the Christian. With Plates. Post 8vo, cloth extra, 4s. 6d.

BREWSTER (Sir DAVID), *continued—*

The Martyrs of Science: Lives of GALILEO, TYCHO BRAHE, and KEPLER. With Portraits. Post 8vo, cloth extra, 4s. 6d.

Letters on Natural Magic. A New Edition, with numerous Illustrations, and Chapters on the Being and Faculties of Man, and Additional Phenomena of Natural Magic, by J. A. SMITH. Post 8vo, cloth extra, 4s. 6d.

Briggs, Memoir of Gen. John.
By Major EVANS BELL. With a Portrait. Royal 8vo, cloth extra, 7s. 6d.

Brillat-Savarin.—Gastronomy
as a Fine Art. By BRILLAT-SAVARIN. Translated by R. E. ANDERSON, M.A. Post 8vo, cloth limp, 2s. 6d.

Buchanan's (Robert) Works:
Crown 8vo, cloth extra, 6s. each.

Ballads of Life, Love, and Humour. Frontispiece by ARTHUR HUGHES.

Undertones.

London Poems.

The Book of Orm.

White Rose and Red: A Love Story.

Idylls and Legends of Inverburn.

Selected Poems of Robert Buchanan. With a Frontispiece by T. DALZIEL.

The Hebrid Isles: Wanderings in the Land of Lorne and the Outer Hebrides. With Frontispiece by WILLIAM SMALL.

A Poet's Sketch-Book: Selections from the Prose Writings of ROBERT BUCHANAN.

The Earthquake; or, Six Days and a Sabbath. Cr. 8vo, cloth extra, 6s.

St. Abe and his Seven Wives: A Tale of Salt Lake City. With a Frontispiece by A. B. HOUGHTON. Crown 8vo, cloth extra, 5s.

Robert Buchanan's Complete Poetical Works. With Steel-plate Portrait. Crown 8vo, cloth extra, 7s. 6d.

Crown 8vo, cloth extra, 3s. 6d. each; post 8vo, illust. boards, 2s. each.

The Shadow of the Sword.

A Child of Nature. With a Frontispiece.

God and the Man. With Illustrations by FRED. BARNARD.

The Martyrdom of Madeline. With Frontispiece by A. W. COOPER.

Love Me for Ever. With a Frontispiece by P. MACNAB.

Annan Water.

The New Abelard.

Crown 8vo, cloth extra, 3s. 6d. each.
Foxglove Manor.
Matt: A Story of a Caravan.

Bunyan's Pilgrim's Progress.
Edited by Rev. T. SCOTT. With 17 Steel Plates by STOTHARD, engraved by GOODALL, and numerous Woodcuts. Crown 8vo, cloth extra, gilt, 7s. 6d.

Burnett (Mrs.), Novels by:
Surly Tim, and other Stories. Post 8vo, illustrated boards, 2s.

Fcap. 8vo, picture cover, 1s. each.
Kathleen Mavourneen.
Lindsay's Luck.
Pretty Polly Pemberton.

Burton (Captain), Works by:
To the Gold Coast for Gold: A Personal Narrative. By RICHARD F. BURTON and VERNEY LOVETT CAMERON. With Maps and Frontispiece. Two Vols., crown 8vo, cloth extra, 21s.
The Book of the Sword: Being a History of the Sword and its Use in all Countries, from the Earliest Times. By RICHARD F. BURTON. With over 400 Illustrations. Square 8vo, cloth extra, 32s.

Burton (Robert):
The Anatomy of Melancholy. A New Edition, complete, corrected and enriched by Translations of the Classical Extracts. Demy 8vo, cloth extra, 7s. 6d.
Melancholy Anatomised: Being an Abridgment, for popular use, of BURTON'S ANATOMY OF MELANCHOLY. Post 8vo, cloth limp, 2s. 6d.

Byron (Lord):
Byron's Childe Harold. An entirely New Edition of this famous Poem, with over One Hundred new Illusts. by leading Artists. (Uniform with the Illustrated Editions of "The Lady of the Lake" and "Marmion.") Elegantly and appropriately bound, small 4to, 16s.
Byron's Letters and Journals. With Notices of his Life. By THOMAS MOORE. A Reprint of the Original Edition, newly revised, with Twelve full-page Plates. Crown 8vo, cloth extra, gilt, 7s. 6d.
Byron's Don Juan. Complete in One Vol., post 8vo, cloth limp, 2s.

Cameron (Commander) and Captain Burton.—To the Gold Coast for Gold: A Personal Narrative. By RICHARD F. BURTON and VERNEY LOVETT CAMERON. Frontispiece and Maps. Two Vols., cr. 8vo, cl. ex., 21s.

Caine.—The Shadow of a Crime: A Novel. By HALL CAINE. Cr. 8vo, cloth extra, 3s. 6d.

Cameron (Mrs. H. Lovett), Novels by:
Crown 8vo, cloth extra, 3s. 6d. each; post 8vo, illustrated boards, 2s. each.
Juliet's Guardian. | Deceivers Ever.

Carlyle (Thomas):
On the Choice of Books. By THOMAS CARLYLE. With a Life of the Author by R. H. SHEPHERD. New and Revised Edition, post 8vo, cloth extra, Illustrated, 1s. 6d.
The Correspondence of Thomas Carlyle and Ralph Waldo Emerson. 1834 to 1872. Edited by CHARLES ELIOT NORTON. With Portraits. Two Vols., crown 8vo, cloth extra, 24s.

Chapman's (George) Works:
Vol. I. contains the Plays complete, including the doubtful ones. Vol. II., the Poems and Minor Translations, with an Introductory Essay by ALGERNON CHARLES SWINBURNE. Vol. III., the Translations of the Iliad and Odyssey. Three Vols., crown 8vo, cloth extra, 18s.; or separately, 6s. each.

Chatto & Jackson.—A Treatise on Wood Engraving, Historical and Practical. By WM. ANDREW CHATTO and JOHN JACKSON. With an Additional Chapter by HENRY G. BOHN; and 450 fine Illustrations. A Reprint of the last Revised Edition. Large 4to, half-bound, 28s.

Chaucer:
Chaucer for Children: A Golden Key. By Mrs. H. R. HAWEIS. With Eight Coloured Pictures and numerous Woodcuts by the Author. New Ed., small 4to, cloth extra, 6s.
Chaucer for Schools. By Mrs. H. R. HAWEIS. Demy 8vo, cloth limp, 2s. 6d.

City (The) of Dream: A Poem. Fcap. 8vo, cloth extra, 6s. [In the press.

Clodd. — Myths and Dreams. By EDWARD CLODD, F.R.A.S., Author of "The Childhood of Religions," &c. Crown 8vo, cloth extra, 5s.

Cobban.—The Cure of Souls: A Story. By J. MACLAREN COBBAN. Post 8vo, illustrated boards, 2s.

Coleman.—Curly: An Actor's Story. By JOHN COLEMAN. Illustrated by J. C. DOLLMAN. Crown 8vo, 1s. cloth, 1s. 6d.

Collins (Mortimer), Novels by:
Crown 8vo, cloth extra, 3s. 6d. each; post 8vo, illustrated boards, 2s. each.
Sweet Anne Page.
Transmigration.
From Midnight to Midnight.
A Fight with Fortune. Post 8vo, illustrated boards, 2s.

Collins (Mortimer & Frances), Novels by:
Crown 8vo, cloth extra, 3s. 6d. each; post 8vo, illustrated boards, 2s. each.
Blacksmith and Scholar.
The Village Comedy.
You Play Me False.
Post 8vo, illustrated boards, 2s. each.
Sweet and Twenty.
Frances.

Collins (Wilkie), Novels by:
Crown 8vo, cloth extra, Illustrated, 3s. 6d. each; post 8vo, illustrated bds., 2s. each; cloth limp, 2s. 6d. each.
Antonina. Illust. by Sir JOHN GILBERT.
Basil. Illustrated by Sir JOHN GILBERT and J. MAHONEY.
Hide and Seek. Illustrated by Sir JOHN GILBERT and J. MAHONEY.
The Dead Secret. Illustrated by Sir JOHN GILBERT.
Queen of Hearts. Illustrated by Sir JOHN GILBERT.
My Miscellanies. With a Steel-plate Portrait of WILKIE COLLINS.
The Woman in White. With Illustrations by Sir JOHN GILBERT and F. A. FRASER.
The Moonstone. With Illustrations by G. Du MAURIER and F. A. FRASER.
Man and Wife. Illust. by W. SMALL.
Poor Miss Finch. Illustrated by G. Du MAURIER and EDWARD HUGHES.
Miss or Mrs.? With Illustrations by S. L. FILDES and HENRY WOODS.
The New Magdalen. Illustrated by G.Du MAURIER and C.S. REINHARDT.
The Frozen Deep. Illustrated by G. Du MAURIER and J. MAHONEY.
The Law and the Lady. Illustrated by S. L. FILDES and SYDNEY HALL.
The Two Destinies.
The Haunted Hotel. Illustrated by ARTHUR HOPKINS.
The Fallen Leaves.
Jezebel's Daughter.
The Black Robe.
Heart and Science: A Story of the Present Time.
"I Say No." Crown 8vo, cloth extra, 3s. 6d.

Collins (C. Allston).—The Bar Sinister: A Story. By C. ALLSTON COLLINS. Post 8vo, illustrated bds., 2s.

Colman's Humorous Works: "Broad Grins," "My Nightgown and Slippers," and other Humorous Works, Prose and Poetical, of GEORGE COLMAN. With Life by G. B. BUCKSTONE, and Frontispiece by HOGARTH. Crown 8vo, cloth extra, gilt, 7s. 6d.

Convalescent Cookery: A Family Handbook. By CATHERINE RYAN. Crown 8vo, 1s.; cloth, 1s. 6d.

Conway (Moncure D.), Works by:
Demonology and Devil Lore. Two Vols., royal 8vo, with 65 Illusts., 28s.
A Necklace of Stories. Illustrated by W. J. HENNESSY. Square 8vo, cloth extra, 6s.

Cook (Dutton), Works by:
Crown 8vo, cloth extra, 6s. each.
Hours with the Players. With a Steel Plate Frontispiece.
Nights at the Play: A View of the English Stage.
Leo: A Novel. Post 8vo, illustrated boards, 2s.
Paul Foster's Daughter. crown 8vo, cloth extra, 3s. 6d.; post 8vo, illustrated boards, 2s.

Copyright. — A Handbook of English and Foreign Copyright in Literary and Dramatic Works. By SIDNEY JERROLD, of the Middle Temple, Esq, Barrister-at-Law. Post 8vo, cloth limp, 2s. 6d.

Cornwall.—PopularRomances of the West of England; or, The Drolls, Traditions, and Superstitions of Old Cornwall. Collected and Edited by ROBERT HUNT, F.R.S. New and Revised Edition, with Additions, and Two Steel-plate Illustrations by GEORGE CRUIKSHANK. Crown 8vo, cloth extra, 7s. 6d.

Craddock. — The Prophet of the Great Smoky Mountains. By CHARLES EGBERT CRADDOCK. Post 8vo, illust. bds., 2s.; cloth limp, 2s. 6d.

Creasy.—Memoirs of Eminent Etonians: with Notices of the Early History of Eton College. By Sir EDWARD CREASY, Author of "The Fifteen Decisive Battles of the World." Crown 8vo, cloth extra, gilt, with 15 Portraits, 7s. 6d.

Cruikshank (George):

The Comic Almanack. Complete in TWO SERIES: The FIRST from 1835 to 1843; the SECOND from 1844 to 1853. A Gathering of the BEST HUMOUR of THACKERAY, HOOD, MAYHEW, ALBERT SMITH, A'BECKETT, ROBERT BROUGH, &c. With 2,000 Woodcuts and Steel Engravings by CRUIKSHANK, HINE, LANDELLS, &c. Crown 8vo, cloth gilt, two very thick volumes, 7s. 6d. each.

The Life of George Cruikshank. By BLANCHARD JERROLD, Author of "The Life of Napoleon III.," &c. With 84 Illustrations. New and Cheaper Edition, enlarged, with Additional Plates, and a very carefully compiled Bibliography. Crown 8vo, cloth extra, 7s. 6d.

Robinson Crusoe. A beautiful reproduction of Major's Edition, with 37 Woodcuts and Two Steel Plates by GEORGE CRUIKSHANK, choicely printed. Crown 8vo, cloth extra, 7s. 6d.

Cumming (C. F. Gordon), Works by:

Demy 8vo, cloth extra, 8s. 6d. each.

In the Hebrides. With Autotype Facsimile and numerous full-page Illustrations.

In the Himalayas and on the Indian Plains. With numerous Illustrations.

Via Cornwall to Egypt. With a Photogravure Frontispiece. Demy 8vo, cloth extra, 7s. 6d.

Cussans.—Handbook of Heraldry; with Instructions for Tracing Pedigrees and Deciphering Ancient MSS., &c. By JOHN E. CUSSANS. Entirely New and Revised Edition, illustrated with over 400 Woodcuts and Coloured Plates. Crown 8vo, cloth extra, 7s. 6d.

Cyples.—Hearts of Gold: A Novel. By WILLIAM CYPLES. Crown 8vo, cloth extra, 3s. 6d., post 8vo, illustrated boards, 2s.

Daniel. — Merrie England in the Olden Time. By GEORGE DANIEL. With Illustrations by ROBT. CRUIKSHANK. Crown 8vo, cloth extra, 3s. 6d.

Daudet.—Port Salvation; or, The Evangelist. By ALPHONSE DAUDET. Translated by C. HARRY MELTZER. With Portrait of the Author. Crown 8vo, cloth extra, 3s. 6d.; post 8vo, illust. boards, 2s.

Davenant. — What shall my Son be? Hints for Parents on the Choice of a Profession or Trade for their Sons. By FRANCIS DAVENANT, M.A. Post 8vo, cloth limp, 2s. 6d.

Davies (Dr. N. E.), Works by:

Crown 8vo, 1s. each; cloth limp, 1s. 6d. each.

One Thousand Medical Maxims.

Nursery Hints: A Mother's Guide.

Aids to Long Life. Crown 8vo, 2s.; cloth limp, 2s. 6d.

Davies' (Sir John) Complete Poetical Works, including Psalms I. to L. in Verse, and other hitherto Unpublished MSS., for the first time Collected and Edited, with Memorial-Introduction and Notes, by the Rev. A. B. GROSART, D.D. Two Vols., crown 8vo, cloth boards, 12s.

De Maistre.—A Journey Round My Room. By XAVIER DE MAISTRE. Translated by HENRY ATTWELL. Post 8vo, cloth limp, 2s. 6d.

De Mille.—A Castle in Spain: A Novel. By JAMES DE MILLE. With a Frontispiece. Crown 8vo, cloth extra, 3s. 6d.; post 8vo, illust. bds., 2s.

Derwent (Leith), Novels by: Crown 8vo, cloth extra, 3s. 6d. each; post 8vo, illustrated boards, 2s. each.

Our Lady of Tears.

Circe's Lovers.

Dickens (Charles), Novels by: Post 8vo, illustrated boards, 2s. each.

Sketches by Boz. | Nicholas Nickleby.
Pickwick Papers. | Oliver Twist.

The Speeches of Charles Dickens, 1841-1870. With a New Bibliography, revised and enlarged. Edited and Prefaced by RICHARD HERNE SHEPHERD. Crown 8vo, cloth extra, 6s.— Also a SMALLER EDITION, in the Mayfair Library. Post 8vo, cloth limp, 2s. 6d.

About England with Dickens. By ALFRED RIMMER. With 57 Illustrations by C. A. VANDERHOOF, ALFRED RIMMER, and others. Sq. 8vo, cloth extra, 10s. 6d.

Dictionaries:

A Dictionary of Miracles: Imitative, Realistic, and Dogmatic. By the Rev. E. C. BREWER, LL.D. Crown 8vo, cloth extra, 7s. 6d.; hf.-bound, 9s.

Dictionaries, *continued*—

The Reader's Handbook of Allusions, References, Plots, and Stories. By the Rev. E. C. Brewer, LL.D. Fourth Edition, revised throughout, with a New Appendix, containing a Complete English Bibliography. Crown 8vo, 1,400 pages, cloth extra, 7s. 6d.

Familiar Allusions: A Handbook of Miscellaneous Information; including the Names of Celebrated Statues, Paintings, Palaces, Country Seats, Ruins, Churches, Ships, Streets, Clubs, Natural Curiosities, and the like. By Wm. A. Wheeler and Charles G. Wheeler. Demy 8vo, cloth extra, 7s. 6d.

Authors and their Works, with the Dates. Being the Appendices to "The Reader's Handbook," separately printed. By the Rev. Dr. Brewer. Crown 8vo, cloth limp, 2s.

Short Sayings of Great Men. With Historical and Explanatory Notes. By Samuel A. Bent, M.A. Demy 8vo, cloth extra, 7s. 6d.

A Dictionary of the Drama: Being a comprehensive Guide to the Plays, Playwrights, Players, and Playhouses of the United Kingdom and America, from the Earliest to the Present Times. By W. Davenport Adams. A thick volume, crown 8vo, half-bound, 12s. 6d. [*In preparation.*]

The Slang Dictionary: Etymological, Historical, and Anecdotal. Crown 8vo, cloth extra, 6s. 6d.

Women of the Day: A Biographical Dictionary. By Frances Hays. Cr. 8vo, cloth extra, 5s.

Words, Facts, and Phrases: A Dictionary of Curious, Quaint, and Out-of-the-Way Matters. By Eliezer Edwards. New and Cheaper Issue. Cr. 8vo, cl. ex., 7s. 6d.; hf.-bd., 9s.

Diderot.—The Paradox of Acting. Translated, with Annotations, from Diderot's "Le Paradoxe sur le Comédien," by Walter Herries Pollock. With a Preface by Henry Irving. Cr. 8vo, in parchment, 4s. 6d.

Dobson (W. T.), Works by:

Post 8vo, cloth limp, 2s. 6d. each.

Literary Frivolities, Fancies, Follies, and Frolics.

Poetical Ingenuities and Eccentricities.

Doran. — Memories of our Great Towns; with Anecdotic Gleanings concerning their Worthies and their Oddities. By Dr. John Doran, F.S.A. With 38 Illustrations. New and Cheaper Ed., cr. 8vo, cl. ex., 7s. 6d.

Drama, A Dictionary of the. Being a comprehensive Guide to the Plays, Playwrights, Players, and Playhouses of the United Kingdom and America, from the Earliest to the Present Times. By W. Davenport Adams. (Uniform with Brewer's "Reader's Handbook.") Crown 8vo, half-bound, 12s. 6d. [*In preparation.*]

Dramatists, The Old. Cr. 8vo, cl. ex., Vignette Portraits, 6s. per Vol.

Ben Jonson's Works. With Notes Critical and Explanatory, and a Biographical Memoir by Wm. Gifford. Edit. by Col. Cunningham. 3 Vols.

Chapman's Works. Complete in Three Vols. Vol. I. contains the Plays complete, including doubtful ones; Vol. II., Poems and Minor Translations, with Introductory Essay by A. C. Swinburne; Vol. III., Translations of the Iliad and Odyssey.

Marlowe's Works. Including his Translations. Edited, with Notes and Introduction, by Col. Cunningham. One Vol.

Massinger's Plays. From the Text of William Gifford. Edited by Col. Cunningham. One Vol.

Dyer. — The Folk Lore of Plants. By Rev. T. F. Thiselton Dyer, M.A. Crown 8vo, cloth extra, 7s. 6d. [*In preparation.*]

Early English Poets. Edited, with Introductions and Annotations, by Rev. A. B. Grosart, D.D. Crown 8vo, cloth boards, 6s. per Volume.

Fletcher's (Giles, B.D.) Complete Poems. One Vol.

Davies' (Sir John) Complete Poetical Works. Two Vols.

Herrick's (Robert) Complete Collected Poems. Three Vols.

Sidney's (Sir Philip) Complete Poetical Works. Three Vols.

Herbert (Lord) of Cherbury's Poems. Edited, with Introduction, by J. Churton Collins. Crown 8vo, parchment, 8s.

Edwardes (Mrs. A.), Novels by:

A Point of Honour. Post 8vo, illustrated boards, 2s.

Archie Lovell. Crown 8vo, cloth extra, 3s. 6d.; post 8vo, illust. bds., 2s.

Eggleston.—Roxy: A Novel. By Edward Eggleston. Post 8vo, illust. boards, 2s.

Emanuel.—On Diamonds and Precious Stones: their History, Value, and Properties; with Simple Tests for ascertaining their Reality. By HARRY EMANUEL, F.R.G.S. With numerous Illustrations, tinted and plain. Crown 8vo, cloth extra, gilt, 6s.

Englishman's House, The: A Practical Guide to all interested in Selecting or Building a House, with full Estimates of Cost, Quantities, &c. By C. J. RICHARDSON. Third Edition. Nearly 600 Illusts. Cr. 8vo, cl. ex., 7s. 6d.

English Merchants: Memoirs in Illustration of the Progress of British Commerce. By H. R. FOX BOURNE. With Illusts. New and Cheaper Edit. revised. Crown 8vo, cloth extra, 7s. 6d. [*Shortly.*

Ewald (Alex. Charles, F.S.A.), Works by:

The Life and Times of Prince Charles Stuart, Count of Albany, commonly called the Young Pretender. From the State Papers and other Sources. New and Cheaper Edition, with a Portrait, crown 8vo, cloth extra, 7s. 6d.

Stories from the State Papers. With an Autotype Facsimile. Crown 8vo, cloth extra, 6s.

Studies Re-studied: Historical Sketches from Original Sources. Demy 8vo cloth extra, 12s.

Eyes, The.—How to Use our Eyes, and How to Preserve Them. By JOHN BROWNING, F.R.A.S., &c. With 52 Illustrations. Crown 8vo, 1s.; cloth, 1s. 6d.

Fairholt.—Tobacco: Its History and Associations; with an Account of the Plant and its Manufacture, and its Modes of Use in all Ages and Countries. By F. W. FAIRHOLT, F.S.A. With upwards of 100 Illustrations by the Author. Crown 8vo, cloth extra, 6s.

Familiar Allusions: A Handbook of Miscellaneous Information; including the Names of Celebrated Statues, Paintings, Palaces, Country Seats, Ruins, Churches, Ships, Streets, Clubs, Natural Curiosities, and the like. By WILLIAM A. WHEELER, Author of "Noted Names of Fiction;" and CHARLES G. WHEELER. Demy 8vo, cloth extra, 7s. 6d.

Faraday (Michael), Works by: Post 8vo, cloth extra, 4s. 6d. each.

The Chemical History of a Candle: Lectures delivered before a Juvenile Audience at the Royal Institution. Edited by WILLIAM CROOKES, F.C.S. With numerous Illustrations.

On the Various Forces of Nature, and their Relations to each other: Lectures delivered before a Juvenile Audience at the Royal Institution. Edited by WILLIAM CROOKES, F.C.S. With numerous Illustrations.

Farrer. — Military Manners and Customs. By J. A. FARRER, Author of "Primitive Manners and Customs," &c. Cr. 8vo, cloth extra, 6s.

Fin-Bec. — The Cupboard Papers: Observations on the Art of Living and Dining. By FIN-BEC. Post 8vo, cloth limp, 2s. 6d.

Fitzgerald (Percy), Works by:

The Recreations of a Literary Man; or, Does Writing Pay? With Recollections of some Literary Men, and a View of a Literary Man's Working Life. Cr. 8vo, cloth extra, 6s.

The World Behind the Scenes. Crown 8vo, cloth extra, 3s. 6d.

Little Essays: Passages from the Letters of CHARLES LAMB. Post 8vo, cloth limp, 2s. 6d.

Post 8vo, illustrated boards, 2s. each.

Bella Donna. | Never Forgotten
The Second Mrs. Tillotson.
Polly.
Seventy-five Brooke Street.
The Lady of Brantome.

Fletcher's (Giles, B.D.) Complete Poems: Christ's Victorie in Heaven, Christ's Victorie on Earth, Christ's Triumph over Death, and Minor Poems. With Memorial-Introduction and Notes by the Rev. A. B. GROSART, D.D. Cr. 8vo, cloth bds., 6s.

Fonblanque.—Filthy Lucre: A Novel. By ALBANY DE FONBLANQUE. Post 8vo, illustrated boards, 2s.

Francillon (R. E.), Novels by: Crown 8vo, cloth extra, 3s. 6d. each; post 8vo, illust. boards, 2s. each.

Olympia. | Queen Cophetua.
One by One. | A Real Queen.

Esther's Glove. Fcap. 8vo, 1s.

French Literature, History of. By HENRY VAN LAUN. Complete in 3 Vols., demy 8vo, cl. bds., 7s. 6d. each.

Frere.—Pandurang Hari; or, Memoirs of a Hindoo. With a Preface by Sir H. BARTLE FRERE, G.C.S.I., &c. Crown 8vo, cloth extra, 3s. 6d.; post 8vo, illustrated boards, 2s.

Friswell.—One of Two: A Novel. By HAIN FRISWELL. Post 8vo, illustrated boards, 2s.

Frost (Thomas), Works by:
Crown 8vo, cloth extra, 3s. 6d. each.
Circus Life and Circus Celebrities.
The Lives of the Conjurers.
The Old Showmen and the Old London Fairs.

Fry's (Herbert) Royal Guide to the London Charities, 1885-6. Showing their Name, Date of Foundation, Objects, Income, Officials, &c. Published Annually. Cr. 8vo, cloth, 1s. 6d.

Gardening Books:
Post 8vo, 1s. each; cl. limp, 1s. 6d. each.
A Year's Work in Garden and Greenhouse: Practical Advice to Amateur Gardeners as to the Management of the Flower, Fruit, and Frame Garden. By GEORGE GLENNY.
Our Kitchen Garden: The Plants we Grow, and How we Cook Them. By TOM JERROLD.
Household Horticulture: A Gossip about Flowers. By TOM and JANE JERROLD. Illustrated.
The Garden that Paid the Rent. By TOM JERROLD.

My Garden Wild, and What I Grew there. By F. G. HEATH. Crown 8vo, cloth extra, 5s.; gilt edges, 6s.

Garrett.—The Capel Girls: A Novel. By EDWARD GARRETT. Cr. 8vo, cl. ex., 3s. 6d.; post 8vo, illust. bds., 2s.

Gentleman's Magazine (The) for 1886. One Shilling Monthly. In addition to the Articles upon subjects in Literature, Science, and Art, for which this Magazine has so high a reputation, "Science Notes," by W. MATTIEU WILLIAMS, F.R.A.S., and "Table Talk," by SYLVANUS URBAN, appear monthly.
⁎ *Just ready, the Volume for* JULY *to* DECEMBER, 1885, *cloth extra, price* 8s. 6d.; *Cases for binding,* 2s. *each.*

Gentleman's Annual (The) for Christmas, 1885. Price 1s. Containing a Complete Novel entitled "A Barren Title," by T. W. SPEIGHT, Author of "The Mysteries of Heron Dyke."

German Popular Stories. Collected by the Brothers GRIMM, and Translated by EDGAR TAYLOR. Edited, with an Introduction, by JOHN RUSKIN. With 22 Illustrations on Steel by GEORGE CRUIKSHANK. Square 8vo, cloth extra, 6s. 6d.; gilt edges, 7s. 6d.

Gibbon (Charles), Novels by:
Crown 8vo, cloth extra, 3s. 6d. each; post 8vo, illustrated boards, 2s. each.

Robin Gray.	The Braes of Yarrow.
For Lack of Gold.	
What will the World Say?	The Flower of the Forest.
In Honour Bound.	A Heart's Problem.
In Love and War.	
Queen of the Meadow.	The Golden Shaft.
	Of High Degree.

Post 8vo, illustrated boards, 2s. each.
For the King.	In Pastures Green
The Dead Heart.	
By Mead and Stream.	[*Preparing.*
A Hard Knot.	[*Preparing.*
Heart's Delight.	[*Preparing.*

Crown 8vo, cloth extra, 3s. 6d. each.
Fancy Free.	Loving a Dream.

Gilbert (William), Novels by:
Post 8vo, illustrated boards, 2s. each.
Dr. Austin's Guests.
The Wizard of the Mountain.
James Duke, Costermonger.

Gilbert (W. S.), Original Plays by: In Two Series, each complete in itself, price 2s. 6d. each.
The FIRST SERIES contains—The Wicked World—Pygmalion and Galatea—Charity—The Princess—The Palace of Truth—Trial by Jury.
The SECOND SERIES contains—Broken Hearts—Engaged—Sweethearts—Gretchen—Dan'l Druce—Tom Cobb—H.M.S. Pinafore—The Sorcerer—The Pirates of Penzance.

Eight Original Comic Operas. Written by W. S. GILBERT. Containing: The Sorcerer—H.M.S. "Pinafore" —The Pirates of Penzance—Iolanthe — Patience — Princess Ida — The Mikado—Trial by Jury. Demy 8vo, cloth limp, 2s. 6d.

Glenny.—A Year's Work in Garden and Greenhouse: Practical Advice to Amateur Gardeners as to the Management of the Flower, Fruit, and Frame Garden. By GEORGE GLENNY. Post 8vo, 1s.; cloth, 1s. 6d.

Godwin.—Lives of the Necro- mancers. By WILLIAM GODWIN. Post 8vo, cloth limp, 2s.

Golden Library, The:

Square 16mo (Tauchnitz size), cloth limp, 2s. per volume.

Bayard Taylor's Diversions of the Echo Club.

Bennett's (Dr. W. C.) Ballad History of England.

Bennett's (Dr.) Songs for Sailors.

Byron's Don Juan.

Godwin's (William) Lives of the Necromancers.

Holmes's Autocrat of the Breakfast Table. Introduction by SALA.

Holmes's Professor at the Breakfast Table.

Hood's Whims and Oddities. Complete. All the original Illustrations.

Irving's (Washington) Tales of a Traveller.

Irving's (Washington) Tales of the Alhambra.

Jesse's (Edward) Scenes and Occupations of a Country Life.

Lamb's Essays of Elia. Both Series Complete in One Vol.

Leigh Hunt's Essays: A Tale for a Chimney Corner, and other Pieces. With Portrait, and Introduction by EDMUND OLLIER.

Mallory's (Sir Thomas) Mort d'Arthur: The Stories of King Arthur and of the Knights of the Round Table. Edited by B. MONTGOMERIE RANKING.

Pascal's Provincial Letters. A New Translation, with Historical Introduction and Notes, by T. M'CRIE, D.D.

Pope's Poetical Works. Complete.

Rochefoucauld's Maxims and Moral Reflections. With Notes, and Introductory Essay by SAINTE-BEUVE.

St. Pierre's Paul and Virginia, and The Indian Cottage. Edited, with Life, by the Rev. E. CLARKE.

Shelley's Early Poems, and Queen Mab. With Essay by LEIGH HUNT.

Shelley's Later Poems: Laon and Cythna, &c.

Shelley's Posthumous Poems, the Shelley Papers, &c.

Shelley's Prose Works, including A Refutation of Deism, Zastrozzi, St. Irvyne, &c.

Golden Treasury of Thought,

The: An ENCYCLOPÆDIA OF QUOTATIONS from Writers of all Times and Countries. Selected and Edited by THEODORE TAYLOR. Crown 8vo, cloth gilt and gilt edges, 7s. 6d.

Graham. — The Professor's

Wife: A Story. By LEONARD GRAHAM. Fcap. 8vo, picture cover, 1s.

Greeks and Romans, The Life

of the, Described from Antique Monuments. By ERNST GUHL and W. KONER. Translated from the Third German Edition, and Edited by Dr. F. HUEFFER. With 545 Illustrations. New and Cheaper Edition, demy 8vo, cloth extra, 7s. 6d.

Greenwood (James), Works by:

Crown 8vo, cloth extra, 3s. 6d. each.

The Wilds of London.

Low-Life Deeps: An Account of the Strange Fish to be Found There.

Dick Temple: A Novel. Post 8vo, illustrated boards, 2s.

Guyot.—The Earth and Man:

or, Physical Geography in its relation to the History of Mankind. By ARNOLD GUYOT. With Additions by Professors AGASSIZ, PIERCE, and GRAY; 12 Maps and Engravings on Steel, some Coloured, and copious Index. Crown 8vo, cloth extra, gilt, 4s. 6d.

Hair (The): Its Treatment in

Health, Weakness, and Disease. Translated from the German of Dr. J. PINCUS. Crown 8vo, 1s; cloth, 1s. 6d.

Hake (Dr. Thomas Gordon),

Poems by:

Crown 8vo, cloth extra, 6s. each.

New Symbols.

Legends of the Morrow.

The Serpent Play.

Maiden Ecstasy. Small 4to, cloth extra, 8s.

Hall.—Sketches of Irish Cha-

racter. By Mrs. S. C. HALL. With numerous Illustrations on Steel and Wood by MACLISE, GILBERT, HARVEY, and G. CRUIKSHANK. Medium 8vo, cloth extra, gilt, 7s. 6d.

Halliday.—Every-day Papers.

By ANDREW HALLIDAY. Post 8vo, illustrated boards, 2s.

Handwriting, The Philosophy

of. With over 100 Facsimiles and Explanatory Text. By DON FELIX DE SALAMANCA. Post 8vo, cl. limp, 2s. 6d.

Hanky-Panky: A Collection of

Very Easy Tricks, Very Difficult Tricks, White Magic, Sleight of Hand, &c. Edited by W. H. CREMER. With 200 Illusts. Crown 8vo, cloth extra, 4s. 6d.

Hardy (Lady Duffus).— Paul
Wynter's Sacrifice: A Story. By
Lady DUFFUS HARDY. Post 8vo, illust.
boards, 2s.

Hardy (Thomas).—Under the
Greenwood Tree. By THOMAS HARDY,
Author of "Far from the Madding
Crowd." With numerous Illustrations.
Crown 8vo, cloth extra, 3s. 6d.; post
8vo, illustrated boards, 2s.

Harwood.—The Tenth Earl
By J. BERWICK HARWOOD. Post 8vo,
illustrated boards, 2s.   [*In the press.*]

Haweis (Mrs. H. R.), Works by:
The Art of Dress. With numerous
Illustrations. Small 8vo, illustrated
cover, 1s.; cloth limp, 1s. 6d.

The Art of Beauty. New and Cheaper
Edition. Crown 8vo, cloth extra,
Coloured Frontispiece and Illusts. 6s.

The Art of Decoration. Square 8vo,
handsomely bound and profusely
Illustrated, 10s. 6d.

Chaucer for Children: A Golden
Key. With Eight Coloured Pictures
and numerous Woodcuts. New
Edition, small 4to, cloth extra, 6s.

Chaucer for Schools. Demy 8vo,
cloth limp, 2s. 6d.

Haweis (Rev. H. R.).—American
Humorists. Including WASHINGTON
IRVING, OLIVER WENDELL HOLMES,
JAMES RUSSELL LOWELL, ARTEMUS
WARD, MARK TWAIN, and BRET HARTE.
By the Rev. H. R. HAWEIS, M.A.
Crown 8vo, cloth extra, 6s.

Hawthorne (Julian), Novels by.
Crown 8vo, cloth extra, 3s. 6d. each;
post 8vo, illustrated boards, 2s. each.

Garth. | Sebastian Strome.
Ellice Quentin. | Dust.
Prince Saroni's Wife.
Fortune's Fool. | Beatrix Randolph.

Crown 8vo, cloth extra, 3s. 6d. each.
Miss Cadogna.
Love—or a Name.   [*Shortly.*]

Mrs. Gainsborough's Diamonds.
Fcap. 8vo, illustrated cover, 1s.

Hays.—Women of the Day: A
Biographical Dictionary of Notable
Contemporaries. By FRANCES HAYS.
Crown 8vo, cloth extra, 5s.

Heath (F. G.). — My Garden
Wild, and What I Grew There. By
FRANCIS GEORGE HEATH, Author of
"The Fern World," &c. Crown 8vo,
cloth extra, 5s.; cl. gilt, gilt edges, 6s.

Helps (Sir Arthur), Works by:
Post 8vo, cloth limp, 2s. 6d. each.
Animals and their Masters.
Social Pressure.

Ivan de Biron: A Novel. Crown 8vo,
cloth extra, 3s. 6d.; post 8vo, illustrated boards, 2s.

Heptalogia (The); or, The
Seven against Sense. A Cap with
Seven Bells. Cr. 8vo, cloth extra, 6s.

Herbert.—The Poems of Lord
Herbert of Cherbury. Edited, with
Introduction, by J. CHURTON COLLINS.
Crown 8vo, bound in parchment, 8s.

Herrick's (Robert) Hesperides,
Noble Numbers, and Complete Collected Poems. With Memorial-Introduction and Notes by the Rev. A. B.
GROSART, D.D., Steel Portrait, Index
of First Lines, and Glossarial Index,
&c. Three Vols., crown 8vo, cloth, 18s.

Hesse - Wartegg   (Chevalier
Ernst von), Works by:
Tunis: The Land and the People.
With 22 Illustrations. Crown 8vo,
cloth extra, 3s. 6d.

The New South-West: Travelling
Sketches from Kansas, New Mexico,
Arizona, and Northern Mexico.
With 100 fine Illustrations and Three
Maps. Demy 8vo, cloth extra,
14s.   [*In preparation.*]

Hindley (Charles), Works by:
Crown 8vo, cloth extra, 3s. 6d. each.
Tavern Anecdotes and Sayings: In-
cluding the Origin of Signs, and
Reminiscences connected with
Taverns, Coffee Houses, Clubs, &c.
With Illustrations.

The Life and Adventures of a Cheap
Jack. By One of the Fraternity.
Edited by CHARLES HINDLEY.

Hoey.—The Lover's Creed.
By Mrs. CASHEL HOEY. With Frontis-
piece by P. MACNAB. New and Cheaper
Edit. Crown 8vo, cloth extra, 3s. 6d.

Holmes (O. Wendell), Works by:
The Autocrat of the Breakfast-
Table. Illustrated by J. GORDON
THOMSON. Post 8vo, cloth limp,
2s. 6d.—Another Edition in smaller
type, with an Introduction by G. A.
SALA. Post 8vo, cloth limp, 2s.

The Professor at the Breakfast-
Table; with the Story of Iris. Post
8vo, cloth limp, 2s.

Holmes. — The Science of Voice Production and Voice Preservation: A Popular Manual for the Use of Speakers and Singers. By GORDON HOLMES, M.D. With Illustrations. Crown 8vo, 1s.; cloth, 1s. 6d.

Hood (Thomas):

Hood's Choice Works, In Prose and Verse. Including the Cream of the COMIC ANNUALS. With Life of the Author, Portrait, and 200 Illustrations. Crown 8vo, cloth extra, 7s. 6d.

Hood's Whims and Oddities. Complete. With all the original Illustrations. Post 8vo, cloth limp, 2s.

Hood (Tom), Works by:

From Nowhere to the North Pole: A Noah's Arkæological Narrative. With 25 Illustrations by W. BRUNTON and E. C. BARNES. Square crown 8vo, cloth extra, gilt edges, 6s.

A Golden Heart: A Novel. Post 8vo, illustrated boards, 2s.

Hook's (Theodore) Choice Humorous Works, including his Ludicrous Adventures, Bons Mots, Puns and Hoaxes. With a New Life of the Author, Portraits, Facsimiles, and Illusts. Cr. 8vo, cl. extra, gilt, 7s. 6d.

Hooper. — The House of Raby: A Novel. By Mrs. GEORGE HOOPER. Post 8vo, illustrated boards, 2s.

Hopkins — "'Twixt Love and Duty:" A Novel. By TIGHE HOPKINS. Crown 8vo, cloth extra, 6s [*In the press.*

Horne. — Orion : An Epic Poem, in Three Books. By RICHARD HENGIST HORNE. With Photographic Portrait from a Medallion by SUMMERS. Tenth Edition, crown 8vo, cloth extra, 7s.

Howell. — Conflicts of Capital and Labour, Historically and Economically considered: Being a History and Review of the Trade Unions of Great Britain. By GEO. HOWELL, M.P. Crown 8vo, cloth extra, 7s. 6d.

Hugo. — The Hunchback of Notre Dame. By VICTOR HUGO. Post 8vo, illustrated boards, 2s.

Hunt. — Essays by Leigh Hunt. A Tale for a Chimney Corner, and other Pieces. With Portrait and Introduction by EDMUND OLLIER. Post 8vo, cloth limp, 2s.

Hunt (Mrs. Alfred), Novels by:
Crown 8vo, cloth extra, 3s. 6d. each; post 8vo, illustrated boards, 2s. each.

Thornicroft's Model.
The Leaden Casket.
Self Condemned

Indoor Paupers. By ONE OF THEMSELVES. With a Preface by GEORGE R. SIMS. Crown 8vo, 1s.: cloth, 1s. 6d. [*In the press.*

Ingelow. — Fated to be Free : A Novel. By JEAN INGELOW. Crown 8vo, cloth extra, 3s. 6d.; post 8vo, illustrated boards, 2s.

Irish Wit and Humour, Songs of. Collected and Edited by A. PERCEVAL GRAVES. Post 8vo, cl. limp, 2s. 6d.

Irving (Washington),Works by:
Post 8vo, cloth limp, 2s. each.
Tales of a Traveller.
Tales of the Alhambra.

Janvier. — Practical Keramics for Students. By CATHERINE A. JANVIER. Crown 8vo, cloth extra, 6s.

Jay (Harriett), Novels by:

The Dark Colleen. Post 8vo, illustrated boards, 2s.

The Queen of Connaught. Crown 8vo, cloth extra, 3s. 6d.; post 8vo, illustrated boards, 2s.

Jefferies (Richard), Works by:
Crown 8vo, cloth extra, 6s. each.
Nature near London.
The Life of the Fields.
The Open Air.

Jennings (H. J.), Works by:

Curiosities of Criticism. Post 8vo, cloth limp, 2s. 6d.

Lord Tennyson: A Biographical Sketch. With a Photograph-Portrait. Crown 8vo, cloth extra, 6s.

Jennings (Hargrave). — The Rosicrucians: Their Rites and Mysteries. With Chapters on the Ancient Fire and Serpent Worshippers. By HARGRAVE JENNINGS. With Five full-page Plates and upwards of 300 Illustrations. A New Edition, crown 8vo, cloth extra, 7s. 6d.

Jerrold (Tom), Works by :
Post 8vo, 1s. each ; cloth, 1s. 6d. each.
The Garden that Paid the Rent.
Household Horticulture : A Gossip about Flowers. Illustrated.
Our Kitchen Garden : The Plants we Grow, and How we Cook Them.

Jesse.—Scenes and Occupations of a Country Life. By EDWARD JESSE. Post 8vo, cloth limp, 2s.

Jeux d'Esprit. Collected and Edited by HENRY S. LEIGH. Post 8vo, cloth limp, 2s. 6d.

Jones (Wm., F.S.A.), Works by :
Crown 8vo, cloth extra, 7s. 6d. each.
Finger-Ring Lore : Historical, Legendary, and Anecdotal. With over Two Hundred Illustrations.
Credulities, Past and Present ; including the Sea and Seamen, Miners, Talismans, Word and Letter Divination, Exorcising and Blessing of Animals, Birds, Eggs, Luck, &c. With an Etched Frontispiece.
Crowns and Coronations : A History of Regalia in all Times and Countries. With One Hundred Illustrations.

Jonson's (Ben) Works. With Notes Critical and Explanatory, and a Biographical Memoir by WILLIAM GIFFORD. Edited by Colonel CUNNINGHAM. Three Vols., crown 8vo, cloth extra, 18s. ; or separately, 6s. each.

Josephus, The Complete Works of. Translated by WHISTON. Containing both "The Antiquities of the Jews" and "The Wars of the Jews." Two Vols., 8vo, with 52 Illustrations and Maps, cloth extra, gilt, 14s.

Kempt.—Pencil and Palette : Chapters on Art and Artists. By ROBERT KEMPT. Post 8vo, cloth limp, 2s. 6d.

Kingsley (Henry), Novels by :
Oakshott Castle. Post 8vo, illustrated boards, 2s.
Number Seventeen. Crown 8vo, cloth extra, 3s. 6d. ; post 8vo, illustrated boards, 2s.

Knight.— The Patient's Vade Mecum : How to get most Benefit from Medical Advice. By WILLIAM KNIGHT, M.R.C.S., and EDWARD KNIGHT, L.R.C.P. Crown 8vo, 1s. ; cloth, 1s. 6d.

Lamb (Charles) :
Lamb's Complete Works, in Prose and Verse, reprinted from the Original Editions, with many Pieces hitherto unpublished. Edited, with Notes and Introduction, by R. H. SHEPHERD. With Two Portraits and Facsimile of Page of the "Essay on Roast Pig." Cr. 8vo, cloth extra, 7s. 6d.
The Essays of Elia. Complete Edition. Post 8vo, cloth extra, 2s.
Poetry for Children, and Prince Dorus. By CHARLES LAMB. Carefully reprinted from unique copies. Small 8vo, cloth extra, 5s.
Little Essays : Sketches and Characters. By CHARLES LAMB. Selected from his Letters by PERCY FITZGERALD. Post 8vo, cloth limp, 2s. 6d.

Lane's Arabian Nights, &c. :
The Thousand and One Nights : commonly called, in England, "THE ARABIAN NIGHTS' ENTERTAINMENTS." A New Translation from the Arabic, with copious Notes, by EDWARD WILLIAM LANE. Illustrated by many hundred Engravings on Wood, from Original Designs by WM. HARVEY. A New Edition, from a Copy annotated by the Translator, edited by his Nephew, EDWARD STANLEY POOLE. With a Preface by STANLEY LANE-POOLE. Three Vols., demy 8vo, cloth extra, 7s. 6d. each.
Arabian Society in the Middle Ages : Studies from "The Thousand and One Nights." By EDWARD WILLIAM LANE, Author of "The Modern Egyptians," &c. Edited by STANLEY LANE-POOLE. Cr. 8vo, cloth extra, 6s.

Lares and Penates ; or, The Background of Life. By FLORENCE CADDY. Crown 8vo, cloth extra, 6s.

Larwood (Jacob), Works by :
The Story of the London Parks. With Illustrations. Crown 8vo, cloth extra, 3s. 6d.
Post 8vo, cloth limp, 2s. 6d. each.
Forensic Anecdotes.
Theatrical Anecdotes.

Life in London ; or, The History of Jerry Hawthorn and Corinthian Tom. With the whole of CRUIKSHANK'S Illustrations, in Colours, after the Originals. Crown 8vo, cloth extra, 7s. 6d.

Linton (E. Lynn), Works by :
Post 8vo, cloth limp, 2s. 6d. each.
Witch Stories.
The True Story of Joshua Davidson.
Ourselves : Essays on Women.

LINTON (E. LYNN), *continued*—

Crown 8vo, cloth extra, 3s 6d. each ; post 8vo, illustrated boards, 2s. each.

Patricia Kemball.
The Atonement of Leam Dundas
The World Well Lost.
Under which Lord ?
With a Silken Thread.
The Rebel of the Family.
" My Love ! "
Ione.

Locks and Keys.—On the Development and Distribution of Primitive Locks and Keys. By Lieut.-Gen. PITT-RIVERS, F.R.S. With numerous Illustrations. Demy 4to, half Roxburghe, 16s.

Longfellow :

Crown 8vo, cloth extra, 7s. 6d. each.

Longfellow's Complete Prose Works. Including " Outre Mer," " Hyperion," " Kavanagh," " The Poets and Poetry of Europe," and " Driftwood." With Portrait and Illustrations by VALENTINE BROMLEY.

Longfellow's Poetical Works. Carefully Reprinted from the Original Editions. With numerous fine Illustrations on Steel and Wood.

Long Life, Aids to: A Medical, Dietetic, and General Guide in Health and Disease. By N. E. DAVIES, L.R.C.P. Crown 8vo, 2s. ; cloth limp, 2s. 6d.

Lucy.—Gideon Fleyce: A Novel. By HENRY W. LUCY. Crown 8vo, cloth extra, 3s. 6d ; post 8vo, illustrated boards, 2s.

Lusiad (The) of Camoens. Translated into English Spenserian Verse by ROBERT FFRENCH DUFF. Demy 8vo, with Fourteen full-page Plates, cloth boards, 18s.

McCarthy (Justin, M.P.),Works by :

A History of Our Own Times, from the Accession of Queen Victoria to the General Election of 1880. Four Vols. demy 8vo, cloth extra, 12s. each.—Also a POPULAR EDITION, in Four Vols. cr. 8vo. cl. extra, 6s each.

A Short History of Our Own Times. One Vol., crown 8vo, cloth extra, 6s.

History of the Four Georges. Four Vols. demy 8vo, cloth extra, 12s. each. [Vol. I. *now ready.*

MCCARTHY (JUSTIN), *continued*—

Crown 8vo, cloth extra, 3s. 6d. each ; post 8vo, illustrated boards, 2s. each.

Dear Lady Disdain.
The Waterdale Neighbours.
My Enemy's Daughter.
A Fair Saxon.
Linley Rochford.
Miss Misanthrope.
Donna Quixote.
The Comet of a Season.
Maid of Athens.

Camiola : A Girl with a Fortune. Three Vols., crown 8vo. Third Edit.

McCarthy (Justin H., M.P.), Works by :

An Outline of the History of Ireland, from the Earliest Times to the Present Day. Cr. 8vo, 1s. ; cloth, 1s. 6d.

England under Gladstone, 1880-85. Second Edition, revised and brought down to the Fall of the Gladstone Administration. Crown 8vo, cloth extra, 6s.

Doomed ! A Novel. Post 8vo, 1s. ; cloth, 1s. 6d. [*Preparing.*

MacDonald (George, LL.D.), Works by :

The Princess and Curdle. With 11 Illustrations by JAMES ALLEN. Small crown 8vo, cloth extra, 5s.

Gutta-Percha Willie, the Working Genius. With 9 Illustrations by ARTHUR HUGHES. Square 8vo, cloth extra, 3s. 6d.

Crown 8vo, cloth extra, 3s 6d. each ; post 8vo, illustrated boards, 2s. each.

Paul Faber, Surgeon. With a Frontispiece by J. E. MILLAIS.

Thomas Wingfold, Curate. With a Frontispiece by C. J. STANILAND.

Macdonell.—Quaker Cousins: A Novel. By AGNES MACDONELL. Crown 8vo, cloth extra, 3s. 6d. ; post 8vo, illustrated boards, 2s.

Macgregor. — Pastimes and Players. Notes on Popular Games. By ROBERT MACGREGOR. Post 8vo, cloth limp, 2s. 6d.

Maclise Portrait-Gallery (The) of Illustrious Literary Characters; with Memoirs—Biographical, Critical, Bibliographical, and Anecdotal—illustrative of the Literature of the former half of the Present Century. By WILLIAM BATES, B.A. With 85 Portraits printed on an India Tint. Crown 8vo, cloth extra, 7s. 6d.

Mackay.—Interludes and Undertones; or, Music at Twilight. By CHARLES MACKAY, LL.D. Crown 8vo, cloth extra, 6s.

Macquoid (Mrs.), Works by:
Square 8vo, cloth extra, 10s. 6d. each.
In the Ardennes. With 50 fine Illustrations by THOMAS R. MACQUOID.
Pictures and Legends from Normandy and Brittany. With numerous Illustrations by THOMAS R. MACQUOID.
About Yorkshire. With 67 Illustrations by T. R. Macquoid.

Crown 8vo, cloth extra, 7s. 6d. each.
Through Normandy. With 90 Illustrations by T. R. MACQUOID.
Through Brittany. With numerous Illustrations by T. R. MACQUOID.

Post 8vo, illustrated boards, 2s. each.
The Evil Eye, and other Stories.
Lost Rose.

Magician's Own Book (The): Performances with Cups and Balls, Eggs, Hats, Handkerchiefs, &c. All from actual Experience. Edited by W. H. CREMER. With 200 Illustrations. Crown 8vo, cloth extra, 4s. 6d.

Magic No Mystery: Tricks with Cards, Dice, Balls, &c., with fully descriptive Directions; the Art of Secret Writing; Training of Performing Animals, &c. With Coloured Frontispiece and many Illustrations. Crown 8vo, cloth extra, 4s. 6d.

Magic Lantern (The), and its Management: including full Practical Directions for producing the Limelight, making Oxygen Gas, and preparing Lantern Slides. By T. C. HEPWORTH. With 10 Illustrations. Crown 8vo, 1s. ; cloth, 1s. 6d.

Magna Charta. An exact Facsimile of the Original in the British Museum, printed on fine plate paper, 3 feet by 2 feet, with Arms and Seals emblazoned in Gold and Colours. 5s.

Mallock (W. H.), Works by:
The New Republic; or, Culture, Faith and Philosophy in an English Country House. Post 8vo, cloth limp, 2s. 6d. ; Cheap Edition, illustrated boards, 2s.
The New Paul and Virginia ; or, Positivism on an Island. Post 8vo, cloth limp, 2s. 6d.
Poems. Small 4to, in parchment, 8s.
Is Life worth Living? Crown 8vo, cloth extra, 6s.

Mallory's (Sir Thomas) Mort d'Arthur: The Stories of King Arthur and of the Knights of the Round Table. Edited by B. MONTGOMERIE RANKING. Post 8vo, cloth limp, 2s.

Marryat (Florence), Novels by:
Crown 8vo, cloth extra, 3s. 6d. each; post 8vo, illustrated boards, 2s. each.
Open! Sesame!
Written in Fire

Post 8vo, illustrated boards, 2s. each.
A Harvest of Wild Oats.
A Little Stepson.
Fighting the Air.

Masterman.—Half a Dozen Daughters: A Novel. By J. MASTERMAN. Post 8vo, illustrated boards, 2s.

Marlowe's Works. Including his Translations. Edited, with Notes and Introductions, by Col. CUNNINGHAM. Crown 8vo, cloth extra, 6s.

Mark Twain, Works by:
The Choice Works of Mark Twain. Revised and Corrected throughout by the Author. With Life, Portrait, and numerous Illustrations. Crown 8vo, cloth extra, 7s. 6d.
The Innocents Abroad ; or, The New Pilgrim's Progress : Being some Account of the Steamship "Quaker City's" Pleasure Excursion to Europe and the Holy Land. With 234 Illustrations. Crown 8vo, cloth extra, 7s. 6d.—Cheap Edition (under the title of "MARK TWAIN'S PLEASURE TRIP"), post 8vo, illust. boards, 2s.
Roughing It, and The Innocents at Home. With 200 Illustrations by F. A. FRASER. Crown 8vo, cloth extra, 7s. 6d.
The Gilded Age. By MARK TWAIN and CHARLES DUDLEY WARNER. With 212 Illustrations by T. COPPIN. Crown 8vo, cloth extra, 7s. 6d.
The Adventures of Tom Sawyer. With 111 Illustrations. Crown 8vo, cloth extra, 7s. 6d.—Cheap Edition, post 8vo, illustrated boards, 2s.
An Idle Excursion, and other Sketches. Post 8vo, illustrated boards, 2s.
The Prince and the Pauper. With nearly 200 Illustrations. Crown 8vo, cloth extra, 7s. 6d.
A Tramp Abroad. With 314 Illustrations. Crown 8vo, cloth extra, 7s. 6d. —Cheap Edition, post 8vo, illustrated boards, 2s.
The Stolen White Elephant, &c. Crown 8vo, cloth extra, 6s.; post 8vo, illustrated boards, 2s.

MARK TWAIN'S WORKS, *continued—*

Life on the Mississippi. With about 300 Original Illustrations. Crown 8vo, cloth extra, 7s. 6d.

The Adventures of Huckleberry Finn. With 174 Illustrations by E. W. KEMBLE. Crown 8vo, cloth extra, 7s. 6d.

Massinger's Plays. From the Text of WILLIAM GIFFORD. Edited by Col. CUNNINGHAM. Crown 8vo, cloth extra, 6s.

Mayfair Library, The :
Post 8vo, cloth limp, 2s. 6d. per Volume.

A Journey Round My Room. By XAVIER DE MAISTRE. Translated by HENRY ATTWELL.

Latter-Day Lyrics. Edited by W DAVENPORT ADAMS.

Quips and Quiddities. Selected by W. DAVENPORT ADAMS.

The Agony Column of "The Times," from 1800 to 1870. Edited, with an Introduction, by ALICE CLAY.

Balzac's "Comedie Humaine" and its Author. With Translations by H. H. WALKER.

Melancholy Anatomised : A Popular Abridgment of "Burton's Anatomy of Melancholy."

Gastronomy as a Fine Art. By BRILLAT-SAVARIN.

The Speeches of Charles Dickens.

Literary Frivolities, Fancies, Follies, and Frolics. By W. T. DOBSON.

Poetical Ingenuities and Eccentricities. Selected and Edited by W. T. DOBSON.

The Cupboard Papers. By FIN-BEC.

Original Plays by W. S. GILBERT. FIRST SERIES. Containing : The Wicked World — Pygmalion and Galatea — Charity — The Princess — The Palace of Truth—Trial by Jury.

Original Plays by W. S. GILBERT. SECOND SERIES. Containing : Broken Hearts — Engaged — Sweethearts — Gretchen—Dan'l Druce—Tom Cobb —H.M.S. Pinafore — The Sorcerer —The Pirates of Penzance.

Songs of Irish Wit and Humour. Collected and Edited by A. PERCEVAL GRAVES.

Animals and their Masters. By Sir ARTHUR HELPS.

Social Pressure. By Sir A. HELPS.

Curiosities of Criticism. By HENRY J. JENNINGS.

The Autocrat of the Breakfast-Table. By OLIVER WENDELL HOLMES. Illustrated by J. GORDON THOMSON.

MAYFAIR LIBRARY, *continued—*

Pencil and Palette. By ROBERT KEMPT.

Little Essays : Sketches and Characters. By CHAS. LAMB. Selected from his Letters by PERCY FITZGERALD.

Forensic Anecdotes; or, Humour and Curiosities of the Law and Men of Law. By JACOB LARWOOD.

Theatrical Anecdotes. By JACOB LARWOOD.

Jeux d'Esprit. Edited by HENRY S. LEIGH.

True History of Joshua Davidson. By E. LYNN LINTON.

Witch Stories. By E. LYNN LINTON.

Ourselves : Essays on Women. By E. LYNN LINTON.

Pastimes and Players. By ROBERT MACGREGOR.

The New Paul and Virginia. By W. H. MALLOCK.

New Republic. By W. H. MALLOCK.

Puck on Pegasus. By H. CHOLMONDELEY-PENNELL.

Pegasus Re-Saddled. By H. CHOLMONDELEY-PENNELL. Illustrated by GEORGE DU MAURIER.

Muses of Mayfair. Edited by H. CHOLMONDELEY-PENNELL.

Thoreau : His Life and Aims. By H. A. PAGE.

Puniana. By the Hon. HUGH ROWLEY.

More Puniana. By the Hon. HUGH ROWLEY.

The Philosophy of Handwriting. By DON FELIX DE SALAMANCA.

By Stream and Sea. By WILLIAM SENIOR.

Old Stories Re-told. By WALTER THORNBURY.

Leaves from a Naturalist's Note-Book. By Dr. ANDREW WILSON.

Mayhew.—London Characters and the Humorous Side of London Life. By HENRY MAYHEW. With numerous Illustrations. Crown 8vo, cloth extra, 3s. 6d.

Medicine, Family.—One Thousand Medical Maxims and Surgical Hints, for Infancy, Adult Life, Middle Age, and Old Age. By N. E. DAVIES, L.R.C.P. Lond. Cr. 8vo, 1s.; cl., 1s. 6d.

Merry Circle (The): A Book of New Intellectual Games and Amusements. By CLARA BELLEW. With numerous Illustrations. Crown 8vo, cloth extra, 4s. 6d.

Mexican Mustang (On a), through Texas, from the Gulf to the Rio Grande. A New Book of American Humour. By ALEX. E. SWEET and J. ARMOY KNOX, Editors of "Texas Siftings." With 265 Illusts. Cr. 8vo, cloth extra, 7s. 6d.

Middlemass (Jean), Novels by: Post 8vo, illustrated boards, 2s. each.
Touch and Go.
Mr. Dorillion.

Miller. — Physiology for the Young; or, The House of Life: Human Physiology, with its application to the Preservation of Health. For Classes and Popular Reading. With numerous Illusts. By Mrs. F. FENWICK MILLER. Small 8vo, cloth limp, 2s. 6d

Milton (J. L.), Works by: Sm. 8vo, 1s. each; cloth ex., 1s. 6d. each.
The Hygiene of the Skin. A Concise Set of Rules for the Management of the Skin; with Directions for Diet, Wines, Soaps, Baths, &c.
The Bath in Diseases of the Skin.
The Laws of Life, and their Relation to Diseases of the Skin.

Molesworth (Mrs.).—Hathercourt Rectory. By Mrs. MOLESWORTH, Author of "The Cuckoo Clock," &c. Crown 8vo, cloth extra, 4s. 6d. [In the press.

Moncrieff. — The Abdication; or, Time Tries All. An Historical Drama. By W. D. SCOTT-MONCRIEFF. With Seven Etchings by JOHN PETTIE, R.A., W. Q. ORCHARDSON, R.A., J. MacWHIRTER, A.R.A., COLIN HUNTER, R. MACBETH, and TOM GRAHAM. Large 4to, bound in buckram, 21s.

Murray (D. Christie), Novels by. Crown 8vo, cloth extra, 3s. 6d. each; post 8vo, illustrated boards, 2s. each.
A Life's Atonement.
A Model Father.
Joseph's Coat.
Coals of Fire.
By the Gate of the Sea.
Val Strange.
Hearts.

Crown 8vo, cloth extra, 3s. 6d. each.
The Way of the World.
A Bit of Human Nature.

First Person Singular: A Novel. Three Vols., cr. 8vo.

North Italian Folk. By Mrs. COMYNS CARR. Illustrated by RANDOLPH CALDECOTT. Square 8vo, cloth extra, 7s. 6d.

Number Nip (Stories about), the Spirit of the Giant Mountains. Retold for Children by WALTER GRAHAME. With Illustrations by J. MOYR SMITH. Post 8vo, cl. extra, 5s.

Nursery Hints: A Mother's Guide in Health and Disease. By N. E. DAVIES. L.R.C.P. Crown 8vo, 1s.; cloth, 1s. 6d.

O'Connor —Lord Beaconsfield A Biography. By T. P. O'CONNOR, M.P. Sixth Edition, with a New Preface, bringing the work down to the Death of Lord Beaconsfield. Crown 8vo, cloth extra, 7s. 6d.

Oliphant (Mrs.) Novels by:
Whiteladies. With Illustrations by ARTHUR HOPKINS and H. WOODS. Crown 8vo, cloth extra, 3s. 6d.; post 8vo, illustrated boards, 2s.

Crown 8vo, cloth extra, 4s. 6d. each.
The Primrose Path.
The Greatest Heiress in England. [Shortly.

O'Hanlon. — The Unforeseen: A Novel. By ALICE O'HANLON. Three Vols., crown 8vo.

O'Reilly.—Phœbe's Fortunes: A Novel. With Illustrations by HENRY TUCK. Post 8vo, illustrated boards, 2s.

O'Shaughnessy (Arth.), Works by:
Songs of a Worker. Fcap. 8vo, cloth extra, 7s. 6d.
Music and Moonlight. Fcap. 8vo, cloth extra, 7s. 6d.
Lays of France. Crown 8vo, cloth extra, 10s. 6d.

Ouida, Novels by. Crown 8vo, cloth extra, 5s. each; post 8vo, illustrated boards, 2s. each.

Held in Bondage.	Pascarel.
Strathmore.	Signa.
Chandos.	In a Winter City.
Under Two Flags.	Ariadne
Cecil Castlemaine's Gage.	Friendship.
	Moths.
Idalia.	Pipistrello.
Tricotrin.	A Village Commune.
Puck.	
Folle Farine.	Bimbi.
TwoLittleWooden Shoes.	In Maremma.
	Wanda.
A Dog of Flanders.	Frescoes.

OUIDA, NOVELS BY, *continued.*

Princess Napraxine. Crown 8vo cloth extra, 5s.

Othmar: A Novel. Second Edition. Three Vols., crown 8vo.

Wisdom, Wit, and Pathos, selected from the Works of OUIDA by F. SYDNEY MORRIS. Small crown 8vo, cloth extra, 5s.

Page (H. A.), Works by:

Thoreau: His Life and Aims: A Study. With a Portrait. Post 8vo, cloth limp, 2s. 6d.

Lights on the Way: Some Tales within a Tale. By the late J. H. ALEXANDER, B.A. Edited by H. A. PAGE. Crown 8vo, cloth extra, 6s.

Pascal's Provincial Letters. A
New Translation, with Historical Introduction and Notes, by T. M'CRIE, D.D. Post 8vo, cloth limp, 2s.

Patient's (The) Vade Mecum:
How to get most Benefit from Medical Advice. By WILLIAM KNIGHT, M.R.C.S., and EDWARD KNIGHT, L.R.C.P. Crown 8vo, 1s; cloth, 1s 6d.

Paul Ferroll:

Post 8vo, illustrated boards, 2s. each.

Paul Ferroll: A Novel.

Why Paul Ferroll Killed his Wife.

Paul.—Gentle and Simple. By
MARGARET AGNES PAUL. With a Frontispiece by HELEN PATERSON. Cr. 8vo, cloth extra, 3s. 6d.; post 8vo, illustrated boards, 2s.

Payn (James), Novels by.
Crown 8vo, cloth extra, 3s. 6d. each; post 8vo, illustrated boards, 2s. each.

Lost Sir Massingberd.

The Best of Husbands.

Walter's Word.

Halves. | **Fallen Fortunes.**

What He Cost Her.

Less Black than we're Painted.

By Proxy. | **High Spirits.**

Under One Roof. | **Carlyon's Year.**

A Confidential Agent.

Some Private Views.

A Grape from a Thorn.

For Cash Only. | **From Exile.**

Kit: A Memory.

The Canon's Ward.

Post 8vo, illustrated boards, 2s. each.

A Perfect Treasure.

Bentinck's Tutor. Murphy's Master

PAYN (JAMES), *continued—*

A County Family. | **At Her Mercy.**

A Woman's Vengeance.

Cecil's Tryst.

The Clyffards of Clyffe.

The Family Scapegrace.

The Foster Brothers.

Found Dead.

Gwendoline's Harvest.

Humorous Stories.

Like Father, Like Son.

A Marine Residence.

Married Beneath Him.

Mirk Abbey.

Not Wooed, but Won.

Two Hundred Pounds Reward

In Peril and Privation: Stories of Marine Adventure Re-told. A Book for Boys. With numerous Illustrations. Crown 8vo, cloth gilt, 6s.

The Talk of the Town: A Novel. With Twelve Illustrations by HARRY FURNISS. Crown 8vo, cloth extra, 3s. 6d.

Pears.—The Present Depression in Trade:
Its Causes and Remedies. Being the "Pears" Prize Essays (of One Hundred Guineas). By EDWIN GOADBY and WILLIAM WATT. With an Introductory Paper by Prof. LEONE LEVI, F.S.A., F.S.S. Demy 8vo, 1s.

Pennell (H. Cholmondeley), Works by:
Post 8vo, cloth limp, 2s. 6d. each.

Puck on Pegasus. With Illustrations.

Pegasus Re-Saddled. With Ten full-page Illusts. by G. DU MAURIER.

The Muses of Mayfair. Vers de Société, Selected and Edited by H. C. PENNELL.

Phelps (E. Stuart), Works by:
Post 8vo, 1s. each; cloth limp, 1s. 6d. each.

Beyond the Gates. By the Author of "The Gates Ajar."

An Old Maid's Paradise.

Pirkis (Mrs. C. L.), Novels by:
Trooping with Crows. Fcap. 8vo, picture cover, 1s.

Lady Lovelace. Post 8vo, illustrated boards, 2s. *[Preparing.*

Plutarch's Lives of Illustrious
Men. Translated from the Greek, with Notes Critical and Historical, and a Life of Plutarch, by JOHN and WILLIAM LANGHORNE. Two Vols., 8vo, cloth extra, with Portraits, 10s. 6d.

Planché (J. R.), Works by :

The Pursuivant of Arms ; or, Heraldry Founded upon Facts. With Coloured Frontispiece and 200 Illustrations. Cr. 8vo, cloth extra, 7s. 6d.

Songs and Poems, from 1819 to 1879. Edited, with an Introduction, by his Daughter, Mrs. MACKARNESS. Crown 8vo, cloth extra, 6s.

Poe (Edgar Allan) :—

The Choice Works, in Prose and Poetry, of EDGAR ALLAN POE. With an Introductory Essay by CHARLES BAUDELAIRE, Portrait and Facsimiles. Crown 8vo, cl. extra, 7s. 6d.

The Mystery of Marie Roget, and other Stories. Post 8vo, illust.bds.,2s.

Pope's Poetical Works. Complete in One Vol. Post 8vo, cl. limp, 2s.

Price (E. C.), Novels by :

Crown 8vo, cloth extra, 3s. 6d. each ; post 8vo, illustrated boards, 2s. each.

Valentina. | The Foreigners.
Mrs. Lancaster's Rival.

Gerald. Post 8vo, illustrated boards, 2s.   [*Preparing.*

Proctor (Richd. A.), Works by :

Flowers of the Sky. With 55 Illusts. Small crown 8vo, cloth extra, 4s. 6d.

Easy Star Lessons. With Star Maps for Every Night in the Year, Drawings of the Constellations, &c. Crown 8vo, cloth extra, 6s.

Familiar Science Studies. Crown 8vo, cloth extra, 7s. 6d.

Saturn and its System. New and Revised Edition, with 13 Steel Plates. Demy 8vo, cloth extra, 10s. 6d.

The Great Pyramid : Observatory, Tomb, and Temple. With Illustrations. Crown 8vo, cloth extra, 6s.

Mysteries of Time and Space. With Illusts. Cr. 8vo, cloth extra, 7s. 6d.

The Universe of Suns, and other Science Gleanings. With numerous Illusts. Cr. 8vo, cloth extra, 7s. 6d.

Wages and Wants of Science Workers. Crown 8vo, 1s. 6d.

Pyrotechnist's Treasury (The); or, Complete Art of Making Fireworks. By THOMAS KENTISH. With numerous Illustrations. Cr. 8vo, cl. extra, 4s. 6d.

Rabelais' Works. Faithfully Translated from the French, with variorum Notes, and numerous characteristic Illustrations by GUSTAVE DORÉ. Crown 8vo, cloth extra, 7s. 6d.

Rambosson.—Popular Astronomy. By J. RAMBOSSON, Laureate of the Institute of France. Translated by C. B. PITMAN. Crown 8vo, cloth gilt, numerous Illusts., and a beautifully executed Chart of Spectra, 7s. 6d.

Reade (Charles), Novels by :

Crown 8vo, cloth extra, illustrated, 3s. 6d. each ; post 8vo, illustrated boards, 2s. each.

Peg Woffington. Illustrated by S. L. FILDES, A.R.A.

Christie Johnstone. Illustrated by WILLIAM SMALL.

It is Never Too Late to Mend. Illustrated by G. J. PINWELL.

The Course of True Love Never did run Smooth. Illustrated by HELEN PATERSON.

The Autobiography of a Thief; Jack of all Trades; and James Lambert. Illustrated by MATT STRETCH.

Love me Little, Love me Long. Illustrated by M. ELLEN EDWARDS.

The Double Marriage. Illust. by Sir JOHN GILBERT, R.A., and C. KEENE.

The Cloister and the Hearth. Illustrated by CHARLES KEENE.

Hard Cash. Illust. by F. W. LAWSON.

Griffith Gaunt. Illustrated by S. L. FILDES, A.R.A., and WM. SMALL.

Foul Play. Illust. by DU MAURIER.

Put Yourself In His Place. Illustrated by ROBERT BARNES.

A Terrible Temptation. Illustrated by EDW. HUGHES and A. W. COOPER.

The Wandering Heir. Illustrated by H. PATERSON, S. L. FILDES, A.R.A., C. GREEN, and H. WOODS, A.R.A.

A Simpleton. Illustrated by KATE CRAUFORD.

A Woman-Hater. Illustrated by THOS. COULDERY.

Readiana. With a Steel-plate Portrait of CHARLES READE.

Singleheart and Doubleface : A Matter-of-fact Romance. Illustrated by P. MACNAB.

Good Stories of Men and other Animals. Illustrated by E. A. ABBEY, PERCY MACQUOID, and JOSEPH NASH.

The Jilt, and other Stories. Illustrated by JOSEPH NASH.

Reader's Handbook (The) of Allusions, References, Plots, and Stories. By the Rev. Dr. BREWER. Fifth Edition, revised throughout, with a New Appendix, containing a COMPLETE ENGLISH BIBLIOGRAPHY. Cr. 8vo, 1,400 pages, cloth extra, 7s. 6d.

Richardson. — A Ministry of Health, and other Papers. By BENJAMIN WARD RICHARDSON, M.D., &c. Crown 8vo, cloth extra, 6s.

Riddell (Mrs. J. H.), Novels by:
Crown 8vo, cloth extra, 3s. 6d. each;
post 8vo, illustrated boards, 2s. each.
Her Mother's Darling.
The Prince of Wales's Garden Party
Weird Stories.

Post 8vo, illustrated boards, 2s. each.
The Uninhabited House.
Fairy Water.

"Right Honourable (The):" A
Novel. Two Vols., crown 8vo, cloth
extra, 12s. [*In the press.*

Rimmer (Alfred), Works by:
Square 8vo, cloth gilt, 10s. 6d. each.
Our Old Country Towns. With over
50 Illustrations.
Rambles Round Eton and Harrow.
With 50 Illustrations.
About England with Dickens. With
58 Illustrations by ALFRED RIMMER
and C. A. VANDERHOOF.

Robinson (F. W.), Novels by:
Crown 8vo, cloth extra, 3s. 6d. each;
post 8vo, illustrated boards, 2s. each.
Women are Strange.
The Hands of Justice.

Robinson (Phil), Works by:
Crown 8vo, cloth extra, 7s. 6d. each.
The Poets' Birds.
The Poets' Beasts.
Poets' Natural History. [*Preparing.*

Robinson Crusoe: A beautiful
reproduction of Major's Edition, with
37 Woodcuts and Two Steel Plates by
GEORGE CRUIKSHANK, choicely printed.
Crown 8vo, cloth extra, 7s. 6d.

Rochefoucauld's Maxims and
Moral Reflections. With Notes, and
an Introductory Essay by SAINTE-
BEUVE. Post 8vo, cloth limp, 2s.

Roll of Battle Abbey, The; or,
A List of the Principal Warriors who
came over from Normandy with William the Conqueror, and Settled in
this Country, A.D. 1066-7. With the
principal Arms emblazoned in Gold
and Colours. Handsomely printed, 5s.

Rowley (Hon. Hugh), Works by:
Post 8vo, cloth limp, 2s. 6d. each.
Puniana: Riddles and Jokes. With
numerous Illustrations.
More Puniana. Profusely Illustrated.

Runciman (James), Stories by:
Post 8vo, illustrated boards, 2s. each;
cloth limp, 2s. 6d. each.
Skippers and Shellbacks.
Grace Balmaign's Sweetheart.

Russell (W. Clark), Works by:
Round the Galley-Fire. Crown 8vo,
cloth extra, 6s.; post 8vo, illustrated
boards, 2s.

Crown 8vo, cloth extra, 6s. each.
On the Fo'k'sle Head: A Collection
of Yarns and Sea Descriptions.
In the Middle Watch.

Sala.—Gaslight and Daylight.
By GEORGE AUGUSTUS SALA. Post
8vo, illustrated boards, 2s.

Sanson.—Seven Generations
of Executioners: Memoirs of the
Sanson Family (1688 to 1847). Edited
by HENRY SANSON. Cr. 8vo, cl. ex. 3s. 6d.

Saunders (John), Novels by:
Crown 8vo, cloth extra, 3s. 6d. each;
post 8vo, illustrated boards, 2s. each.
Bound to the Wheel.
One Against the World.
Guy Waterman.
The Lion in the Path.
The Two Dreamers.

Saunders (Katharine), Novels
by: Cr. 8vo, cloth extra, 3s. 6d. each;
post 8vo, illustrated boards, 2s. each.
Joan Merryweather.
Margaret and Elizabeth.
The High Mills.

Crown 8vo, cloth extra, 3s. 6d. each.
Heart Salvage. | Sebastian.
Gideon's Rock.

Science Gossip: An Illustrated
Medium of Interchange for Students
and Lovers of Nature. Edited by J. E.
TAYLOR, F.L.S., &c. Devoted to Geo-
logy, Botany, Physiology, Chemistry,
Zoology, Microscopy, Telescopy, Phy-
siography, &c. Price 4d. Monthly; or
5s. per year, post free. Vols. I. to
XIV. may be had at 7s. 6d. each; and
Vols. XV. to XXI. (1835), at 5s. each.
Cases for Binding, 1s. 6d. each.

Scott's (Sir Walter) Marmion.
A New Edition of this famous Poem,
with over 100 new Illustrations by leading Artists. Small 4to, cloth extra, 16s.

"Secret Out" Series, The:
Crown 8vo, cloth extra, profusely Illus-
trated, 4s. 6d. each.
The Secret Out: One Thousand
Tricks with Cards, and other Re-
creations; with Entertaining Experi-
ments in Drawing-room or "White
Magic." By W. H. CREMER. 300
Engravings.
The Pyrotechnist's Treasury; or,
Complete Art of Making Fireworks.
By THOMAS KENTISH. With numer-
ous Illustrations.

"SECRET OUT" SERIES, *continued*—

The Art of Amusing: A Collection of Graceful Arts, Games, Tricks, Puzzles, and Charades. By FRANK BELLEW. With 300 Illustrations.

Hanky-Panky: Very Easy Tricks, Very Difficult Tricks, White Magic Sleight of Hand. Edited by W. H. CREMER. With 200 Illustrations.

The Merry Circle: A Book of New Intellectual Games and Amusements. By CLARA BELLEW. Many Illusts.

Magician's Own Book: Performances with Cups and Balls, Eggs, Hats, Handkerchiefs, &c. All from actual Experience. Edited by W. H. CREMER. 200 Illustrations.

Magic No Mystery: Tricks with Cards, Dice, Balls, &c., with fully descriptive Directions; the Art of Secret Writing; Training of Performing Animals, &c. With Coloured Frontis. and many Illusts.

Senior.—By Stream and Sea. By WILLIAM SENIOR. Post 8vo, cloth limp, 2s. 6d.

Seven Sagas (The) of Prehistoric Man. By JAMES H. STODDART, Author of "The Village Life." Crown 8vo, cloth extra, 6s.

Shakespeare:

The First Folio Shakespeare.—MR. WILLIAM SHAKESPEARE'S Comedies, Histories, and Tragedies. Published according to the true Original Copies. London, Printed by ISAAC IAGGARD and ED. BLOUNT. 1623.—A Reproduction of the extremely rare original, in reduced facsimile, by a photographic process—ensuring the strictest accuracy in every detail. Small 8vo, half-Roxburghe, 7s. 6d.

The Lansdowne Shakespeare. Beautifully printed in red and black, in small but very clear type. With engraved facsimile of DROESHOUT'S Portrait. Post 8vo, cloth extra, 7s. 6d.

Shakespeare for Children: Tales from Shakespeare. By CHARLES and MARY LAMB. With numerous Illustrations, coloured and plain, by J. MOYR SMITH. Cr. 4to, cl. gilt, 6s.

The Dramatic Works of Shakespeare: The Text of the First Edition, carefully reprinted. Eight Vols., demy 8vo, cloth boards. 40s.

The Handbook of Shakespeare Music. Being an Account of 350 Pieces of Music, set to Words taken from the Plays and Poems of Shakespeare, the compositions ranging from the Elizabethan Age to the Present Time. By ALFRED ROFFE. 4to, half-Roxburghe, 7s.

SHAKESPEARE, *continued*—

A Study of Shakespeare. By ALGERNON CHARLES SWINBURNE. Crown 8vo, cloth extra, 8s.

Shelley's Complete Works, in Four Vols., post 8vo, cloth limp, 8s; or separately, 2s. each. Vol. I. contains his Early Poems, Queen Mab, &c., with an Introduction by LEIGH HUNT; Vol. II., his Later Poems, Laon and Cythna, &c.; Vol. III., Posthumous Poems, the Shelley Papers, &c.; Vol. IV., his Prose Works, including A Refutation of Deism, Zastrozzi, St. Irvyne, &c.

Sheridan:—

Sheridan's Complete Works, with Life and Anecdotes. Including his Dramatic Writings, printed from the Original Editions, his Works in Prose and Poetry, Translations, Speeches, Jokes, Puns, &c. With a Collection of Sheridaniana. Crown 8vo, cloth extra, gilt, with 10 full-page Tinted Illustrations, 7s. 6d.

Sheridan's Comedies: The Rivals, and The School for Scandal. Edited, with an Introduction and Notes to each Play, and a Biographical Sketch of Sheridan, by BRANDER MATTHEWS. With Decorative Vignettes and 10 full-page Illusts. Demy 8vo, half-parchment, 12s. 6d.

Short Sayings of Great Men. With Historical and Explanatory Notes by SAMUEL A. BENT, M.A. Demy 8vo, cloth extra, 7s. 6d.

Sidney's (Sir Philip) Complete Poetical Works, including all those in "Arcadia." With Portrait, Memorial-Introduction, Notes, &c., by the Rev. A. B. GROSART, D.D. Three Vols., crown 8vo, cloth boards, 18s.

Signboards: Their History. With Anecdotes of Famous Taverns and Remarkable Characters. By JACOB LARWOOD and JOHN CAMDEN HOTTEN. Crown 8vo, cloth extra, with 100 Illustrations, 7s. 6d.

Sims (George R.), Works by:

How the Poor Live. With 60 Illusts. by FRED. BARNARD. Large 4to, 1s.

Rogues and Vagabonds. Post 8vo, illust. boards, 2s.; cloth limp, 2s. 6d.

A Ring o' Bells. Post 8vo, illust. bds., 2s.; cloth, 2s. 6d.   [*In the press.*

Sketchley.—A Match in the Dark. By ARTHUR SKETCHLEY. Post 8vo, illustrated boards, 2s.

Slang Dictionary, The: Etymological, Historical, and Anecdotal. Crown 8vo, cloth extra, gilt, 6s. 6d.

Smith (J. Moyr), Works by:
The Prince of Argolis: A Story of the Old Greek Fairy Time. Small 8vo, cloth extra, with 130 Illusts., 3s. 6d.
Tales of Old Thule. With numerous Illustrations. Cr. 8vo, cloth gilt, 6s.
The Wooing of the Water Witch: A Northern Oddity. With numerous Illustrations. Small 8vo, cl. ex., 6s.

Society in London. By A FOREIGN RESIDENT. New and Cheaper (the Ninth) Edition, Revised. Post 8vo, 1s.; cloth, 1s. 6d. [*Preparing.*

Spalding.—Elizabethan Demonology: An Essay in Illustration of the Belief in the Existence of Devils, and the Powers possessed by Them. By T. ALFRED SPALDING, LL.B. Crown 8vo, cloth extra, 5s.

Spanish Legendary Tales. By Mrs. S. G. C. MIDDLEMORE, Author of "Round a Posada Fire." Crown 8vo, cloth extra, 6s.

Speight (T. W.), Novels by:
The Mysteries of Heron Dyke. With a Frontispiece by M. ELLEN EDWARDS. Crown 8vo, cloth extra, 3s. 6d.; post 8vo, illustrated bds., 2s.
A Barren Title. Demy 8vo, illustrated cover, 1s.

Spenser for Children. By M. H. TOWRY. With Illustrations by WALTER J. MORGAN. Crown 4to, with Coloured Illustrations, cloth gilt, 6s.

Staunton.—Laws and Practice of Chess; Together with an Analysis of the Openings, and a Treatise on End Games. By HOWARD STAUNTON. Edited by ROBERT B. WORMALD. New Edition, small cr. 8vo, cloth extra, 5s.

Stedman.— The Poets of America. With full Notes in Margin, and careful Analytical Index. By EDMUND CLARENCE STEDMAN, Author of "Victorian Poets." Cr. 8vo, cl. ex., 9s.

Sterndale.—The Afghan Knife: A Novel. By ROBERT ARMITAGE STERNDALE. Cr. 8vo, cloth extra, 3s. 6d.; post 8vo, illustrated boards, 2s.

Stevenson (R. Louis), Works by:
Travels with a Donkey in the Cevennes. Frontispiece by WALTER CRANE. Post 8vo, cloth limp, 2s. 6d.
An Inland Voyage. With Front. by W. CRANE. Post 8vo, cl. lp., 2s. 6d.

STEVENSON (R. LOUIS), *continued—*
Virginibus Puerisque, and other Papers. Crown 8vo, cloth extra, 6s.
Familiar Studies of Men and Books. Crown 8vo, cloth extra, 6s.
New Arabian Nights. Crown 8vo, cl. extra, 6s.; post 8vo, illust. bds., 2s.
The Silverado Squatters. With Frontispiece. Cr. 8vo, cloth extra, 6s.
Prince Otto: A Romance. Second Edition. Crown 8vo, cloth extra, 6s.

St. John.—A Levantine Family. By BAYLE ST. JOHN. Post 8vo, illustrated boards, 2s.

Stoddard.—Summer Cruising in the South Seas. By CHARLES WARREN STODDARD. Illust. by WALLIS MACKAY. Crown 8vo, cl. extra, 3s. 6d.

Stories from Foreign Novelists. With Notices of their Lives and Writings. By HELEN and ALICE ZIMMERN. With a Frontispiece. Crown 8vo, cloth extra, 3s. 6d.; post 8vo, illustrated boards, 2s.

St. Pierre.—Paul and Virginia, and The Indian Cottage. By BERNARDIN ST. PIERRE. Edited, with Life, by Rev. E. CLARKE. Post 8vo, cl. lp., 2s.

Strutt's Sports and Pastimes of the People of England; including the Rural and Domestic Recreations, May Games, Mummeries, Shows, Processions, Pageants, and Pompous Spectacles, from the Earliest Period to the Present Time. With 140 Illustrations. Edited by WILLIAM HONE. Crown 8vo, cloth extra, 7s. 6d.

Suburban Homes (The) of London: A Residential Guide to Favourite London Localities, their Society, Celebrities, and Associations. With Notes on their Rental, Rates, and House Accommodation. With Map of Suburban London. Cr. 8vo cl. ex., 7s. 6d.

Swift's Choice Works, in Prose and Verse. With Memoir, Portrait, and Facsimiles of the Maps in the Original Edition of "Gulliver's Travels." Cr. 8vo, cloth extra, 7s. 6d.

Swinburne (Algernon C.), Works by:
The Queen Mother and Rosamond. Fcap. 8vo, 5s.
Atalanta in Calydon. Crown 8vo, 6s.
Chastelard. A Tragedy. Cr. 8vo, 7s.
Poems and Ballads. FIRST SERIES. Fcap. 8vo, 9s. Cr. 8vo, same price.
Poems and Ballads. SECOND SERIES. Fcap. 8vo, 9s. Cr. 8vo, same price.
Notes on Poems and Reviews. 8vo, 1s.
Songs before Sunrise. Cr. 8vo, 10s. 6d.
Bothwell: A Tragedy. Cr. 8vo, 12s. 6d.

SWINBURNE'S (A. C.) WORKS, *continued.*
George Chapman : An Essay. Crown 8vo, 7s.
Songs of Two Nations. Cr. 8vo, 6s.
Essays and Studies. Crown 8vo, 12s.
Erechtheus : A Tragedy. Cr. 8vo, 6s.
Note of an English Republican on the Muscovite Crusade. 8vo, 1s.
A Note on Charlotte Bronte. Crown 8vo, 6s.
A Study of Shakespeare. Cr. 8vo, 8s.
Songs of the Springtides. Cr. 8vo, 6s.
Studies in Song. Crown 8vo, 7s.
Mary Stuart : A Tragedy. Cr. 8vo, 8s.
Tristram of Lyonesse, and other Poems. Crown 8vo, 9s.
A Century of Roundels. Small 4to, 8s.
A Midsummer Holiday, and other Poems. Crown 8vo, 7s.
Marino Faliero : A Tragedy. Cr.8vo,6s.
A Study of Victor Hugo. Crown 8vo, 6s. [*Shortly.*

Symonds.—Wine, Women and Song: Mediæval Latin Students' Songs. Now first translated into English Verse, with Essay by J. ADDINGTON SYMONDS. Small 8vo, parchment, 6s.

Syntax's (Dr.) Three Tours : In Search of the Picturesque, in Search of Consolation, and in Search of a Wife. With the whole of ROWLANDSON's droll page Illustrations in Colours and a Life of the Author by J. C. HOTTEN. Med. 8vo, cloth extra, 7s. 6d.

Taine's History of English Literature. Translated by HENRY VAN LAUN. Four Vols., small 8vo, cloth boards, 30s.—POPULAR EDITION, Two Vols., crown 8vo, cloth extra, 15s.

Taylor's (Bayard) Diversions of the Echo Club: Burlesques of Modern Writers. Post 8vo, cl. limp, 2s.

Taylor (Dr. J. E., F.L.S.), Works by : Crown 8vo, cloth ex., 7s. 6d. each.
The Sagacity and Morality of Plants: A Sketch of the Life and Conduct of the Vegetable Kingdom. Coloured Frontispiece and 100 Illust.
Our Common British Fossils, and Where to Find Them : A Handbook for Students. With 331 Illustrations.

Taylor's (Tom) Historical Dramas: "Clancarty," "Jeanne Darc," "'Twixt Axe and Crown," "The Fool's Revenge," "Arkwright's Wife," "Anne Boleyn," "Plot and Passion." One Vol., cr. 8vo, cloth extra, 7s. 6d.
⁎ The Plays may also be had separately, at 1s. each.

Tennyson (Lord): A Biographical Sketch. By H. J. JENNINGS. With a Photograph-Portrait. Crown 8vo, cloth extra, 6s.

Thackerayana: Notes and Anecdotes. Illustrated by Hundreds of Sketches by WILLIAM MAKEPEACE THACKERAY, depicting Humorous Incidents in his School-life, and Favourite Characters in the books of his every-day reading. With Coloured Frontispiece. Cr. 8vo, cl. extra, 7s 6d.

Thomas (Bertha), Novels by : Crown 8vo, cloth extra, 3s. 6d. each ; post 8vo, illustrated boards, 2s. each.
Cressida. | Proud Maisie.
The Violin-Player.

Thomas (M.).—A Fight for Life : A Novel. By W. MOY THOMAS. Post 8vo, illustrated boards, 2s.

Thomson's Seasons and Castle of Indolence. With a Biographical and Critical Introduction by ALLAN CUNNINGHAM, and over 50 fine Illustrations on Steel and Wood. Crown 8vo, cloth extra, gilt edges, 7s. 6d.

Thornbury (Walter), Works by :
Haunted London. Edited by EDWARD WALFORD, M.A. With Illustrations by F. W. FAIRHOLT, F.S.A. Crown 8vo, cloth extra, 7s. 6d.
The Life and Correspondence of J. M. W. Turner. Founded upon Letters and Papers furnished by his Friends and fellow Academicians. With numerous Illusts. in Colours, facsimiled from Turner's Original Drawings. Cr. 8vo, cl. extra, 7s. 6d.
Old Stories Re-told. Post 8vo, cloth limp, 2s. 6d.
Tales for the Marines. Post 8vo, illustrated boards, 2s.

Timbs (John), Works by : Crown 8vo, cloth extra, 7s. 6d. each.
The History of Clubs and Club Life in London. With Anecdotes of its Famous Coffee-houses, Hostelries, and Taverns. With many Illusts.
English Eccentrics and Eccentricities: Stories of Wealth and Fashion, Delusions, Impostures, and Fanatic Missions, Strange Sights and Sporting Scenes, Eccentric Artists, Theatrical Folk, Men of Letters, &c. With nearly 50 Illusts.

Trollope (Anthony), Novels by : Crown 8vo, cloth extra, 3s. 6d. each ; post 8vo, illustrated boards, 2s. each.
The Way We Live Now.
Kept in the Dark.
Frau Frohmann. | Marion Fay.
Mr. Scarborough's Family.
The Land-Leaguers.

Post 8vo, illustrated boards, 2s each.
The Golden Lion of Granpere.
John Caldigate. | American Senator

Trollope (Frances E.), Novels by
Crown 8vo, cloth extra, 3s. 6d. each ;
post 8vo, illustrated boards, 2s. each.
  Like Ships upon the Sea.
  Mabel's Progress. | Anne Furness.

Trollope (T. A.).—Diamond Cut
Diamond, and other Stories. By
T. ADOLPHUS TROLLOPE. Cr. 8vo, cl.
ex., 3s. 6d.; post 8vo, illust. boards, 2s.

Trowbridge.—Farnell's Folly:
A Novel. By J. T. TROWBRIDGE. Post
8vo, illustrated boards, 2s. [*Preparing.*

Turgenieff. — Stories from
Foreign Novelists. By IVAN TURGE-
NIEFF, and others. Crown 8vo, cloth
extra, 3s. 6d.; post 8vo, illustrated
boards, 2s.

Tytler (C. C. Fraser-). — Mis-
tress Judith: A Novel. By C. C.
FRASER TYTLER. Cr. 8vo, cloth extra,
3s. 6d ; post 8vo, illust boards, 2s.

Tytler (Sarah), Novels by:
Crown 8vo, cloth extra, 3s. 6d. each ;
post 8vo, illustrated boards, 2s. each.
  What She Came Through.
  The Bride's Pass.

Crown 8vo, cloth extra, 3s. 6d. each.
  Saint Mungo's City.
  Beauty and the Beast. With a
  Front'spiece by P. MACNAB.
  Noblesse Oblige. With Illustrations.
  Citoyenne Jacqueline. Illustrated
  by A. B. HOUGHTON.
  The Huguenot Family. With Illusts.
  Lady Bell. Illustrated by R. MACBETH.

  Buried Diamonds: A Novel. Three
  Vols., crown 8vo. [*Shortly.*

Van Laun.—History of French
Literature. By H. VAN LAUN. Three
Vols , demy 8vo, cl. bds., 7s. 6d. each.

Villari.— A Double Bond: A
Story. By LINDA VILLARI. Fcap.
8vo, picture cover, 1s.

Walford (Edw., M.A.), Works by :
  The County Families of the United
  Kingdom. Containing Notices of
  the Descent, Birth, Marriage, Educa-
  tion, &c., of more than 12,000 dis-
  tinguished Heads of Families, their
  Heirs Apparent or Presumptive, the
  Offices they hold or have held, their
  Town and Country Addresses, Clubs,
  &c. Twenty-sixth Annual Edition,
  for 1886, cloth gilt, 50s. [*Preparing.*
  The Shilling Peerage (1886). Con-
  taining an Alphabetical List of the
  House of Lords, Dates of Creation,
  Lists of Scotch and Irish Peers,
  Addresses, &c. 32mo, cloth, 1s.
  Published annually. [*Preparing.*

WALFORD'S (EDW.) WORKS, continued—
  The Shilling Baronetage (1886).
  Containing an Alphabetical List of
  the Baronets of the United Kingdom,
  short Biographical Notices, Dates
  of Creation, Addresses, &c. 32mo,
  cloth, 1s. [*Preparing.*
  The Shilling Knightage (1886). Containing an Alphabetical List of the
  Knights of the United Kingdom,
  short Biographical Notices, Dates
  of Creation, Addresses, &c. 32mo,
  cloth, 1s. [*Preparing.*
  The Shilling House of Commons
  (1886). Containing a List of all the
  Members of Parliament, their Town
  and Country Addresses, &c. 32mo,
  cloth, 1s. Published annually.
  The Complete Peerage, Baronetage, Knightage, and House of
  Commons (1886). In One Volume,
  royal 32mo, cloth extra, gilt edges,
  5s. [*Preparing.*

Haunted London. By WALTER
THORNBURY. Edited by EDWARD
WALFORD, M.A. With Illustrations
by F. W. FAIRHOLT, F.S.A. Crown
8vo, cloth extra, 7s. 6d.

Walton and Cotton's Complete
Angler; or, The Contemplative Man's
Recreation ; being a Discourse of
Rivers, Fishponds, Fish and Fishing,
written by IZAAK WALTON; and In-
structions how to Angle for a Trout or
Grayling in a clear Stream, by CHARLES
COTTON. With Original Memoirs and
Notes by Sir HARRIS NICOLAS, and
61 Copperplate Illustrations. Large
crown 8vo, cloth antique, 7s. 6d.

Wanderer's Library, The :
Crown 8vo, cloth extra, 3s. 6d. each.
  Wanderings in Patagonia; or, Life
  among the Ostrich-Hunters. By
  JULIUS BEERBOHM. Illustrated.
  Camp Notes: Stories of Sport and
  Adventure in Asia, Africa, and
  America. By FREDERICK BOYLE.
  Savage Life. By FREDERICK BOYLE.
  Merrie England in the Olden Time
  By GEORGE DANIEL. With Illustra-
  tions by ROBT. CRUIKSHANK.
  Circus Life and Circus Celebrities.
  By THOMAS FROST.
  The Lives of the Conjurers. By
  THOMAS FROST.
  The Old Showmen and the Old
  London Fairs. By THOMAS FROST.
  Low-Life Deeps. An Account of the
  Strange Fish to be found there. By
  JAMES GREENWOOD.
  The Wilds of London. By JAMES
  GREENWOOD.
  Tunis: The Land and the People.
  By the Chevalier de HESSE-WAR-
  TEGG. With 22 Illustrations.

WANDERER'S LIBRARY, THE, *continued—*

The World Behind the Scenes. By PERCY FITZGERALD.

Tavern Anecdotes and Sayings: Including the Origin of Signs, and Reminiscences connected with Taverns, Coffee Houses, Clubs, &c. By CHARLES HINDLEY. With Illusts.

The Genial Showman: Life and Adventures of Artemus Ward. By E. P. HINGSTON. With a Frontispiece.

The Story of the London Parks. By JACOB LARWOOD. With Illusts.

London Characters. By HENRY MAYHEW. Illustrated.

Seven Generations of Executioners: Memoirs of the Sanson Family (1688 to 1847). Edited by HENRY SANSON.

Summer Cruising in the South Seas. By C. WARREN STODDARD. Illustrated by WALLIS MACKAY.

Warner.—A Roundabout Journey. By CHARLES DUDLEY WARNER, Author of "My Summer in a Garden." Crown 8vo, cloth extra, 6s.

Warrants, &c. :—

Warrant to Execute Charles I. An exact Facsimile, with the Fifty-nine Signatures, and corresponding Seals. Carefully printed on paper to imitate the Original, 22 in. by 14 in. Price 2s.

Warrant to Execute Mary Queen of Scots. An exact Facsimile, including the Signature of Queen Elizabeth, and a Facsimile of the Great Seal. Beautifully printed on paper to imitate the Original MS. Price 2s.

Magna Charta. An exact Facsimile of the Original Document in the British Museum, printed on fine plate paper, nearly 3 feet long by 2 feet wide, with the Arms and Seals emblazoned in Gold and Colours. Price 5s.

The Roll of Battle Abbey; or, A List of the Principal Warriors who came over from Normandy with William the Conqueror, and Settled in this Country, A.D. 1066-7. With the principal Arms emblazoned in Gold and Colours. Price 5s.

Weather, How to Foretell the, with the Pocket Spectroscope. By F. W. CORY, M.R.C.S. Eng., F.R.Met. Soc., &c. With 10 Illustrations. Crown 8vo, 1s.; cloth, 1s. 6d.

Westropp.—Handbook of Pottery and Porcelain: or, History of those Arts from the Earliest Period. By HODDER M. WESTROPP. With numerous Illustrations and a List of Marks. Crown 8vo, cloth limp, 4s. 6d.

Williams (W. Mattieu, F.R.A.S.), Works by :

Science Notes. See the GENTLEMAN'S MAGAZINE. 1s. Monthly.

Science in Short Chapters. Crown 8vo, cloth extra, 7s. 6d.

A Simple Treatise on Heat. Crown 8vo, cloth limp, with Illusts., 2s. 6d.

The Chemistry of Cookery. Crown 8vo, cloth extra, 6s.

Wilson (Dr. Andrew, F.R.S.E.), Works by :

Chapters on Evolution: A Popular History of the Darwinian and Allied Theories of Development. Second Edition. Crown 8vo, cloth extra, with 259 Illustrations, 7s. 6d.

Leaves from a Naturalist's Notebook. Post 8vo, cloth limp, 2s. 6d.

Leisure-Time Studies, chiefly Biological. Third Edition, with a New Preface. Crown 8vo, cloth extra, with Illustrations, 6s.

Studies in Life and Sense. With numerous Illustrations. Crown 8vo, cloth extra, 6s. [*Preparing.*

Common Accidents, and How to Treat them. With numerous Illustrations. Crown 8vo, 1s.; cloth limp, 1s. 6d. [*Preparing.*

Winter (J. S.), Stories by : Crown 8vo, cloth extra, 3s. 6d. each; post 8vo, illustrated boards, 2s. each.

Cavalry Life. | Regimental Legends.

Women of the Day: A Biographical Dictionary of Notable Contemporaries. By FRANCES HAYS. Crown 8vo, cloth extra, 5s.

Wood.—Sabina: A Novel. By Lady WOOD. Post 8vo, illust. bds., 2s.

Words, Facts, and Phrases: A Dictionary of Curious, Quaint, and Out-of-the-Way Matters. By ELIEZER EDWARDS. New and cheaper issue. cr. 8vo, cl. ex., 7s. 6d.; half-bound, 9s.

Wright (Thomas), Works by : Crown 8vo, cloth extra, 7s. 6d. each.

Caricature History of the Georges. (The House of Hanover.) With 400 Pictures, Caricatures, Squibs, Broadsides, Window Pictures, &c.

History of Caricature and of the Grotesque in Art, Literature, Sculpture, and Painting. Profusely Illustrated by F. W. FAIRHOLT, F.S.A.

Yates (Edmund), Novels by : Post 8vo, illustrated boards, 2s. each. Castaway | The Forlorn Hope. Land at Last.

NEW THREE-VOLUME NOVELS.

OUIDA'S NEW NOVEL.

Othmar. (A Sequel to " Princess Napraxine.") By OUIDA. Three Vols., crown 8vo.

CHRISTIE MURRAY'S NEW NOVEL

First Person Singular. By D. CHRISTIE MURRAY, Author of " Joseph's Coat," &c. Three Vols., crown 8vo.

MISS O'HANLON'S NEW NOVEL.

The Unforeseen. By ALICE O'HANLON. Three Vols., crown 8vo.

SARAH TYTLER'S NEW NOVEL.

Buried Diamonds. By SARAH TYTLER, Author of " Saint Mango's City," &c. Three Vols., crown 8vo. [*Shortly*

JUSTIN McCARTHY'S NEW NOVEL

Camiola. By JUSTIN McCARTHY, Author of " Dear Lady Disdain," &c. Three Vols., crown 8vo.

"**The Right Honourable.**" Two Vols., Crown 8vo.

THE PICCADILLY NOVELS.

Popular Stories by the Best Authors. LIBRARY EDITIONS, many Illustrated, crown 8vo, cloth extra, 3s. 6d. each.

BY MRS. ALEXANDER.

Maid, Wife, or Widow?

BY GRANT ALLEN.

Philistia.

BY BASIL.

A Drawn Game.
"The Wearing of the Green."

BY W. BESANT & JAMES RICE.

Ready-Money Mortiboy.
My Little Girl.
The Case of Mr. Lucraft.
This Son of Vulcan.
With Harp and Crown.
The Golden Butterfly.
By Celia's Arbour.
The Monks of Thelema.
'Twas in Trafalgar's Bay.
The Seamy Side.
The Ten Years' Tenant.
The Chaplain of the Fleet.

BY WALTER BESANT.

All Sorts and Conditions of Men.
The Captains' Room.
All in a Garden Fair.
Dorothy Forster.
Uncle Jack.

BY ROBERT BUCHANAN.

A Child of Nature.
God and the Man.
The Shadow of the Sword.
The Martyrdom of Madeline.
Love Me for Ever.
Annan Water. | The New Abelard.
Matt. | Foxglove Manor.

BY HALL CAINE.

The Shadow of a Crime.

BY MRS. H. LOVETT CAMERON.

Deceivers Ever. | Juliet's Guardian.

BY MORTIMER COLLINS.

Sweet Anne Page.
Transmigration.
From Midnight to Midnight.

MORTIMER & FRANCES COLLINS.

Blacksmith and Scholar.
The Village Comedy.
You Play me False.

BY WILKIE COLLINS.

Antonina. | New Magdalen.
Basil. | The Frozen Deep.
Hide and Seek. | The Law and the
The Dead Secret. | Lady.
Queen of Hearts. | The Two Destinies
My Miscellanies. | Haunted Hotel.
Woman in White. | The Fallen Leaves
The Moonstone. | Jezebel's Daughter
Man and Wife. | The Black Robe.
Poor Miss Finch. | Heart and Science
Miss or Mrs.? | I Say No.

BY DUTTON COOK.

Paul Foster's Daughter.

BY WILLIAM CYPLES.

Hearts of Gold.

BY ALPHONSE DAUDET.

Port Salvation.

BY JAMES DE MILLE.

A Castle in Spain.

PICCADILLY NOVELS, *continued—*

BY J LEITH DERWENT.
Our Lady of Tears. | Circe's Lovers.

BY M. BETHAM-EDWARDS.
Felicia. | Kitty.

BY MRS. ANNIE EDWARDES.
Archie Lovell.

BY R. E. FRANCILLON.
Olympia. | One by One.
Queen Cophetua. | A Real Queen.

Prefaced by Sir BARTLE FRERE.
Pandurang Hari.

BY EDWARD GARRETT.
The Capel Girls.

BY CHARLES GIBBON.
Robin Gray. | For Lack of Gold.
In Love and War.
What will the World Say?
In Honour Bound.
Queen of the Meadow.
The Flower of the Forest.
A Heart's Problem.
The Braes of Yarrow.
The Golden Shaft. | Of High Degree.
Fancy Free. | Loving a Dream.

BY THOMAS HARDY.
Under the Greenwood Tree.

BY JULIAN HAWTHORNE.
Garth. | Ellice Quentin.
Sebastian Strome.
Prince Saroni's Wife.
Dust. | Fortune's Fool.
Beatrix Randolph.
Miss Cadogna.
Love—or a Name.

BY SIR A. HELPS.
Ivan de Biron.

BY MRS. CASHEL HOEY.
The Lover's Creed.

BY MRS. ALFRED HUNT.
Thornicroft's Model.
The Leaden Casket.
Self Condemned.

BY JEAN INGELOW.
Fated to be Free.

BY HARRIETT JAY.
The Queen of Connaught

BY HENRY KINGSLEY.
Number Seventeen.

PICCADILLY NOVELS, *continued—*

BY E. LYNN LINTON.
Patricia Kemball.
Atonement of Leam Dundas.
The World Well Lost.
Under which Lord?
With a Silken Thread.
The Rebel of the Family
"My Love!" | Ione.

BY HENRY W. LUCY.
Gideon Fleyce.

BY JUSTIN McCARTHY, M.P.
The Waterdale Neighbours.
My Enemy's Daughter.
Linley Rochford. | A Fair Saxon
Dear Lady Disdain.
Miss Misanthrope. | Donna Quixot
The Comet of a Season.
Maid of Athens.

BY GEORGE MACDONALD.
Paul Faber, Surgeon.
Thomas Wingfold, Curate.

BY MRS. MACDONELL.
Quaker Cousins.

BY FLORENCE MARRYAT.
Open! Sesame! | Written in Fir

BY D. CHRISTIE MURRAY.
Life's Atonement. | Coals of Fire.
Joseph's Coat. | Val Strange.
A Model Father. | Hearts.
By the Gate of the Sea
The Way of the World.
A Bit of Human Nature.

BY MRS. OLIPHANT.
Whiteladies.

BY MARGARET A. PAUL.
Gentle and Simple.

BY JAMES PAYN.
Lost Sir Massing- | A Confidential
berd. | Agent.
Best of Husbands | From Exile.
Fallen Fortunes. | A Grape from
Halves. | Thorn.
Walter's Word. | For Cash Only.
What He Cost Her | Some Private
Less Black than | Views.
We're Painted. | Kit: A Memory.
By Proxy. | The Canon's
High Spirits. | Ward.
Under One Roof. | The Talk of th
Carlyon's Year. | Town.

PICCADILLY NOVELS, *continued*—

BY E. C. PRICE.
Valentina. | The Foreigners.
Mrs. Lancaster's Rival.

BY CHARLES READE.
It Is Never Too Late to Mend.
Hard Cash.
Peg Woffington.
Christie Johnstone.
Griffith Gaunt. | Foul Play.
The Double Marriage.
Love Me Little, Love Me Long.
The Cloister and the Hearth.
The Course of True Love.
The Autobiography of a Thief.
Put Yourself in His Place.
A Terrible Temptation.
The Wandering Heir. | A Simpleton.
A Woman-Hater. | Readiana.
Singleheart and Doubleface.
The Jilt.
Good Stories of Men and other Animals.

BY MRS. J. H. RIDDELL.
Her Mother's Darling.
Prince of Wales's Garden-Party.
Weird Stories.

BY F. W. ROBINSON.
Women are Strange.
The Hands of Justice.

BY JOHN SAUNDERS.
Bound to the Wheel.
Guy Waterman.
Two Dreamers.
One Against the World.
The Lion in the Path.

PICCADILLY NOVELS, *continued*—

BY KATHARINE SAUNDERS.
Joan Merryweather.
Margaret and Elizabeth.
Gideon's Rock. | Heart Salvage.
The High Mills. | Sebastian.

BY T. W. SPEIGHT.
The Mysteries of Heron Dyke.

BY R. A. STERNDALE.
The Afghan Knife.

BY BERTHA THOMAS.
Proud Maisie. | Cressida.
The Violin-Player.

BY ANTHONY TROLLOPE.
The Way we Live Now.
Frau Frohmann. | Marion Fay.
Kept in the Dark.
Mr. Scarborough's Family.
The Land-Leaguers.

BY FRANCES E. TROLLOPE.
Like Ships upon the Sea.
Anne Furness.
Mabel's Progress.

BY T. A. TROLLOPE.
Diamond Cut Diamond.

By IVAN TURGENIEFF, &c.
Stories from Foreign Novelists.

BY SARAH TYTLER.
What She Came Through.
The Bride's Pass.
Saint Mungo's City.
Beauty and the Beast.

BY C. C. FRASER-TYTLER.
Mistress Judith.

BY J. S. WINTER.
Cavalry Life.
Regimental Legends.

CHEAP EDITIONS OF POPULAR NOVELS.
Post 8vo, illustrated boards, 2s. each.

BY EDMOND ABOUT.
The Fellah.

BY HAMILTON AÏDÉ.
Carr of Carrlyon. | Confidences.

BY MRS. ALEXANDER.
Maid, Wife, or Widow?
Valerie's Fate.

BY SHELSLEY BEAUCHAMP.
Grantley Grange.

BY W. BESANT & JAMES RICE.
Ready-Money Mortiboy.
With Harp and Crown.
This Son of Vulcan. | My Little Girl.
The Case of Mr. Lucraft.

BY BESANT AND RICE, *continued*—
The Golden Butterfly.
By Celia's Arbour.
The Monks of Thelema.
'Twas in Trafalgar's Bay.
The Seamy Side.
The Ten Years' Tenant.
The Chaplain of the Fleet.

BY WALTER BESANT.
All Sorts and Conditions of Men.
The Captains' Room.
All in a Garden Fair.

BY FREDERICK BOYLE.
Camp Notes. | Savage Life.
Chronicles of No-man's Land.

CHEAP POPULAR NOVELS, *continued—*

BY BRET HARTE.
An Heiress of Red Dog.
The Luck of Roaring Camp.
Californian Stories.
Gabriel Conroy. | Flip.
Maruja.

BY ROBERT BUCHANAN.
The Shadow of the Sword. | The Martyrdom of Madeline.
A Child of Nature. | Annan Water.
God and the Man. | The New Abelard.
Love Me for Ever.

BY MRS. BURNETT.
Surly Tim.

BY MRS. LOVETT CAMERON.
Deceivers Ever. | Juliet's Guardian.

BY MACLAREN COBBAN.
The Cure of Souls.

BY C. ALLSTON COLLINS.
The Bar Sinister.

BY WILKIE COLLINS.
Antonina. | Miss or Mrs. ?
Basil. | New Magdalen.
Hide and Seek. | The Frozen Deep.
The Dead Secret. | Law and the Lady.
Queen of Hearts. | The Two Destinies
My Miscellanies. | Haunted Hotel.
Woman in White. | The Fallen Leaves.
The Moonstone. | Jezebel's Daughter
Man and Wife. | The Black Robe.
Poor Miss Finch. | Heart and Science

BY MORTIMER COLLINS.
Sweet Anne Page. | From Midnight to
Transmigration. | Midnight.
A Fight with Fortune.

MORTIMER & FRANCES COLLINS.
Sweet and Twenty. | Frances.
Blacksmith and Scholar.
The Village Comedy.
You Play me False.

BY DUTTON COOK.
Leo. | Paul Foster's Daughter.

BY C. EGBERT CRADDOCK.
The Prophet of the Great Smoky Mountains.

BY WILLIAM CYPLES.
Hearts of Gold.

BY ALPHONSE DAUDET.
The Evangelist; or, Port Salvation.

BY JAMES DE MILLE.
A Castle in Spain.

BY J. LEITH DERWENT.
Our Lady of Tears. | Circe's Lovers.

BY CHARLES DICKENS.
Sketches by Boz. | Oliver Twist.
Pickwick Papers. | Nicholas Nickleby

CHEAP POPULAR NOVELS, *continued—*

BY MRS. ANNIE EDWARDES.
A Point of Honour. | Archie Lovell

BY M. BETHAM-EDWARDS.
Felicia. | Kitty.

BY EDWARD EGGLESTON.
Roxy.

BY PERCY FITZGERALD.
Bella Donna. | Never Forgotten.
The Second Mrs. Tillotson.
Polly.
Seventy-five Brooke Street.
The Lady of Brantome.

BY ALBANY DE FONBLANQUE.
Filthy Lucre.

BY R. E. FRANCILLON.
Olympia. | Queen Cophetua
One by One. | A Real Queen.

Prefaced by Sir H. BARTLE FRERE
Pandurang Hari.

BY HAIN FRISWELL.
One of Two.

BY EDWARD GARRETT.
The Capel Girls.

BY CHARLES GIBBON.
Robin Gray. | Queen of the Meadow.
For Lack of Gold.
What will the World Say? | The Flower of the Forest.
In Honour Bound. | A Heart's Problem
The Dead Heart. | The Braes of Yarrow.
In Love and War.
For the King. | The Golden Shaft.
In Pastures Green. | Of High Degree.

BY WILLIAM GILBERT.
Dr. Austin's Guests.
The Wizard of the Mountain.
James Duke.

BY JAMES GREENWOOD.
Dick Temple.

BY ANDREW HALLIDAY.
Every-Day Papers.

BY LADY DUFFUS HARDY.
Paul Wynter's Sacrifice.

BY THOMAS HARDY.
Under the Greenwood Tree.

BY JULIAN HAWTHORNE.
Garth. | Sebastian Strome
Ellice Quentin. | Dust.
Prince Saroni's Wife.
Fortune's Fool. | Beatrix Randolph.

BY SIR ARTHUR HELPS.
Ivan de Biron.

BY TOM HOOD.
A Golden Heart.

BY MRS. GEORGE HOOPER.
The House of Raby.

CHEAP POPULAR NOVELS, *continued—*

BY VICTOR HUGO.
The Hunchback of Notre Dame.

BY MRS. ALFRED HUNT.
Thornicroft's Model.
The Leaden Casket.
Self-Condemned.

BY JEAN INGELOW.
Fated to be Free.

BY HARRIETT JAY.
The Dark Colleen.
The Queen of Connaught.

BY HENRY KINGSLEY.
Oakshott Castle. | Number Seventeen

BY E. LYNN LINTON.
Patricia Kemball.
The Atonement of Leam Dundas.
The World Well Lost.
Under which Lord?
With a Silken Thread.
The Rebel of the Family.
"My Love!" | Ione.

BY HENRY W. LUCY.
Gideon Fleyce.

BY JUSTIN McCARTHY, M.P.
Dear Lady Disdain. | Linley Rochford.
The Waterdale Neighbours. | Miss Misanthrope.
My Enemy's Daughter. | Donna Quixote.
A Fair Saxon. | The Comet of a Season.
| Maid of Athens.

BY GEORGE MACDONALD.
Paul Faber, Surgeon.
Thomas Wingfold, Curate.

BY MRS. MACDONELL.
Quaker Cousins.

BY KATHARINE S. MACQUOID.
The Evil Eye. | Lost Rose.

BY W. H. MALLOCK.
The New Republic.

BY FLORENCE MARRYAT.
Open! Sesame! | A Little Stepson.
A Harvest of Wild Oats. | Fighting the Air
| Written in Fire.

BY J. MASTERMAN.
Half-a-dozen Daughters.

BY JEAN MIDDLEMASS.
Touch and Go. | Mr. Dorillion.

BY D. CHRISTIE MURRAY.
A Life's Atonement. | By the Gate of the Sea.
A Model Father. | Val Strange.
Joseph's Coat. | Hearts.
Coals of Fire. |

BY MRS. OLIPHANT.
Whiteladies.

BY MRS. ROBERT O'REILLY.
Phœbe's Fortunes

CHEAP POPULAR NOVELS, *continued—*

BY OUIDA.
Held in Bondage. | Two Little Wooden Shoes.
Strathmore. | In a Winter City.
Chandos. | Ariadne.
Under Two Flags. | Friendship.
Idalia. | Moths.
Cecil Castle-maine's Gage. | Pipistrello.
Tricotrin. | A Village Com-
Puck. | rune.
Folle Farine. | Bimbi.
A Dog of Flanders. | In Maremma.
Pascarel. | Wanda.
Signa. | Frescoes.

BY MARGARET AGNES PAUL.
Gentle and Simple.

BY JAMES PAYN.
Lost Sir Massing-berd. | Like Father, Like Son.
A Perfect Trea-sure. | A Marine Resi-dence.
Bentinck's Tutor. | Married Beneath Him.
Murphy's Master. | Mirk Abbey.
A County Family. | Not Wooed, but Won.
At Her Mercy. | Less Black than We're Painted.
A Woman's Ven-geance. | By Proxy.
Cecil's Tryst. | Under One Roof.
Clyffards of Clyffe | High Spirits.
The Family Scape-grace. | Carlyon's Year.
Foster Brothers. | A Confidential Agent.
Found Dead. | Some Private Views.
Best of Husbands. | From Exile.
Walter's Word. | A Grape from a Thorn.
Halves. |
Fallen Fortunes. | For Cash Only.
What He Cost Her | Kit: A Memory.
Humorous Stories | The Canon's Ward
Gwendoline's Har-vest. |
£200 Reward. |

BY EDGAR A. POE.
The Mystery of Marie Roget.

BY E. C. PRICE.
Valentina. | The Foreigners.
Mrs. Lancaster's Rival.

BY CHARLES READE.
It is Never Too Late to Mend
Hard Cash. | Peg Woffington
Christie Johnstone.
Griffith Gaunt.
Put Yourself in His Place.
The Double Marriage.
Love Me Little, Love Me Long.
Foul Play.
The Cloister and the Hearth
The Course of True Love.
Autobiography of a Thief.
A Terrible Temptation.
The Wandering Heir.

Cheap Popular Novels, *continued*—
By CHARLES READE, *continued.*
A Simpleton. | A Woman-Hater.
Readiana. | The Jilt.
Singleheart and Doubleface.
Good Stories of Men and other Animals.

BY MRS. J. H. RIDDELL.
Her Mother's Darling.
Prince of Wales's Garden Party
Weird Stories.
The Uninhabited House.
Fairy Water.

BY F. W. ROBINSON.
Women are Strange.
The Hands of Justice.

BY JAMES RUNCIMAN.
Skippers and Shellbacks.

BY W. CLARK RUSSELL.
Round the Galley Fire.

BY BAYLE ST. JOHN.
A Levantine Family.

BY GEORGE AUGUSTUS SALA.
Gaslight and Daylight.

BY JOHN SAUNDERS.
Bound to the Wheel.
One Against the World.
Guy Waterman.
The Lion in the Path.
Two Dreamers.

BY KATHARINE SAUNDERS.
Joan Merryweather.
Margaret and Elizabeth.
The High Mills.

BY GEORGE R. SIMS.
Rogues and Vagabonds.

BY ARTHUR SKETCHLEY.
A Match in the Dark.

BY T. W. SPEIGHT.
The Mysteries of Heron Dyke.

BY R. A. STERNDALE.
The Afghan Knife.

BY R. LOUIS STEVENSON.
New Arabian Nights.

BY BERTHA THOMAS.
Cressida. | Proud Maisie.
The Violin-Player.

BY W. MOY THOMAS.
A Fight for Life.

BY WALTER THORNBURY.
Tales for the Marines.

BY T. ADOLPHUS TROLLOPE.
Diamond Cut Diamond.

BY ANTHONY TROLLOPE.
The Way We Live Now.
The American Senator.
Frau Frohmann.

Cheap Popular Novels, *continued*—
By ANTHONY TROLLOPE, *continued.*
Marion Fay.
Kept in the Dark.
Mr. Scarborough's Family.
The Land-Leaguers.
The Golden Lion of Granpere.
John Caldigate.

By FRANCES ELEANOR TROLLOPE
Like Ships upon the Sea.
Anne Furness.
Mabel's Progress.

BY IVAN TURGENIEFF, &c.
Stories from Foreign Novelists

BY MARK TWAIN.
Tom Sawyer.
An Idle Excursion.
A Pleasure Trip on the Continent of Europe.
A Tramp Abroad.
The Stolen White Elephant.

BY C. C. FRASER-TYTLER.
Mistress Judith.

BY SARAH TYTLER.
What She Came Through.
The Bride's Pass.

BY J. S. WINTER.
Cavalry Life. | Regimental Legends.

BY LADY WOOD.
Sabina.

BY EDMUND YATES.
Castaway. | The Forlorn Hope.
Land at Last.

ANONYMOUS.
Paul Ferroll.
Why Paul Ferroll Killed his Wife.

Fcap. 8vo, picture covers, 1s. each.
Jeff Briggs's Love Story. By BRET HARTE.
The Twins of Table Mountain. By BRET HARTE.
Mrs. Gainsborough's Diamonds. By JULIAN HAWTHORNE.
Kathleen Mavourneen. By Author of " That Lass o' Lowrie's."
Lindsay's Luck. By the Author of " That Lass o' Lowrie's."
Pretty Polly Pemberton. By the Author of " That Lass o' Lowrie's."
Trooping with Crows. By Mrs. PIRKIS.
The Professor's Wife. By LEONARD GRAHAM.
A Double Bond. By LINDA VILLARI.
Esther's Glove. By R. E. FRANCILLON.
The Garden that Paid the Rent. By TOM JERROLD.
Curly. By JOHN COLEMAN. Illustrated by J. C. DOLLMAN.
Beyond the Gates. By E. S. PHELPS.
An Old Maid's Paradise. By E. S. PHELPS.
Doomed ! By JUSTIN H. MACCARTHY.

J. OGDEN AND CO., PRINTERS, 172, ST. JOHN STREET, E.C.

THE BEST REMEDY FOR INDIGESTION.

www.ingramcontent.com/pod-product-compliance
Lightning Source LLC
Chambersburg PA
CBHW021111270326
41929CB00009B/824